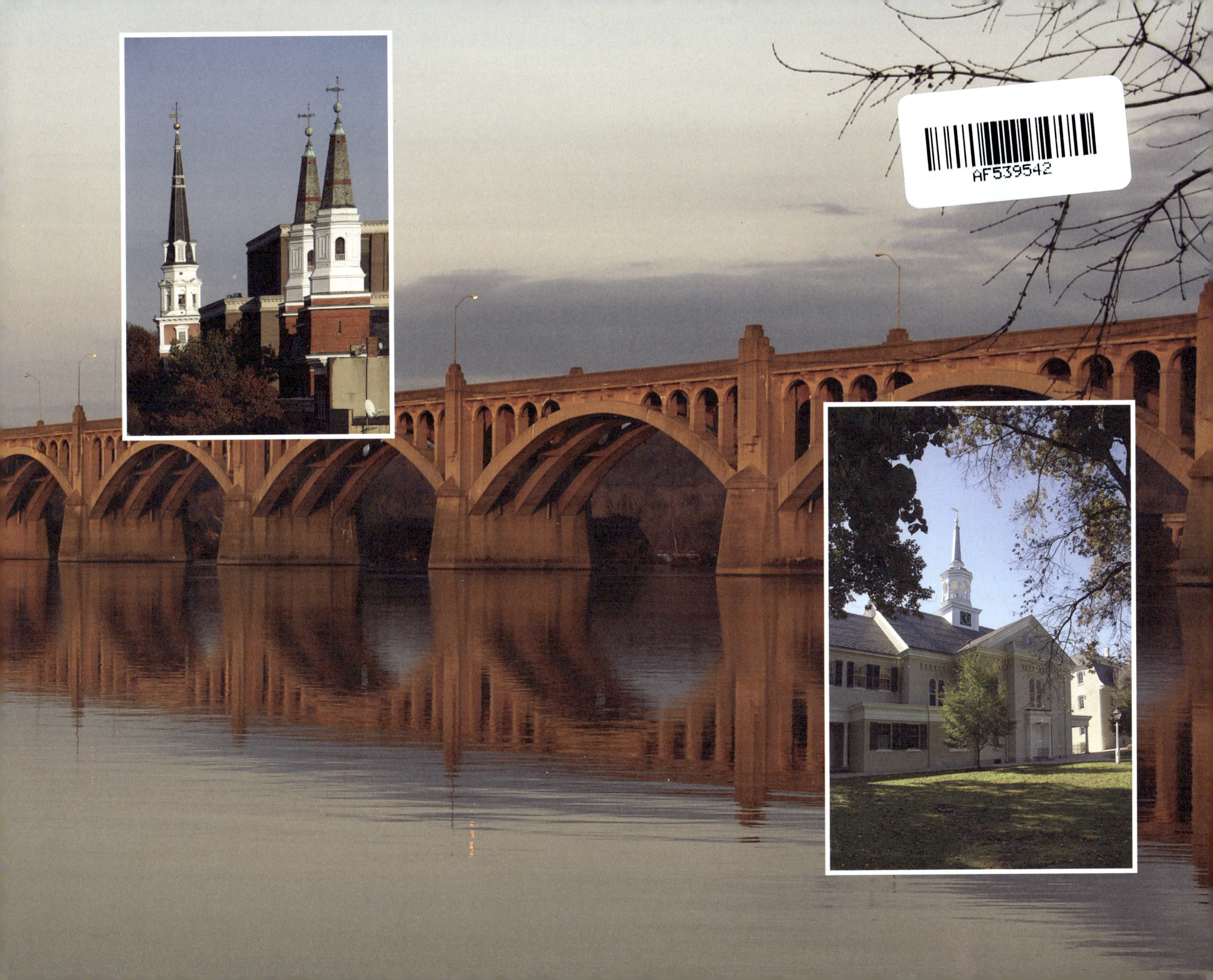
AF539542

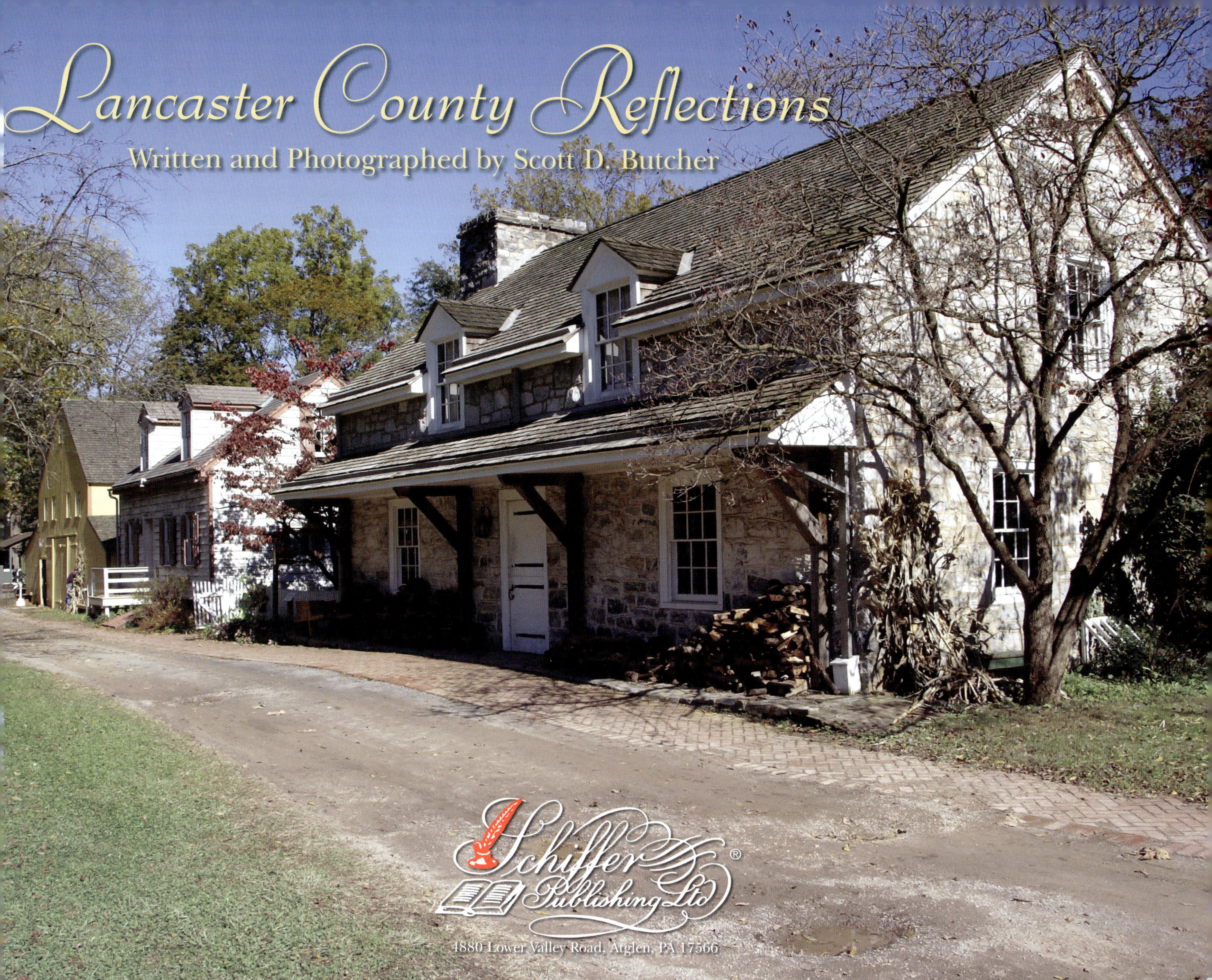

Lancaster County Reflections

Written and Photographed by Scott D. Butcher

Schiffer® Publishing Ltd

4880 Lower Valley Road, Atglen, PA 17566

Other Schiffer Books By The Author:

Tombstone: Relive the Gunfight at the OK Corral, 978-0-7643-3425-2, $9.99

York: America's Historic Crossroads, 978-0-7643-3012-4, $29.99

Delaware Reflections, 978-0-7643-3200-5, $29.99

Gettysburg Perspectives, 978-0-7643-3296-8, $9.99

Library of Congress Control Number: 2010928195

Designed by John P. Cheek
Type set in New Baskerville BT/Bembo Std

ISBN: 978-0-7643-3584-6
Printed in China

Schiffer Books are available at special discounts for bulk purchases for sales promotions or premiums. Special editions, including personalized covers, corporate imprints, and excerpts can be created in large quantities for special needs. For more information contact the publisher:

Published by Schiffer Publishing Ltd.
4880 Lower Valley Road
Atglen, PA 19310
Phone: (610) 593-1777; Fax: (610) 593-2002
E-mail: Info@schifferbooks.com

For the largest selection of fine reference books on this and related subjects, please visit our web site at **www.schifferbooks.com**
We are always looking for people to write books on new and related subjects. If you have an idea for a book please contact us at the above address.

This book may be purchased from the publisher.
Include $5.00 for shipping.
Please try your bookstore first.
You may write for a free catalog.

In Europe, Schiffer books are distributed by
Bushwood Books
6 Marksbury Ave.
Kew Gardens
Surrey TW9 4JF England
Phone: 44 (0) 20 8392 8585; Fax: 44 (0) 20 8392 9876
E-mail: info@bushwoodbooks.co.uk
Website: www.bushwoodbooks.co.uk

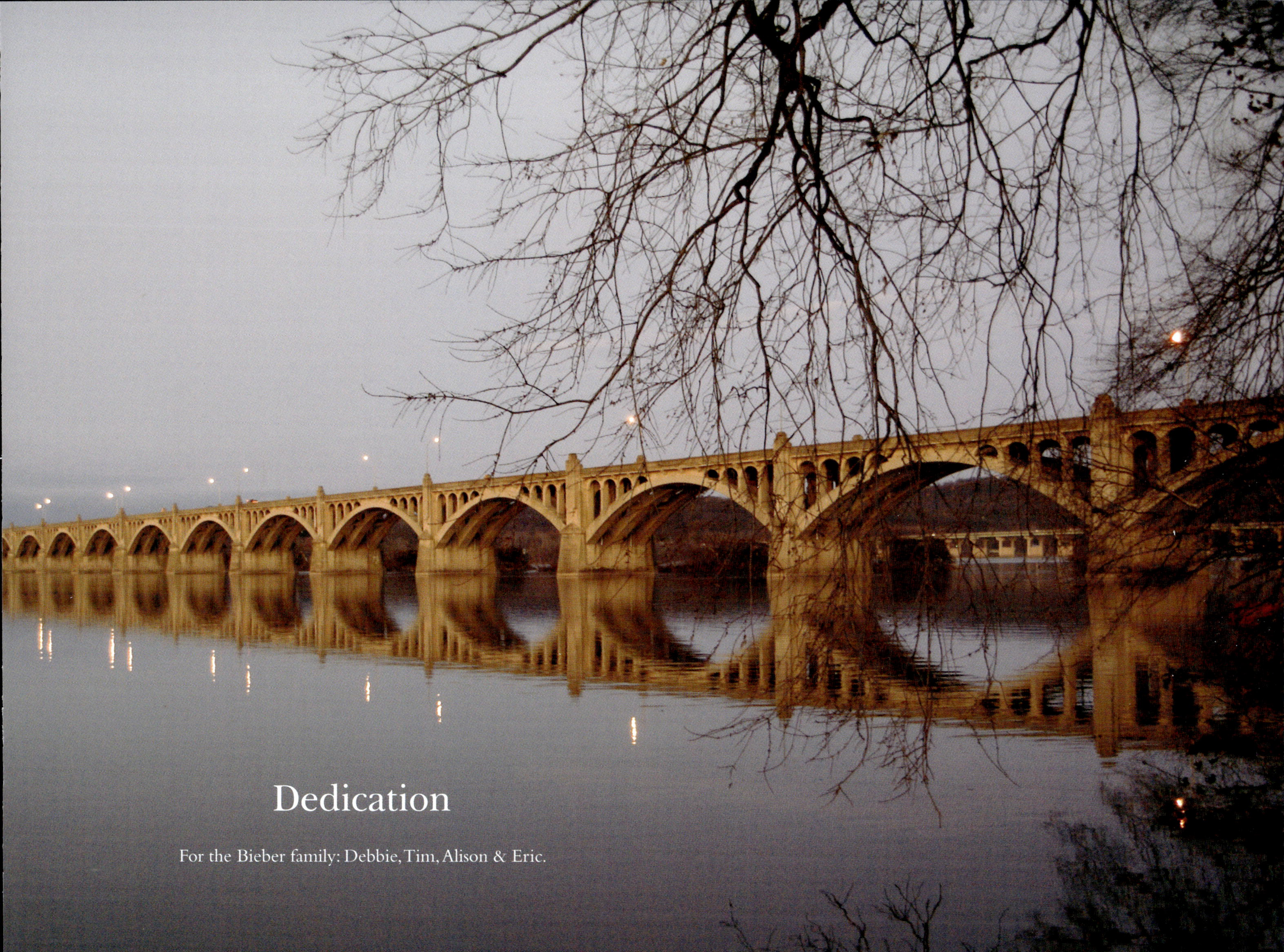

Dedication

For the Bieber family: Debbie, Tim, Alison & Eric.

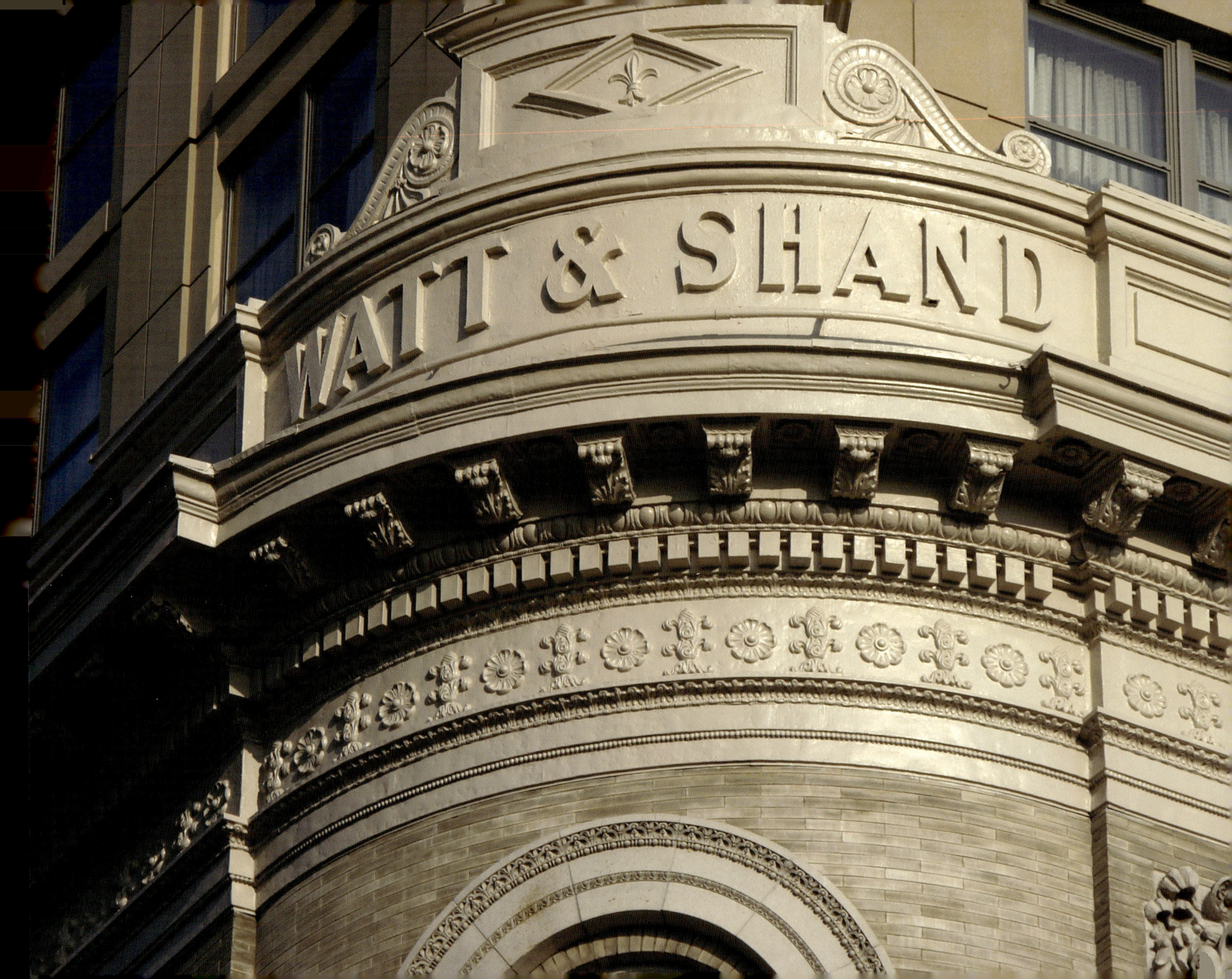
WATT & SHAND

Contents

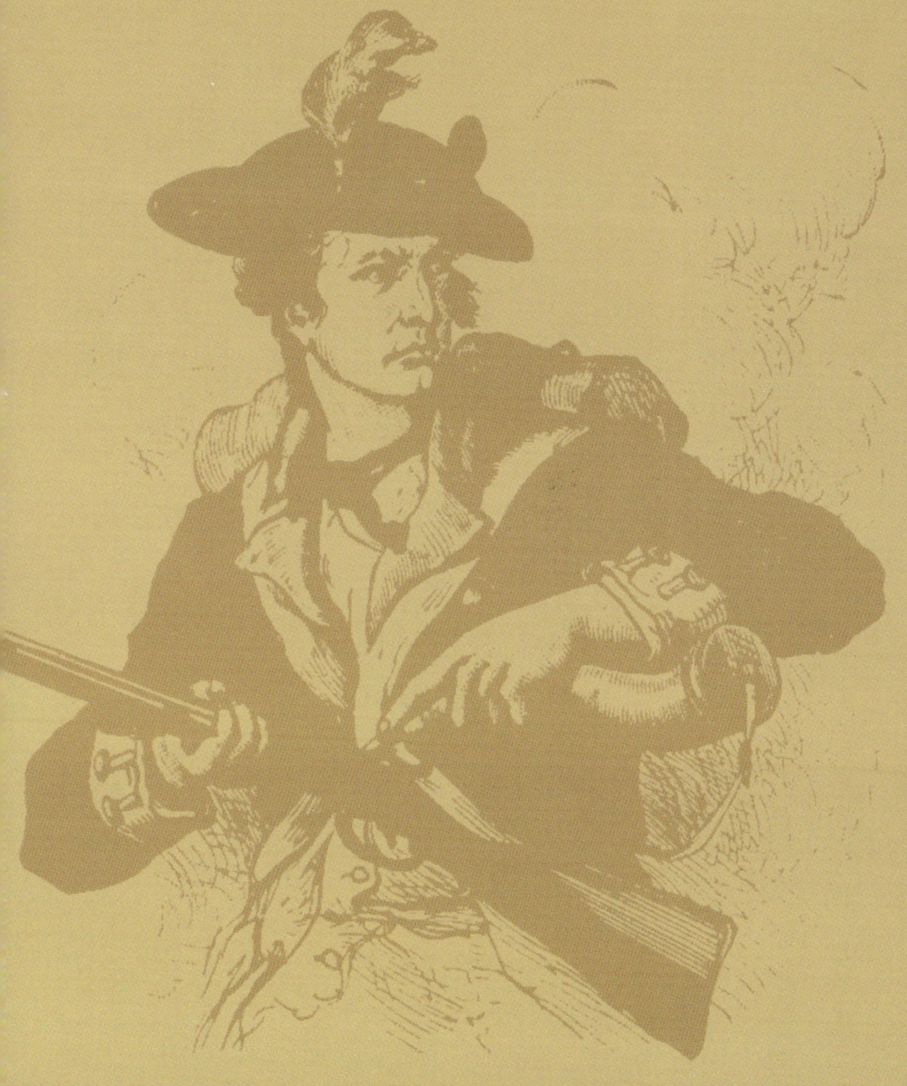

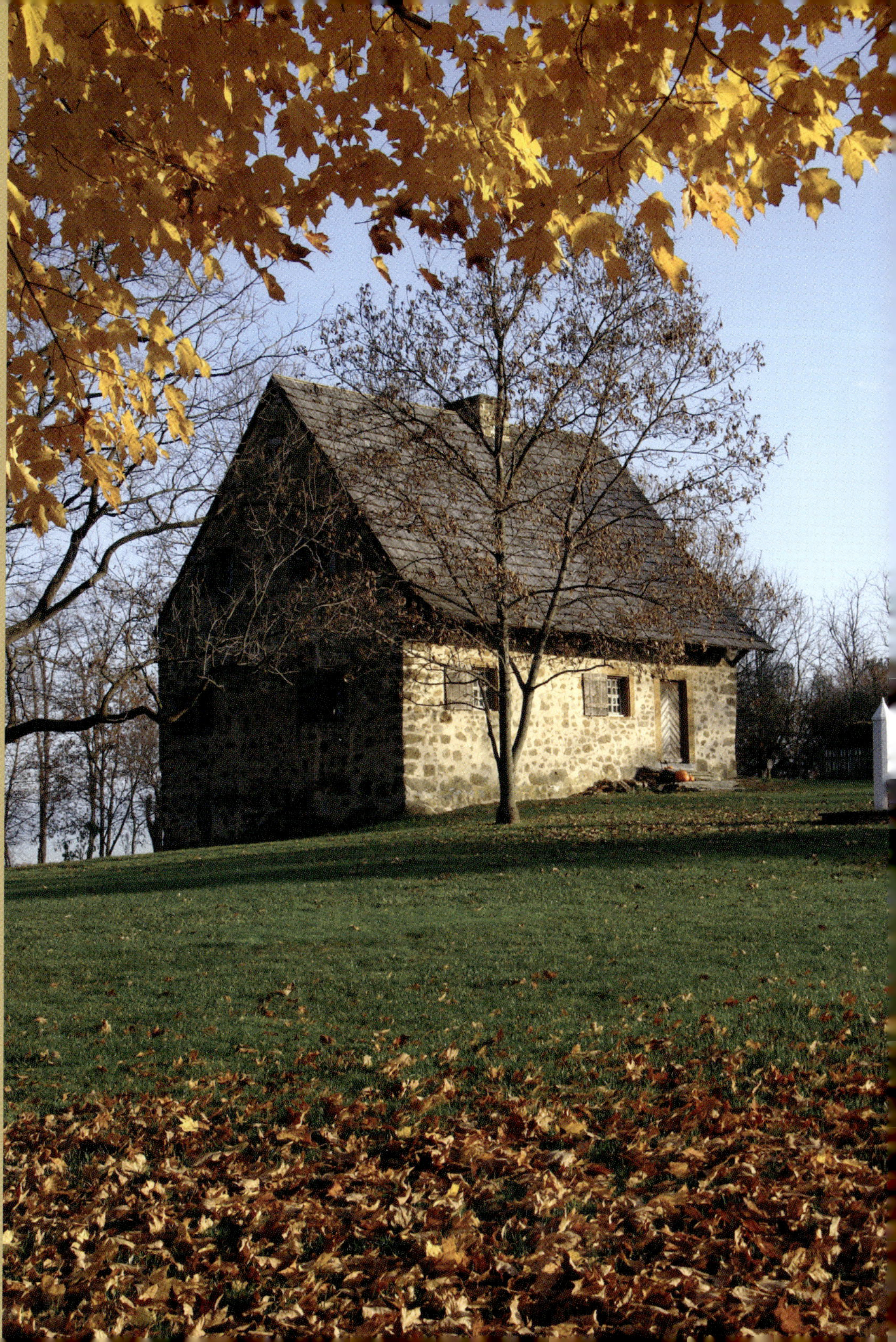

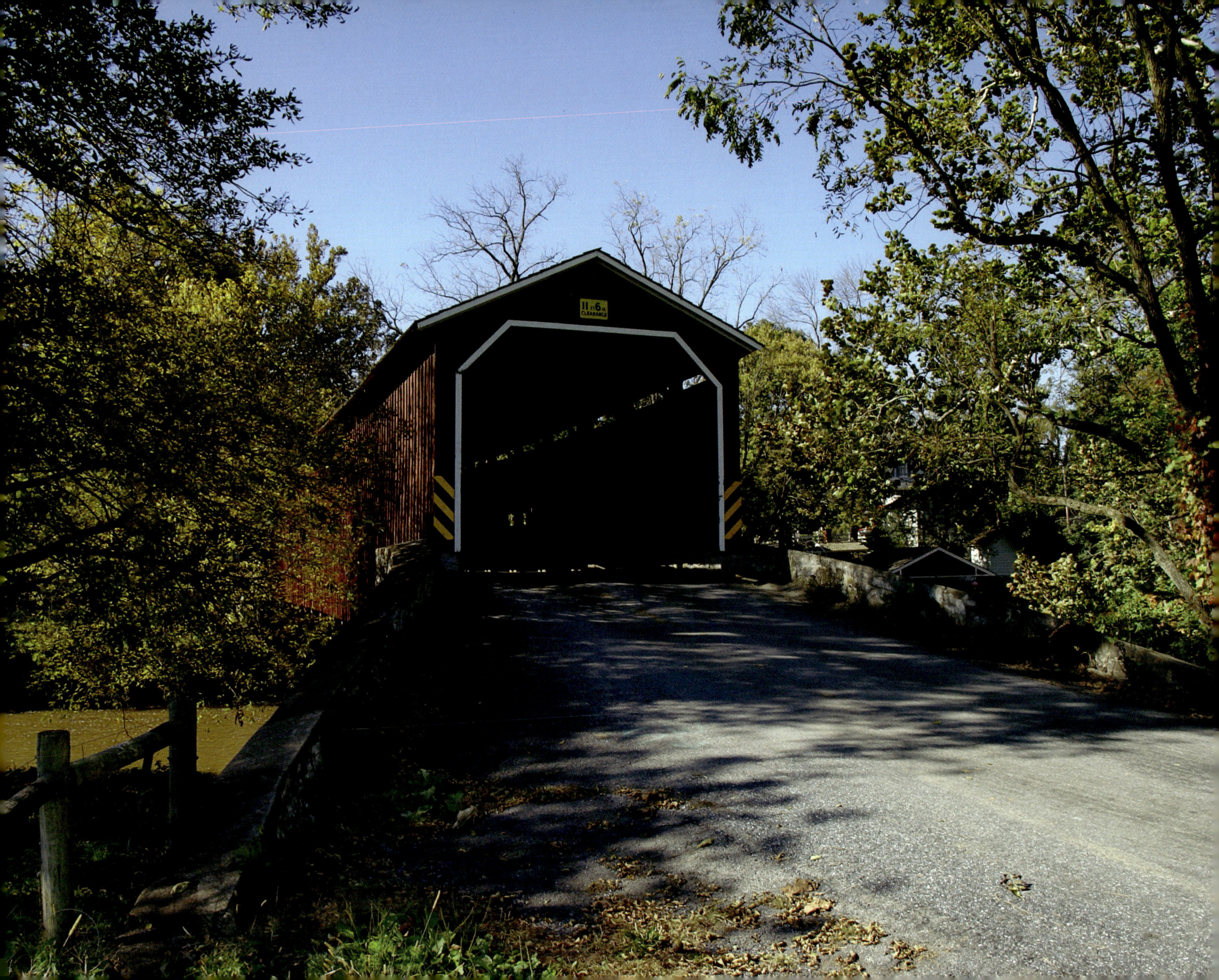
11 FT 6 IN
CLEARANCE

Acknowledgments

Lancaster County Reflections was an enjoyable project, but also somewhat daunting. How can you take a county the size of Lancaster, Pennsylvania, with a vibrant city, picturesque towns, colorful covered bridges, sprawling farms, and a major river, and capture it in about 200 photographs? Not very easily, as it turned out! I had the fortune of talking with several county residents and picking their brains with one or two simple (or not so simple) questions: "What are your favorite buildings?" and "What are your favorite settings?" I am grateful for the input of Hunter Johnson, John Yoder, Betty Helms, Jodi Kreider, Brian Schulman, and Scott Martin, who all steered me in the right direction. I am also indebted to my son, Jonathan, and my wife, Debbie, who accompanied me on several of my photo-shooting expeditions and put up with my continued promises of, "Just one more photo–I'm almost finished. No really, this is it!" Finally, a special thanks to all my friends at Schiffer Publishing for believing in another photography book project.

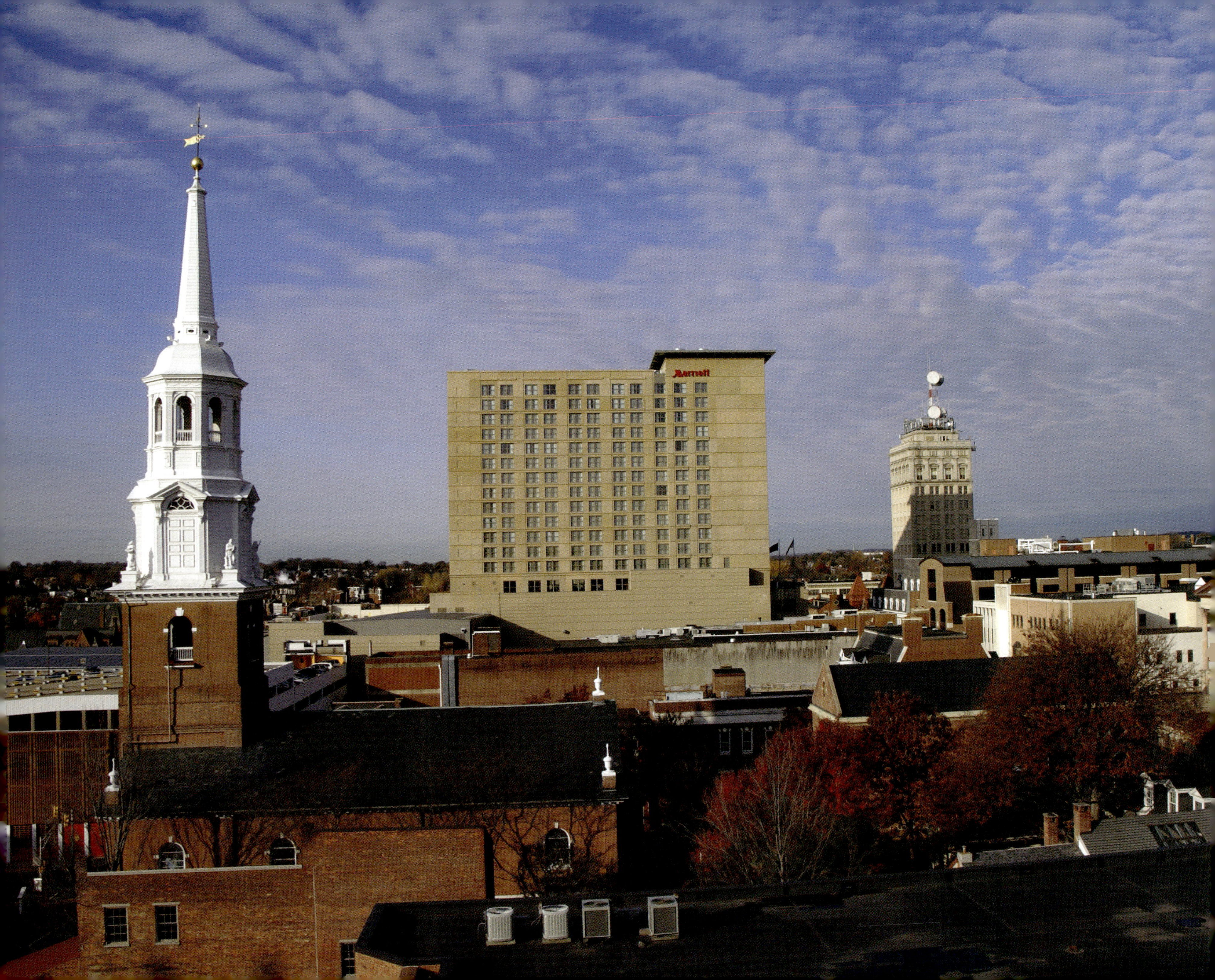
Marriott

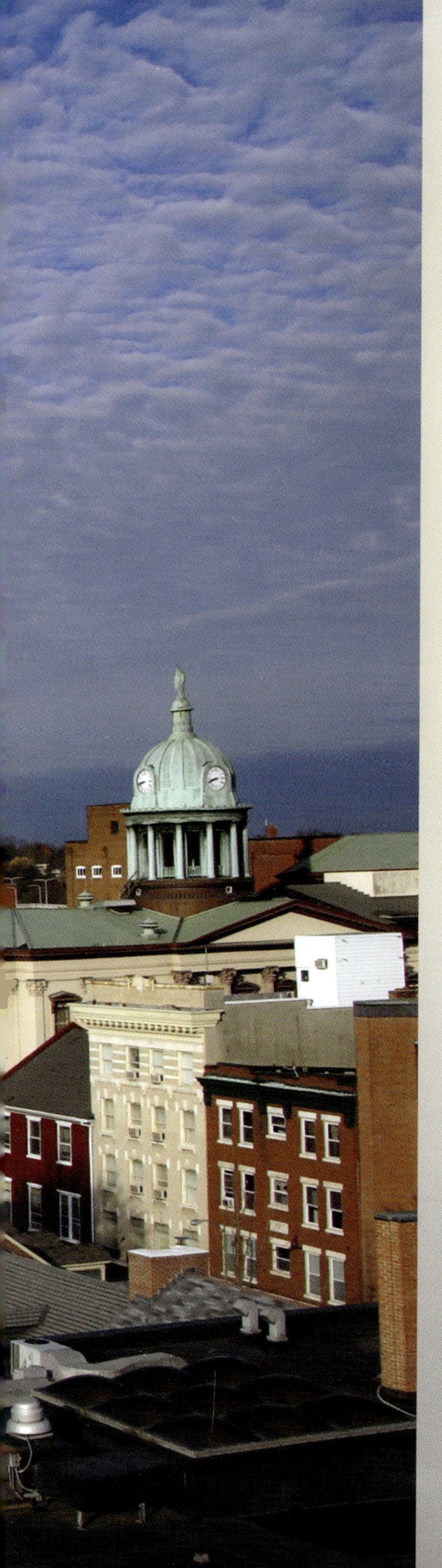

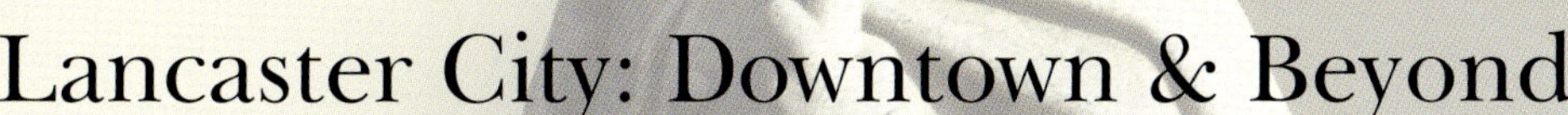

Lancaster City: Downtown & Beyond

Once known as Hickory Town, Lancaster was renamed for the English town of Lancaster, located in the northwestern county of Lancashire. The Pennsylvania town was laid out in the early-1730s by James Hamilton. Streets were designed in grid formation, with a large square, originally called Centre Square, marking the center of town.

Lancaster became a borough in 1742, when it was home to almost 1,500 residents. By 1760, Lancaster was the largest inland city in the colonies, and served as the capital of the Commonwealth of Pennsylvania (1799-1813) *and* the national capital. Forced to flee the British Army descending upon Philadelphia, the Second Continental Congress moved to Lancaster for one day in September 1777. In the brief period when Lancaster was the capital, the Congress' only order of business was to resolve to relocate to nearby York, Pennsylvania. Located on the west side of the Susquehanna River, York provided further distance and protection from the British.

Major national political figures like President James Buchanan and Thaddeus Stevens, the "Great Commoner," called Lancaster home in the nineteenth century. Today, Lancaster is a shining example of urban renewal. More than 13,400 buildings and structures are part of Pennsylvania's largest National Register of Historic Places historic district. The downtown has become a vibrant arts destination, anchored by the Fulton Opera House and Pennsylvania College of Art & Design. The Lancaster County Convention Center has given new life to a vacant quadrant of Penn Square, and resulted in construction of Lancaster's second skyscraper. And one of Lancaster's long-time draws, Lancaster Central Market, is today recognized as one of the top public gathering spaces in the United States.

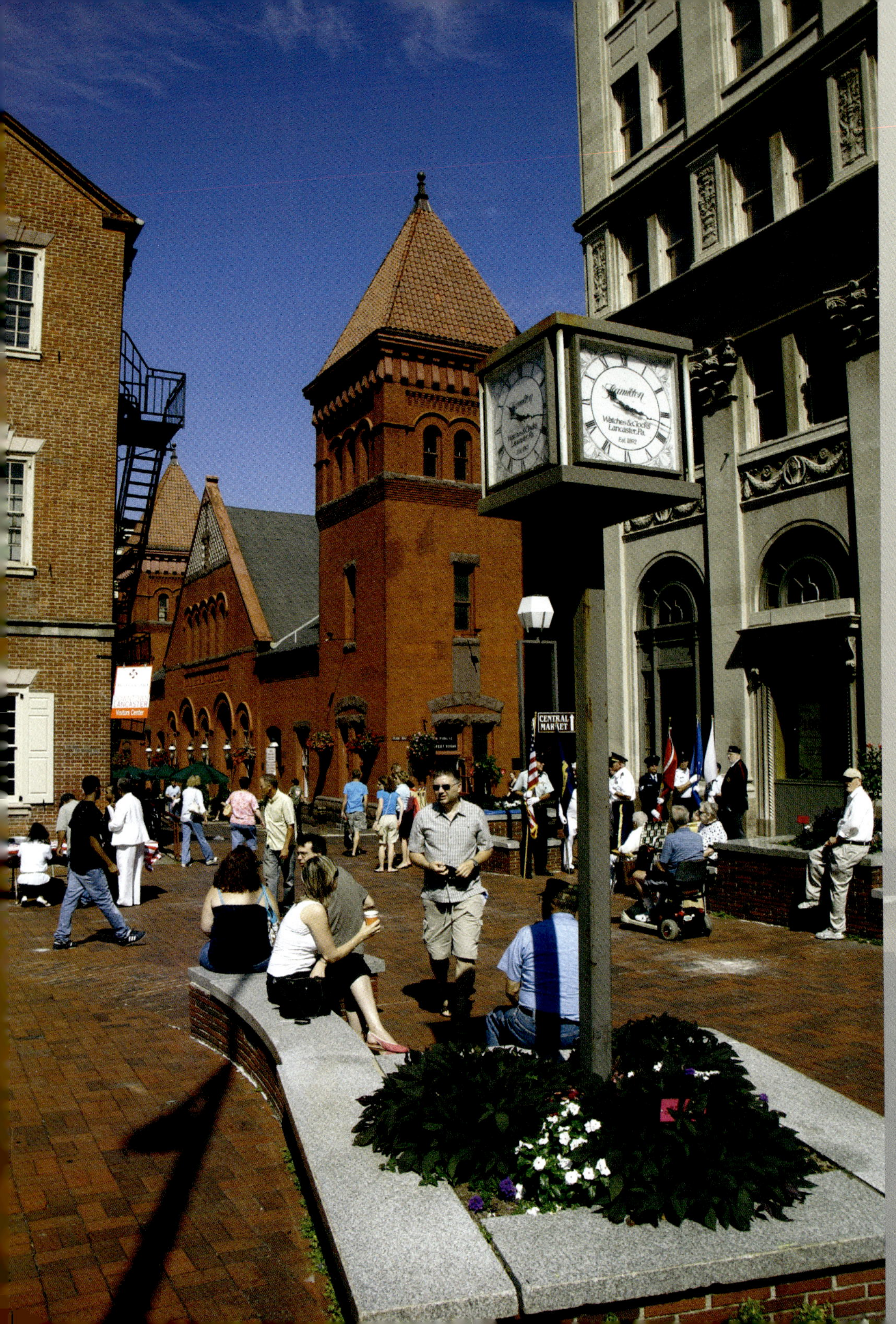

Penn Square

James Hamilton's 1730s plan for Lancaster's streets was a grid pattern similar to Philadelphia's. At the intersection of High (renamed King) and Queen Streets, a town square was established. This square was originally known as Centre Square, a name that it retained throughout the eighteenth century, and much of the nineteenth. In 1737, a county courthouse was constructed in the middle of the square—a common practice in Pennsylvania communities. Throughout the centuries, Centre/Penn Square has been the heart of Lancaster. The Second Continental Congress met in the Square, as did the government of the Commonwealth of Pennsylvania. An outdoor farmers' market began in the Square before relocating to a nearby building. Prominent businesses and retailers have called the Square home since Lancaster was established. Today, Penn Square offers a remarkable juxtaposition of past and present, ranging from the late-eighteenth-century Old City Hall building to the modern twenty-first-century Lancaster County Convention Center.

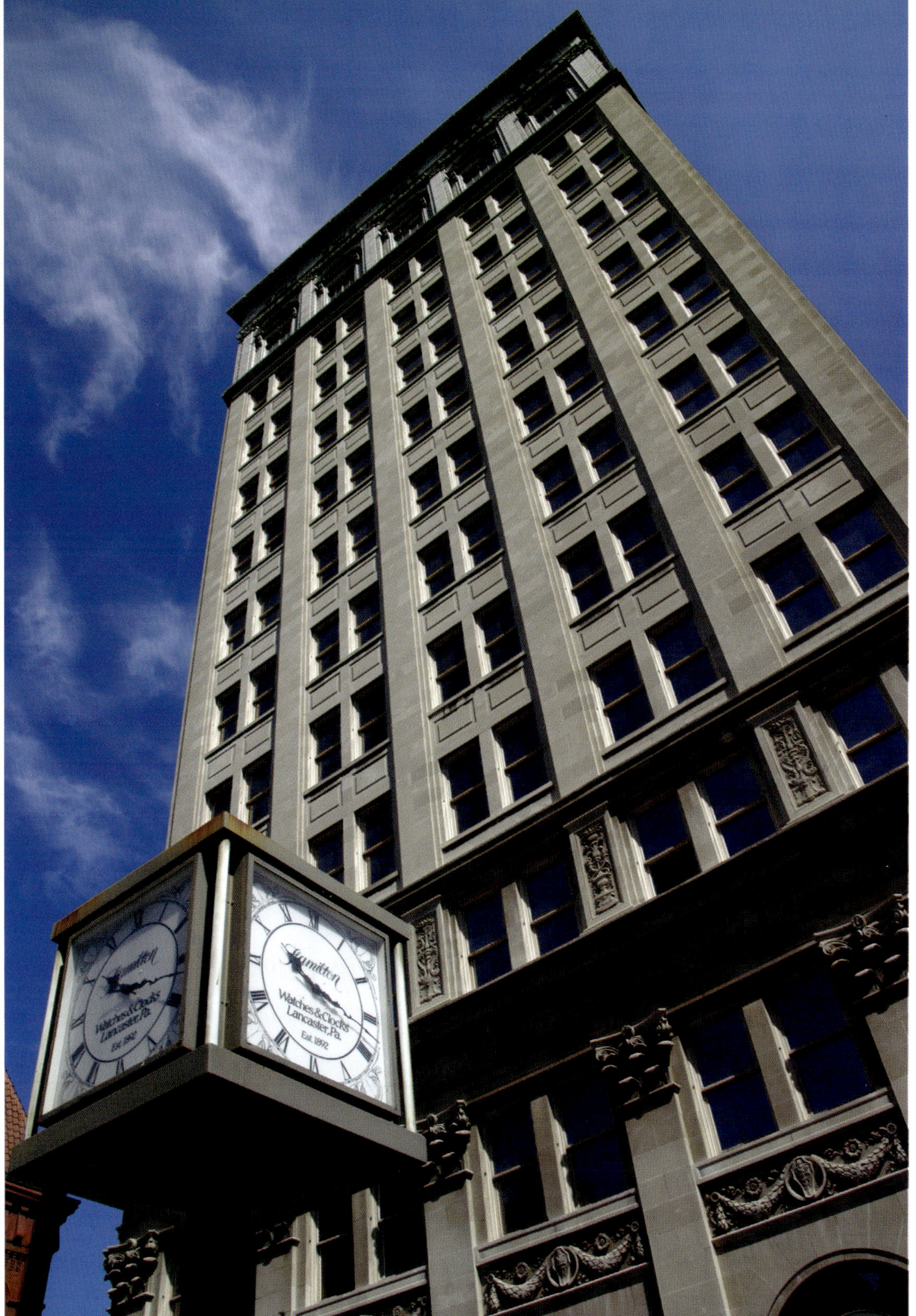

For more than eighty-five years the W.W. Griest Building on Penn Square was Lancaster's only skyscraper. The 14-story building was constructed in 1925 from a design by noted Lancaster architect C. Emlen Urban. Italian Renaissance Revival in style, the building was originally home to Lancaster's public utilities, which were led by William Walton Griest, for whom the building is named. Griest also served in the U.S. House of Representatives from 1909 to 1929.

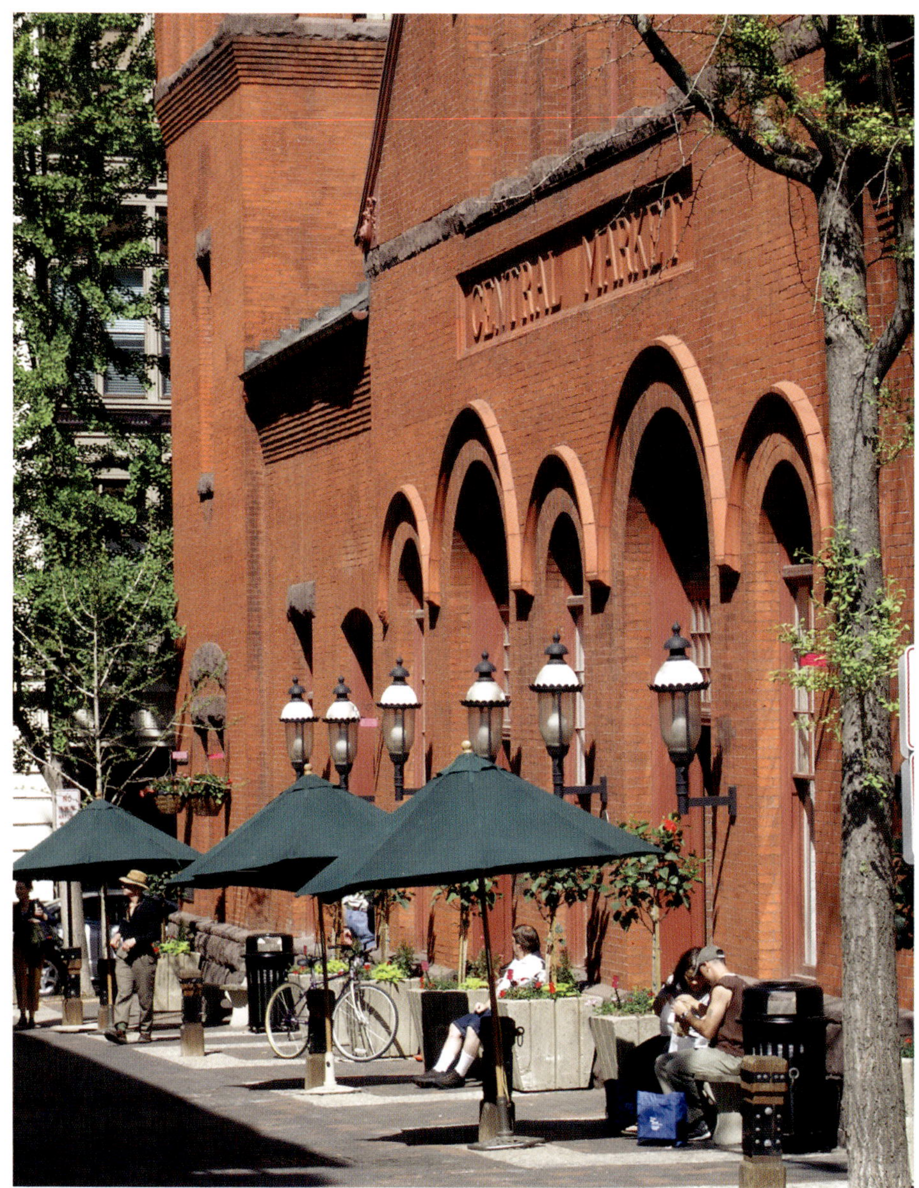

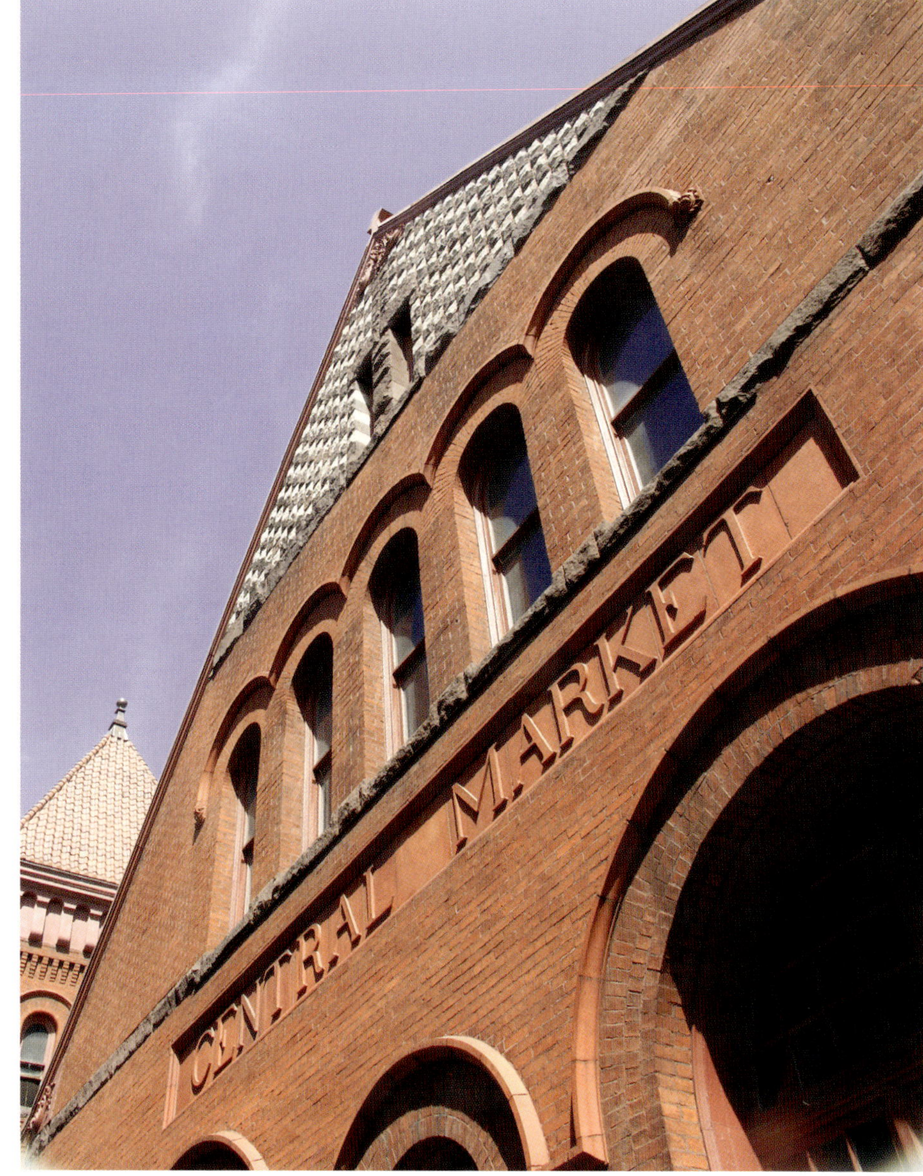

Built in 1889 in the Romanesque Revival style of architecture, the Lancaster Central Market is located on a tract of land that was set aside for a farmers' market in 1730. The Central Market was established by King George II in 1742 and the first market house was built in 1757. James H. Warner was the architect of the present building, which features twin seventy-two-foot towers and a terra cotta roof. In 2009, Central Market was recognized as one of America's Great Public Spaces by the American Planning Association.

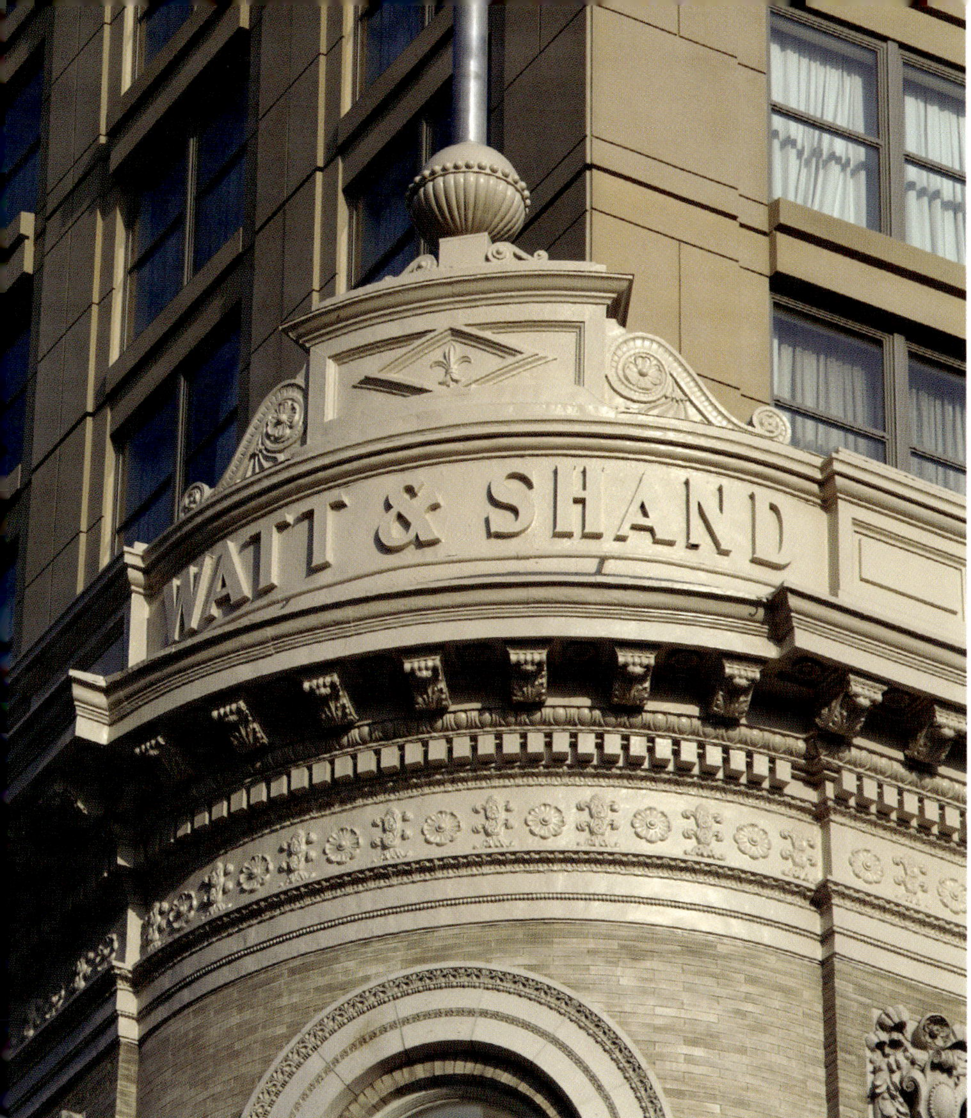

The Watt and Shand Department Store in Penn Square was the heart of Lancaster's commercial district for more than 100 years. The store was opened in 1878 by Peter Watt, James Shand, and Gilbert Thompson (Thompson died one year later). Lancaster's largest department store was constructed in several major phases as the store grew in size. The well-known Beaux-Arts appearance is the result of a new building designed by C. Emlen Urban and constructed in 1898. Upon completion of the new building, the earlier buildings occupied by the department store on East King Street were upgraded with façades that matched the new building. As the store expanded on Penn Square and South Queen Street, the façade was maintained so the buildings would look as one from the exterior. In 1992, Watt & Shand was acquired by York-based The Bon-Ton, which closed the store in 1995. After standing vacant for a decade, the façade found new life as part of the Lancaster County Convention Center—a modern building and hotel tower constructed behind the historic façade.

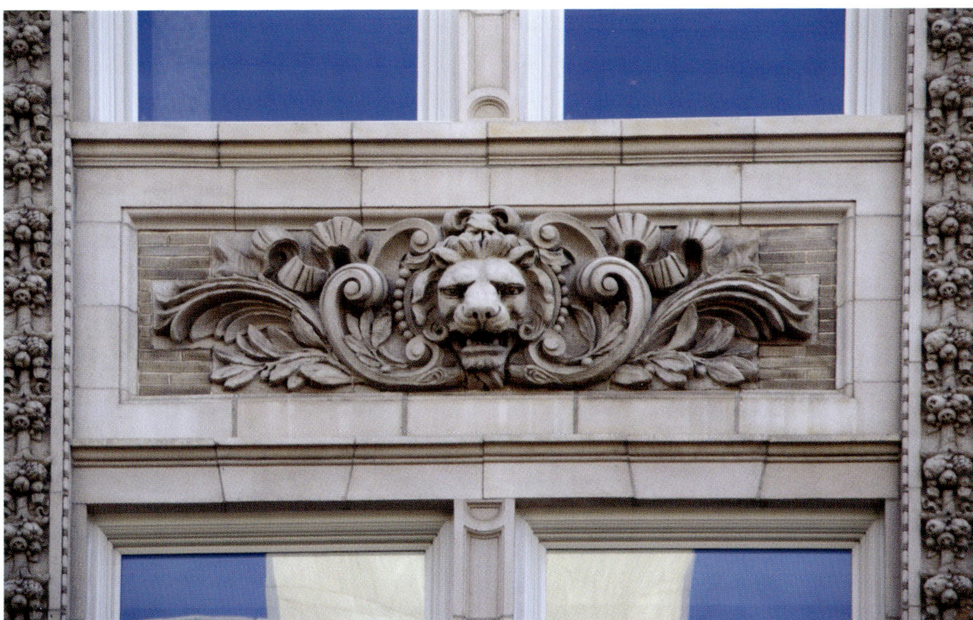

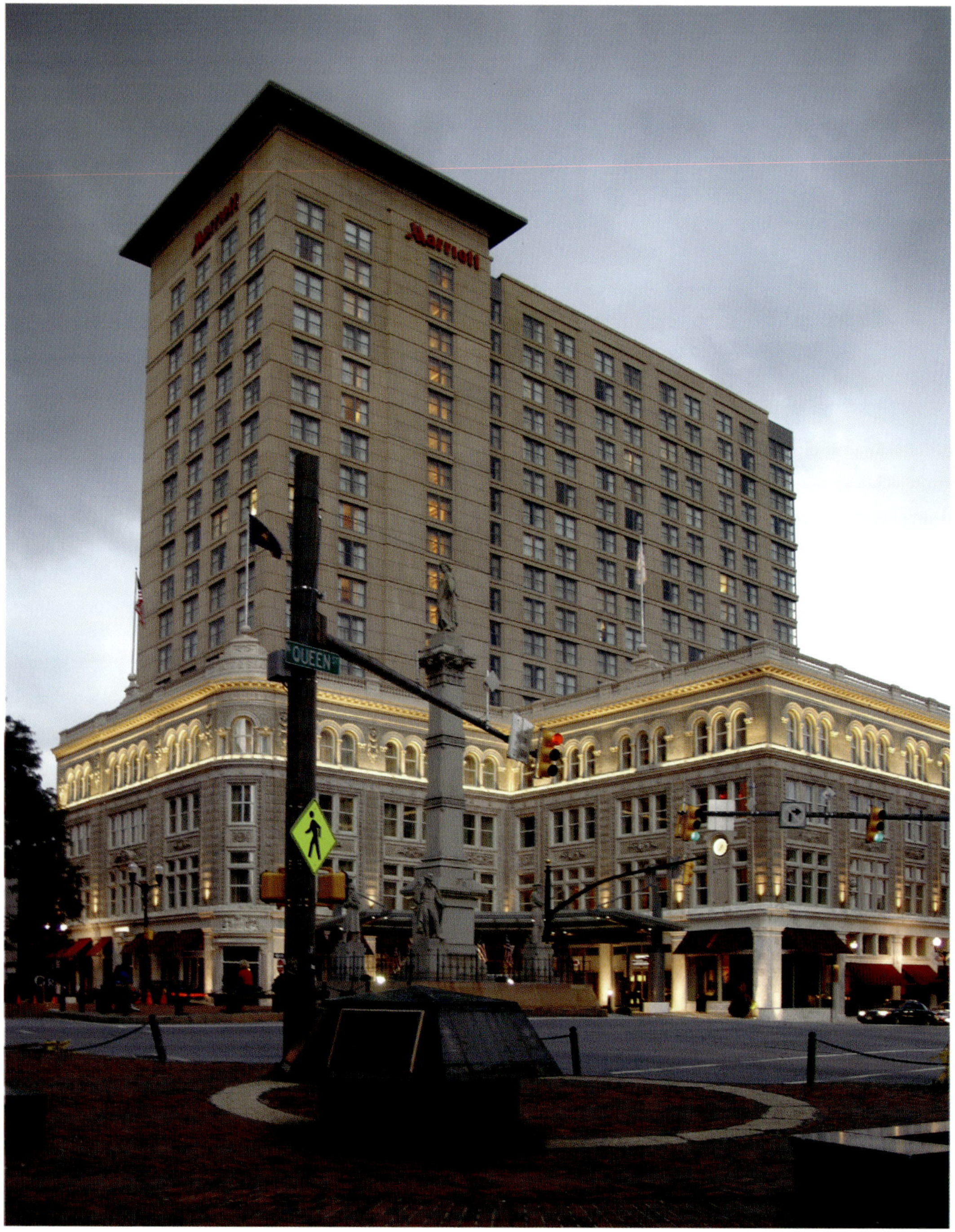

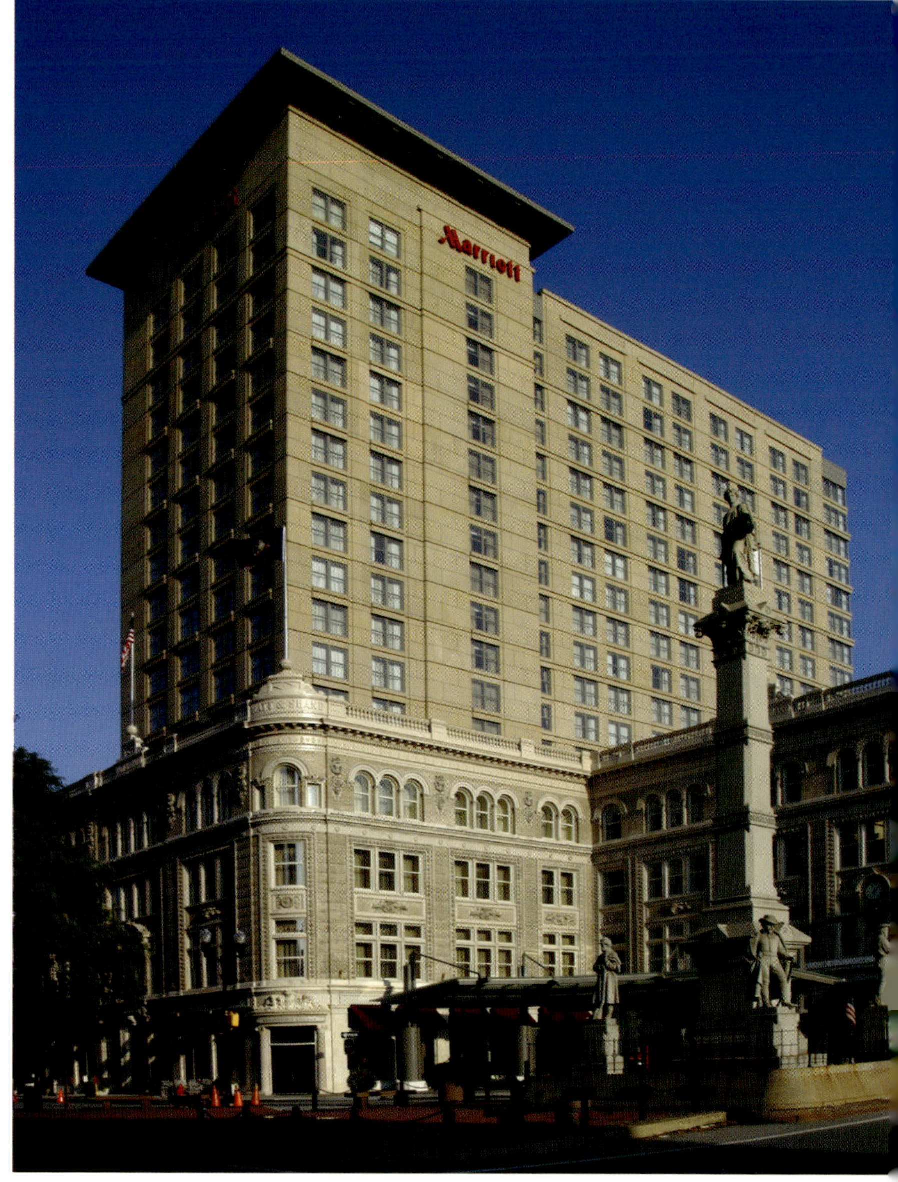

The $174 million Lancaster County Convention Center was completed in 2009. The integrated facility includes 90,000 square feet of meeting and convention space, as well as a new 300-room, eighteen-story Marriott Hotel—Lancaster's second skyscraper.

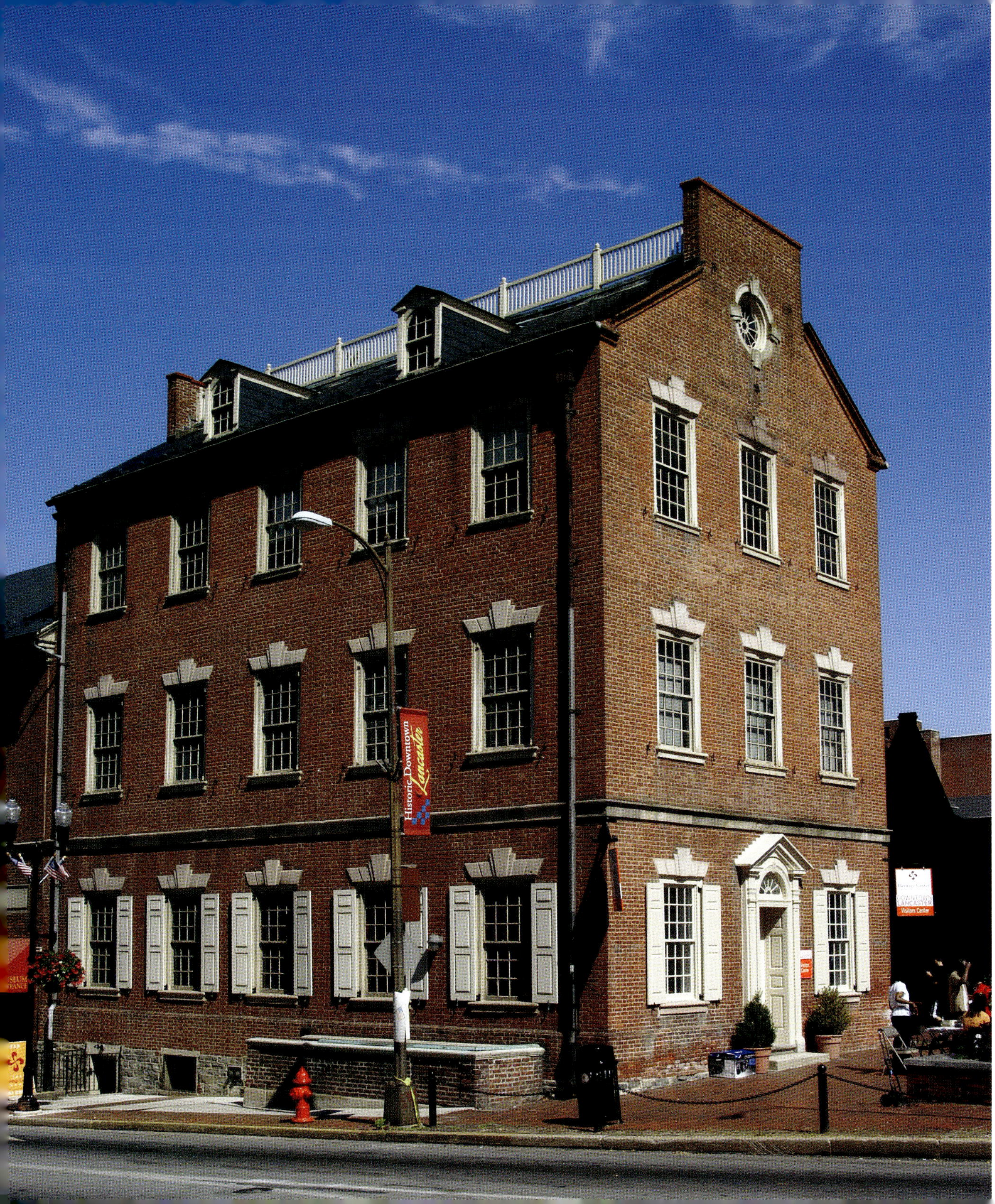

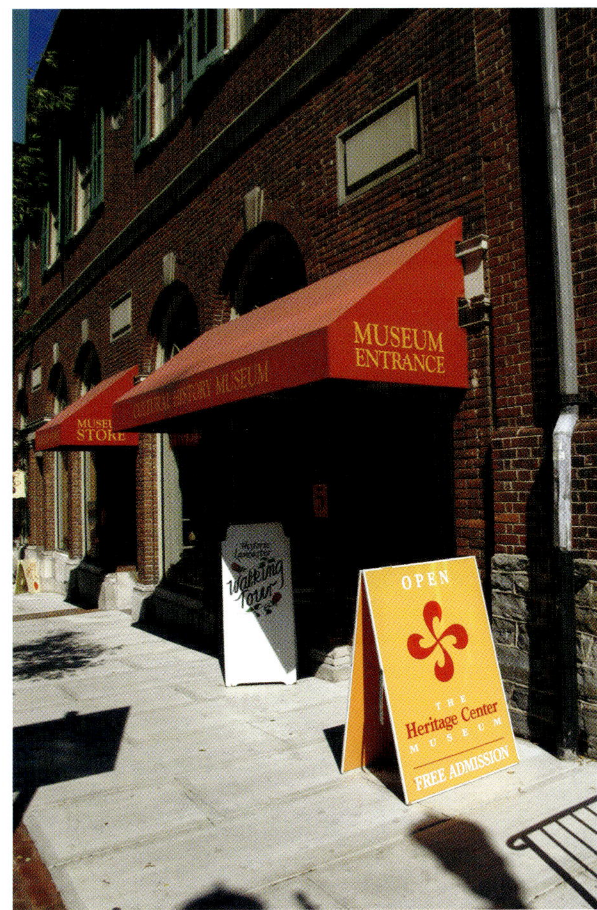

Construction on this building began in 1795 and was completed two years later. Originally the Public Office House, the three and a half-story building is a prominent example of Federal-style architecture with Flemish-bond brickwork, keystones, and a belt course. The main entrance was originally located on the south side of the building fronting West King Street. From 1799 to 1812, when Lancaster was the state capital, the building was home to the government of the Commonwealth of Pennsylvania. Through the years the building also housed city and county government offices, a Masonic Lodge, Post Office, and library. Today the building is home to the Lancaster Visitors Center, as well as the Heritage Center Museum, a steward of Lancaster County's past that collects, preserves, and interprets history and decorative arts.

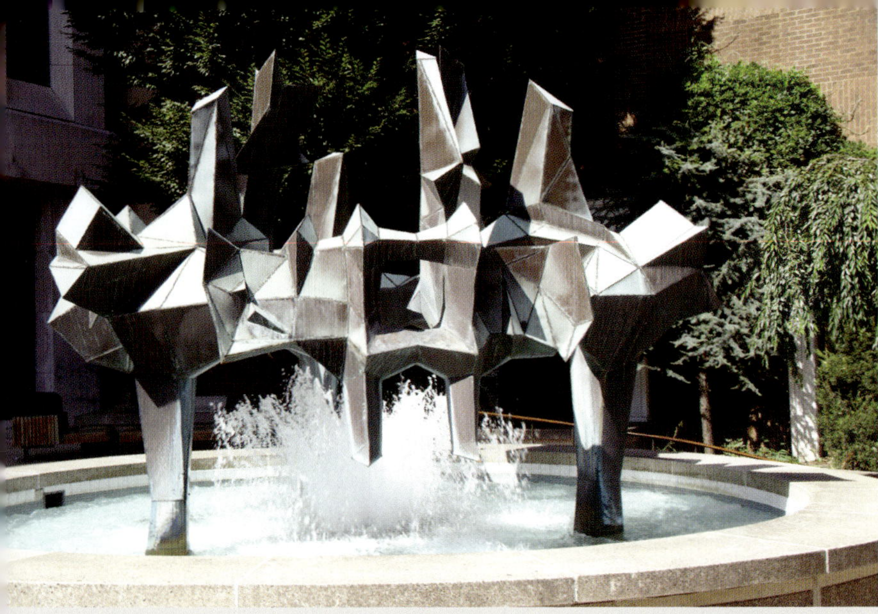

This modern fountain is located on the southwest quadrant of Penn Square.

This building, located on the southwest quadrant of Penn Square, was built in 1921 for the Keystone Furniture Company. In the mid-1940s, the building became home to Harold's Furniture Store.

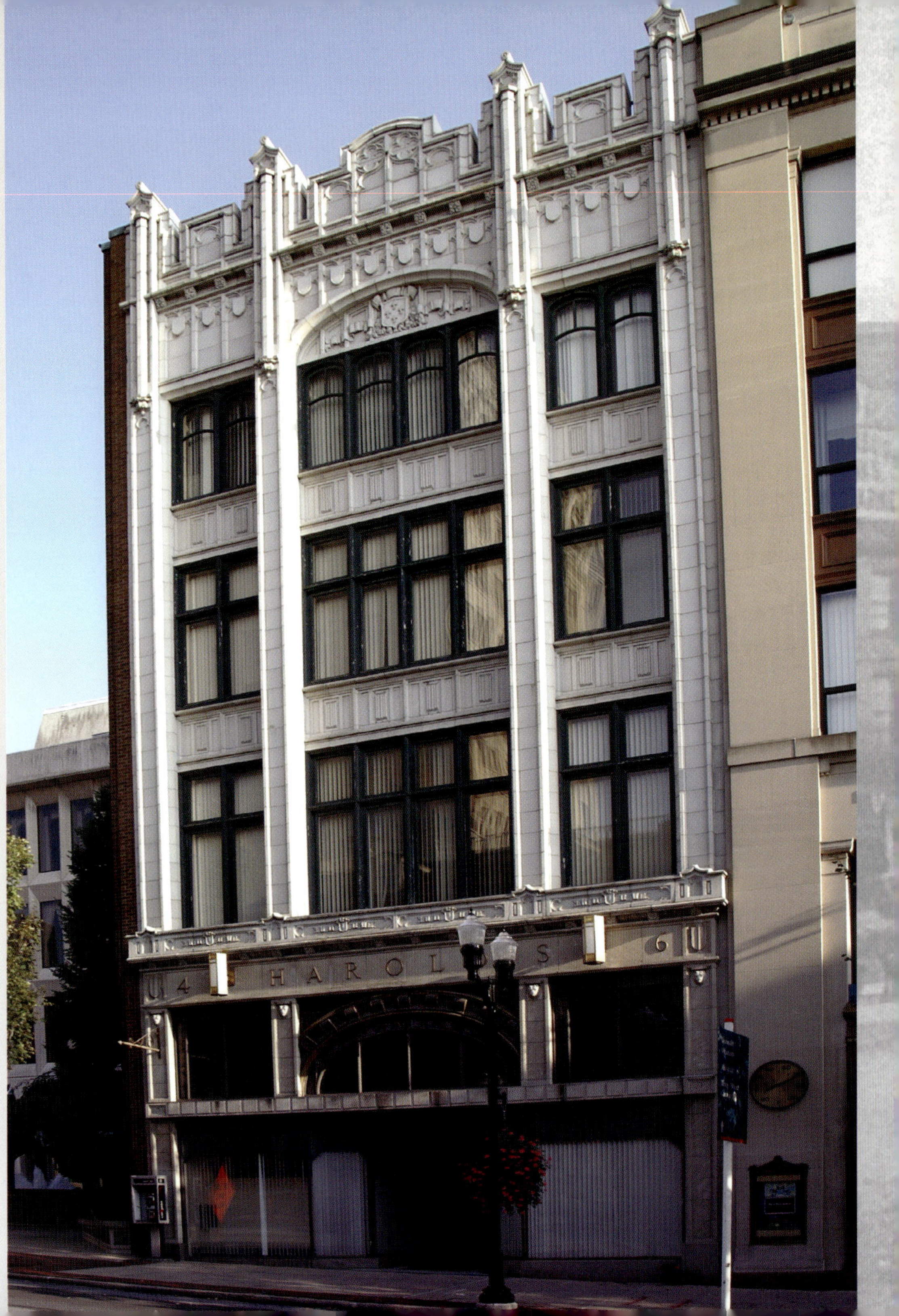

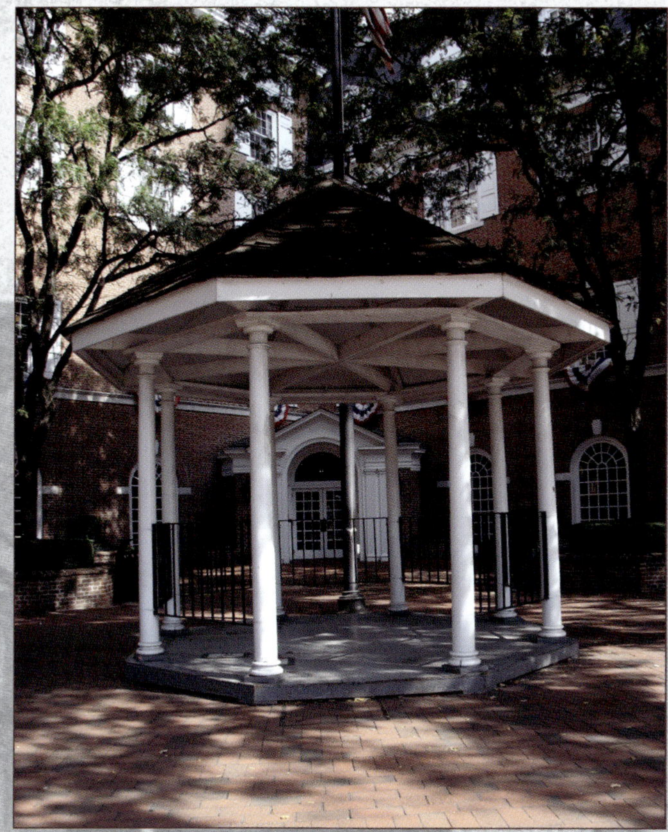

The Penn Square gazebo stands on the northeast quadrant of the square.

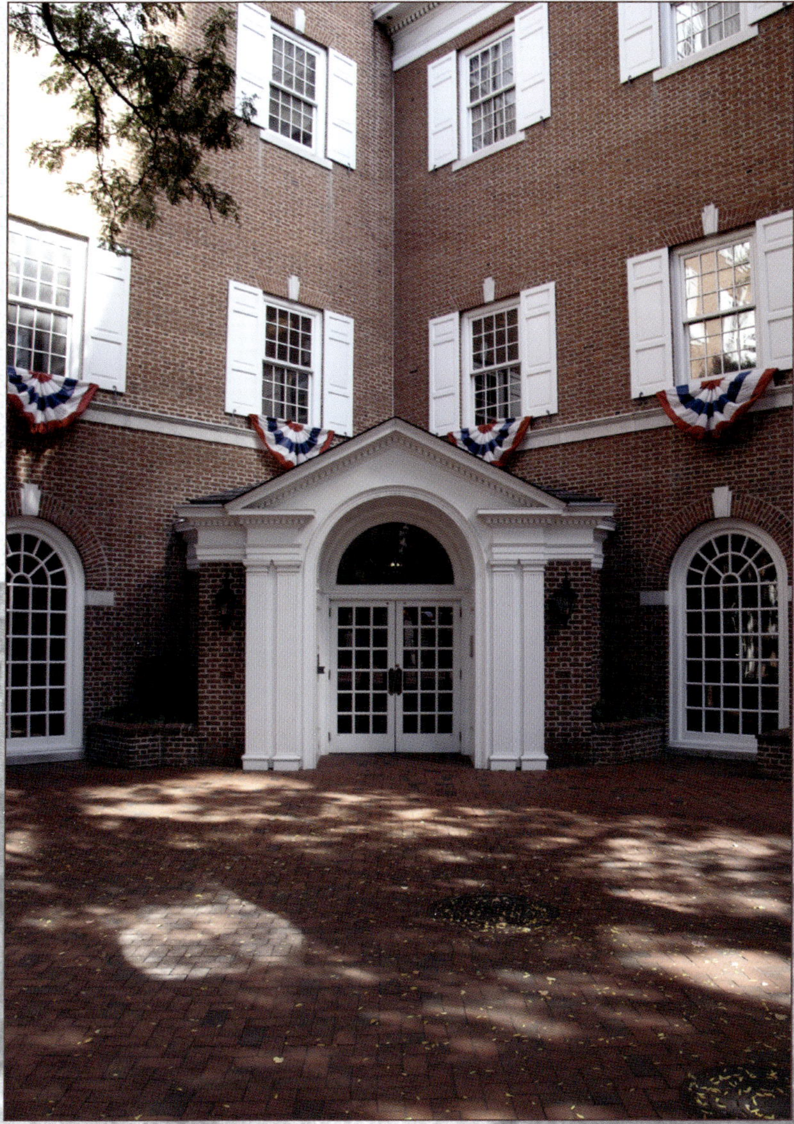

In 1882, Lancaster merchants and farmers organized Fulton National Bank, named to honor Robert Fulton, a Lancaster County native best known for building the first successful steamboat. For several decades Fulton Bank occupied a large Art Deco building in Penn Square. The building was renovated in 1976, losing the geometric façade and gaining a Neo-Colonial appearance with an exaggerated mansard roof.

The Lancaster *Intelligencer Journal* traces its roots to *The Lancaster Journal,* which was founded in 1794, making it one of the oldest operating newspapers in the United States. By the end of the Civil War, the newspaper was in decline and Andrew Jackson Steinman took it over and brought it back to prominence. This building was constructed in 1927 and is today home to Lancaster Newspapers, publishers of the *Intelligencer Journal* and *Lancaster New Era*, which were merged in 2009.

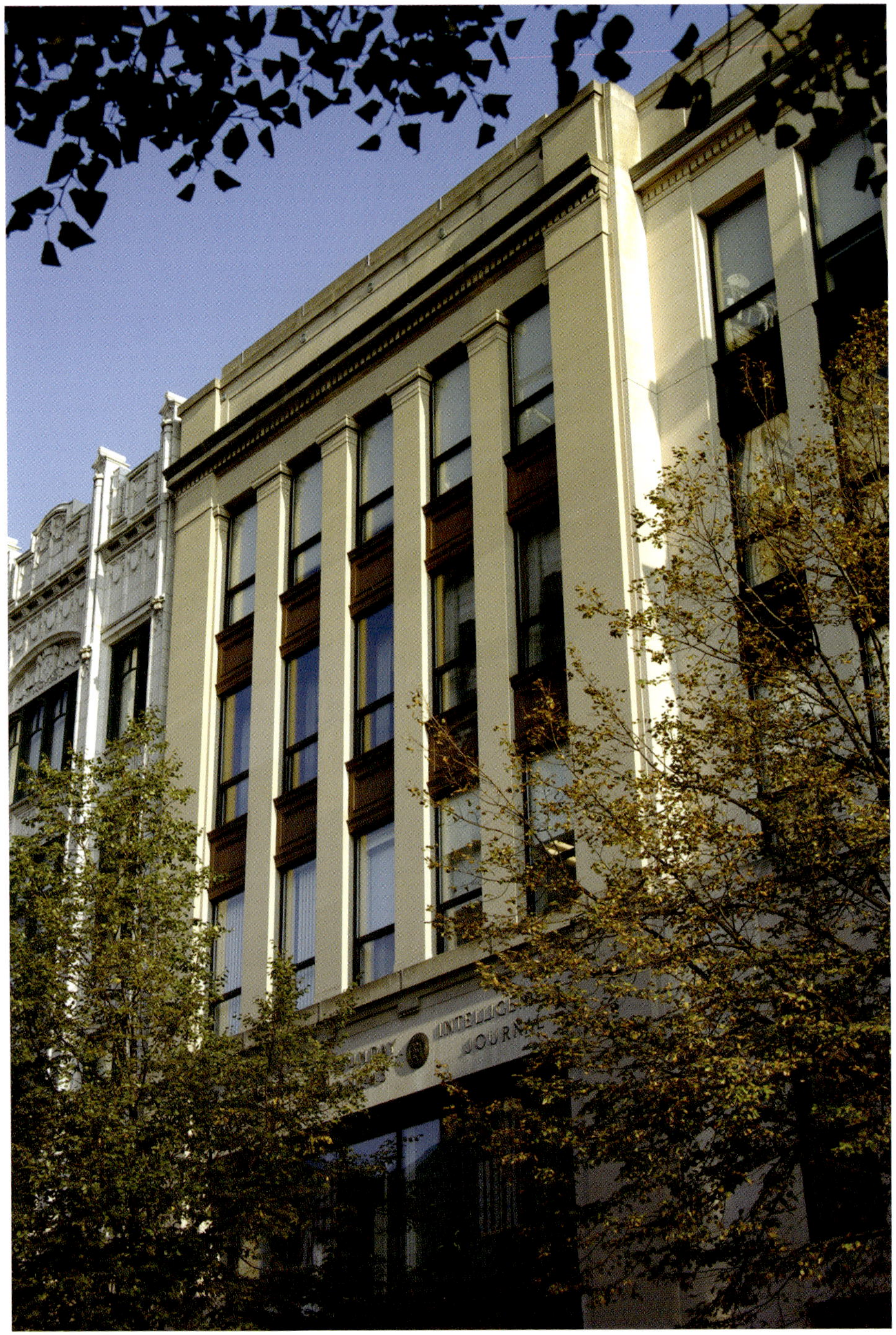

Located in the center of Penn Square, the Soldiers and Sailors Monument was dedicated on July 4, 1874. The Civil War monument features granite statues of four servicemen representing infantry, artillery, cavalry, and navy. The memorial is topped by a statue representing the Genius of Liberty. The location of the statue also marks the location of two county courthouses that stood in Center Square. The first Lancaster County Courthouse was home to the Second Continental Congress, which occupied the building for one day in September 1777.

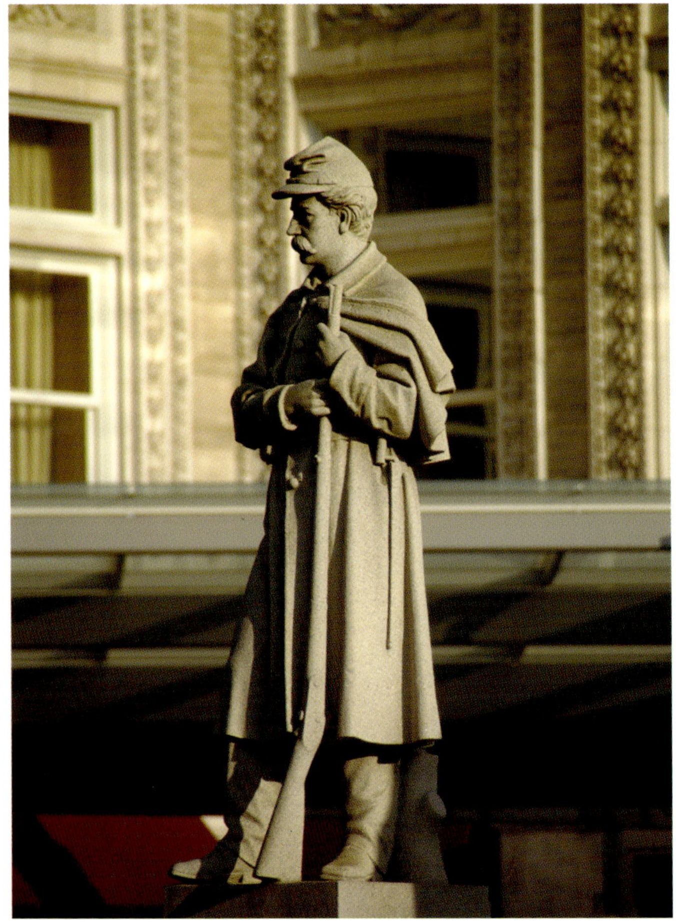

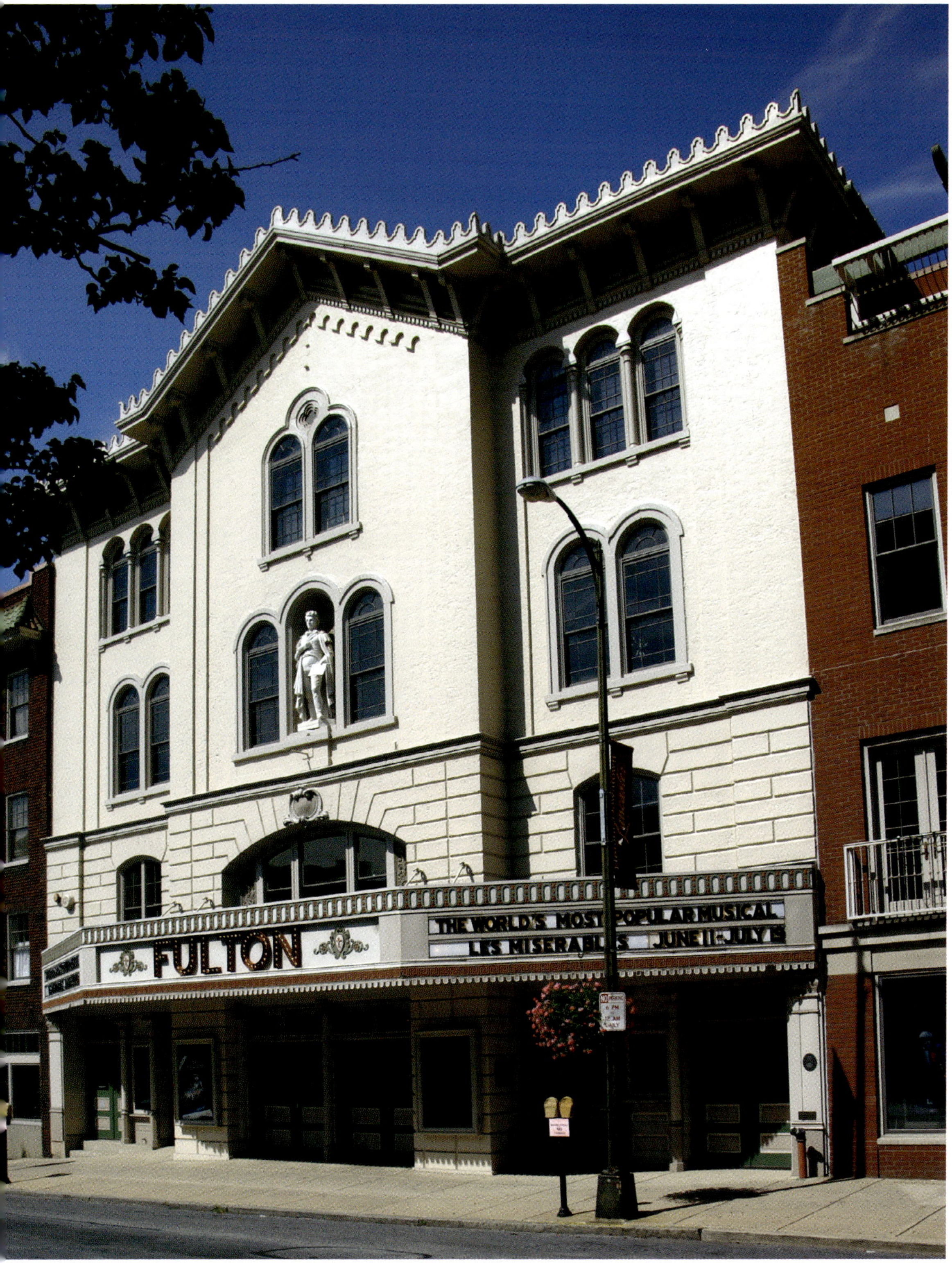

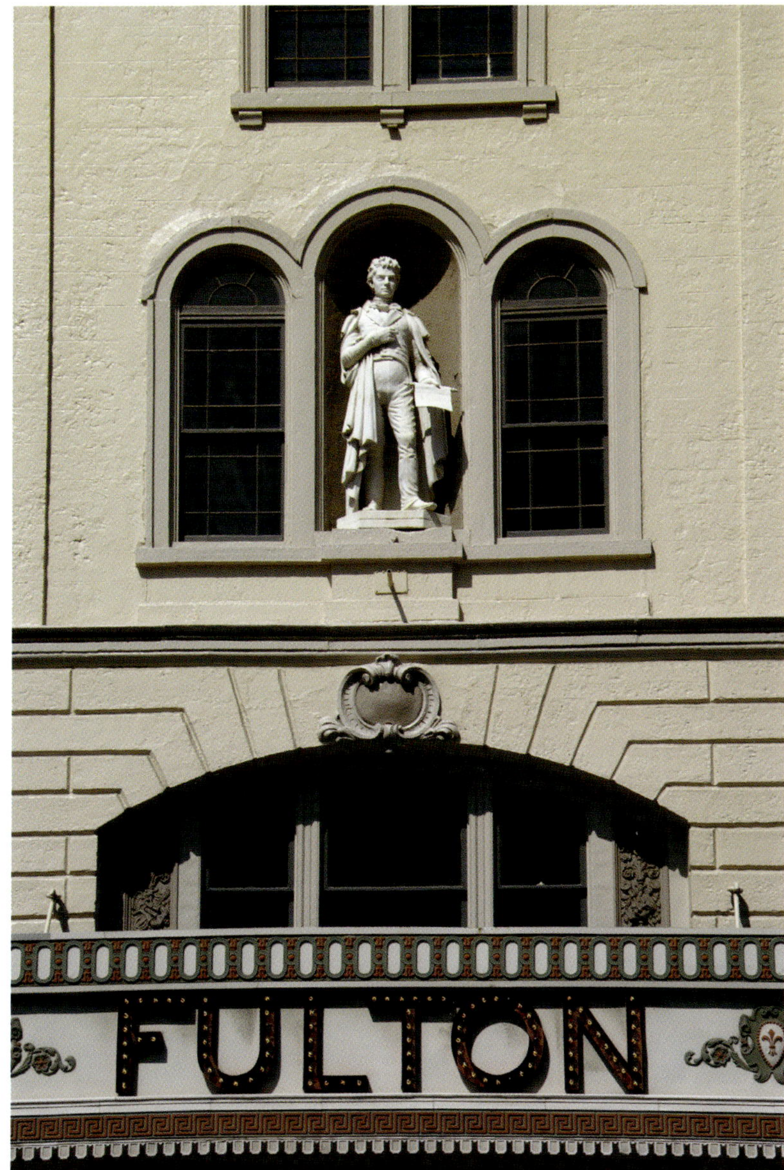

Located on the first block of North Prince Street, the Fulton Opera House is a community gem and one of the anchors of Lancaster's arts community. The Italianate building was constructed in 1852 as Fulton Hall then remodeled in 1873 as the Fulton Opera House. Known as "The Grand Old Lady," the theater is a National Historic Landmark and recognized as the nation's oldest continually operating theater. The building's architect was Samuel Sloan, who also designed the Lancaster County Courthouse.

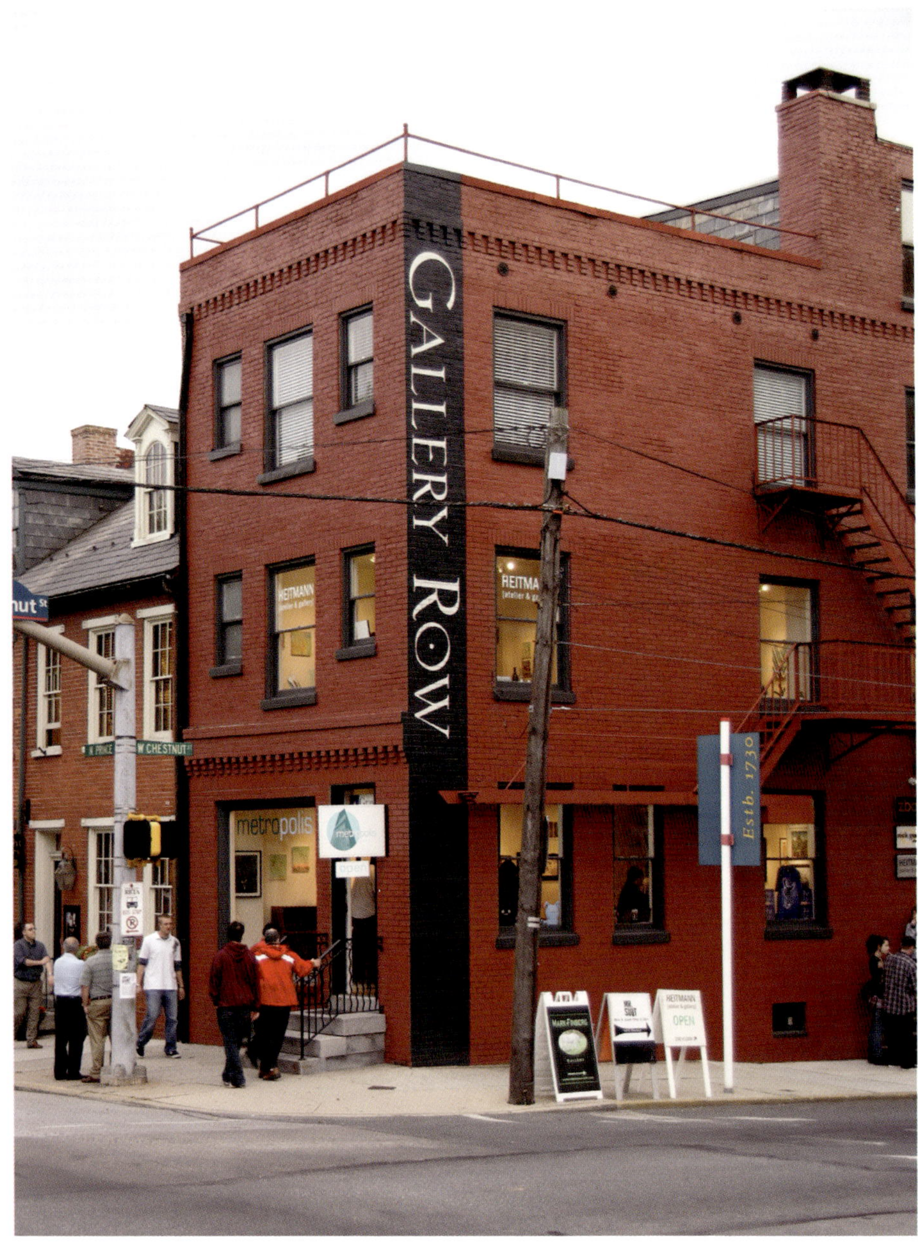

Gallery Row is a popular arts destination in downtown Lancaster. Anchored by Fulton Opera House and Pennsylvania College of Art & Design, the "Avenue of the Arts" features a colorful blend of galleries and shops.

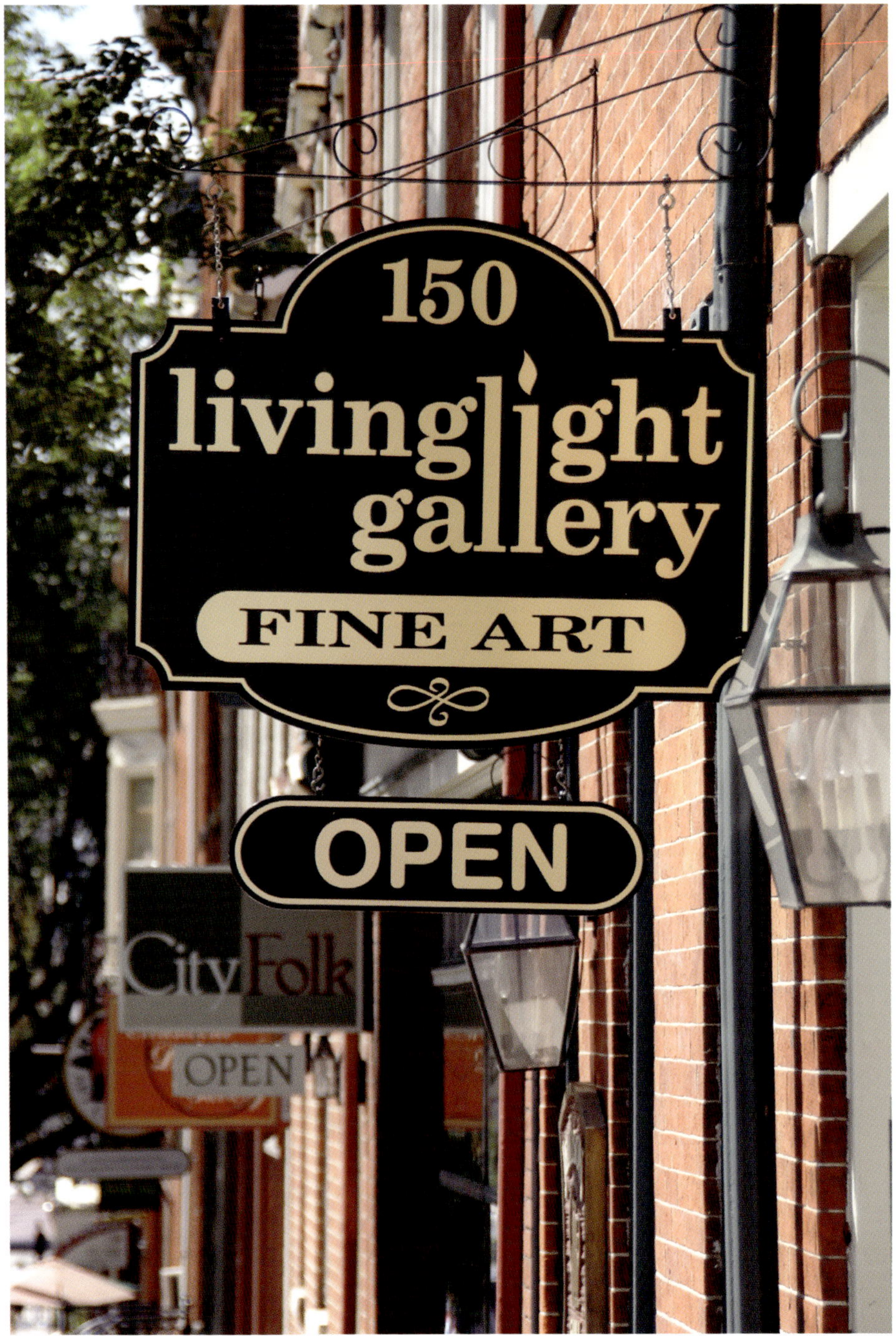

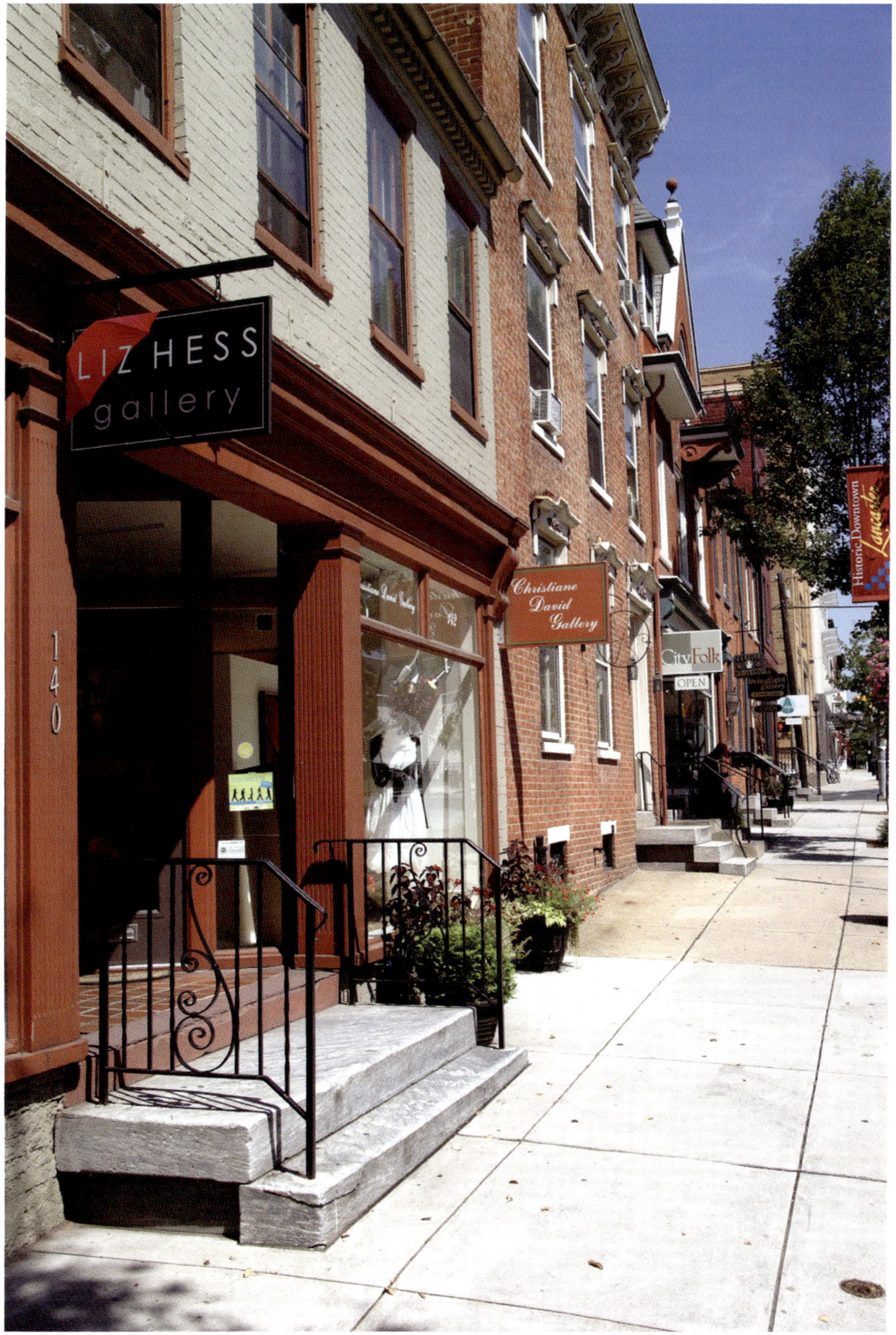

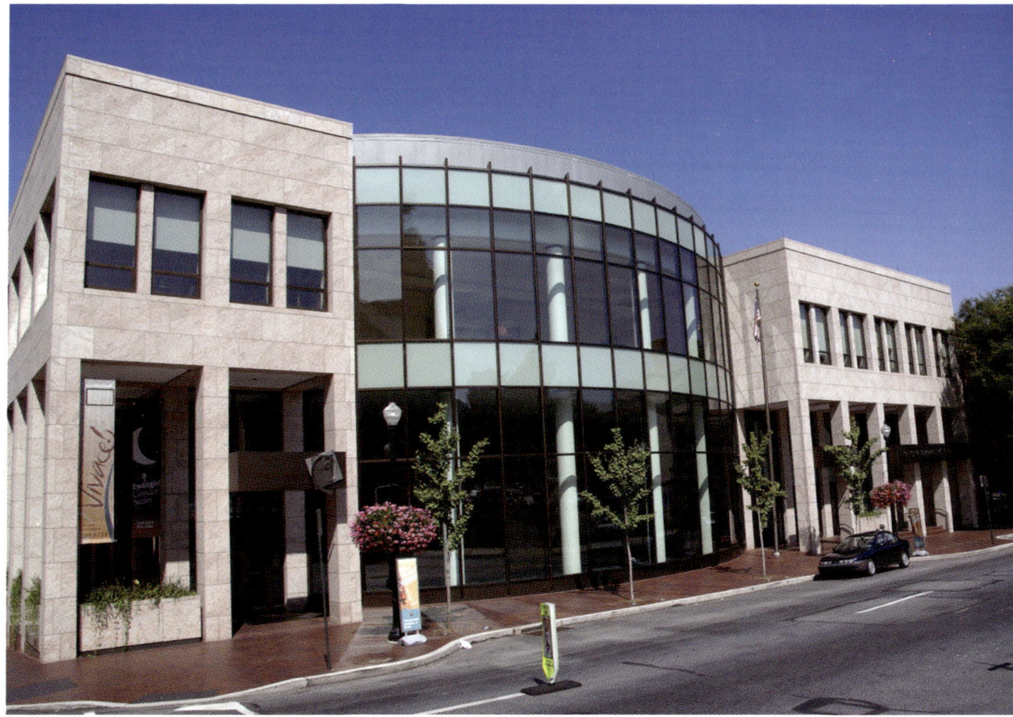

The Pennsylvania Academy of Music opened in 1991 and one year later moved into a building on North Prince Street. In 2008, a modern glass and stone building was constructed on North Prince Street, allowing the Academy to serve up to 600 student musicians. The building was designed by internationally renowned architects Philip Johnson and Alan Ritchie and featured the 367-seat Steinman Concert Hall.

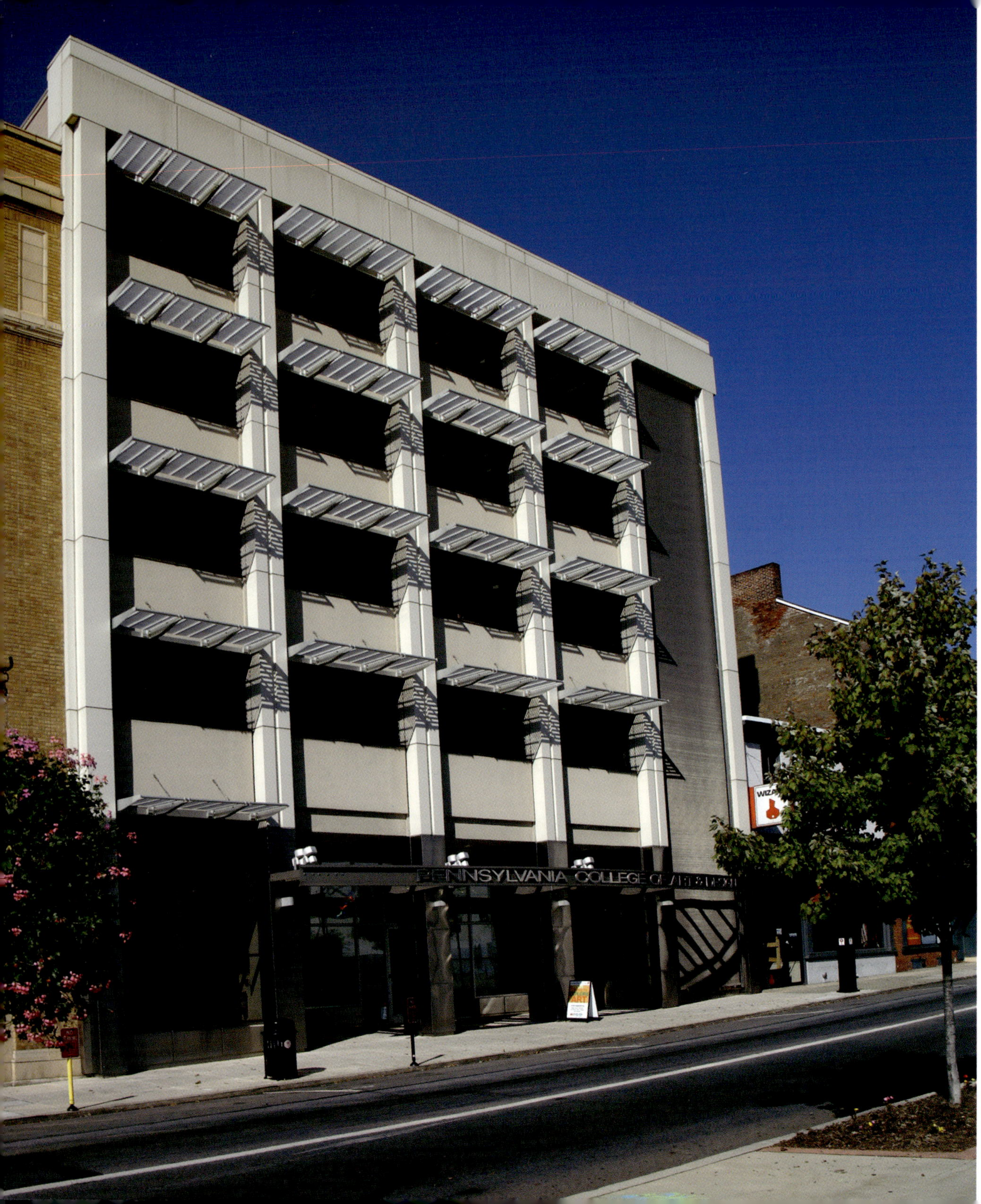

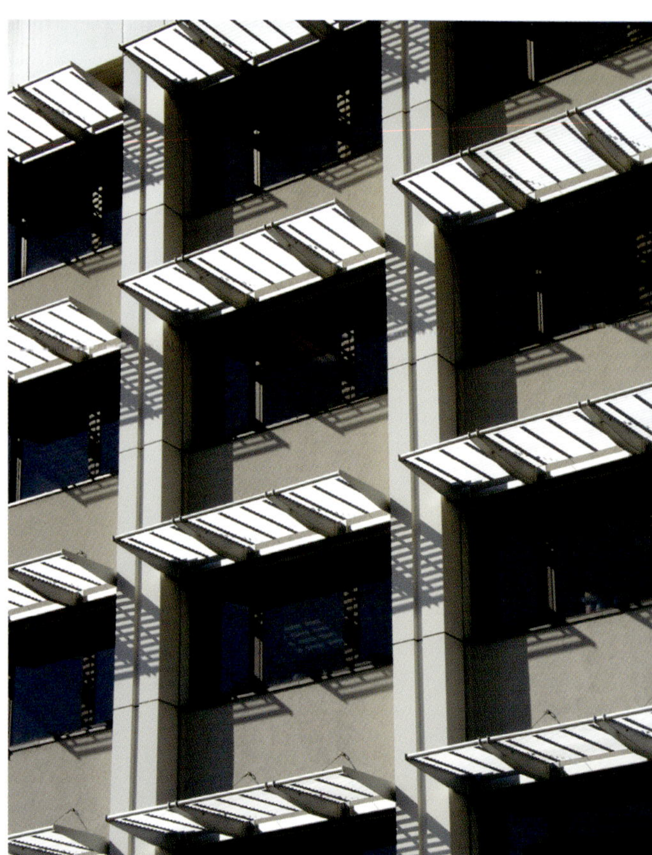

The Pennsylvania School of the Arts was founded in 1982 and relocated to North Prince Street in Lancaster City five years later. The school became a degree-granting college in 1999, offering a Bachelor of Fine Arts Program. Now known as the Pennsylvania College of Art & Design, the institution offers training in fine art, graphic design, photography, and illustratio In 2004, the college updated its façade, creating a focal point with metal skin, glass, and sun canopies. The drama is enhance after dark, when the building is bathed in a rotating palette of color.

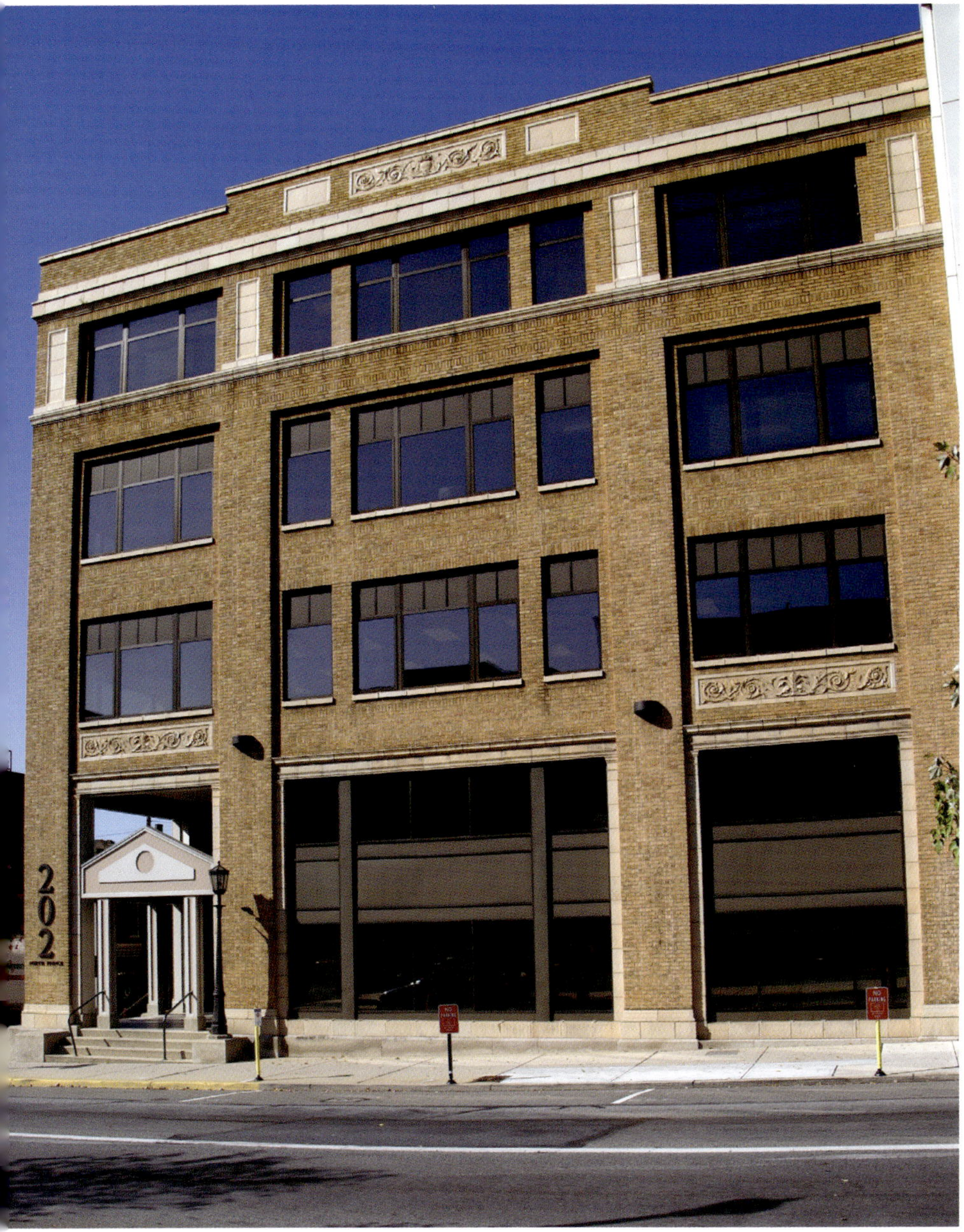

Previously home to Educator's Mutual Insurance Co., this historic building is today part of the Pennsylvania College of Art & Design. The 1920s-era building was originally home to Herr and Company.

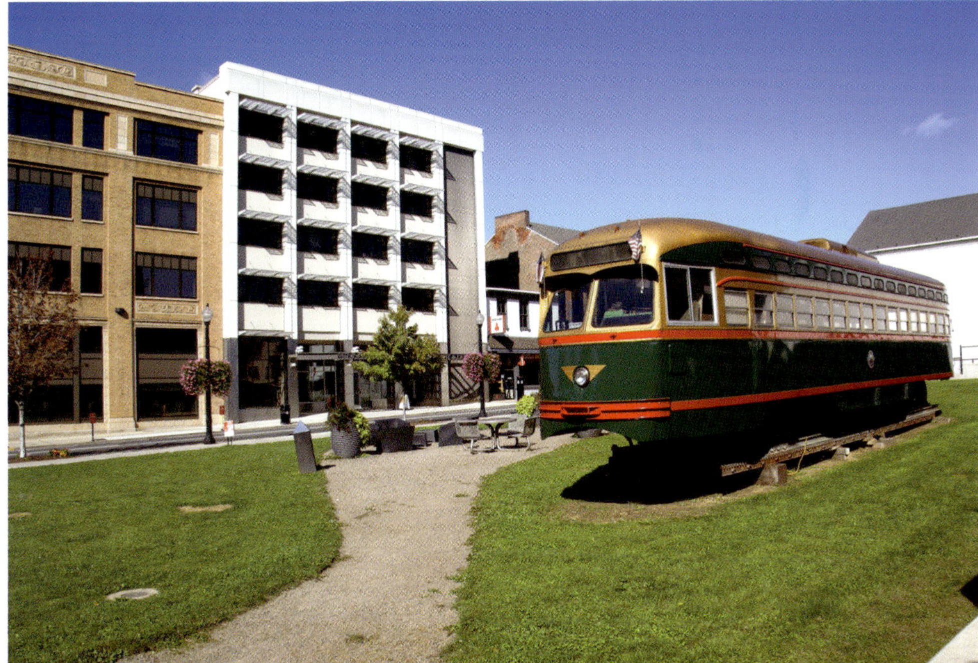

Located across from the Pennsylvania College of Art & Design, the Art Park features a restored vintage streetcar that was unveiled in 2008.

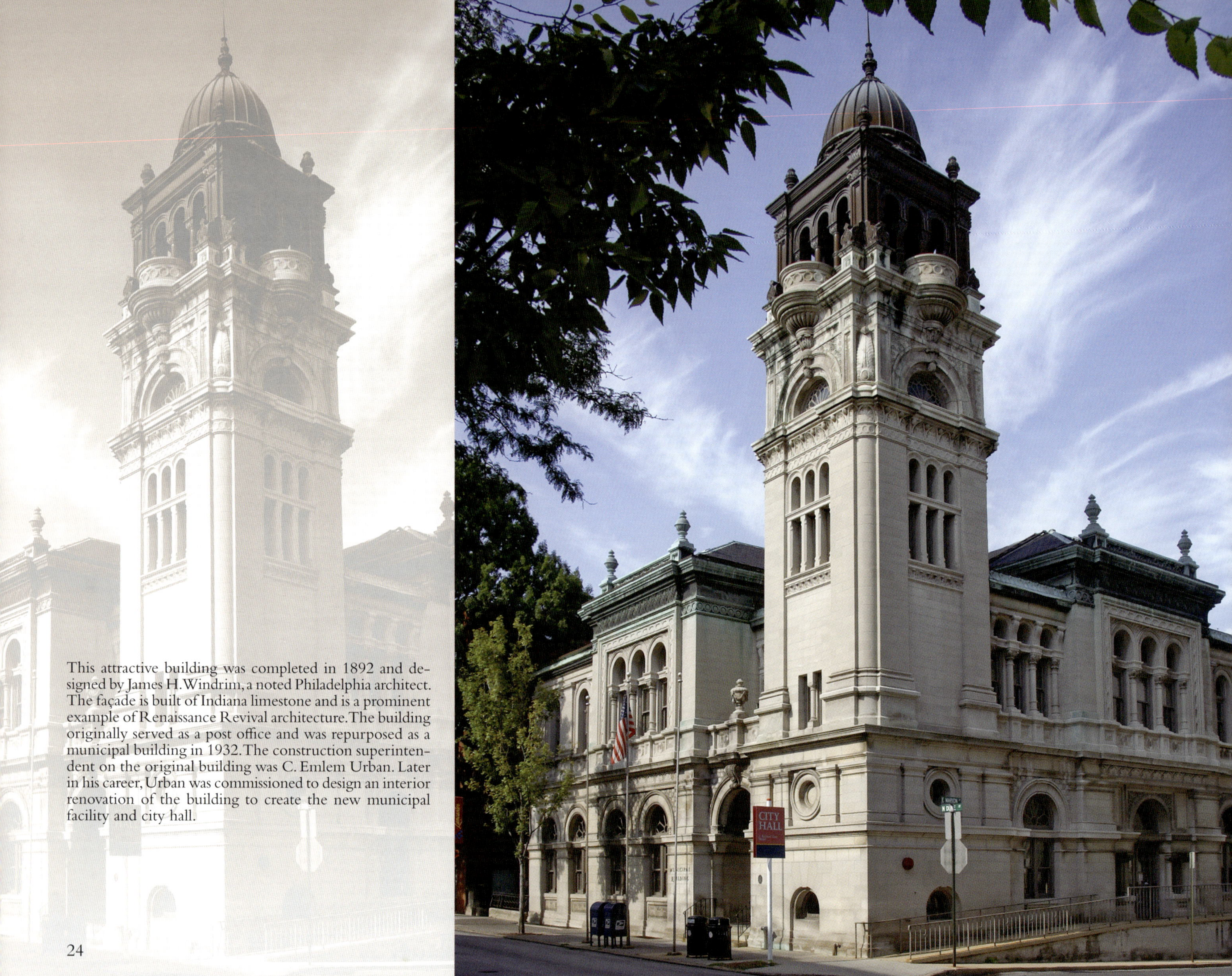

This attractive building was completed in 1892 and designed by James H. Windrim, a noted Philadelphia architect. The façade is built of Indiana limestone and is a prominent example of Renaissance Revival architecture. The building originally served as a post office and was repurposed as a municipal building in 1932. The construction superintendent on the original building was C. Emlem Urban. Later in his career, Urban was commissioned to design an interior renovation of the building to create the new municipal facility and city hall.

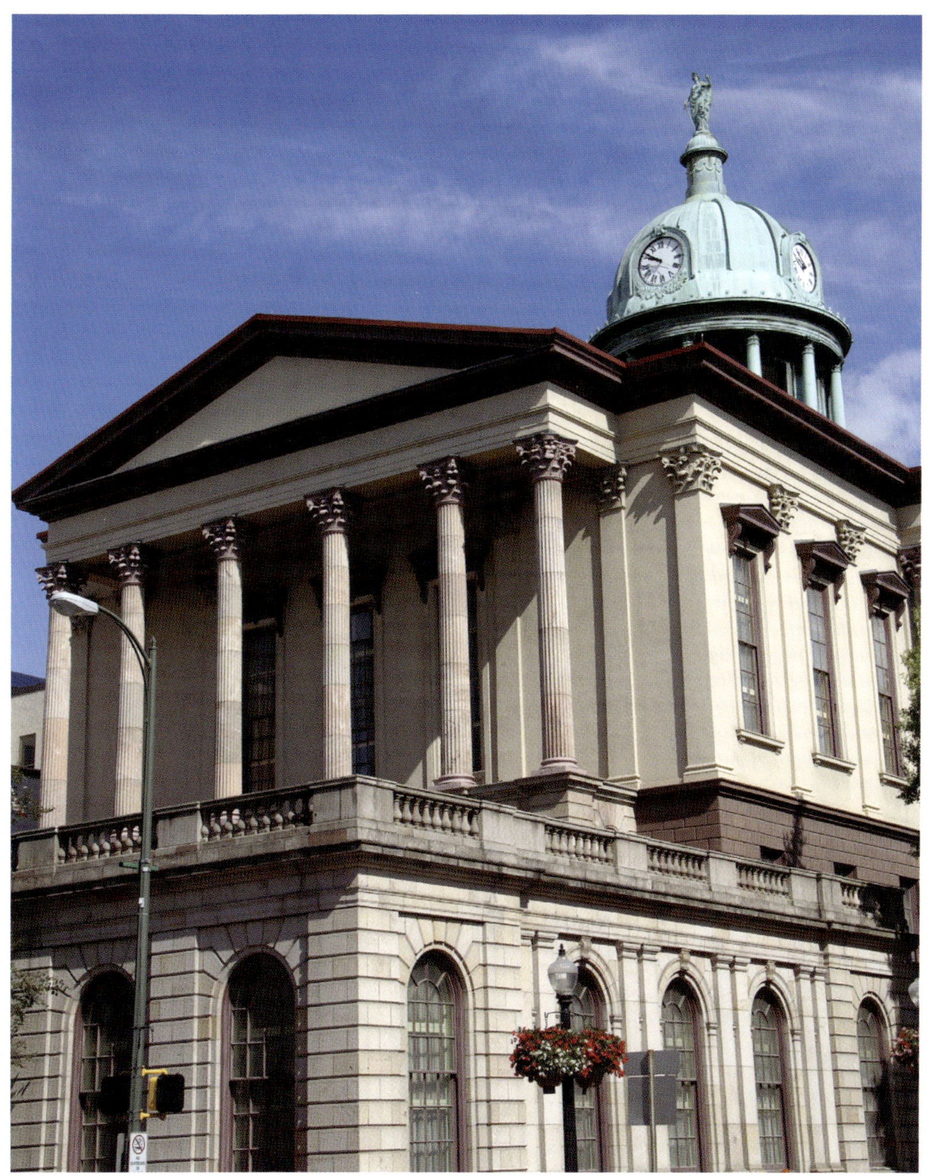

The original portion of the present-day Lancaster County Courthouse was constructed from 1852 to 1855 from a design by Philadelphia architect Samuel Sloan. Its design is somewhat unique in that Sloan used Roman architecture as his inspiration, instead of the Greek precedent that many courthouses built during the same era used. James H. Warner designed a north addition, which was constructed in 1898, and C. Emlen Urban designed the low wings, which were built in 1927. The building's notable features include Corinthian columns and a copper dome topped by a statue of Justice.

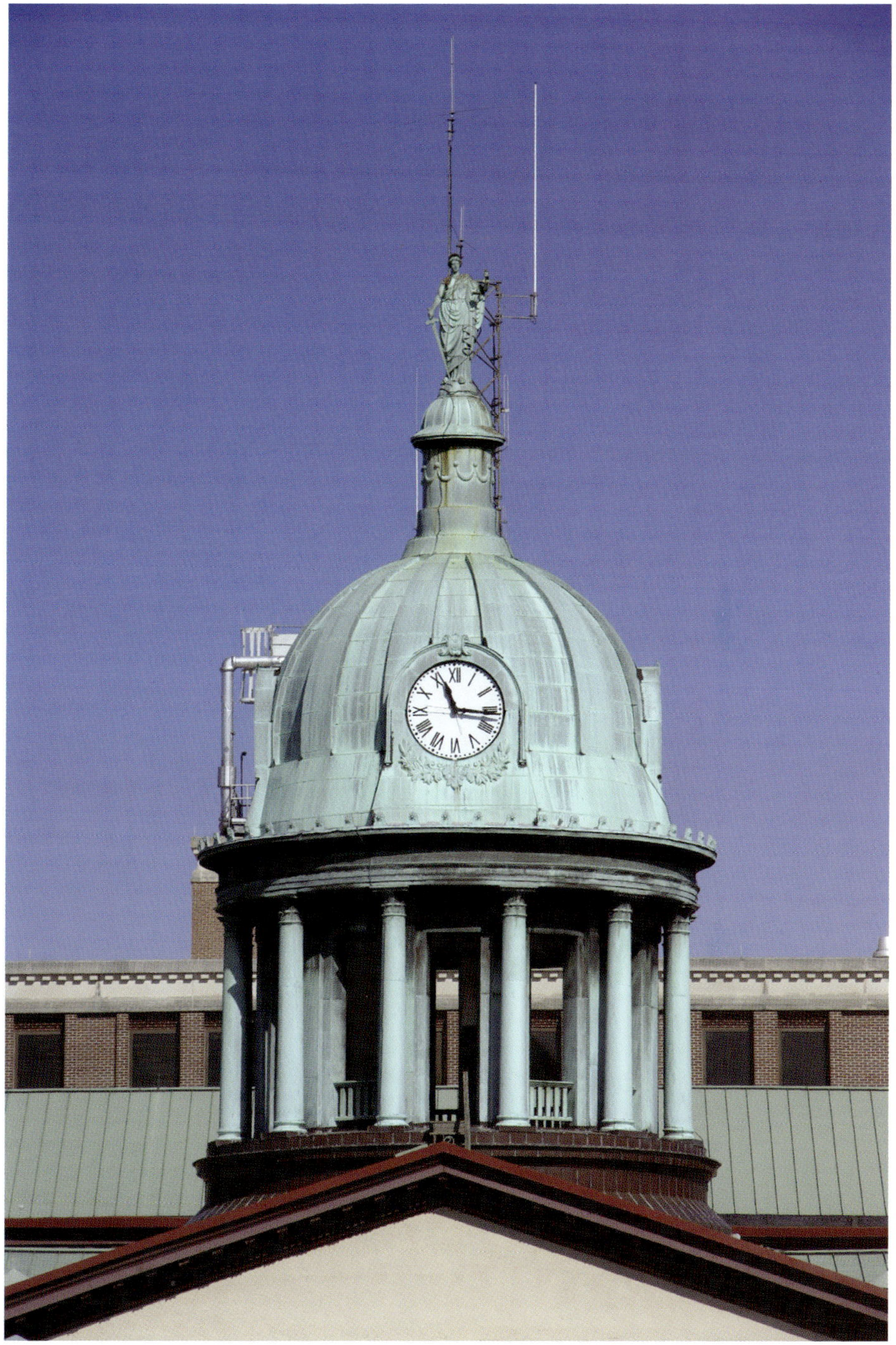

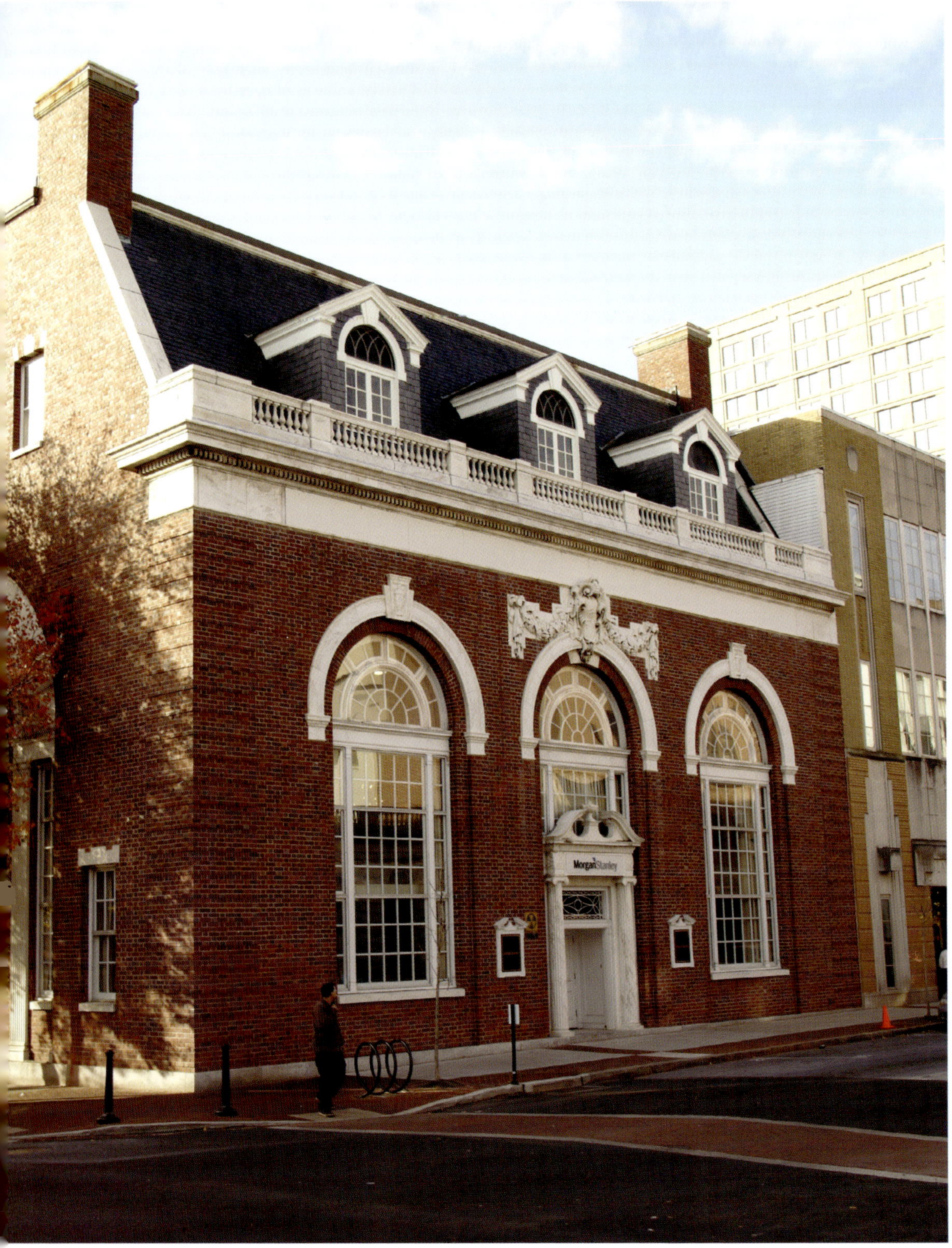

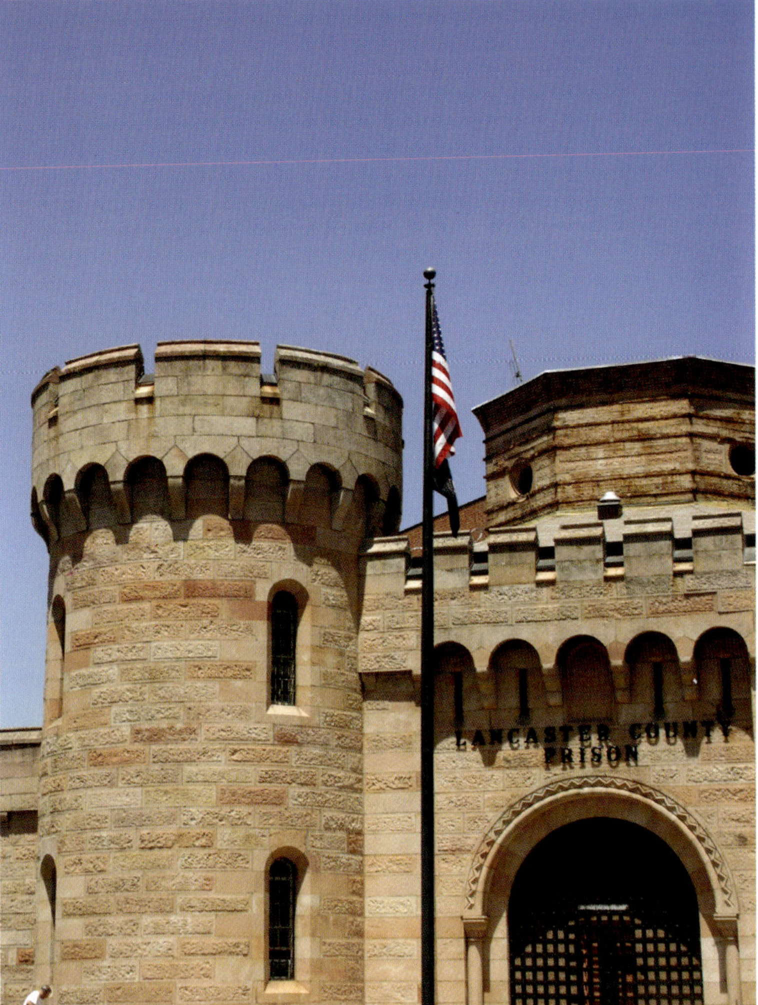

The Lancaster County Prison on East King Street showcases a unique style of architecture for the area: Norman Revival. Inspired by the European castles of the Norman period, architect John Haviland designed this red sandstone building in 1851. Haviland is best known as architect of the Eastern State Penitentiary in Philadelphia. He used a castle in Lancashire, England, as the template for this design.

This attractive Colonial Revival building was built for Farmer's Trust Company of Lancaster in 1929. The East King Street Building was designed by Melvern R. Evans and is topped with a mansard roof, which is uncommon for Colonial architecture.

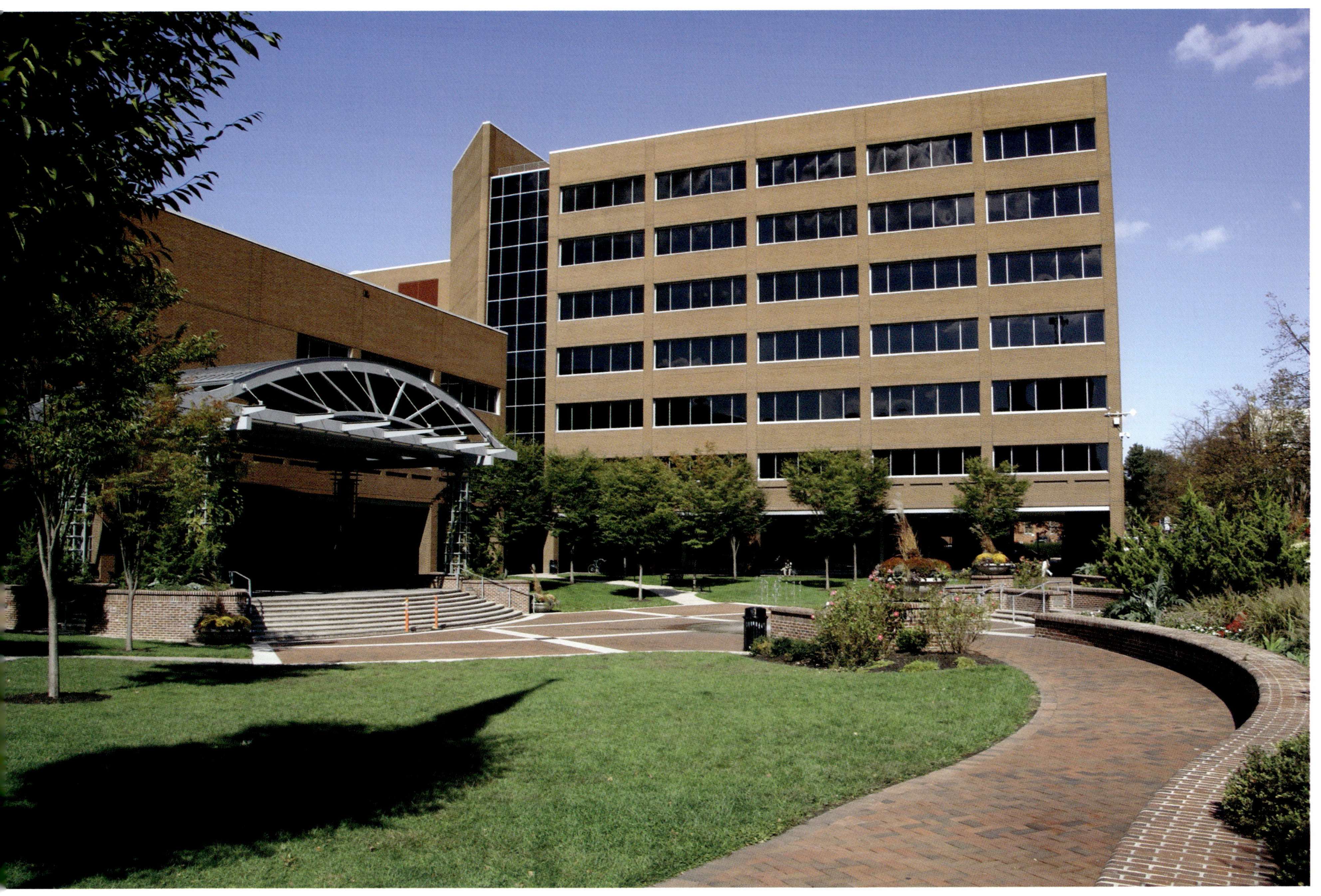

Dedicated in 2005, Binn's Park is a public gathering space with a fountain, stage, and gardens located adjacent to a seven-story building that was formerly home to Armstrong World Industries. Today the building is occupied by the government of Lancaster County.

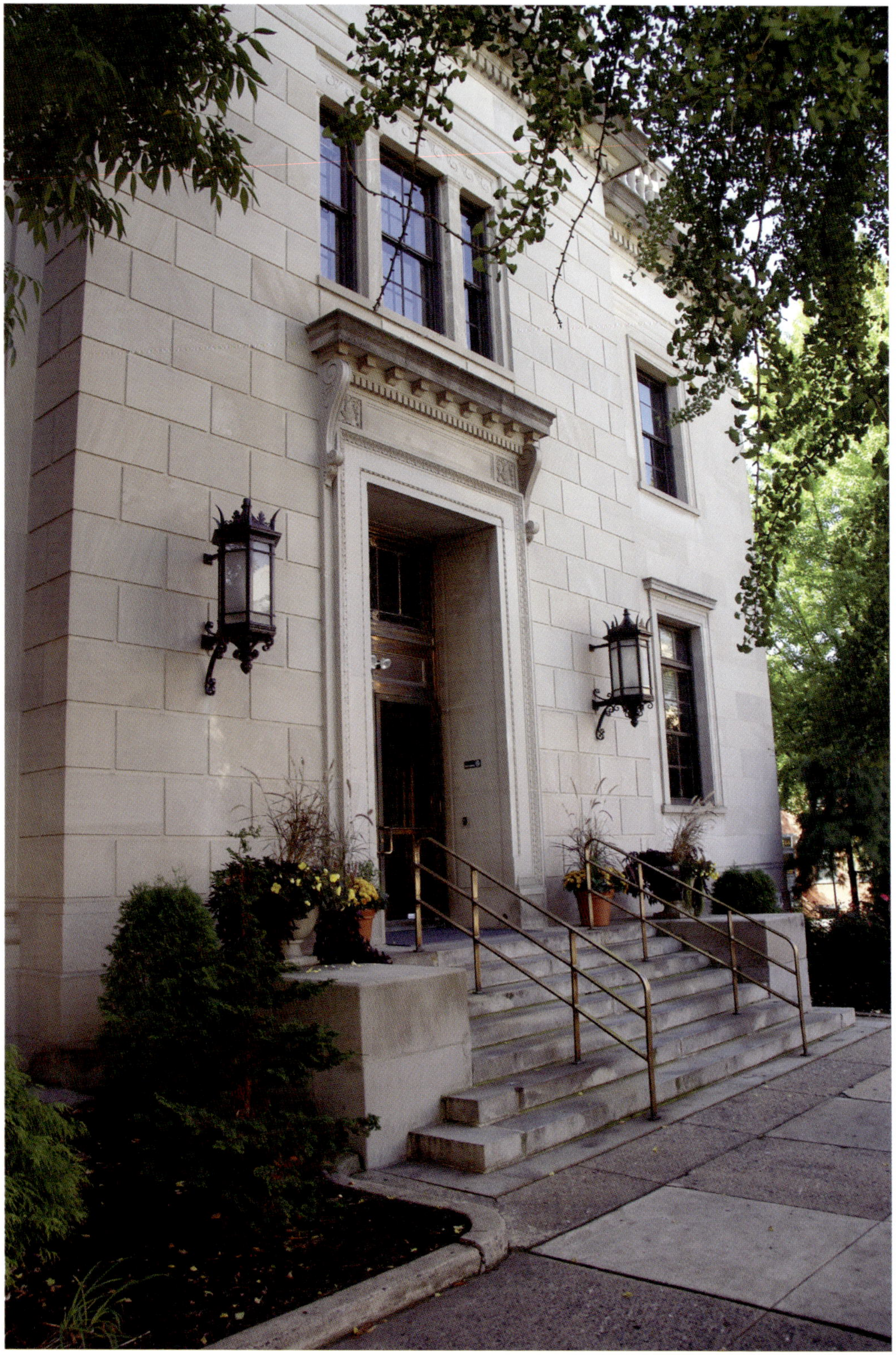

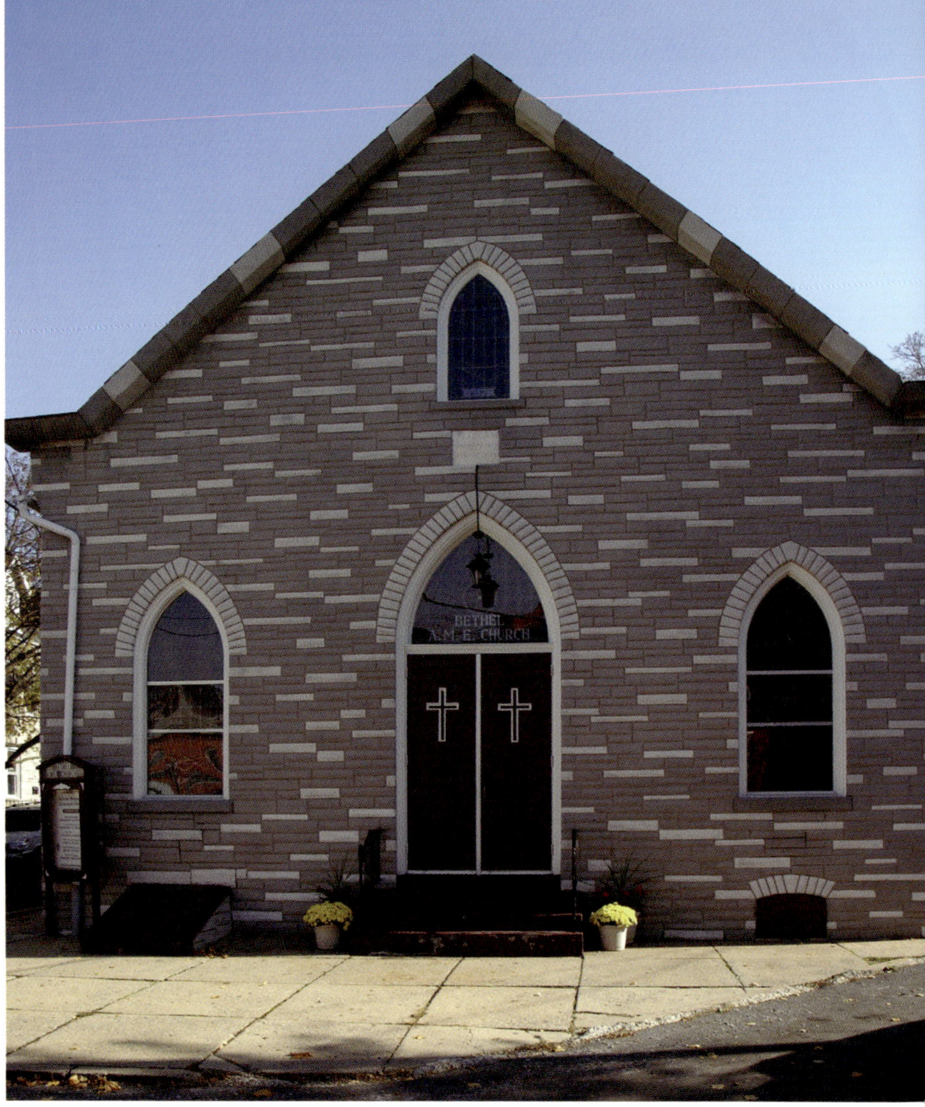

To serve the growing African-American population in Lancaster, members of St. James Episcopal and Trinity Lutheran Church helped establish Bethel African Methodist Episcopal Church in 1818. *Living the Experience*, an interactive spiritual journey that interprets the Underground Railroad, is a historical dramatization performed here regularly by Bethel Harambee Historical Services.

The Lancaster Post Office building is a notable example of Beaux-Arts Classicism architecture. Designed by James A. Westmore, the building is constructed of Indiana limestone and was dedicated in 1930. The site on which the building and parking lot sit were formerly home to a Moravian graveyard, Continental Army warehouse, and the Lancastrian School.

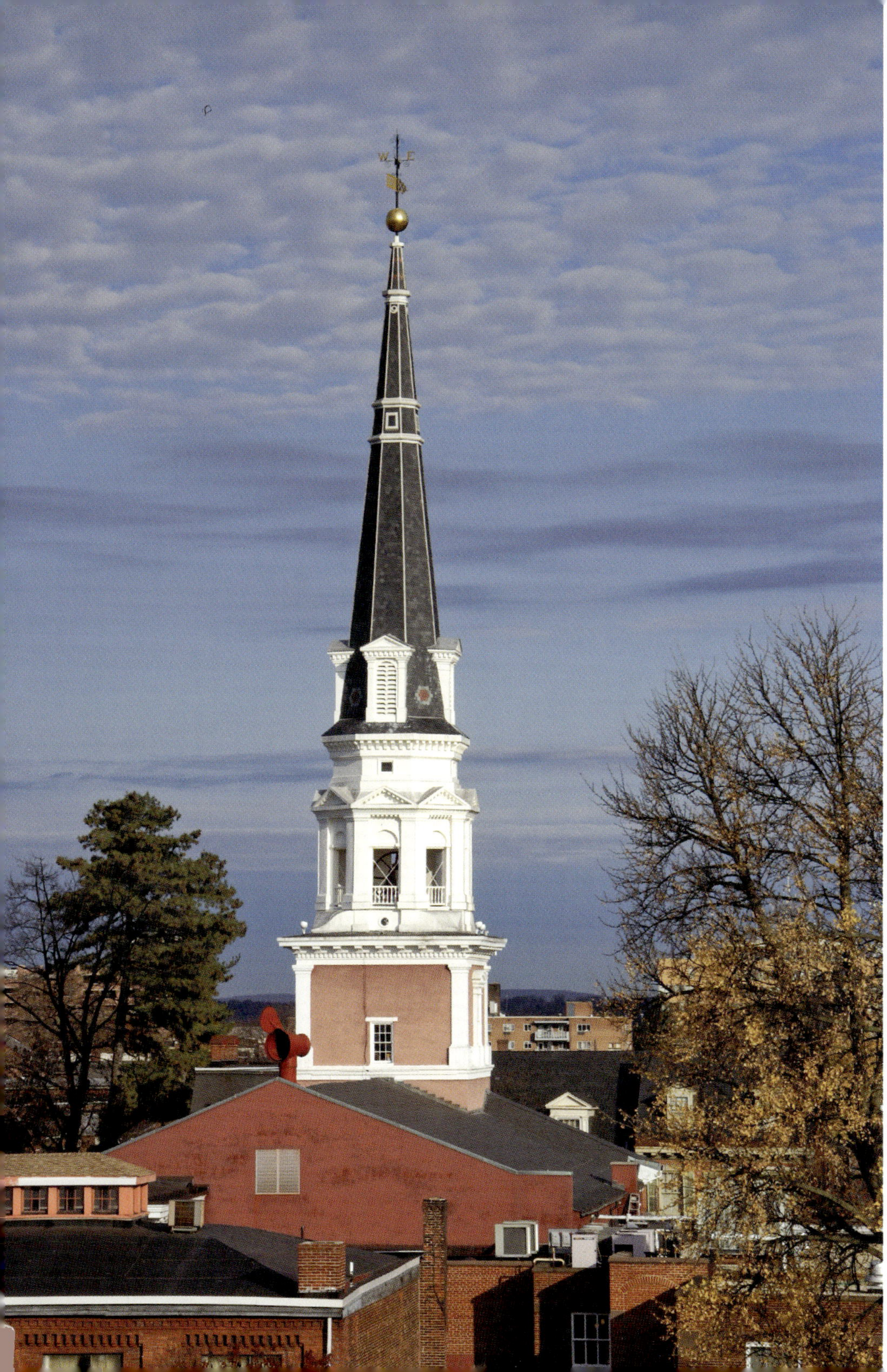

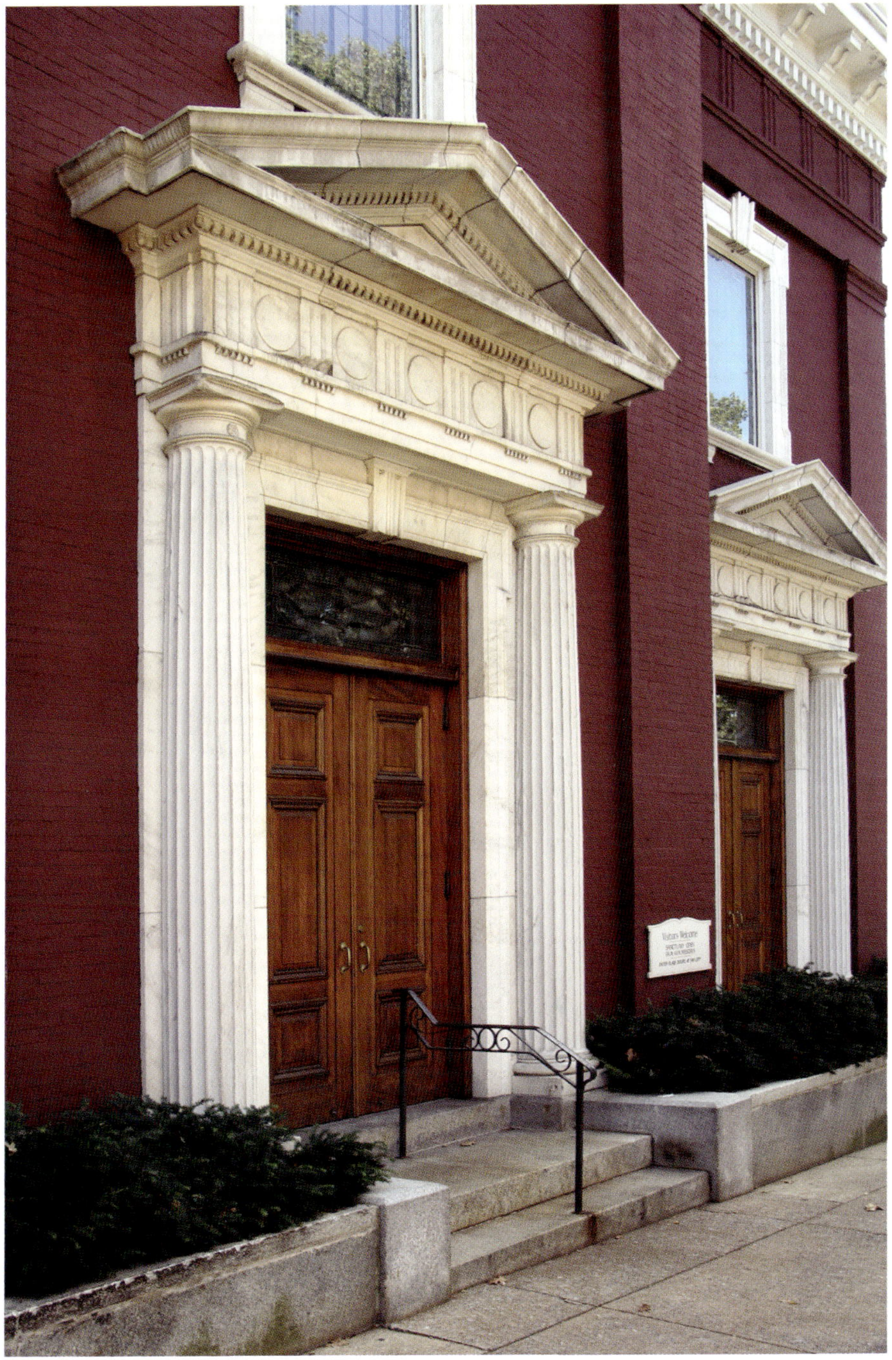

Lancaster Presbyterians first worshipped at the original Lancaster County Courthouse, then built a church on East Orange Street in 1770. The current Greek Revival-style First Presbyterian Church building was constructed in 1851. James Buchanan and Thaddeus Stevens worshipped here.

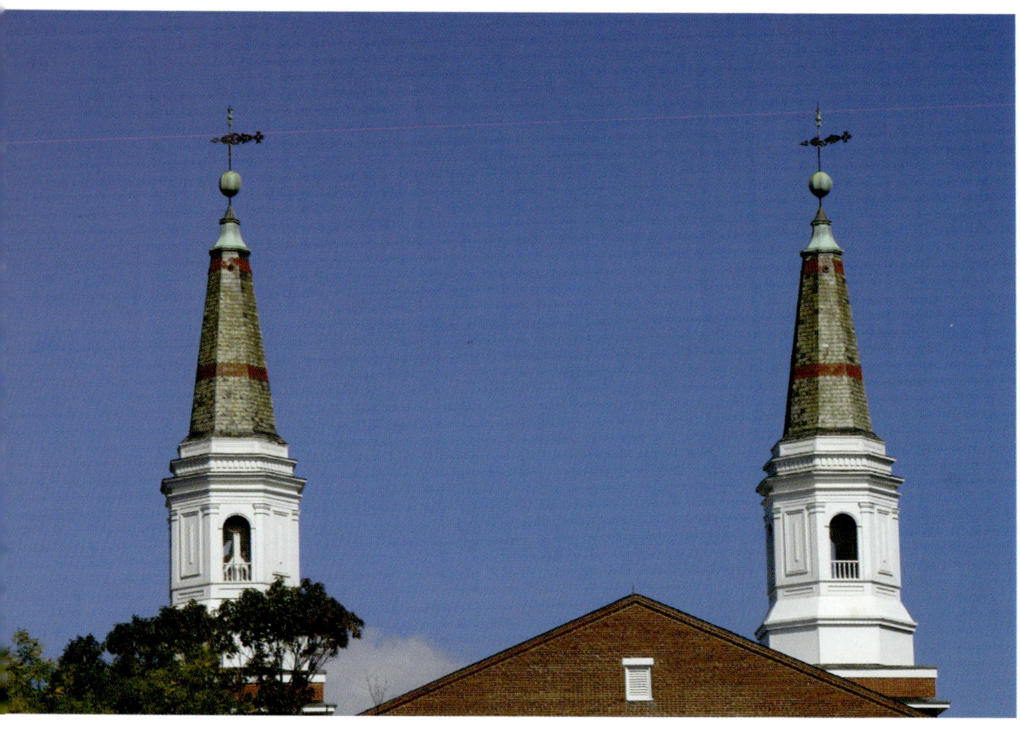

The twin spires of First Reformed Church have watched over Lancaster since 1852. The congregation originally comprised German, Swiss, and French settlers, who built the first church in Lancaster City in 1736. When this building was constructed almost 120 years later, services were still being conducted in German.

Designed by C. Emlen Urban, the Grace Lutheran Church was constructed in 1906 and built of Hummelstown brownstone. The Late Gothic Revival-style building cost $70,000 to construct and originally featured an auditorium with seating for 850 people.

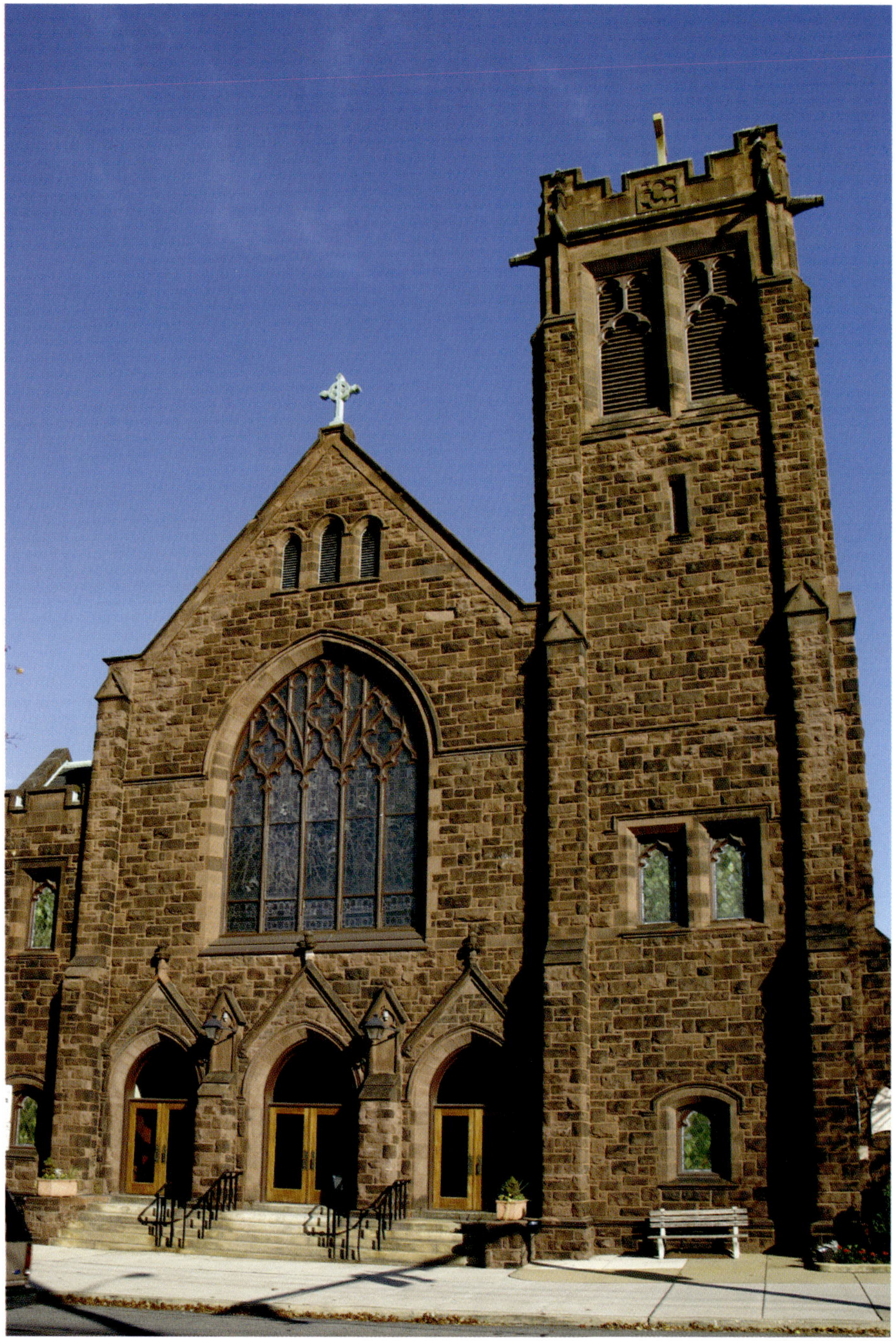

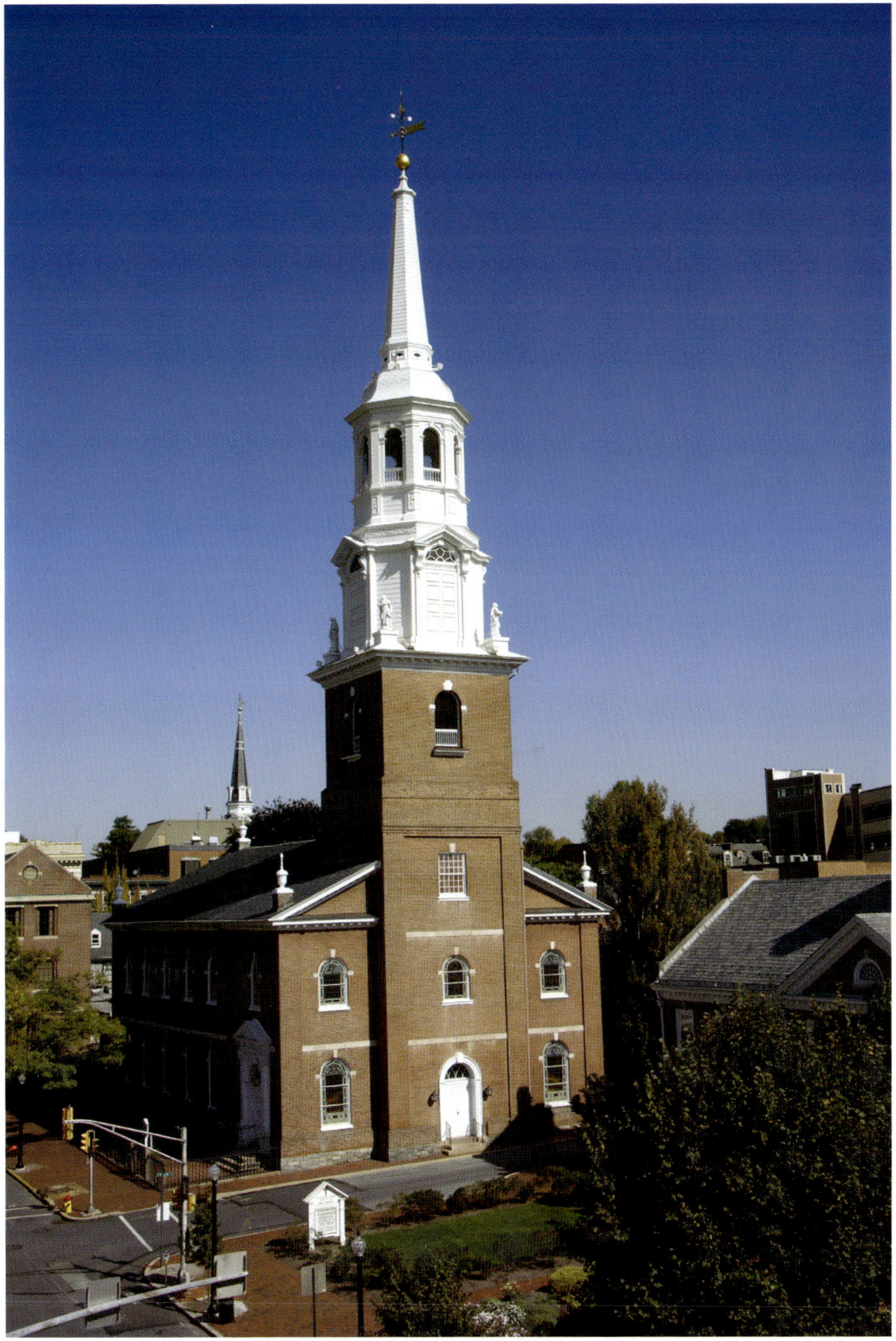

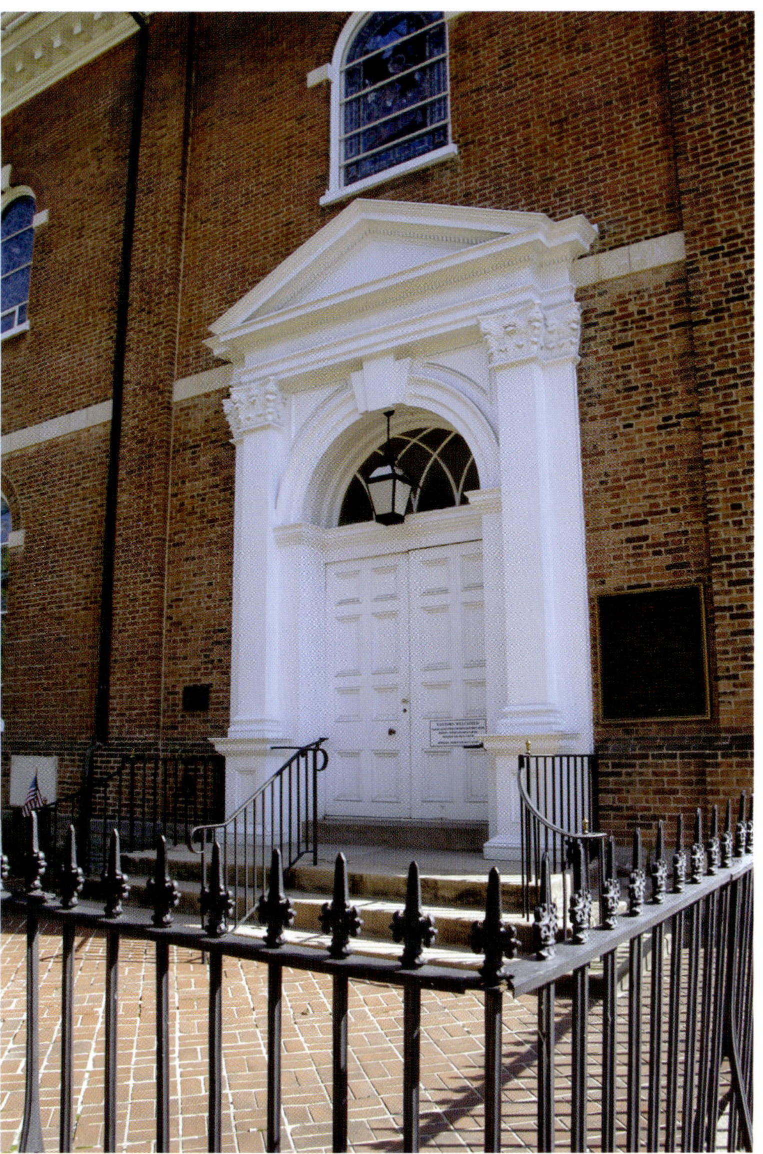

Evangelical Lutheran Church of the Holy Trinity was built from 1761 to 1766 and is a prominent example of Georgian-style architecture. A Tannenberg Organ, built by eighteenth-century master organ builder David Tannenberg, was installed in 1774. The prominent steeple was added in 1794, making the church the tallest structure west of Philadelphia at the time. Trinity Lutheran Church has the distinction of being the oldest house of worship in Lancaster.

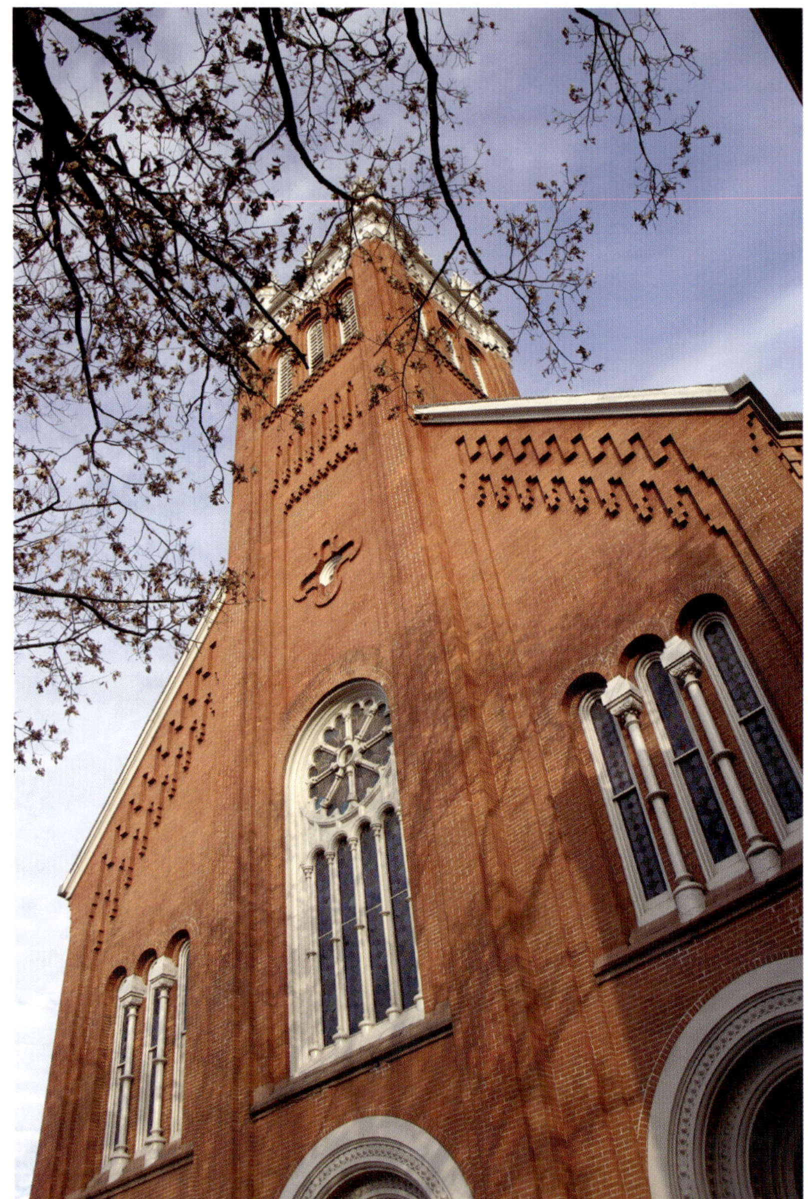

In 1828 the New High German Evangelical Lutheran Church was founded by members of Trinity Lutheran Church who wanted to maintain German language for services. The name was later changed to Zion Lutheran Church. This East Vine Street building was completed in 1871, and the prominent central tower was constructed in 1897. The congregation ceased operation in 1983, and the building is now occupied by the Lord's House of Prayer.

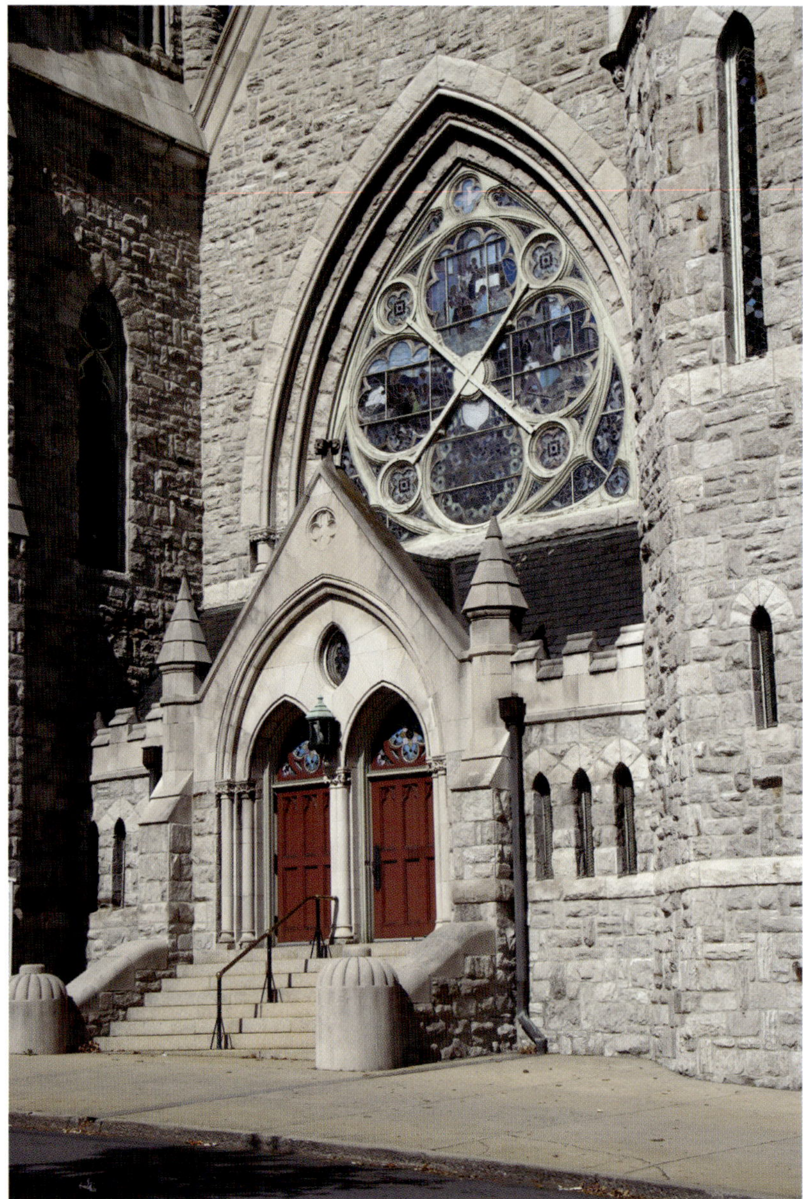

Located on West Orange Street, St. John Lutheran Church operates a community food bank as part of their outreach program. The building was designed in the Late Gothic Revival style of architecture, a style common for Christian churches. The pointed arch, known as a lancet arch, is a defining characteristic of the style. The attractive stone building also features a rose window and two monumental towers—one has a pyramidal roof, pinnacles, and finials, while the other features a copper roof and triangular parapets.

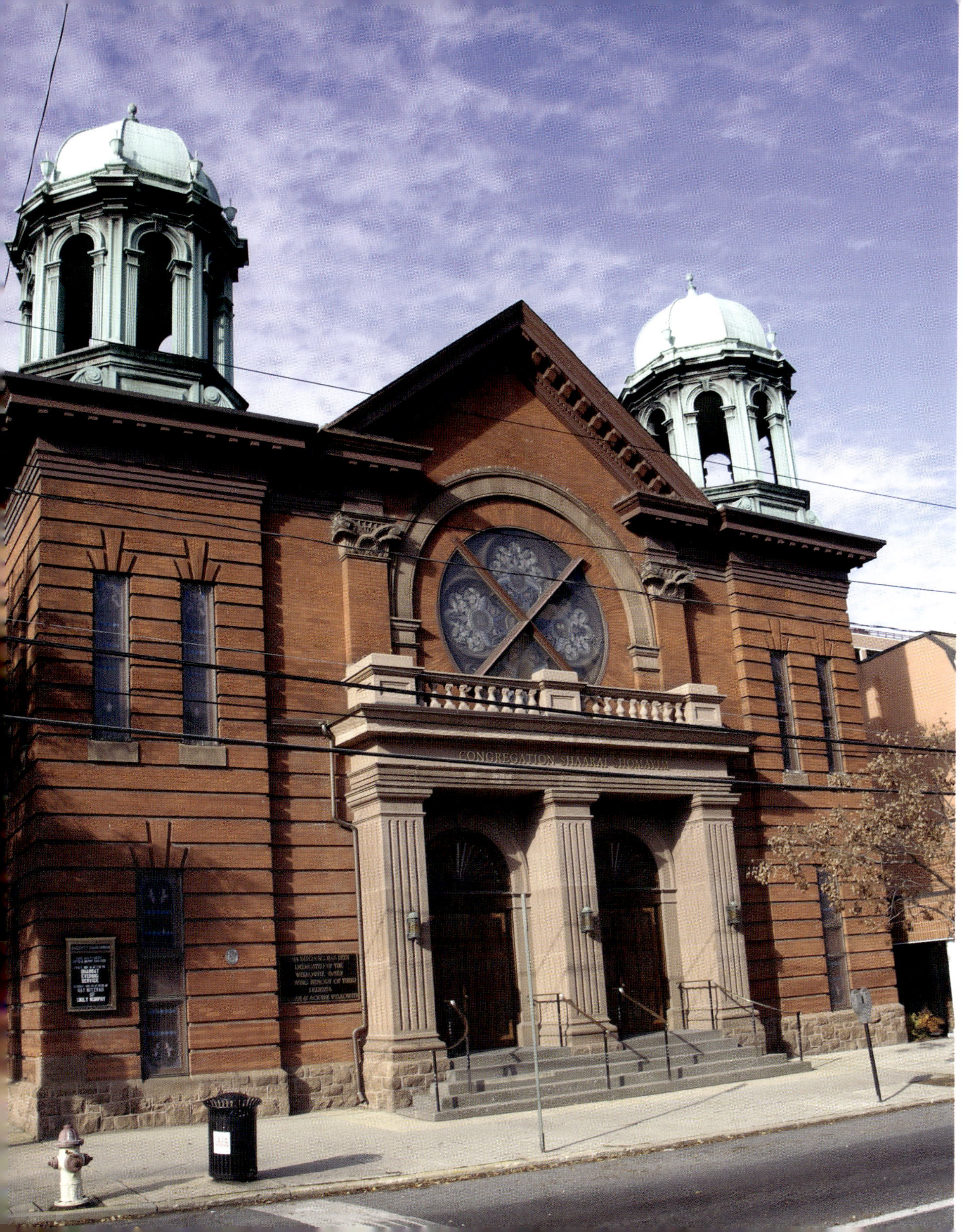

Congregation Shaarai Shomayim was established in 1856, when the Commonwealth of Pennsylvania granted a charter to members of Lancaster's Jewish community looking to establish a congregation. The first synagogue was located on East Orange Street. The eclectic Duke Street Temple was dedicated in 1896 and continues to serve as home to the fourth oldest Jewish congregation in North America.

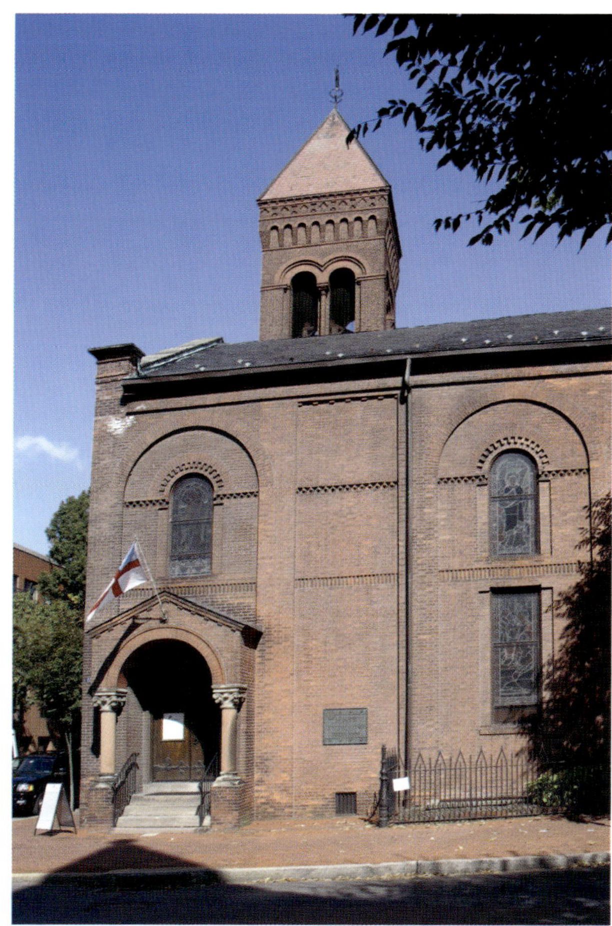

St. James Episcopal Church was established in 1744 but closed during the American Revolution because the pastor was a British loyalist. Parishioners included General Edward Hand and George Ross, signer of the Declaration of Independence. The current church was built in 1820 and expanded in 1880.

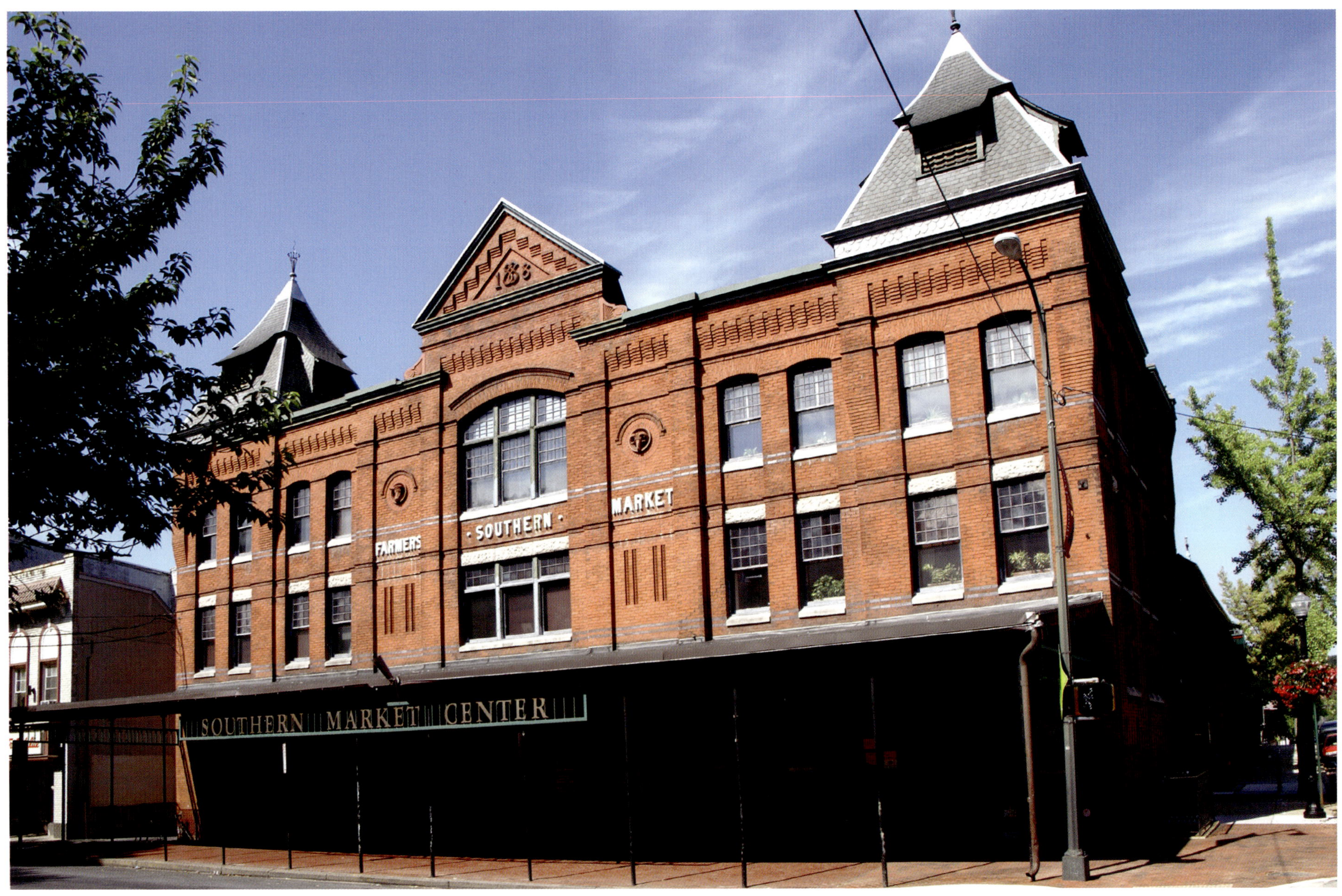

Farmers' Southern Market was established at the intersection of South Queen and West Vine Streets in 1888. One of C. Emlen Urban's early design commissions, the three-story head house was constructed in the Queen Anne style. The ornamental brickwork and towers with pyramidal roofs, coupled with the terra cotta ram and bull heads on the façade, display an intricate level of craftsmanship. The market was built for $75,000 to serve the southern portion of Lancaster City. It operated for ninety-eight years, closing in 1986.

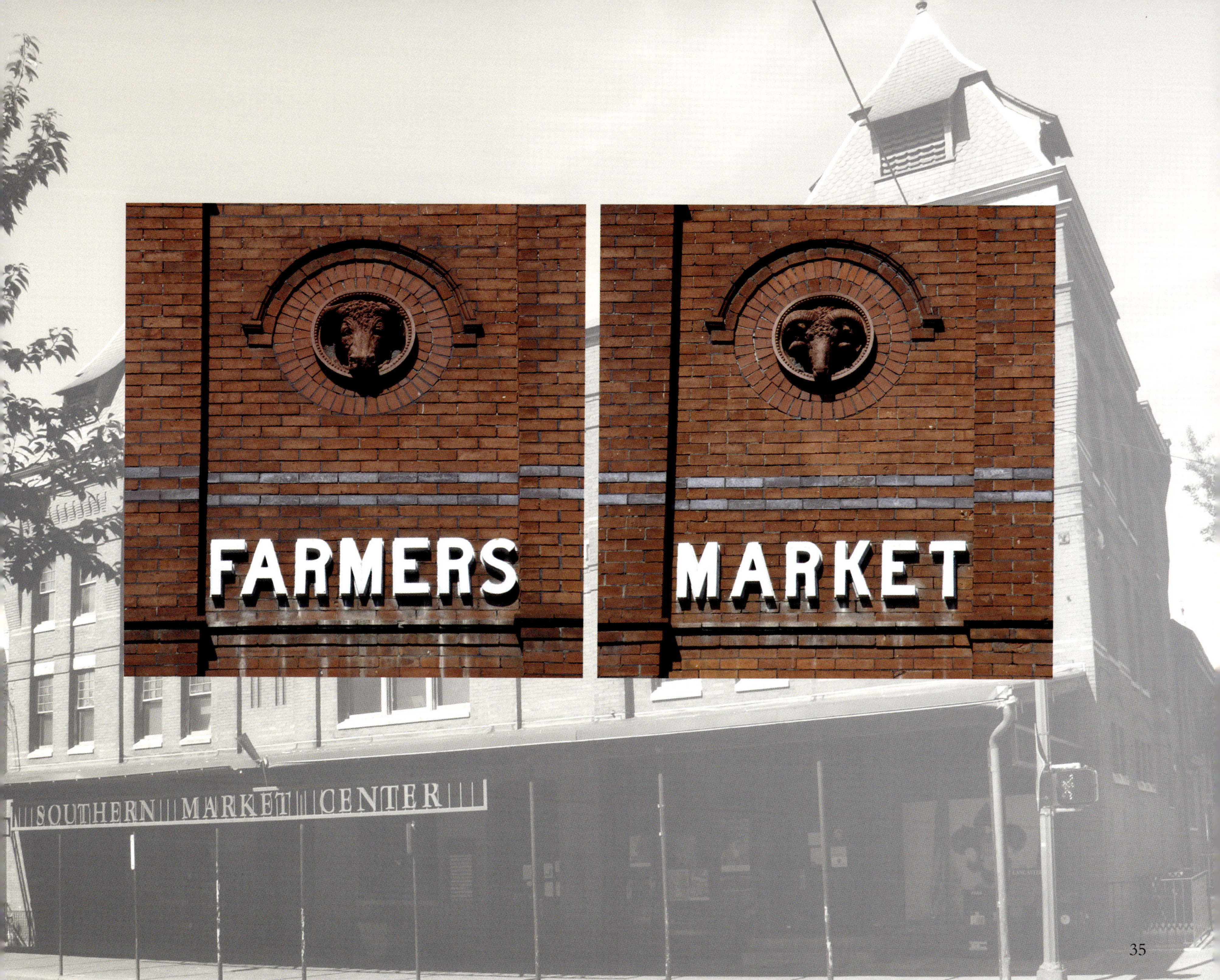
FARMERS
MARKET
SOUTHERN MARKET CENTER

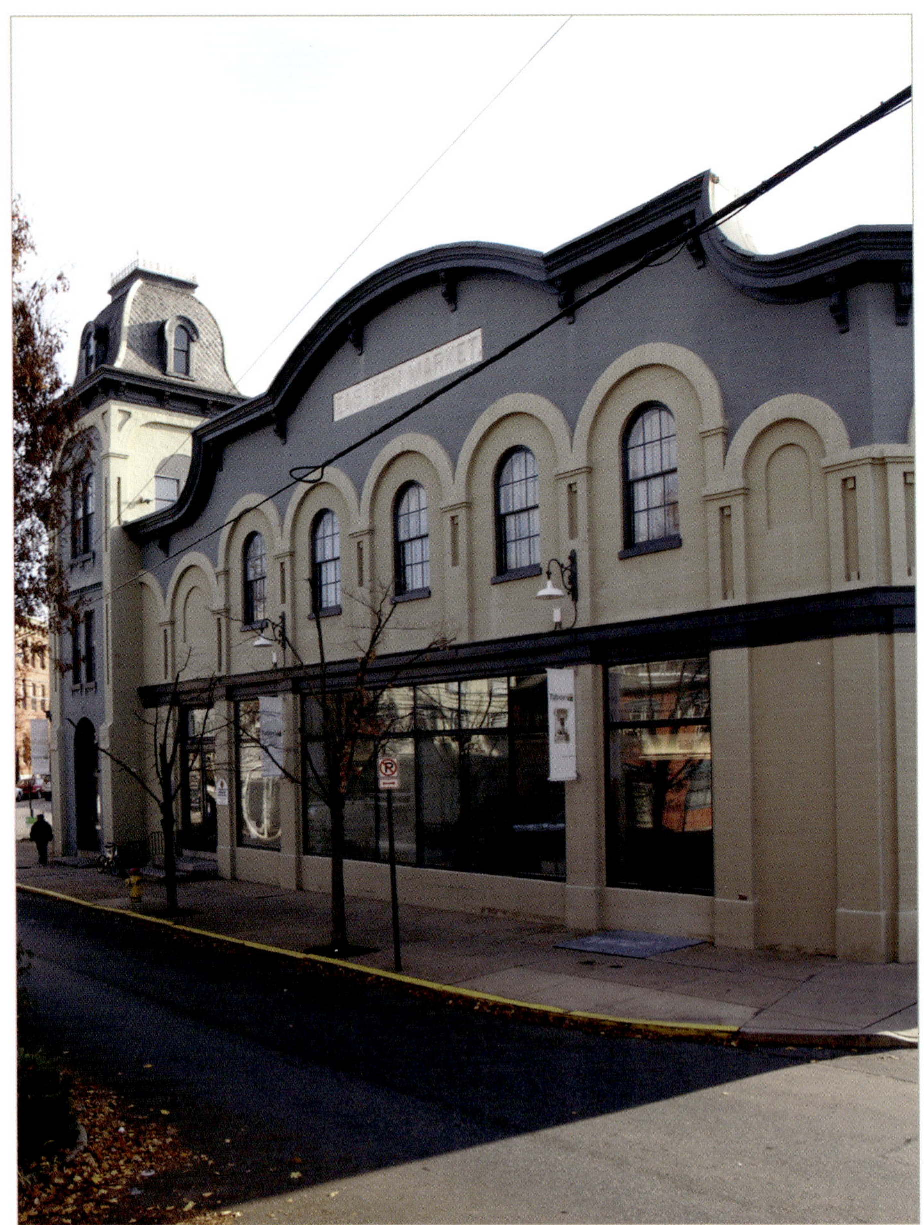

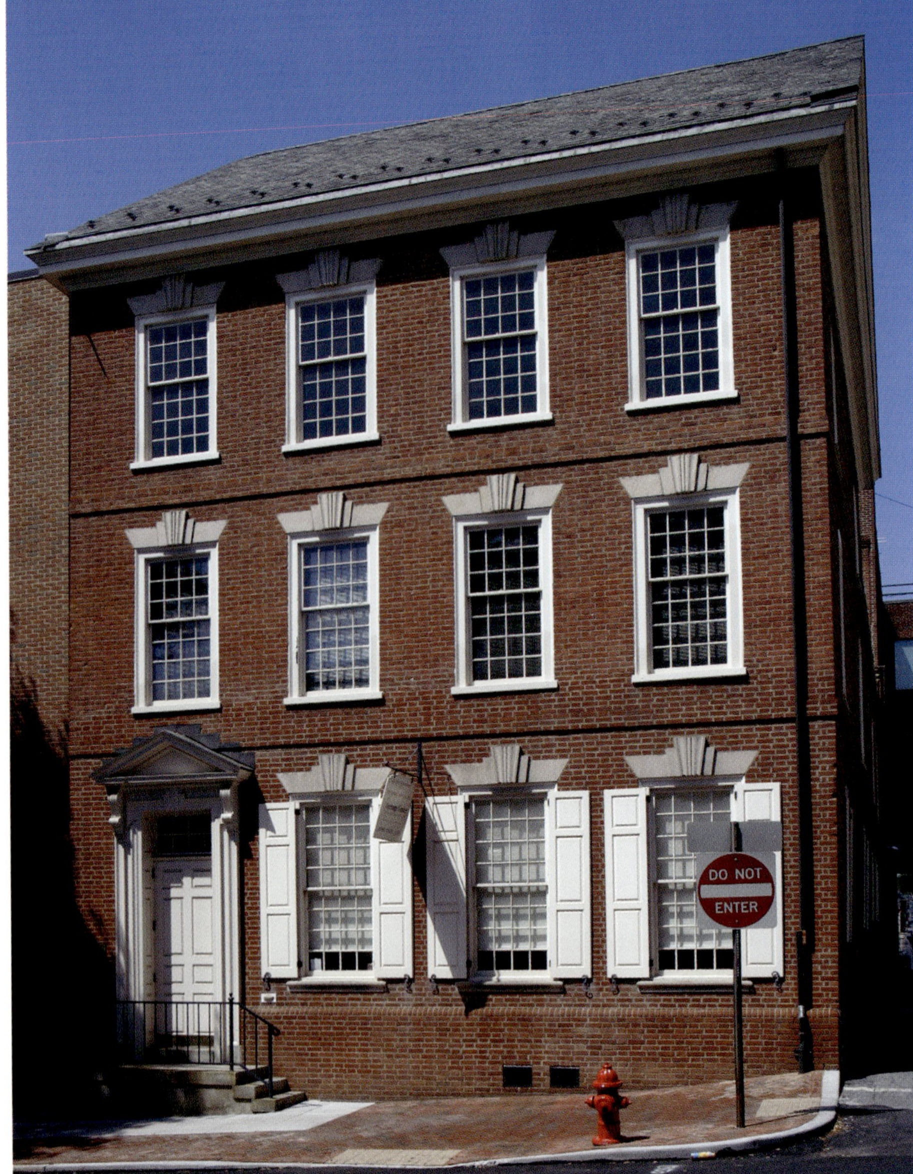

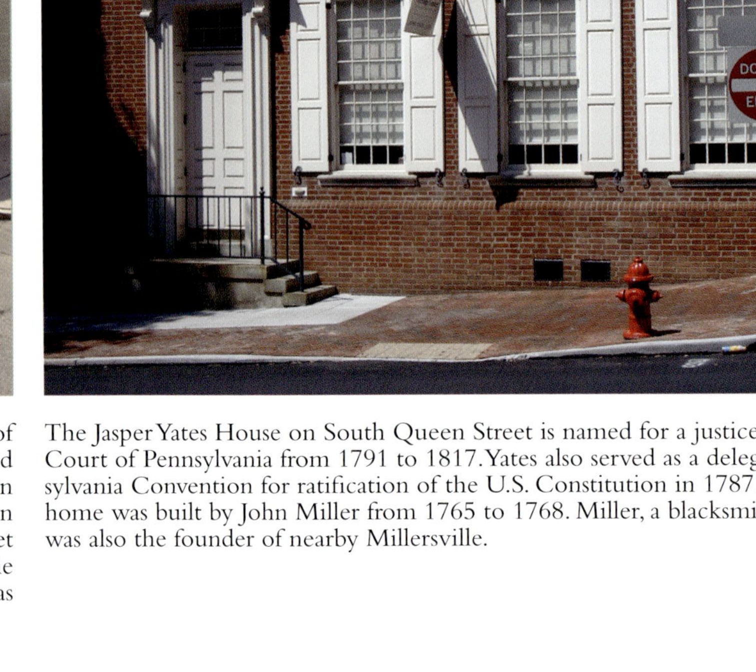

The Eastern Market House was built in 1883 to serve residents of the eastern portion of Lancaster City. The unique structure includes a prominent tower designed in the Second Empire style. Other markets built in the late nineteenth century include the Southern Market on South Queen Street (1888), Central Market on Penn Square (1889), Western Market on West Orange Street (1882), and Northern Market on North Queen Street (1872). The Western Market became a one-story building as the result of a 1942 fire while the Northern Market was demolished in 1958. An early twentieth-century market was the Fulton Market, constructed on North Plum Street in 1907.

The Jasper Yates House on South Queen Street is named for a justice of the Supreme Court of Pennsylvania from 1791 to 1817. Yates also served as a delegate to the Pennsylvania Convention for ratification of the U.S. Constitution in 1787. The Georgian home was built by John Miller from 1765 to 1768. Miller, a blacksmith and merchant, was also the founder of nearby Millersville.

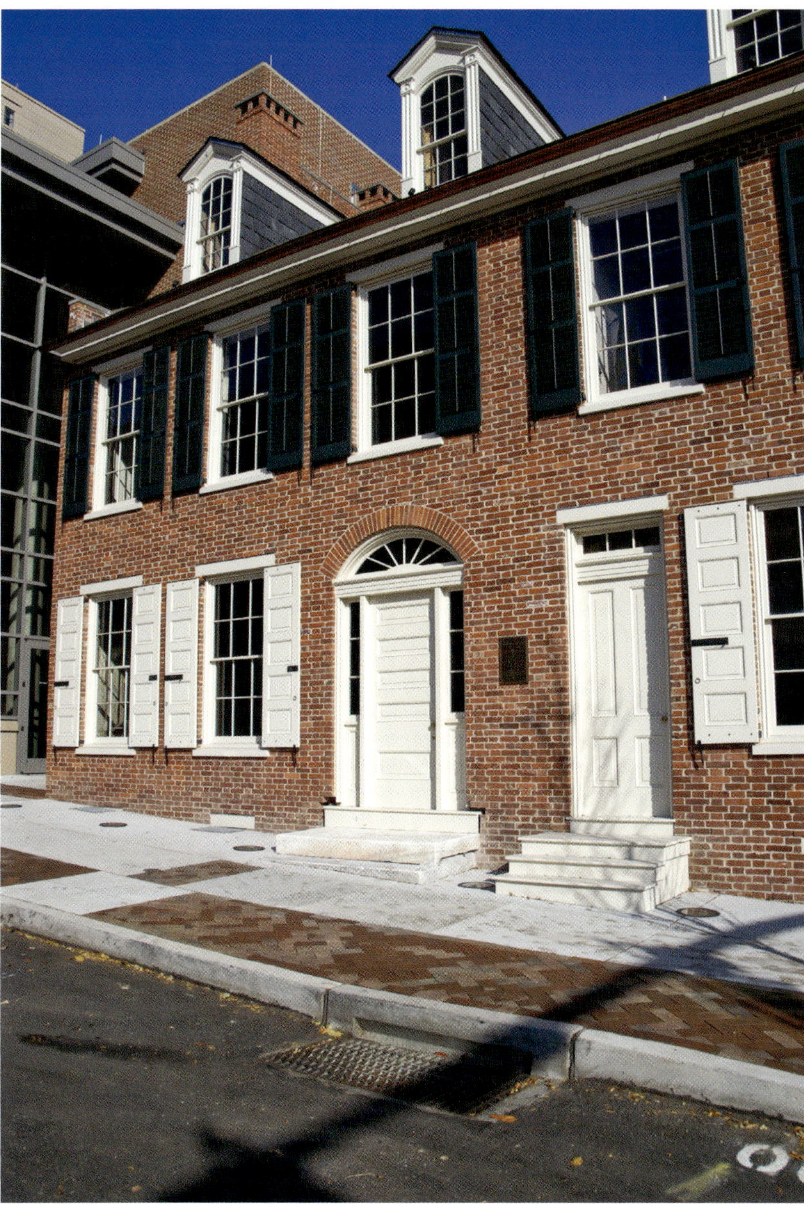

From 1843 until 1868, Thaddeus Stevens was one of Lancaster's most prominent residents. He studied law in nearby York, and then spent his early career practicing in Gettysburg, Pennsylvania, where he was elected to the Pennsylvania House of Representatives. After moving to Lancaster, Stevens became involved in the abolition movement and returned to politics, serving in the U.S. House of Representatives from 1848 to 1853, then again from 1859 until his death in 1868. By the time the Civil War began, Stevens had become one of the most powerful men in Congress, serving as chairman of the Ways and Means Committee. The Radical Republican, who along with his housekeeper, Lydia Smith, was active with the Underground Railroad, was instrumental in writing and passing the thirteenth, fourteenth, and fifteenth amendments to the U.S. Constitution, which abolished slavery, extended equal rights protection, and expanded voting rights to all men. Stevens lived here from 1843 until his death in 1868.

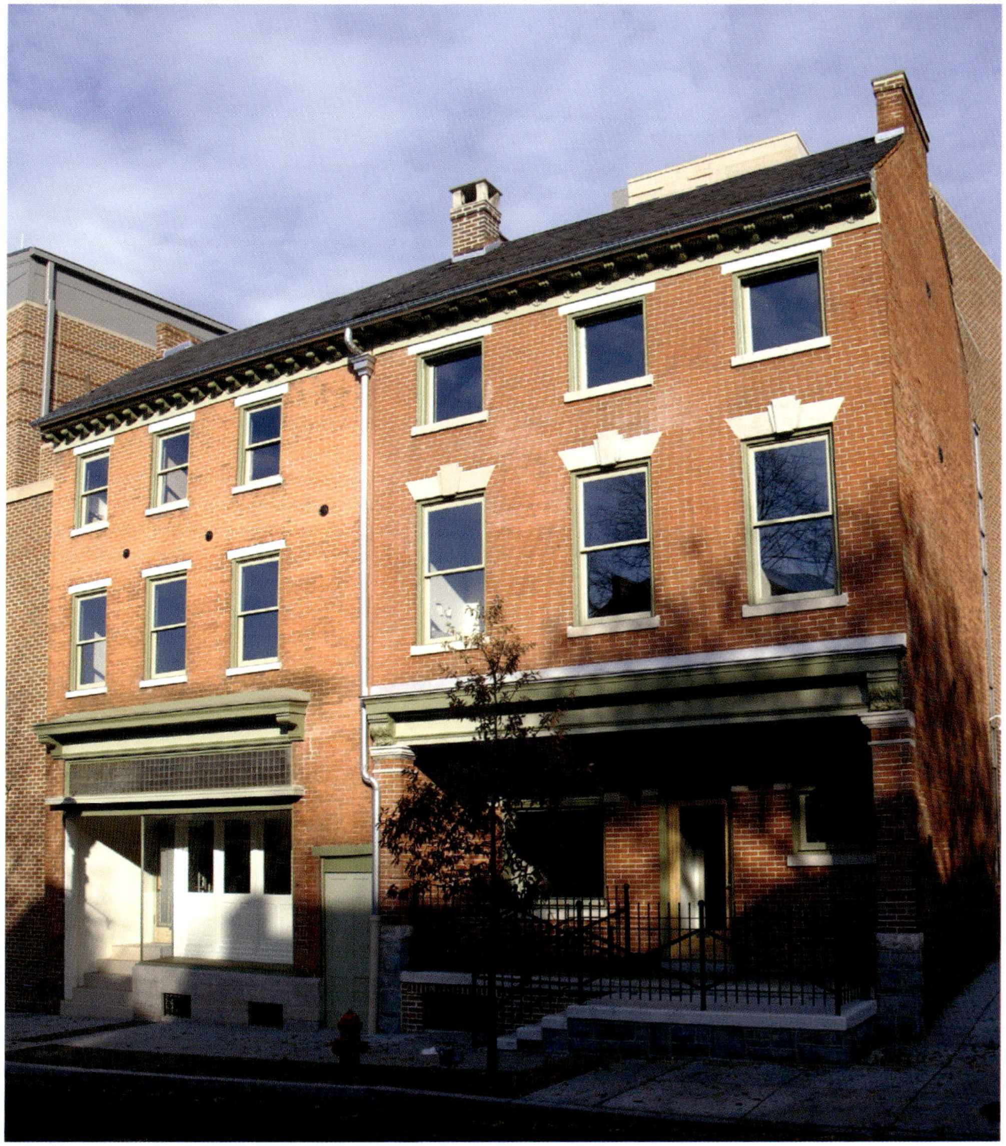

Lydia Hamilton Smith was Thaddeus Stevens' housekeeper for more than two decades. Progressive for the time, Smith, who was African-American, maintained a remarkable partnership with Stevens and became a successful businesswoman and owner of several properties, including these. She is also believed to have been a conductor on the Underground Railroad.

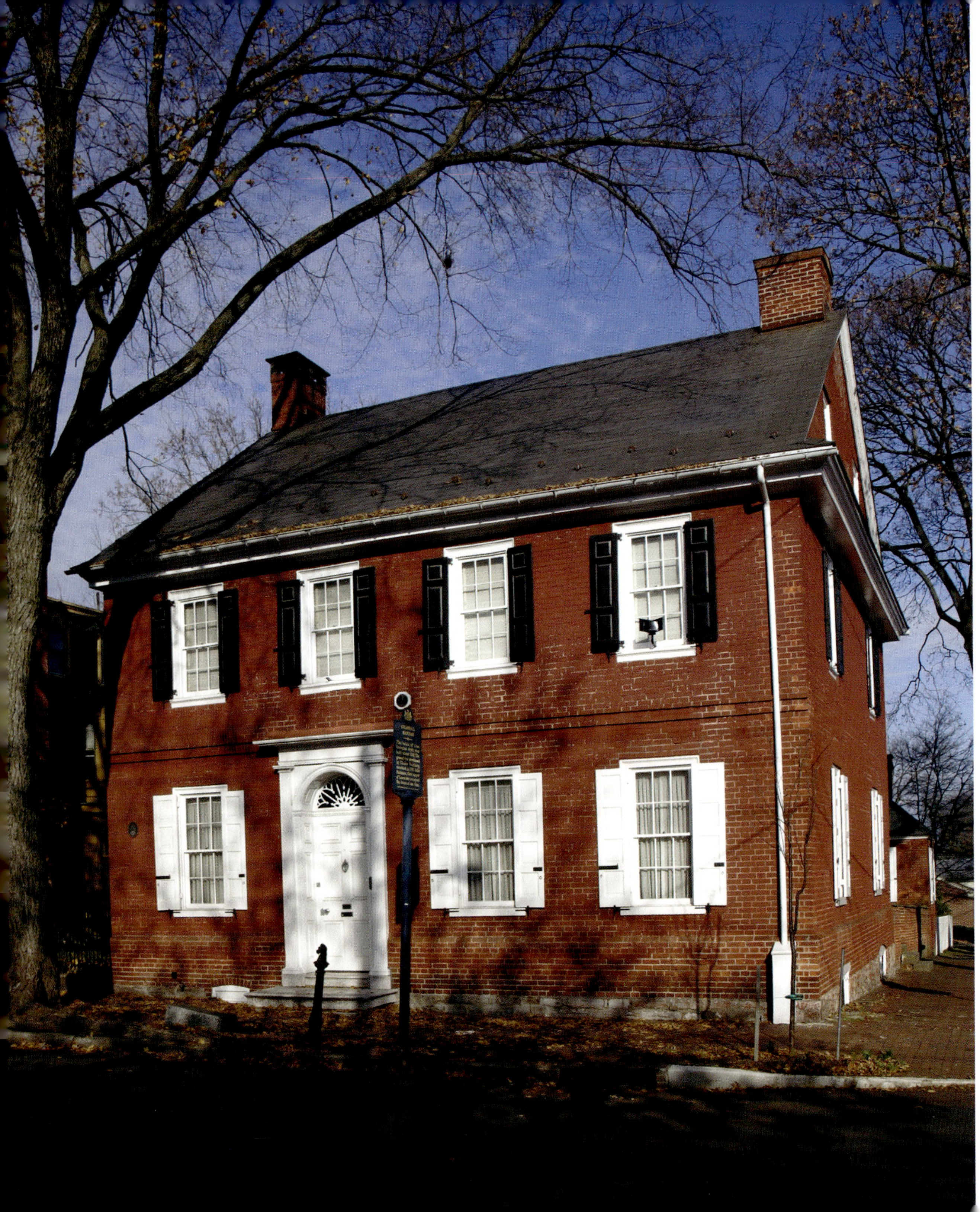

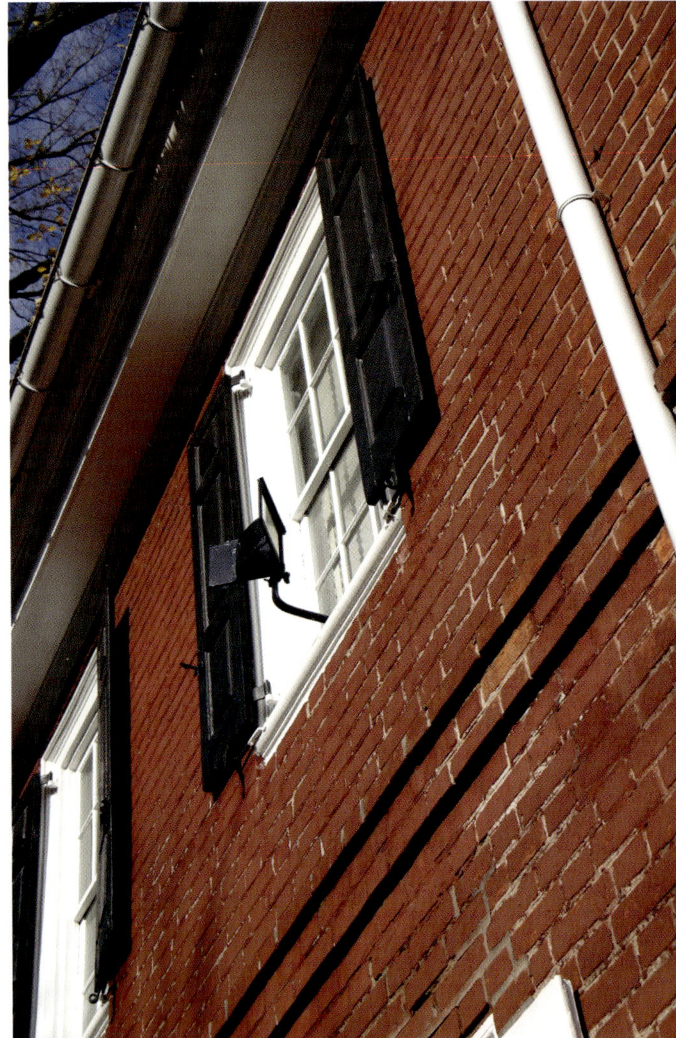

Sometimes called the Colonial Mansion, this Georgian home is known as the Neff-Passmore House. The 1785 house was built by Dr. Christian Neff and was later home to John Passmore, Lancaster's first mayor. Among its notable features is a busybody, a second-floor mirror that allows occupants to look down on the street below to see who is standing at the front door.

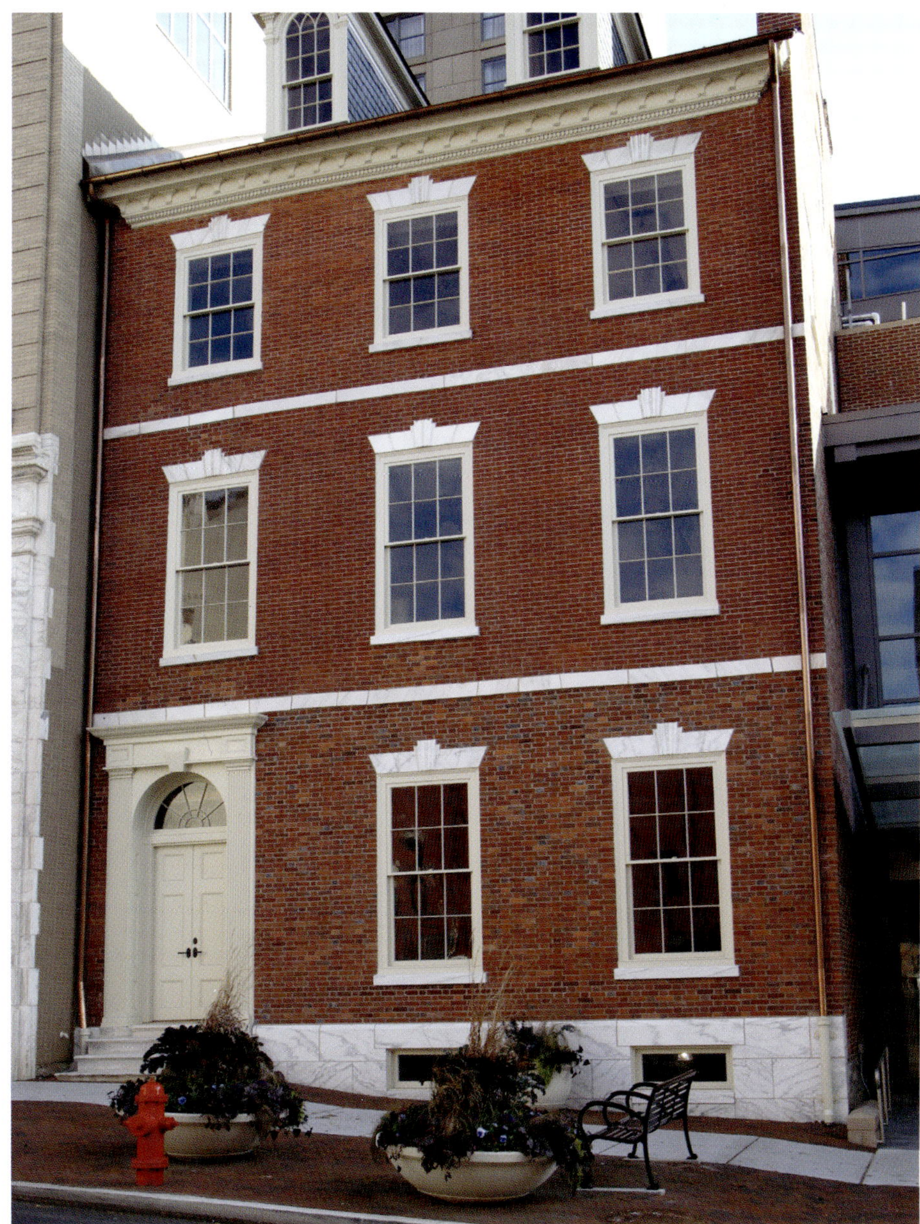

The William Montgomery House on South Queen Street was built in 1804 in the Federal style. Today, the historic home is part of the Lancaster County Convention Center, which was literally built around the Montgomery House—the rear of the building is exposed on the interior of the convention center, across from the main convention halls. The Montgomery House was designed by architect Stephen Hills, who also designed the original capitol building in Harrisburg.

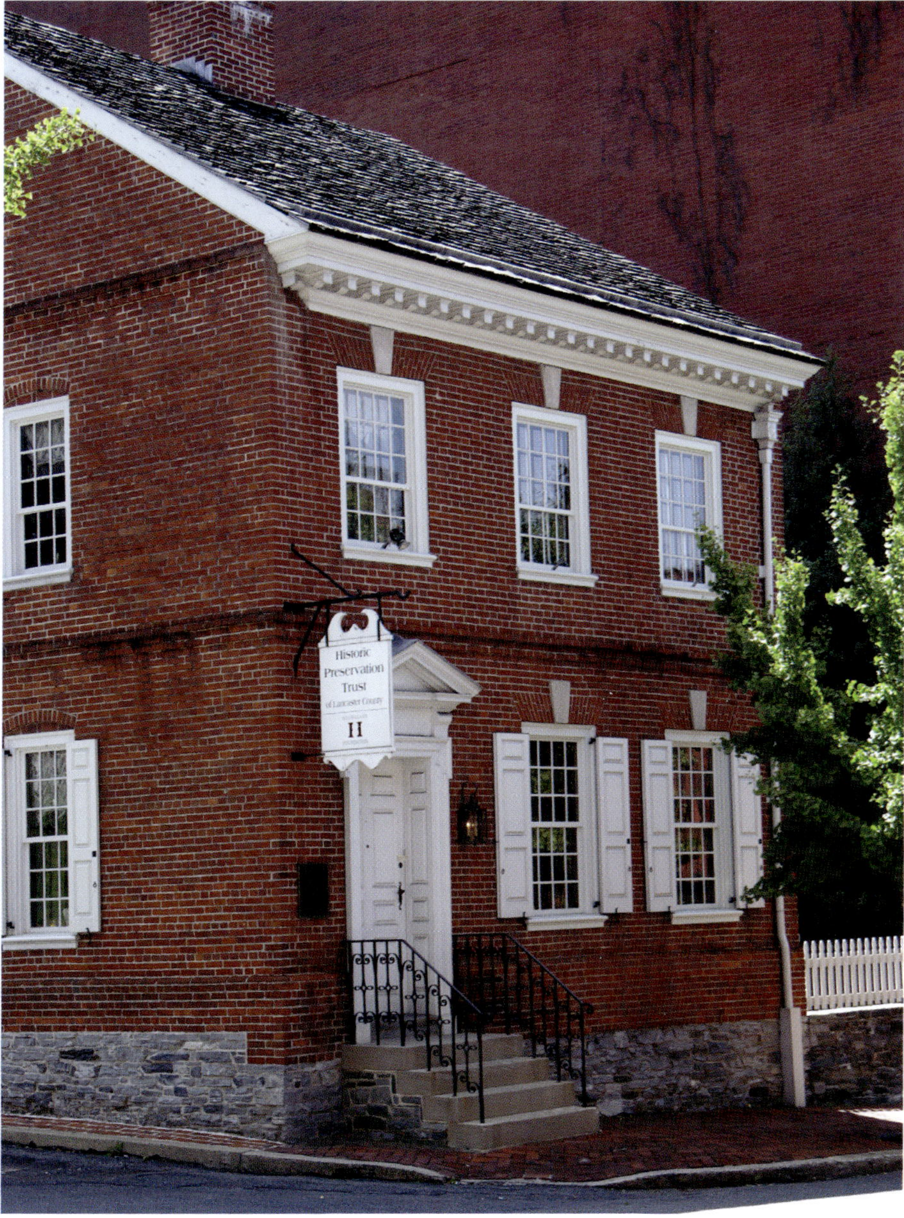

In 1966, a group of historic preservationists banded together to save this home from demolition. The group became the Historic Preservation Trust of Lancaster County. The home was saved and restored, and is today known as the Sehner-Ellicott-von Hess House, named for several notable occupants. The most famous resident was Andrew Ellicott, who surveyed the District of Columbia and helped establish the Mason-Dixon Line. The home was constructed in 1789 and was designed in the Georgian style, sometimes referred to as "half-Georgian" because it lacks the trademark symmetry of the style. Half-Georgian homes were popular for row houses and in urban environments.

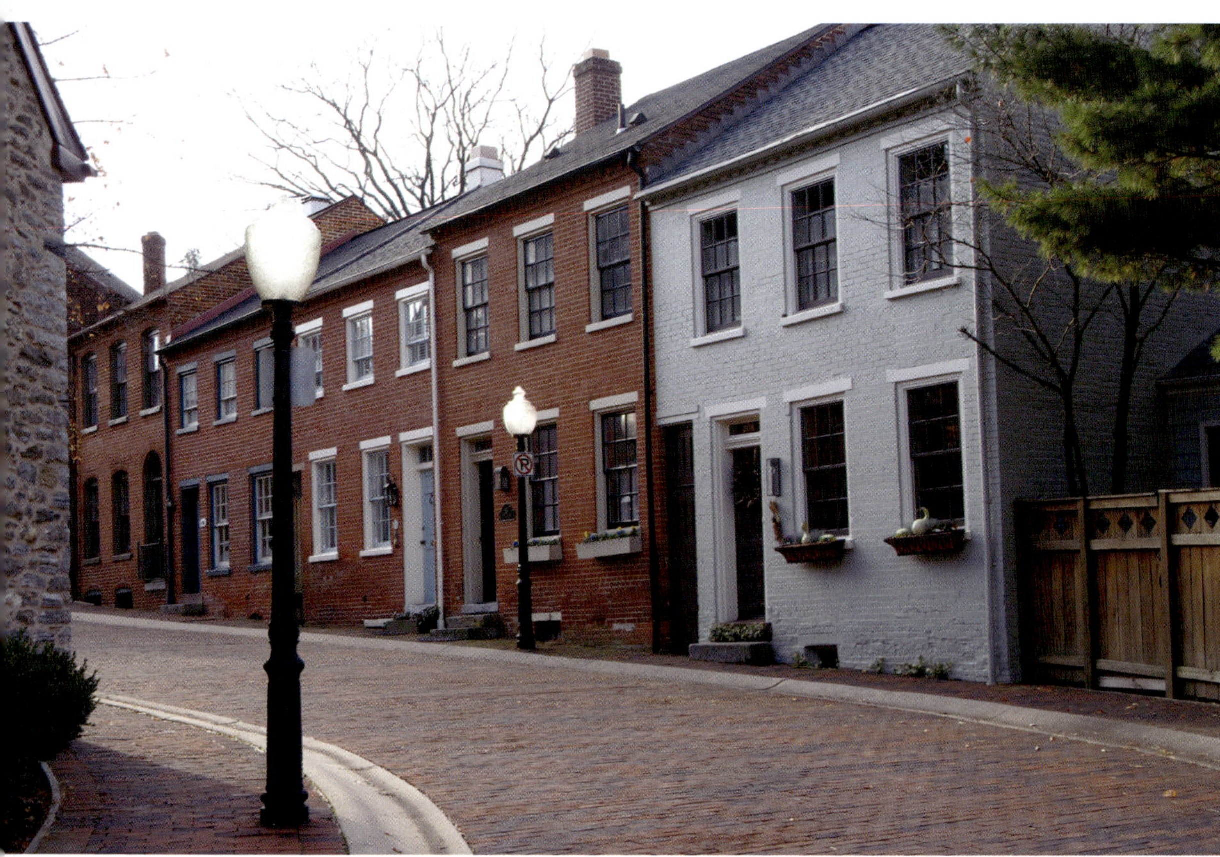

The area south of downtown is known as Old Town Lancaster. It was one of the earliest areas of development in the city, with buildings dating from the Colonial Era into the twentieth century. As listed on the National Register of Historic Places, the historic district includes East Vine Street, South Duke Street, Old Trinity Place, and South Christian Street. At one time the neighborhood was located on the edge of the town of Lancaster, bordering Adamstown and Mussertown, two small towns that were later incorporated into Lancaster City. Though the streets were laid out in 1730, the majority of the buildings date from 1840 to 1910. By the 1960s, the area was blighted, with vacant and boarded properties. An urban renewal project saved and restored the neighborhood, which received a design award from the National Association of Home Builders in 1980.

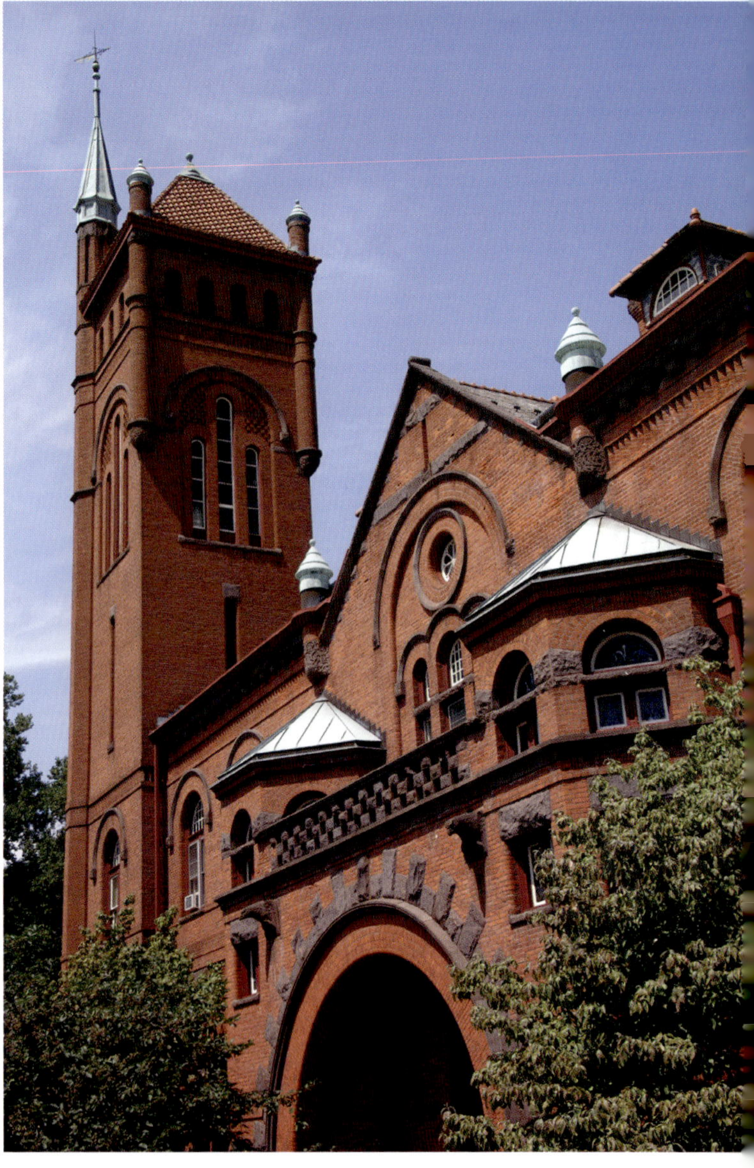

The Seminary of the Reformed Church in the United States opened in 1825 in Carlisle, Pennsylvania. It subsequently relocated to York, then to Mercersburg, Pennsylvania, before finding a permanent home in Lancaster in 1871. Now known as the Lancaster Theological Seminary, the institution constructed the picturesque Victorian Romanesque Lark Building in 1894.

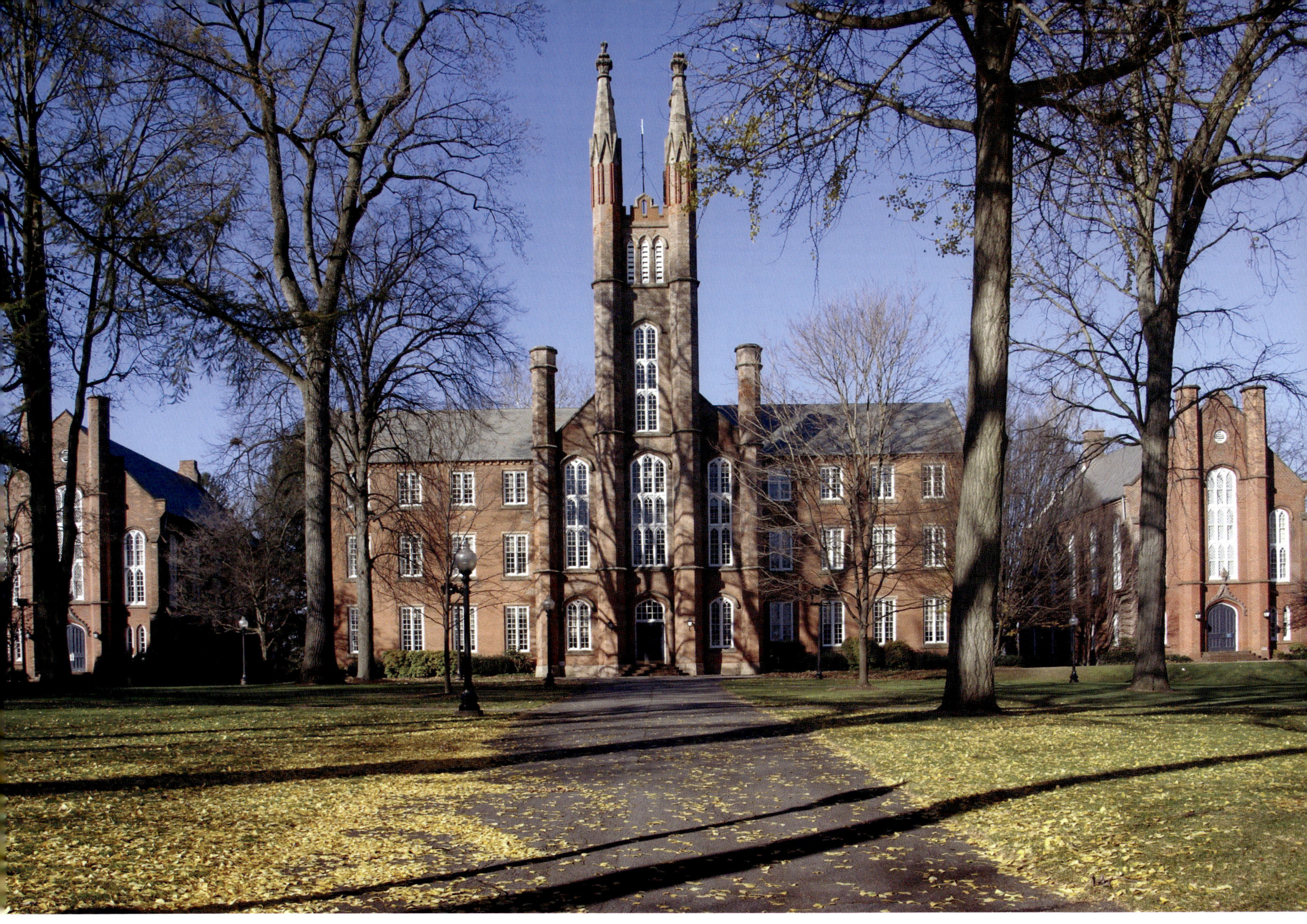

Franklin and Marshall College's Old Main building was dedicated in 1856 and designed by the Baltimore architectural firm of Dixon, Balburnie, and Dixon. The brick and sandstone Gothic Revival building is an early example of Collegiate Gothic architecture and was previously known as Recitation Hall, or simply the College Building. The imposing building is flanked by Goethean Hall and Diagnothian Hall—both were originally built to house literary societies that relocated from Mercersburg.

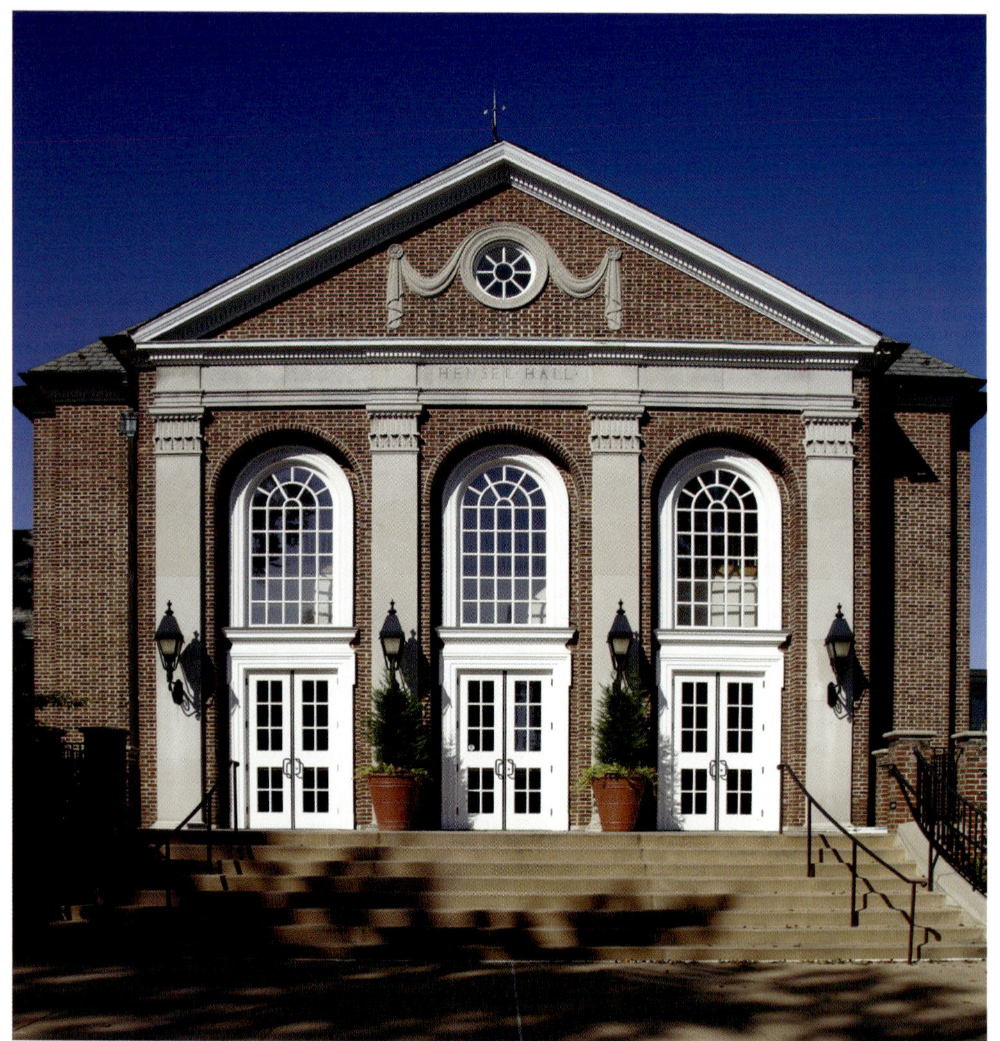

In 1923, Charles Zeller Klauder was selected as planner and architect for Franklin & Marshall. He designed several buildings including two dormitories, Biesecker Gymnasium, Fackenthal Laboratories, and this building, Hensel Hall. His vision moved the College away from its Gothic Revival roots and focused on Colonial Revival, which was a very popular style at the time and probably the most common style in Lancaster. Completed in 1927, Hensel Hall was built for a cost of $650,000 and named for W.U. Hensel, president of the College's Board of Trustees.

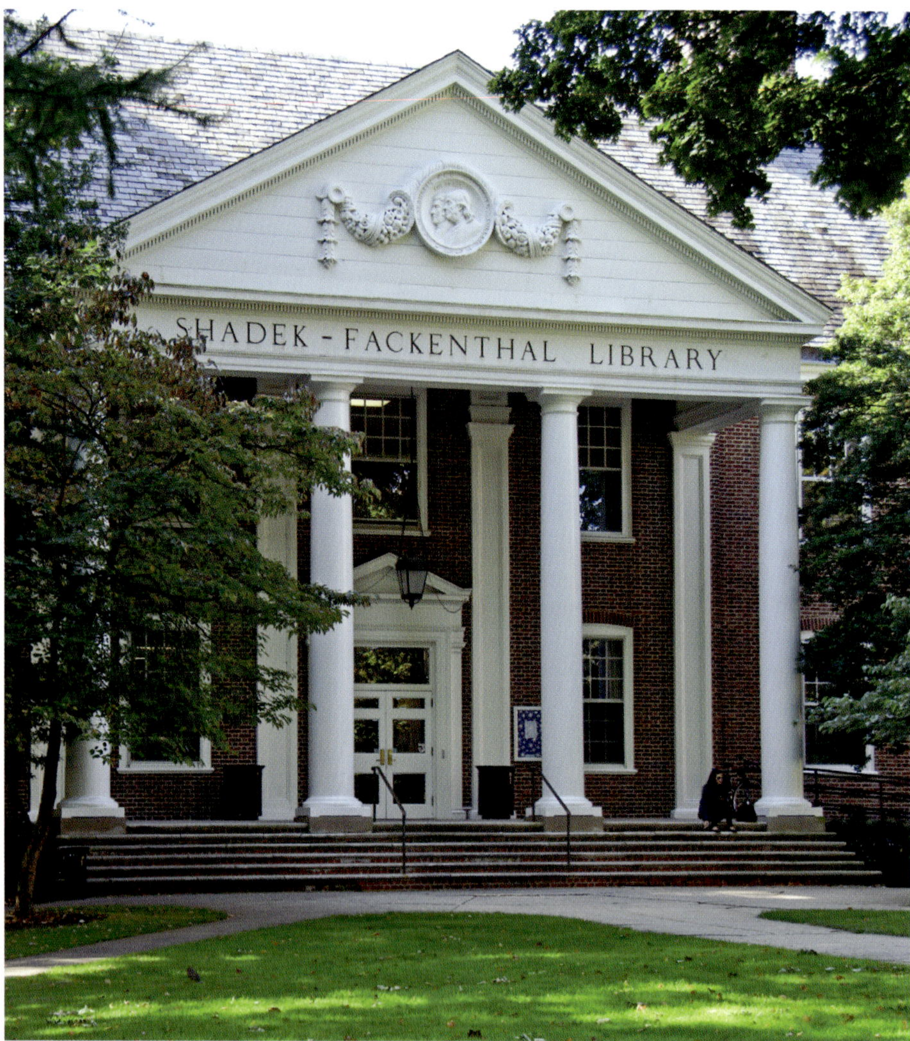

The Shadek-Fackenthal Library at Franklin & Marshall College was constructed in 1938 from a design by Philadelphia architect William H. Lee. The prominent building features a Neoclassical portico and is named for Arthur Shadek and Dr. Benjamin Franklin Fackenthal, who were both members of the Board of Trustees that contributed funds in different eras to build (and later renovate) the building.

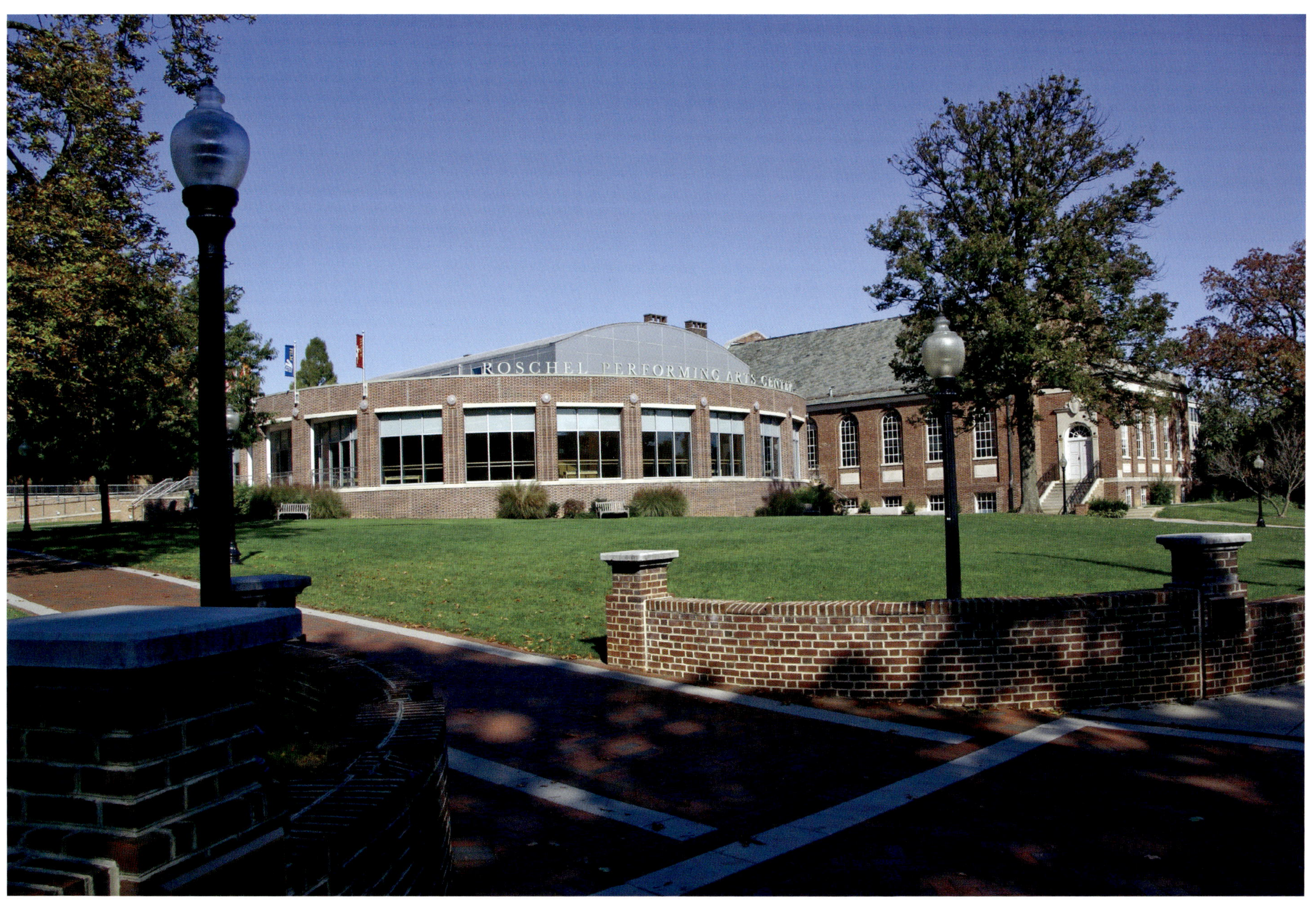

Roshel Performing Arts Center opened on the campus of Franklin and Marshall College in 2003. The 38,000 square foot facility includes the 305-seat Schnader Theater.

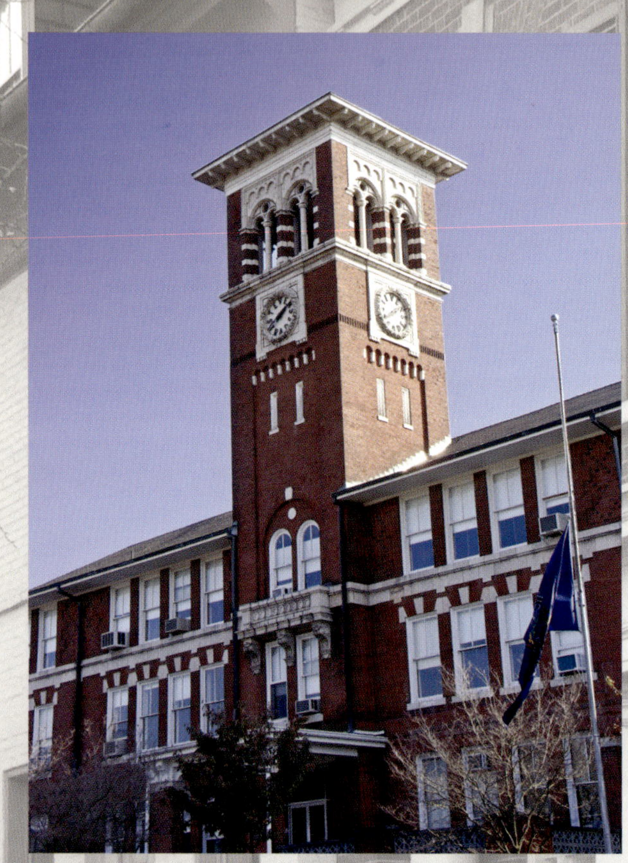

Founded in 1905, the Thaddeus Stevens College of Technology is located on thirty-two and a half acres east of downtown Lancaster. The main building was completed in 1908. Today, the college, which is owned by the Commonwealth of Pennsylvania, includes eighteen buildings. The college is named for the "Great Commoner," who died in 1868 and left a bequest that led to the creation of the Stevens School of Trade for "all industrial trades and pursuits."

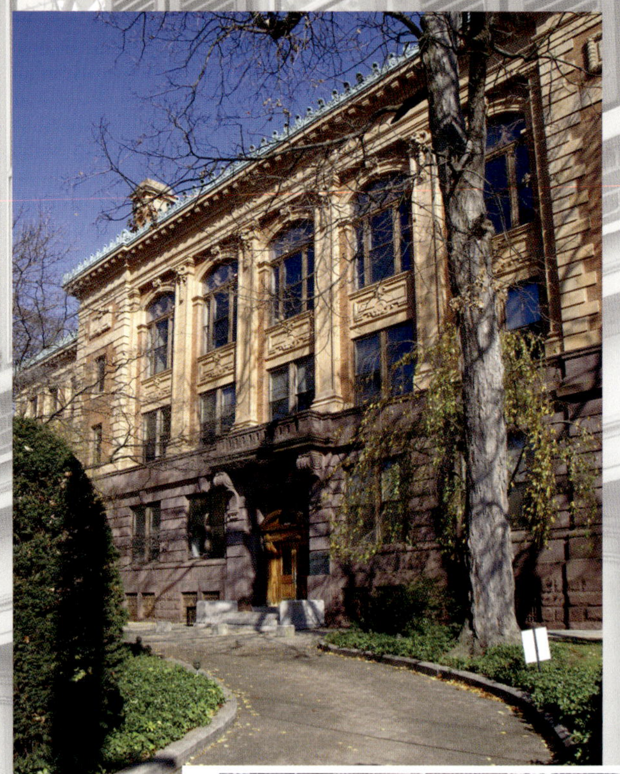

Completed in 1905 for a cost of $215,000, Stevens High School was the first high school in Lancaster built for girls. C. Emlen Urban designed the Renaissance Revival building, which was constructed of brownstone and gold roman brick with terra cotta ornamentation. One of the building's original features was a third floor auditorium with seating for 600 people. From 1938 to 1983 the building was home to Stevens Elementary School. Today, the building is home to the residences at Stevens School.

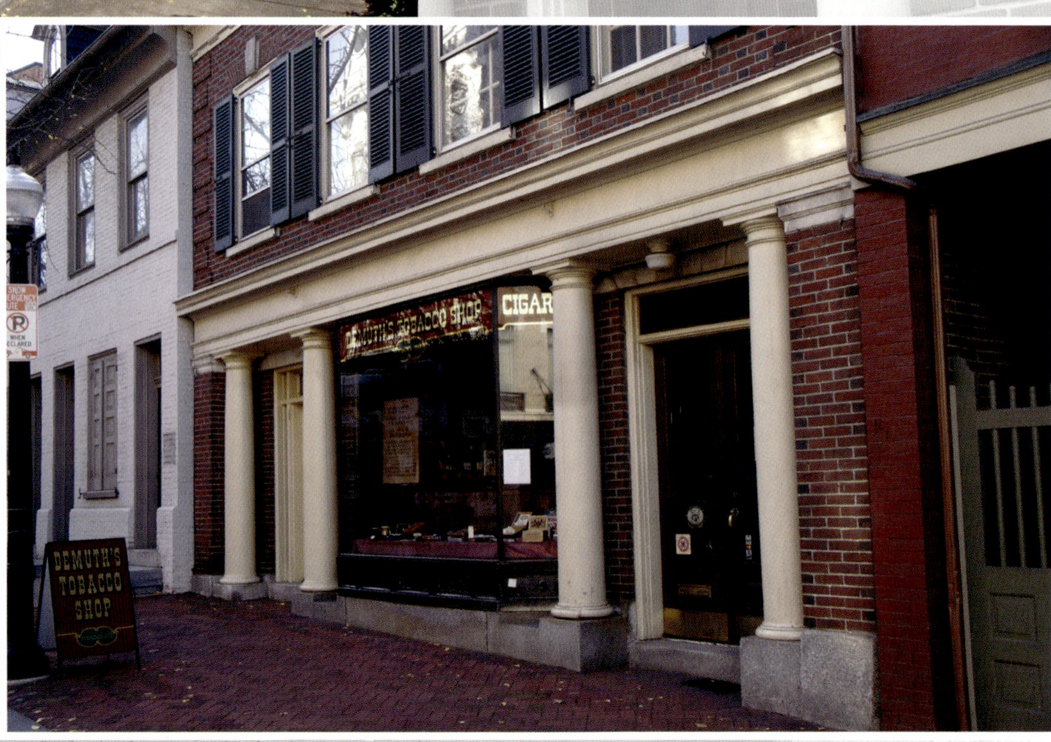

The Demuth Tobacco Shop on East King Street opened in 1770 and remained in the family for the next 200 years. It is still in operation today, making it the oldest tobacco shop in America. Charles Demuth (1883-1935) lived next door in a building that once served as a Colonial tavern. Demuth was a famous American artist who produced more than 1,000 paintings, mostly in watercolor, in a style known as Precisionism. His former residence is today a museum dedicated to promoting his work and preserving his home.

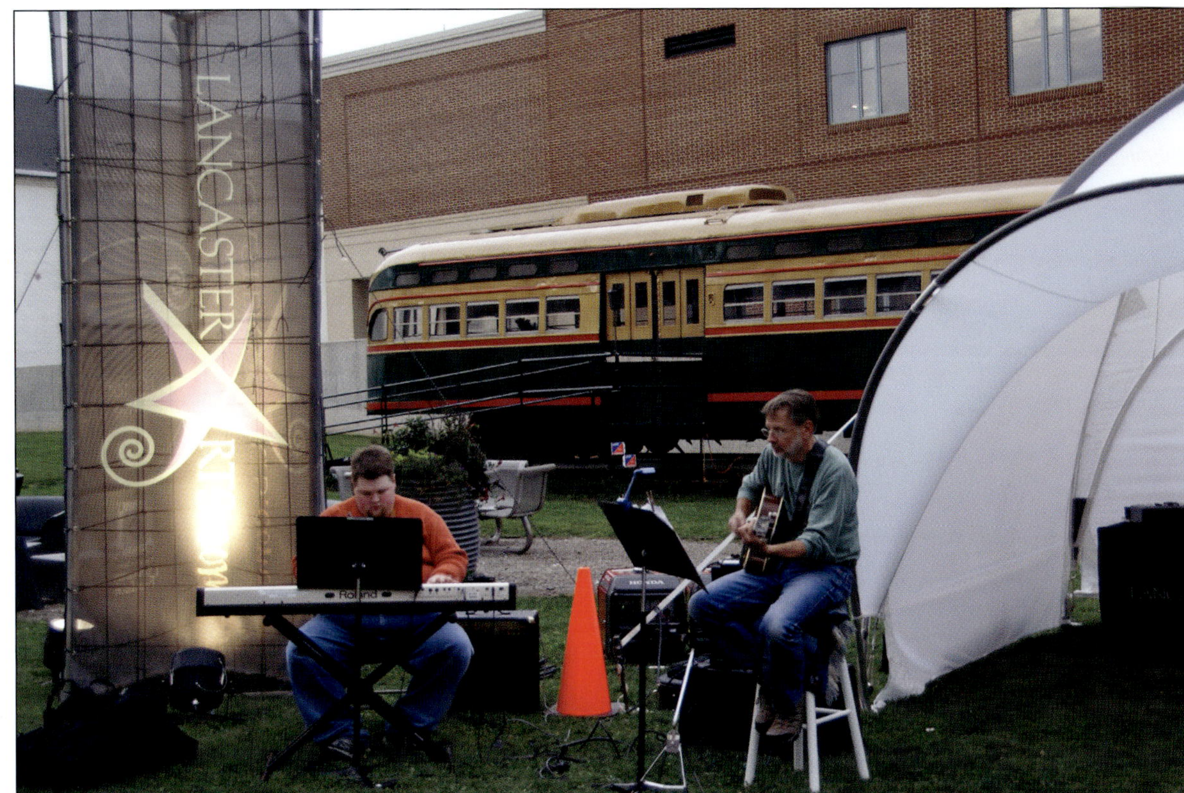

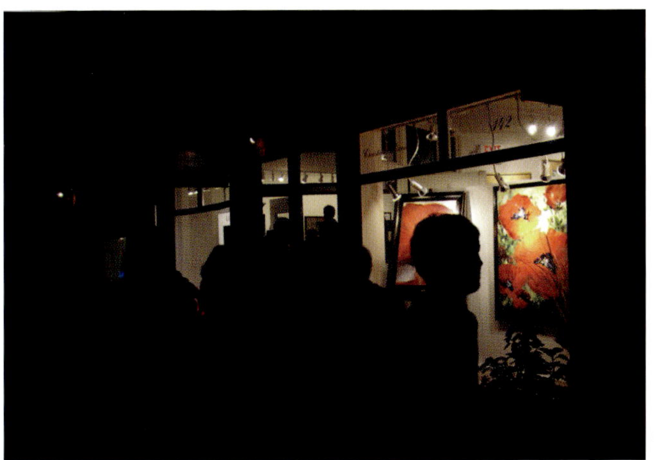

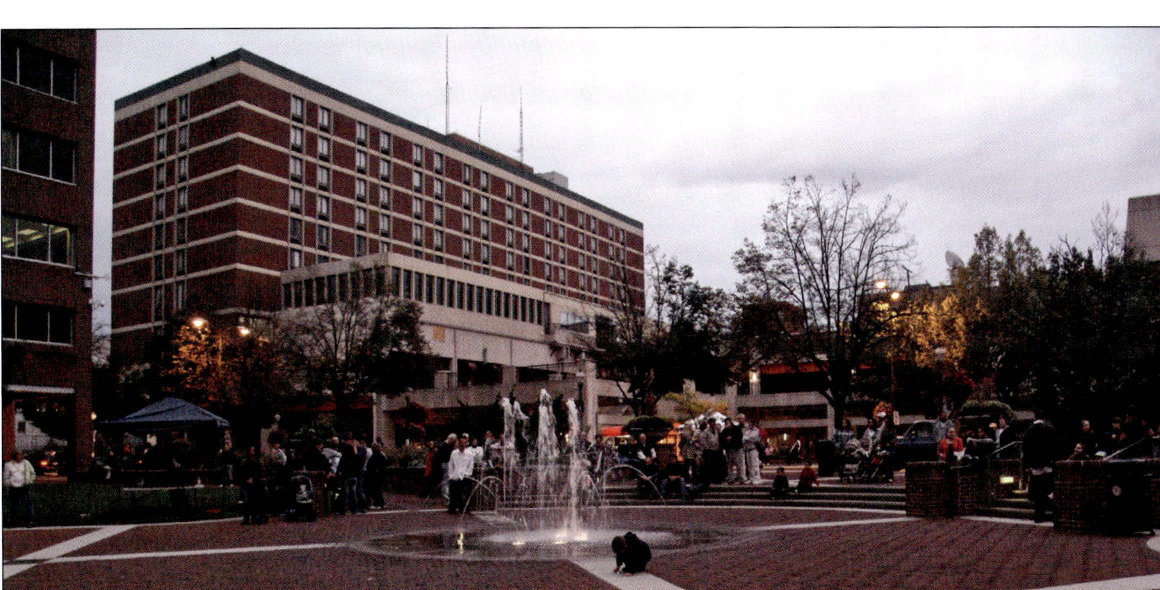

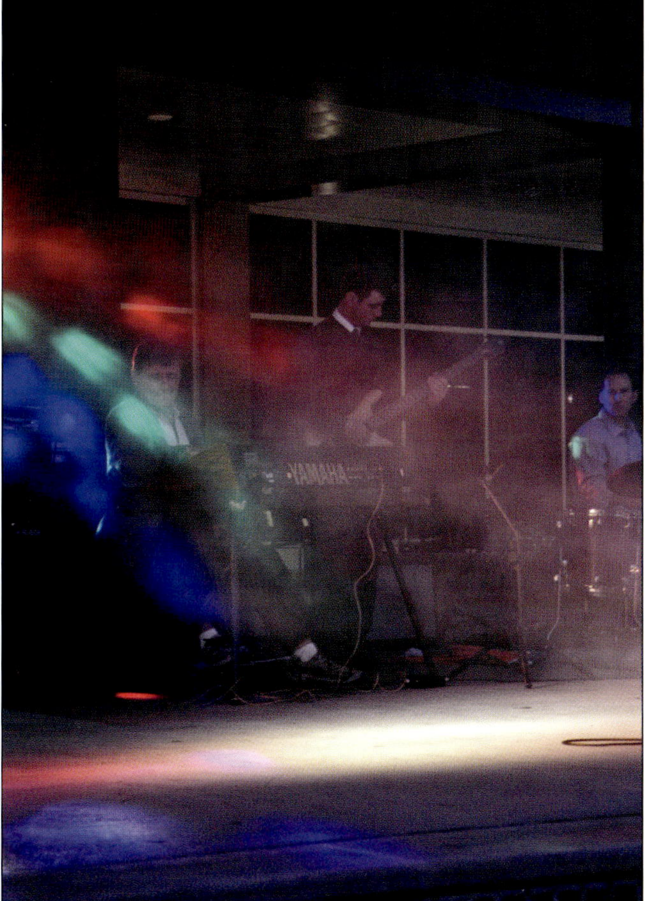

LancasterARTS exists to cultivate an environment where the arts can flourish. One of their popular programs is First Friday, a monthly event that fills the streets of Lancaster on the first Friday of every month. Over seventy arts venues stay open late and offer new exhibits and opportunities to meet the artists. Live music is performed in Binn's Park and at other locations, and many restaurants, businesses, and even churches participate in the popular event.

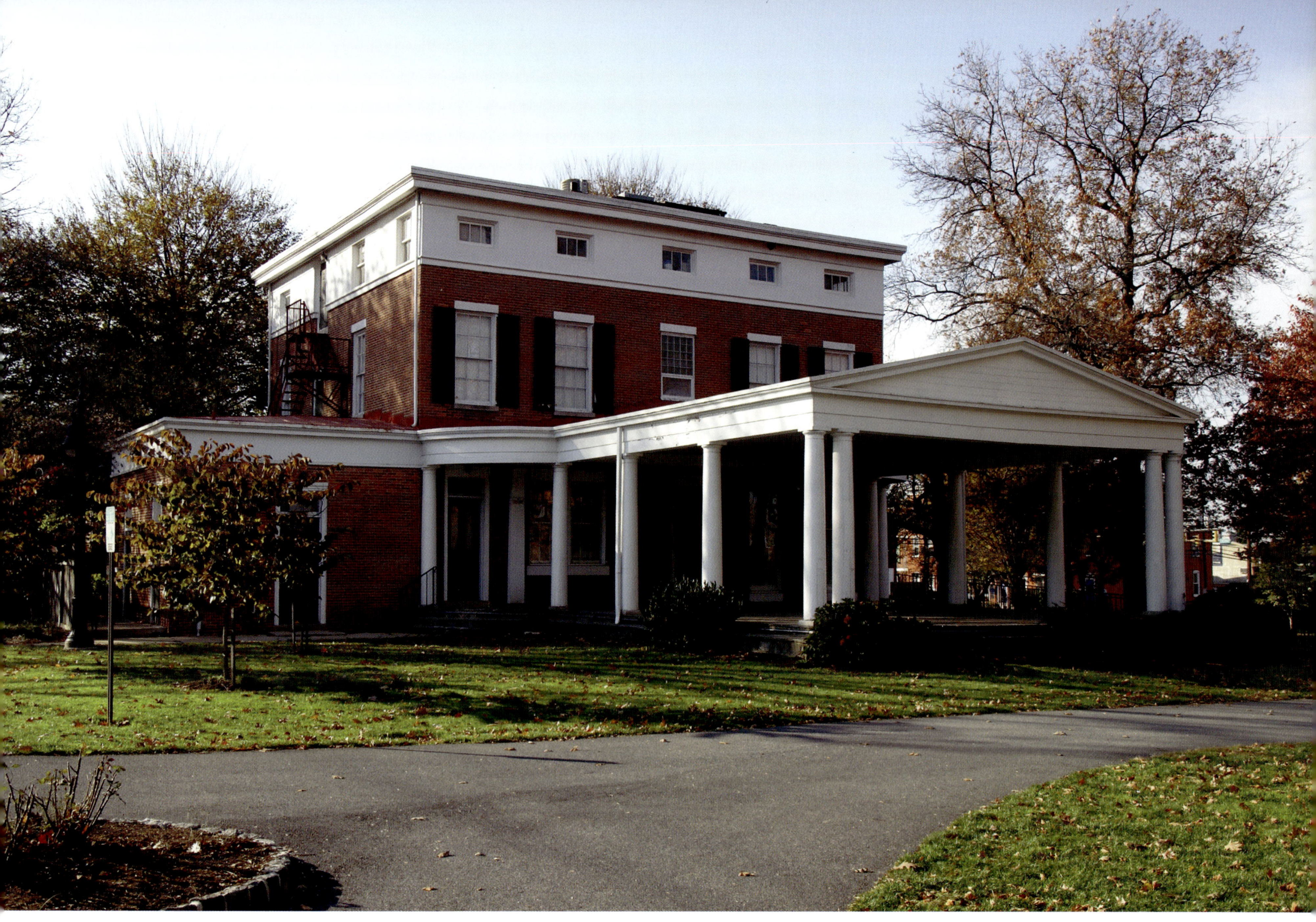

The Lancaster Museum of Art is located in the historic Grubb Mansion at Musser Park. Constructed by Clement Bates Grubb, ironmaster of Mount Hope Furnace, the Greek Revival mansion was built in 1846 for $1,500. In 1979, the striking building became home to the Community Gallery, which is today the Lancaster Museum of Art. Here residents and visitors enjoy permanent and visiting collections of art created by local, regional, and national artists.

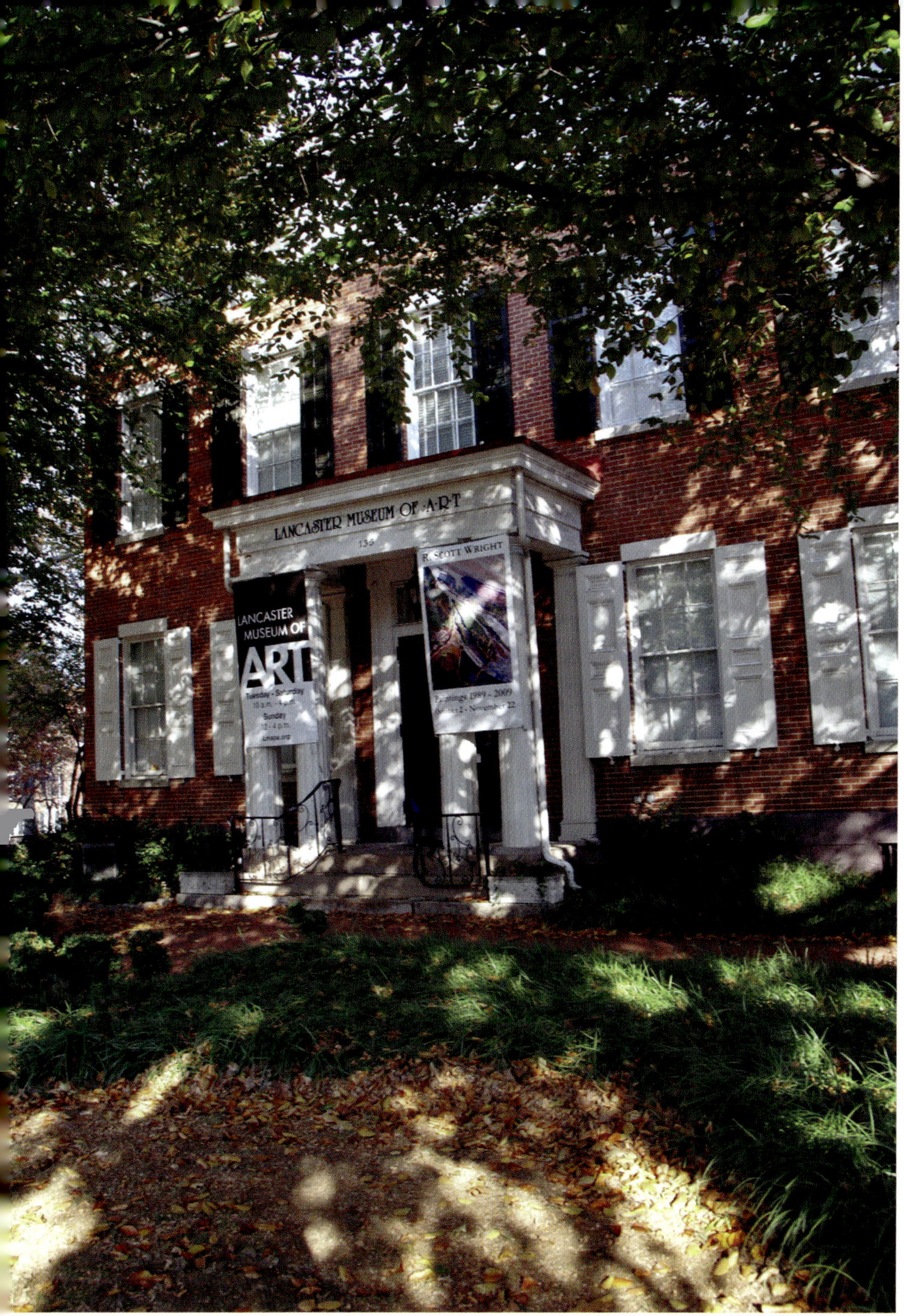

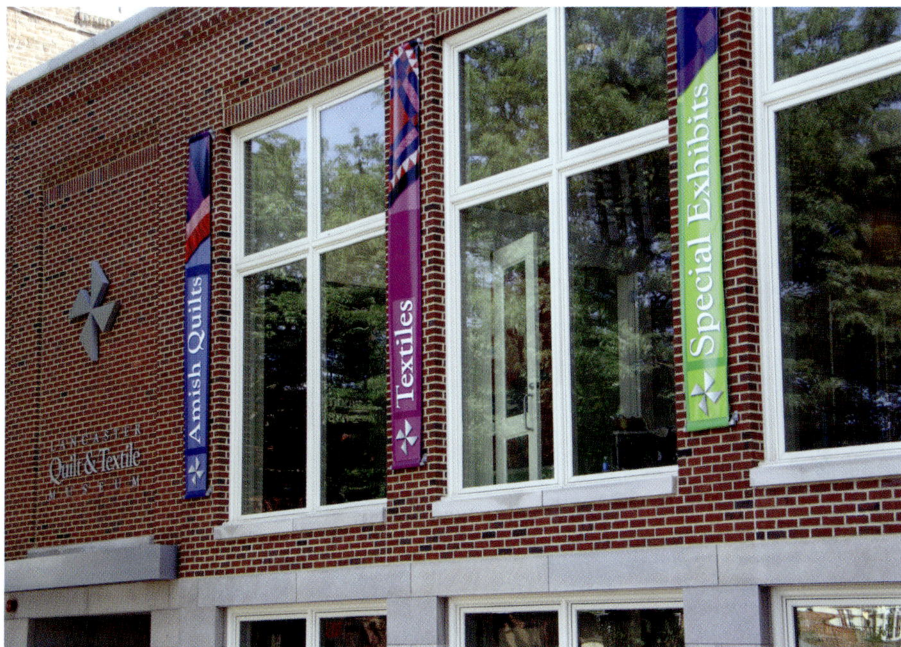

The Lancaster Quilt & Textile Museum is managed by the Heritage Center of Lancaster County. The museum opened in 2004 and occupies the former Lancaster Trust Building near Central Market. Constructed in 1912, the building was expanded in 2007 to accommodate an extensive and nationally recognized collection of quilts and textiles from the nineteenth and twentieth centuries.

The 6,000 seat Clipper Magazine Stadium opened to great fanfare in May 2005. The stadium is home to the Lancaster Barnstormers, an Atlantic League team that played its inaugural game the same year the stadium opened. Prior to the formation of the Barnstormers, Lancaster had gone more than forty years without a professional baseball team. Throughout much of the twentieth century the Lancaster Red Roses had provided entertainment for Lancastrians, but the team folded after the 1961 season.

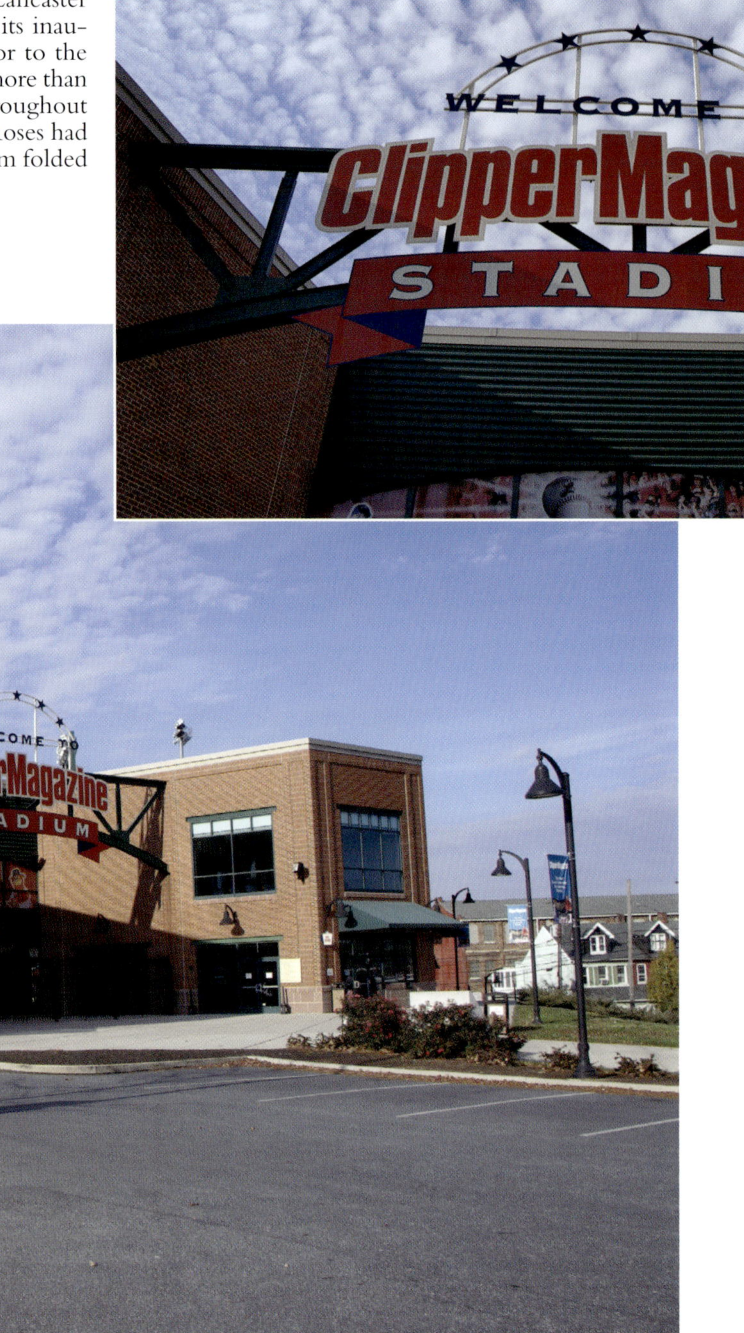

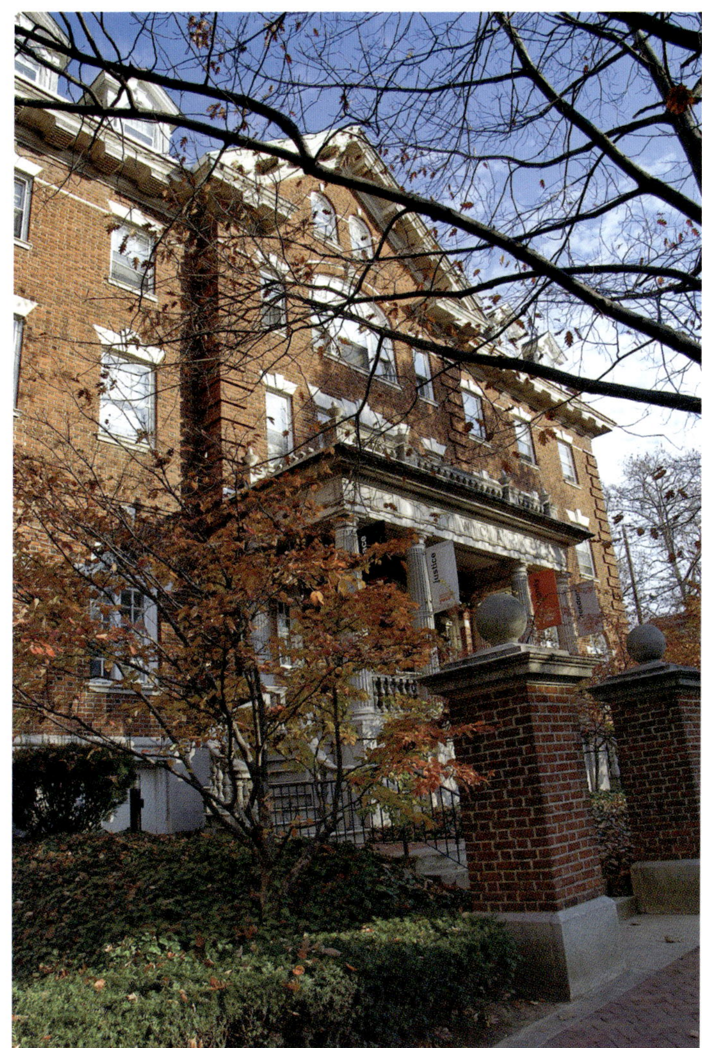

The YWCA of Lancaster was founded in 1889 and constructed this building in 1918. Located at the intersection of East Orange and North Lime Streets, the building is a prominent example of Colonial Revival architecture.

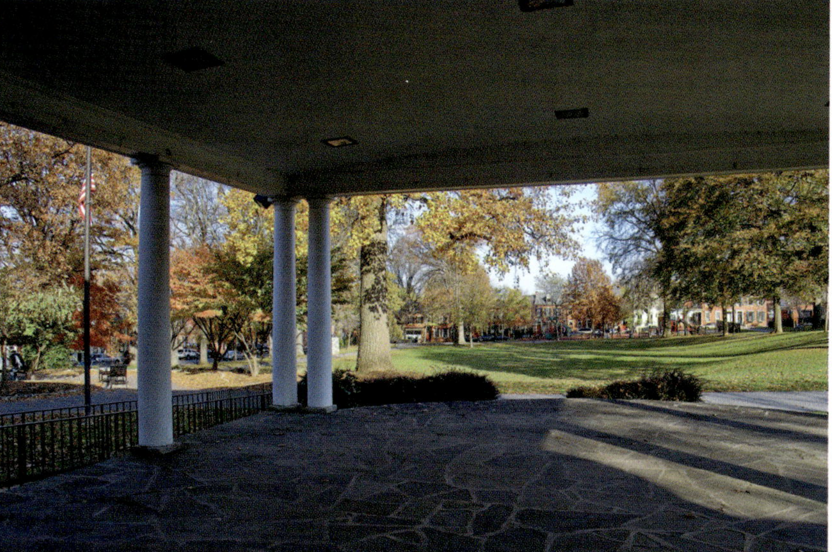

The three acre Musser Park, located near downtown Lancaster, became a public park in 1949. Funding for the park was made possible via a bequest by Harry M. Musser, a successful manufacturer of umbrella handles, who died in 1928 but directed his executors to purchase land for use as a public park.

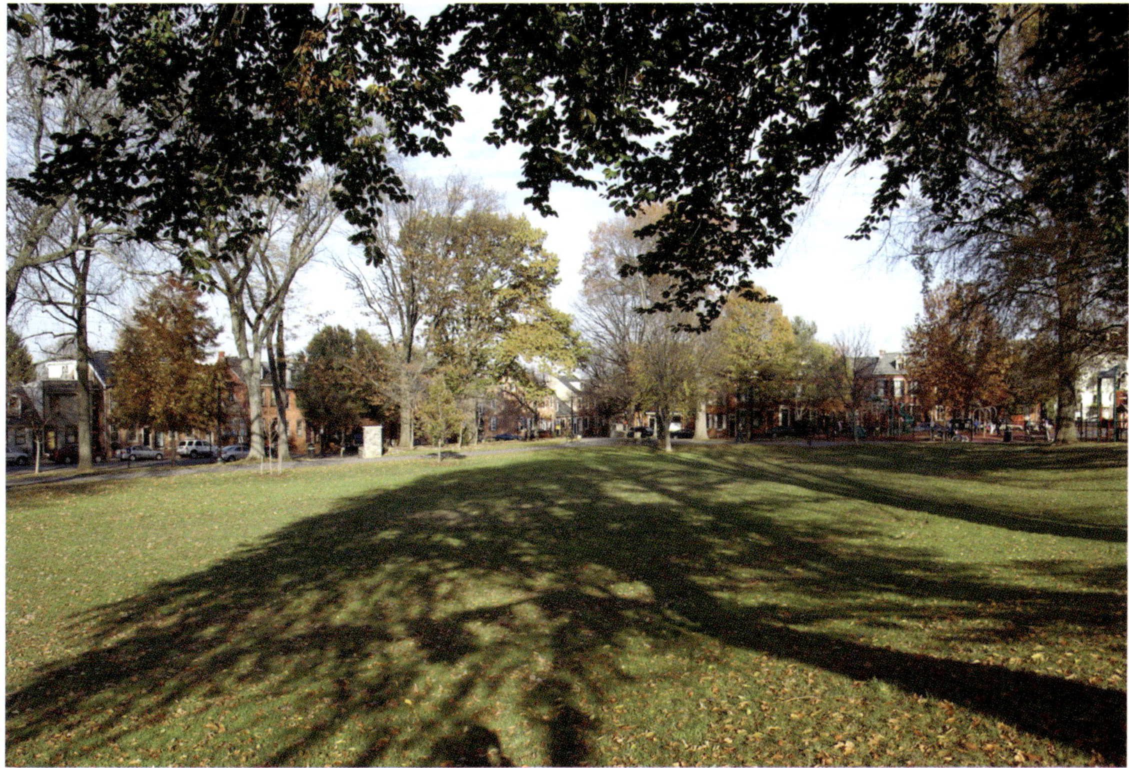

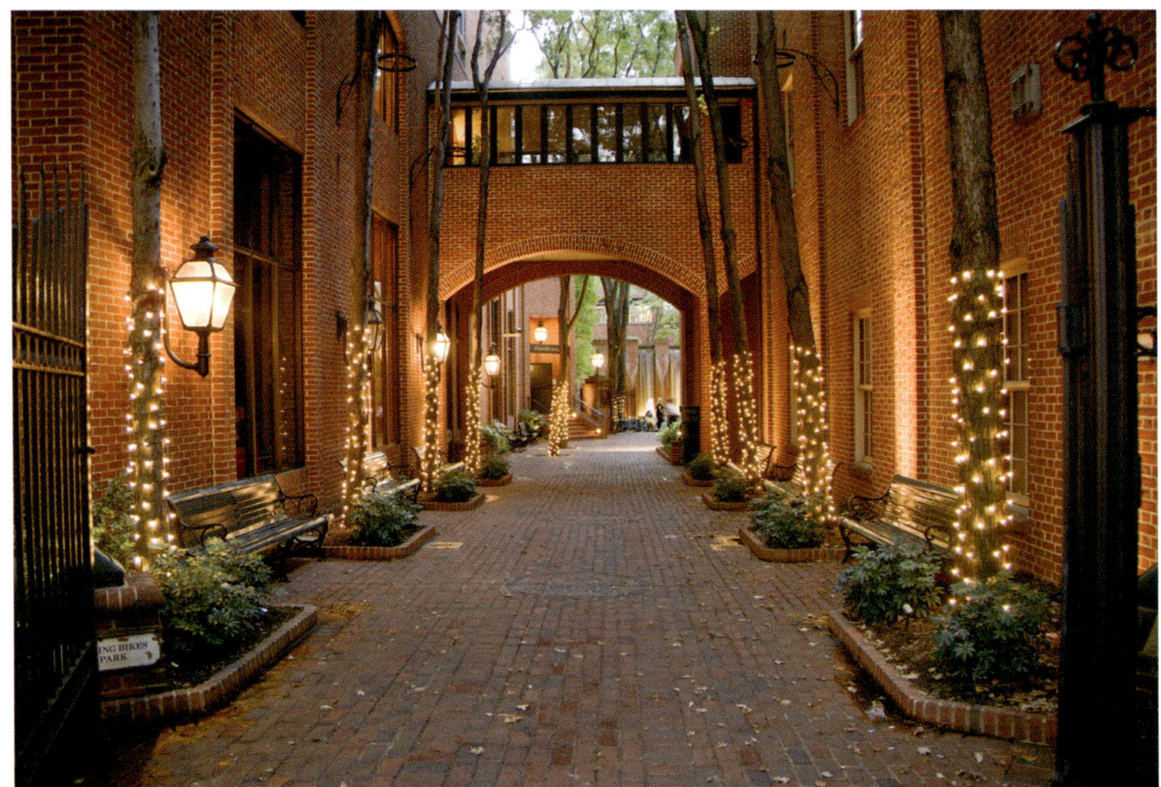

Steinman Park is a unique asset for a downtown area—an urban oasis located not far from the town square. The park was the result of the efforts of the Steinman family, owners of Lancaster Newspapers, Inc., who in the early 1980s decided to restore several nearby buildings and construct a park. The most striking feature of the brick-lined park is a twenty-foot waterfall and fountain, which creates a pleasant white noise that helps drown out the sounds of the surrounding city. The park is dedicated to the memory of James Hale Steinman and John Frederick Steinman, co-publishers of Lancaster Newspapers.

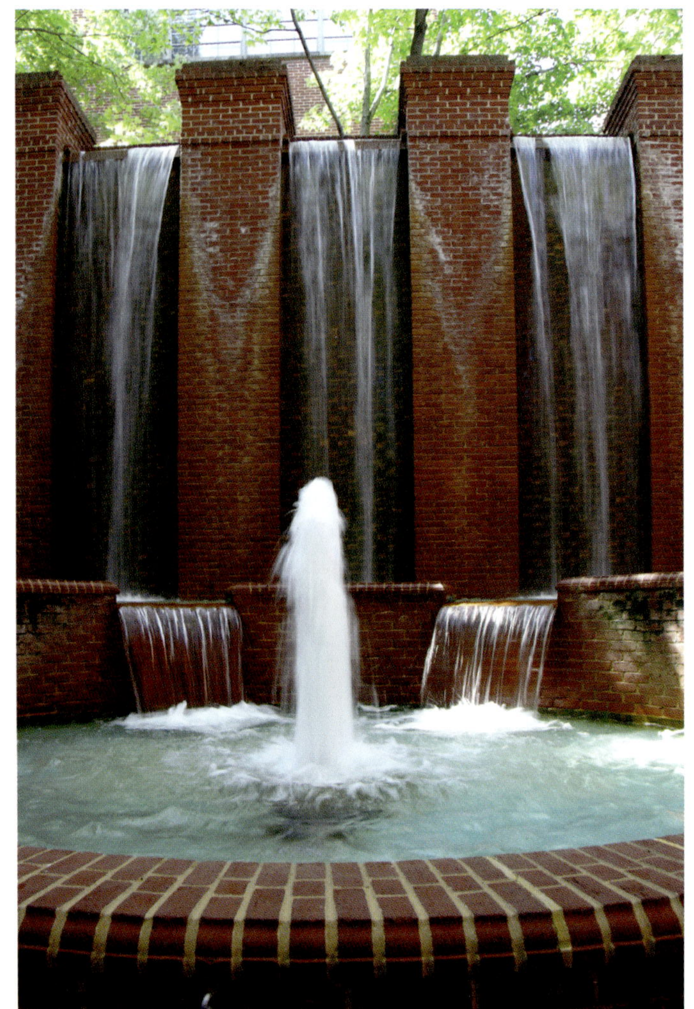

This 1866 commercial Queen Anne-style building was home of the Steinman Hardware Store. Founded in 1744, the store had the distinction of being the oldest operating hardware store in the country when it closed in 1965. Today the Victorian building is home to the Pressroom Restaurant, a newspaper-themed restaurant whose slogan is, "Where Great Food and Drink Make Headlines."

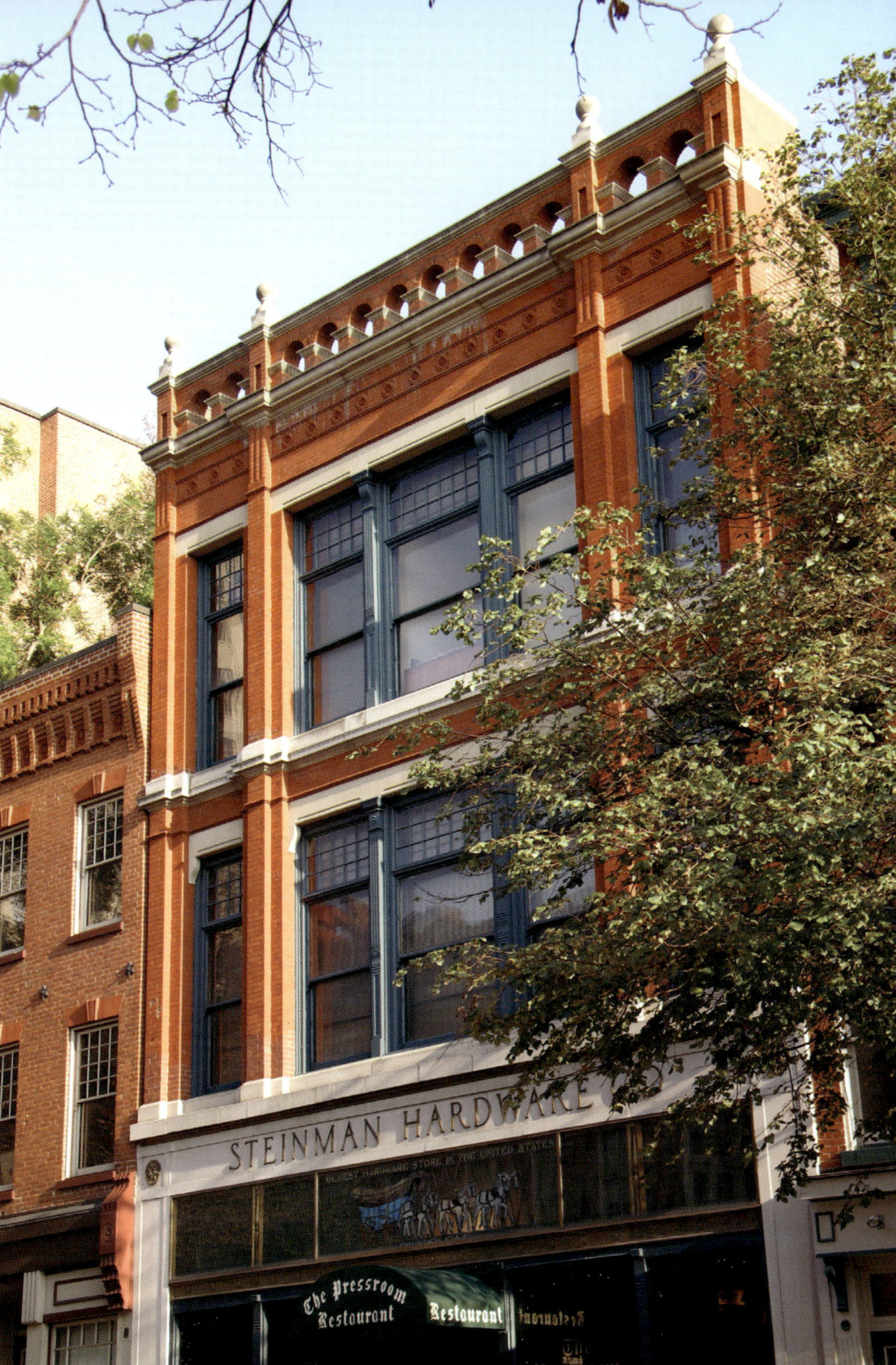

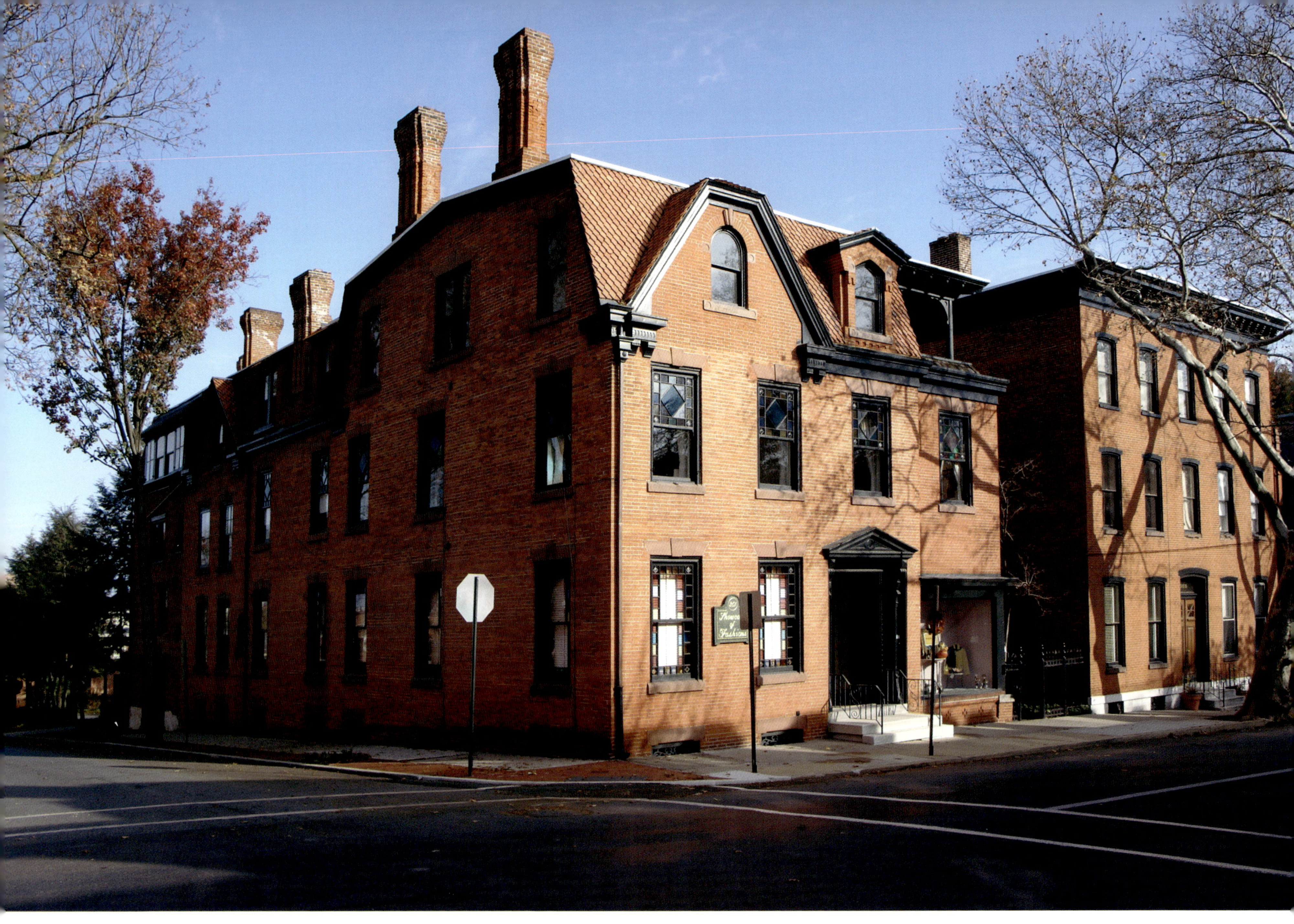

The Andrew Jackson Steinman Mansion is located at 301 East Orange Street. The building is one of Lancaster's most outstanding examples of Queen Anne architecture and was built in 1882. Steinman was the first family member involved with the newspaper business, which he entered in 1866, when he purchased the struggling *Intelligencer* newspaper. Today the Steinman family owns Lancaster Newspapers, Inc.

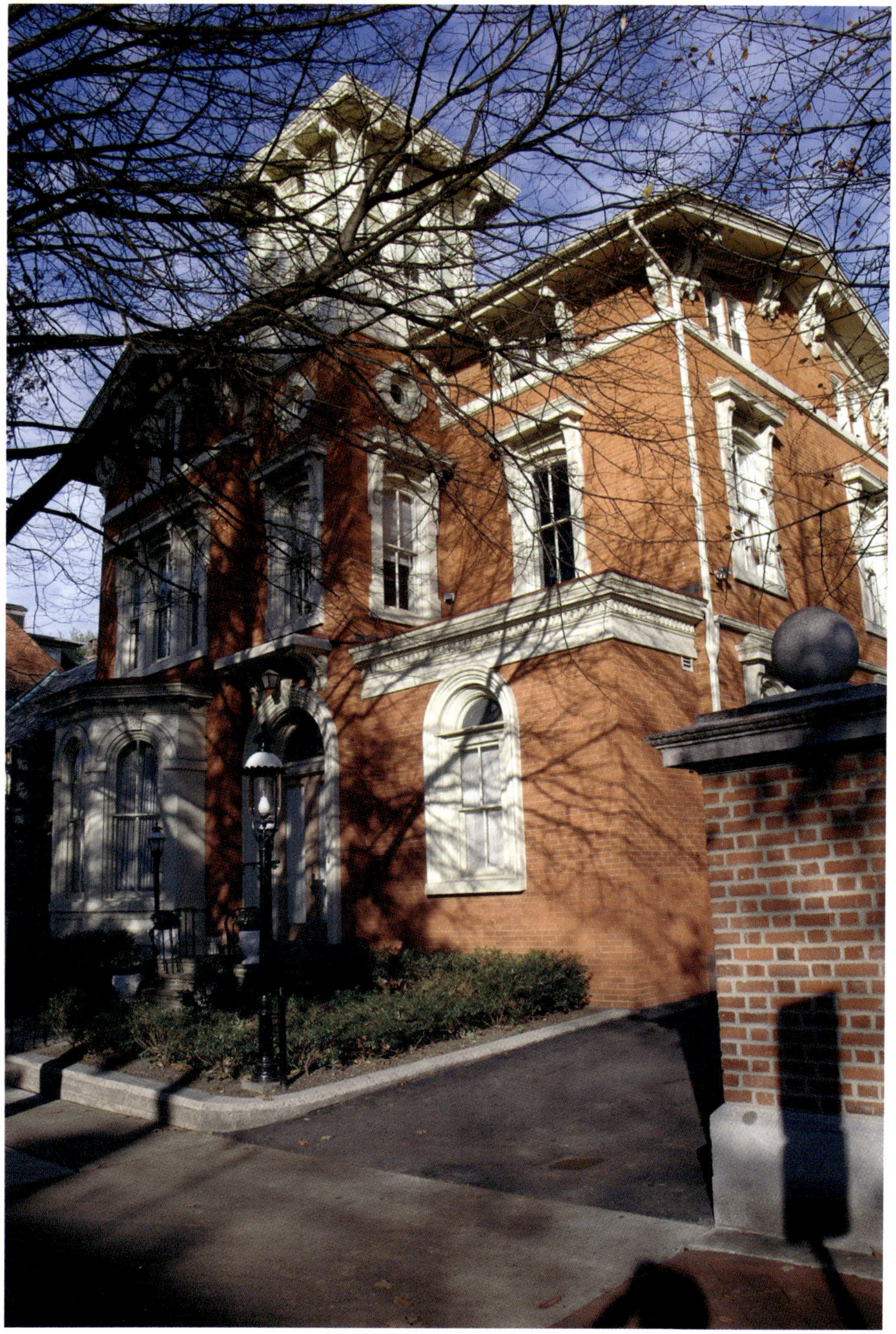

The Reuban Baer Mansion on East Orange Street is one of Lancaster's best examples of Italianate-style architecture. Constructed in 1874, the asymmetrical building with decorative brackets showcases the Italian Villa subtype of the style. Today the picturesque structure is home to the Snyder Funeral Home.

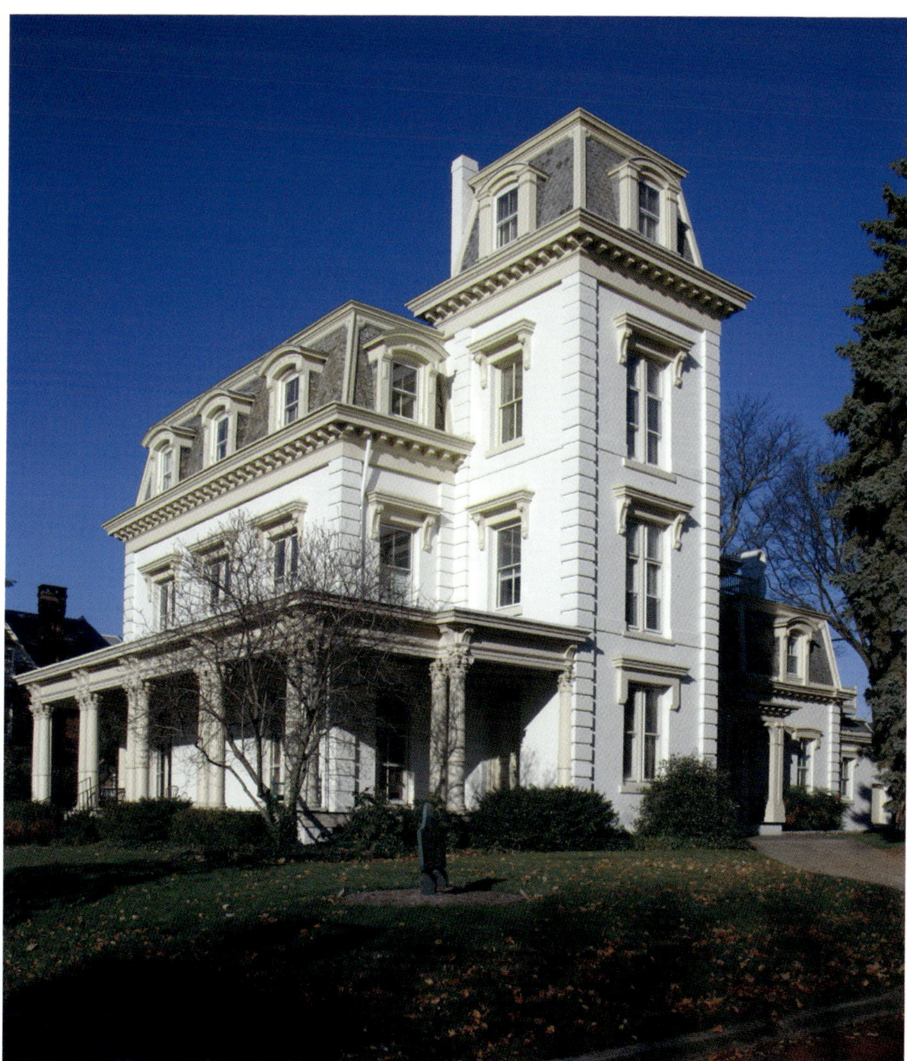

This stately mansion is known as West Lawn and was built in 1874 for Barton Bowman Martin, a leading lumber merchant and one of the founders of Millersville Normal School. The West Chestnut Street home is one of Lancaster's best examples of Second Empire architecture, with mansard roof and projecting central pavilion.

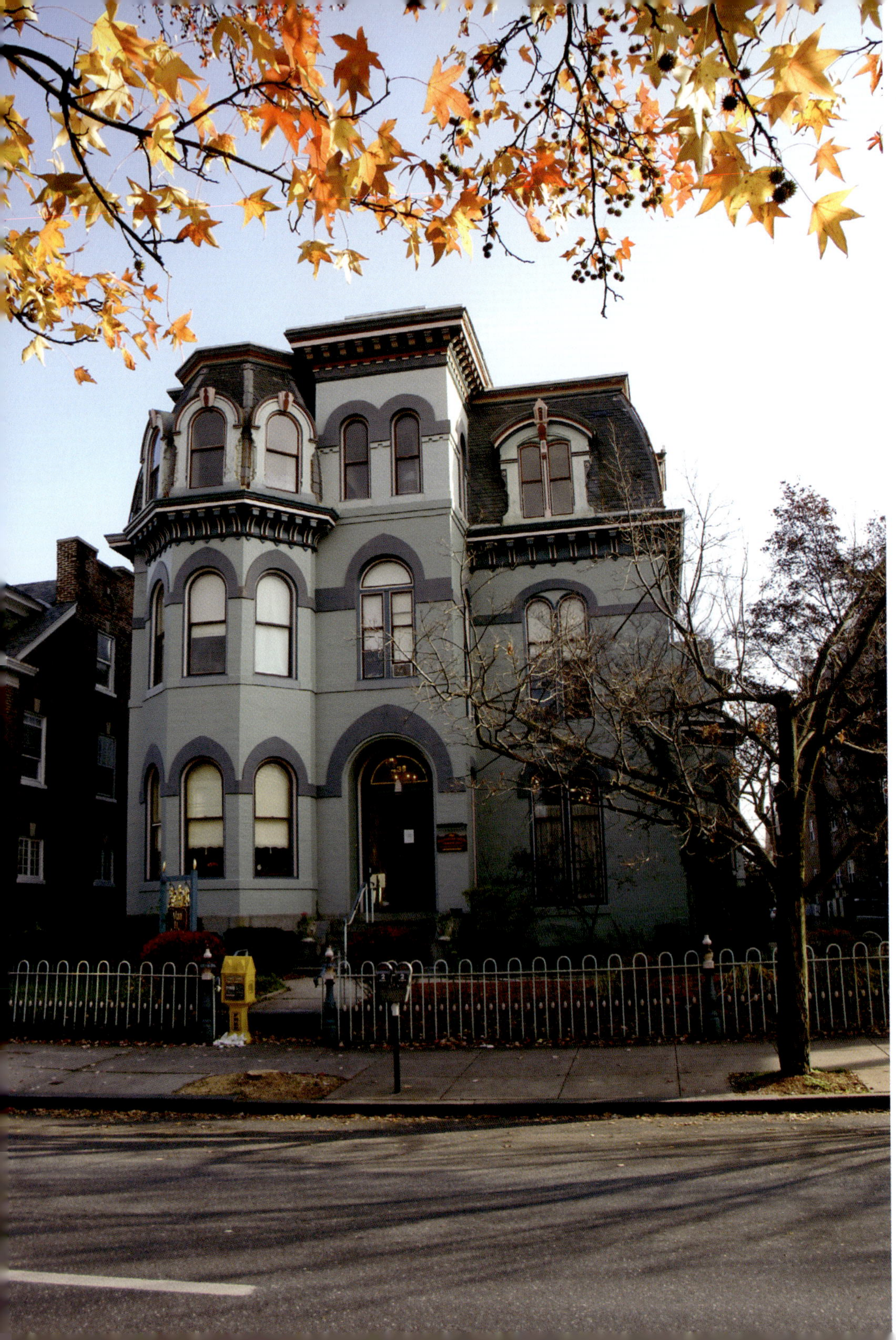

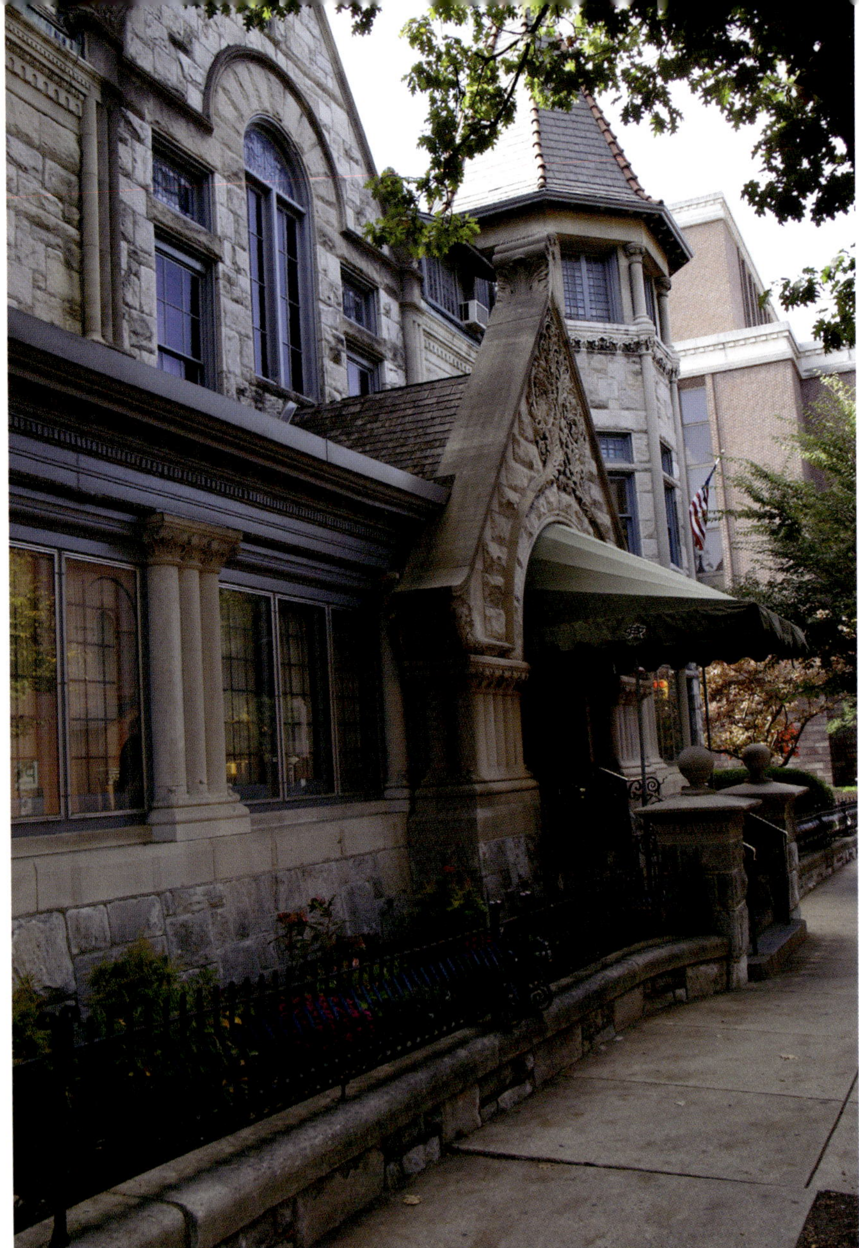

Founded in 1889 by prominent local citizens, the Hamilton Club is a private social club named for James Hamilton, who laid out Lancaster in the 1730s. Their stone Chateauesque building on East Orange Street was built as a private residence in 1890 and acquired by the club in 1912.

The John Ives Hartman Mansion is located at 439 North Duke Street. It is a striking example of Second Empire architecture constructed in the late 1870s. Today the building is home to several businesses.

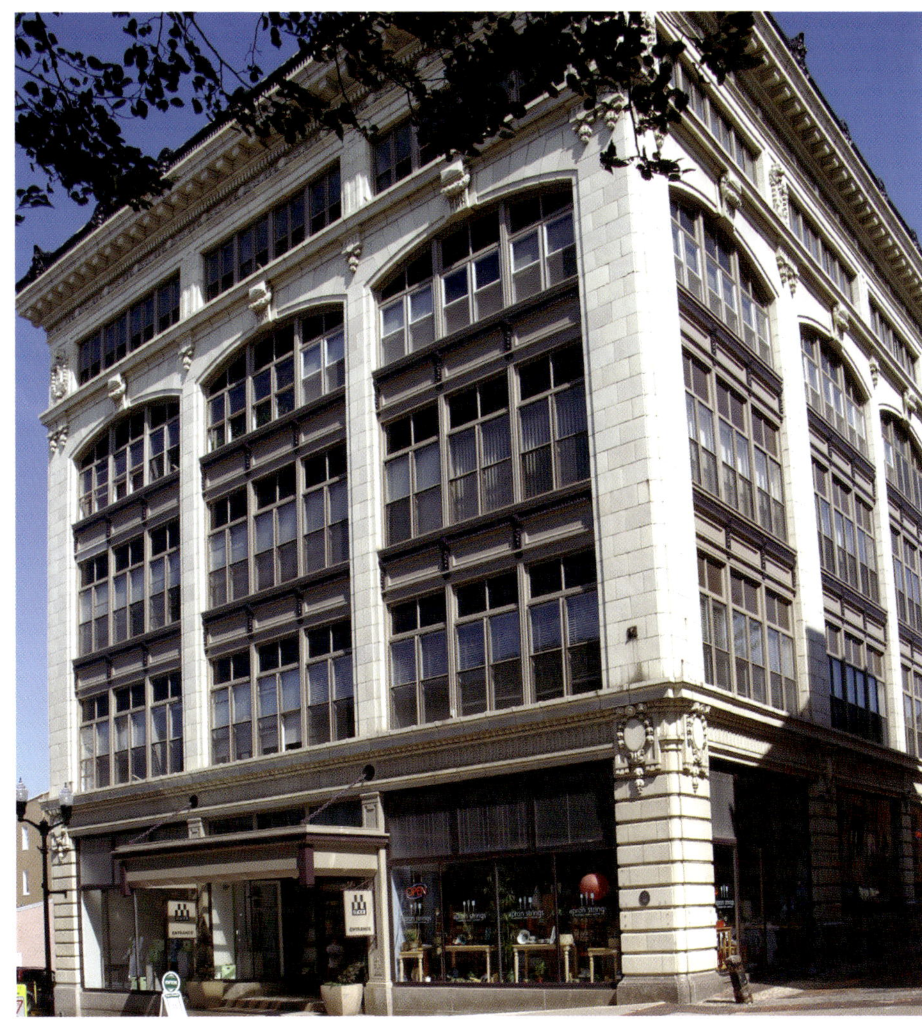

The Hager Store opened in 1823 on West King Street and remained in business until 1977. Lancaster architect C. Emlen Urban was commissioned to design a major expansion to the Hager Store, including a total redesign of the existing King Street building. The new store opened in 1911 and featured extensive use of natural light. While the building features Beaux-Arts-style ornamentation, Urban incorporated the popular Commercial style of architecture by designing a skeletal structure with large banks of windows. The style originated with Chicago department stores and had a functional purpose: more light meant better-lit merchandise, which improved sales.

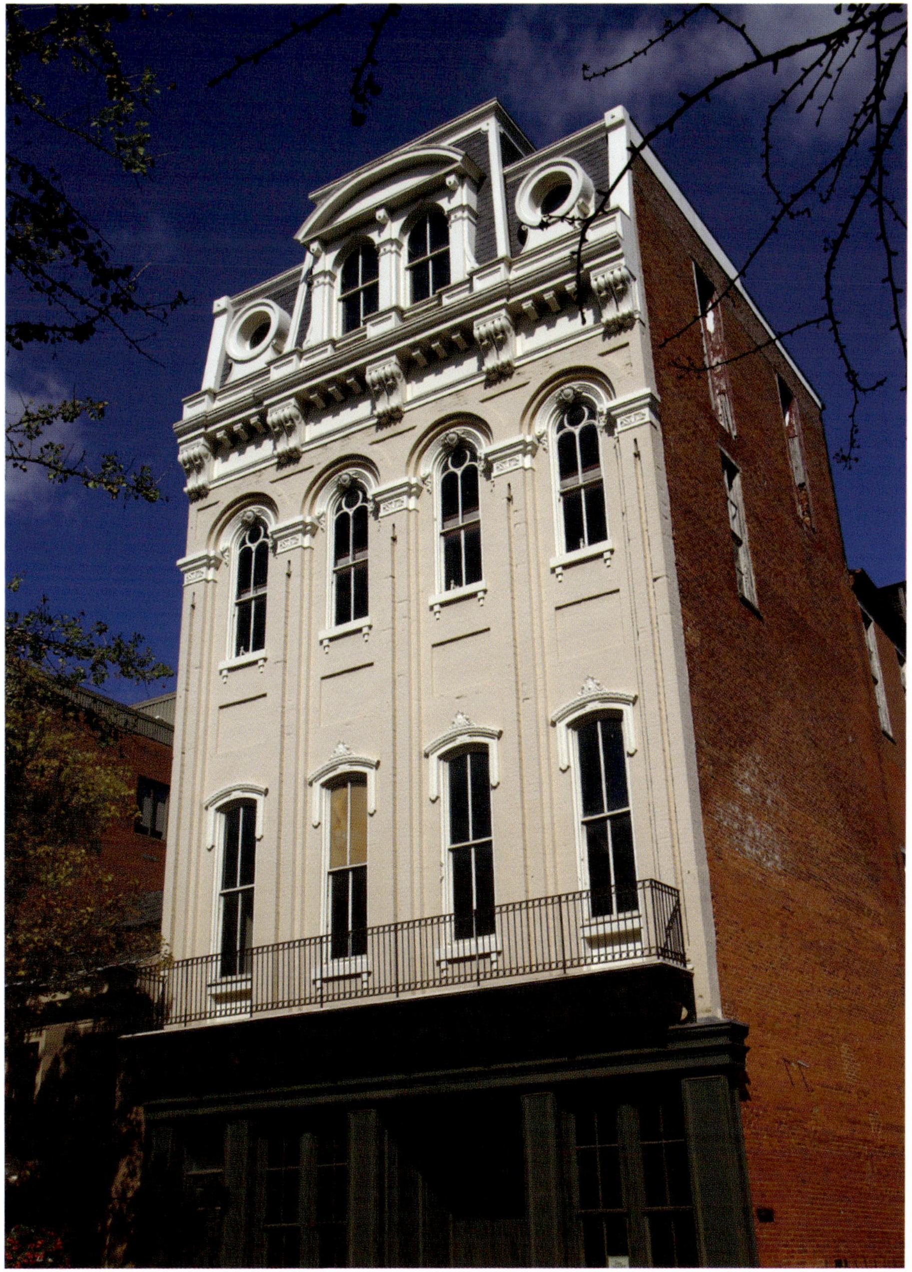

In the late nineteenth century, the Sprenger Brewery complex occupied several buildings on East King Street. The largest of these was known as Excelsior Hall, a four-story building constructed in 1873 and designed in the Second Empire style. The building housed a saloon on the ground floor and meeting halls for societies on the upper floors.

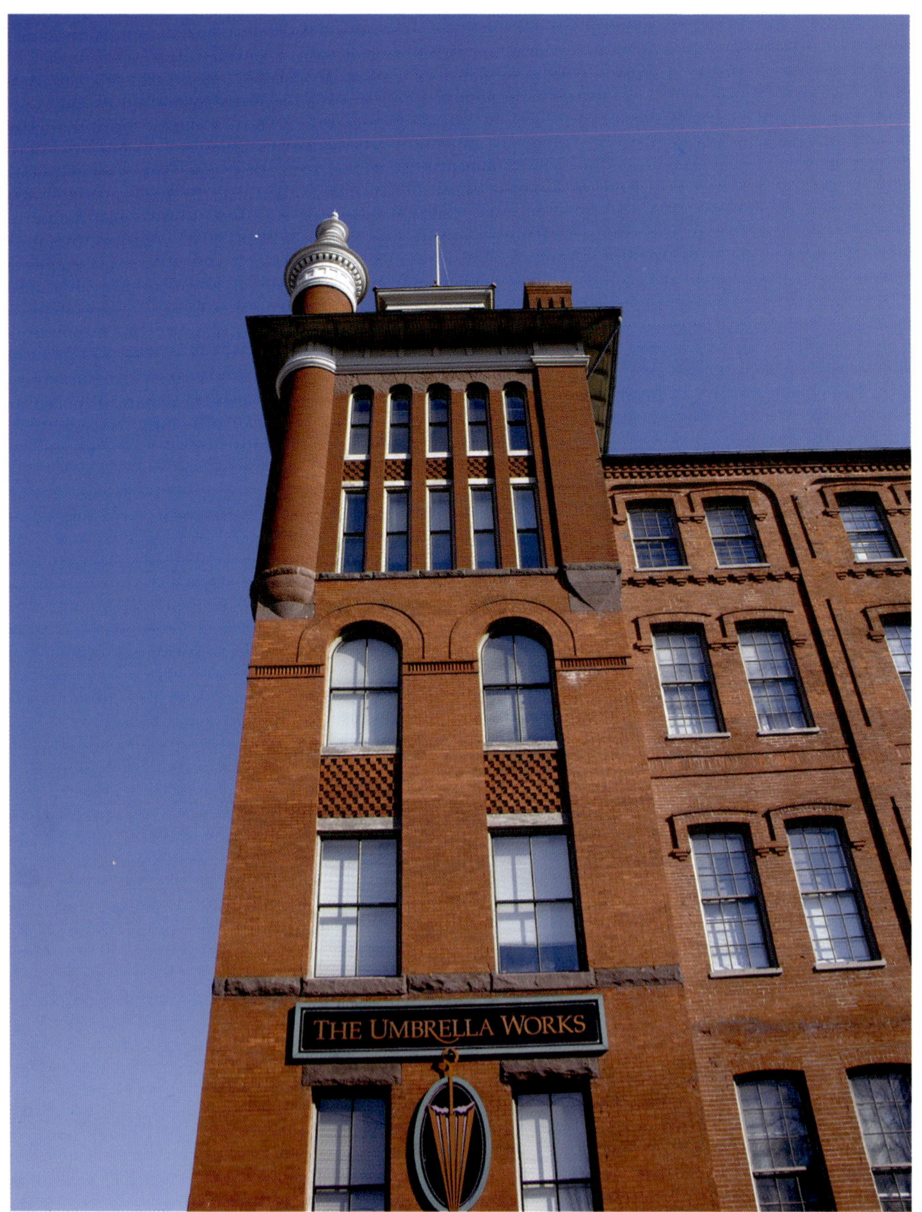

Built as the Follmer, Clogg & Company Umbrella Factory between 1880 and 1905, this building, known today as the Umbrella Works, was also home to the Van Sciver Furniture Company. Silk umbrellas were manufactured in the complex beginning in 1892, when the portion of the building fronting West King Street was constructed. By 1910 the factory was one of the largest umbrella producers in the world. After sitting vacant for several years, the building was adaptively reused for apartments in 1986. The prominent corner tower was reconstructed at that time.

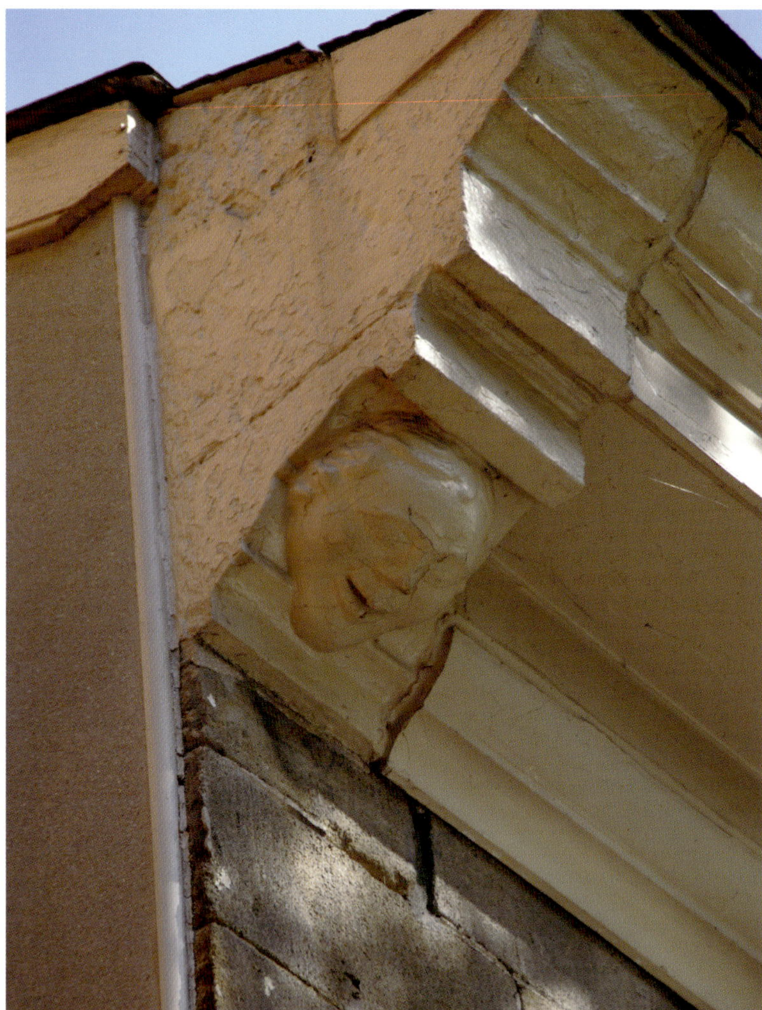

Hidden in plain sight, several stories above East King Street, is the Eavesdropper, a sculpted head projecting from the corner cornice of the Bausman House. The home dates from 1762 and was the residence of William Bausman, chief burgess of Lancaster.

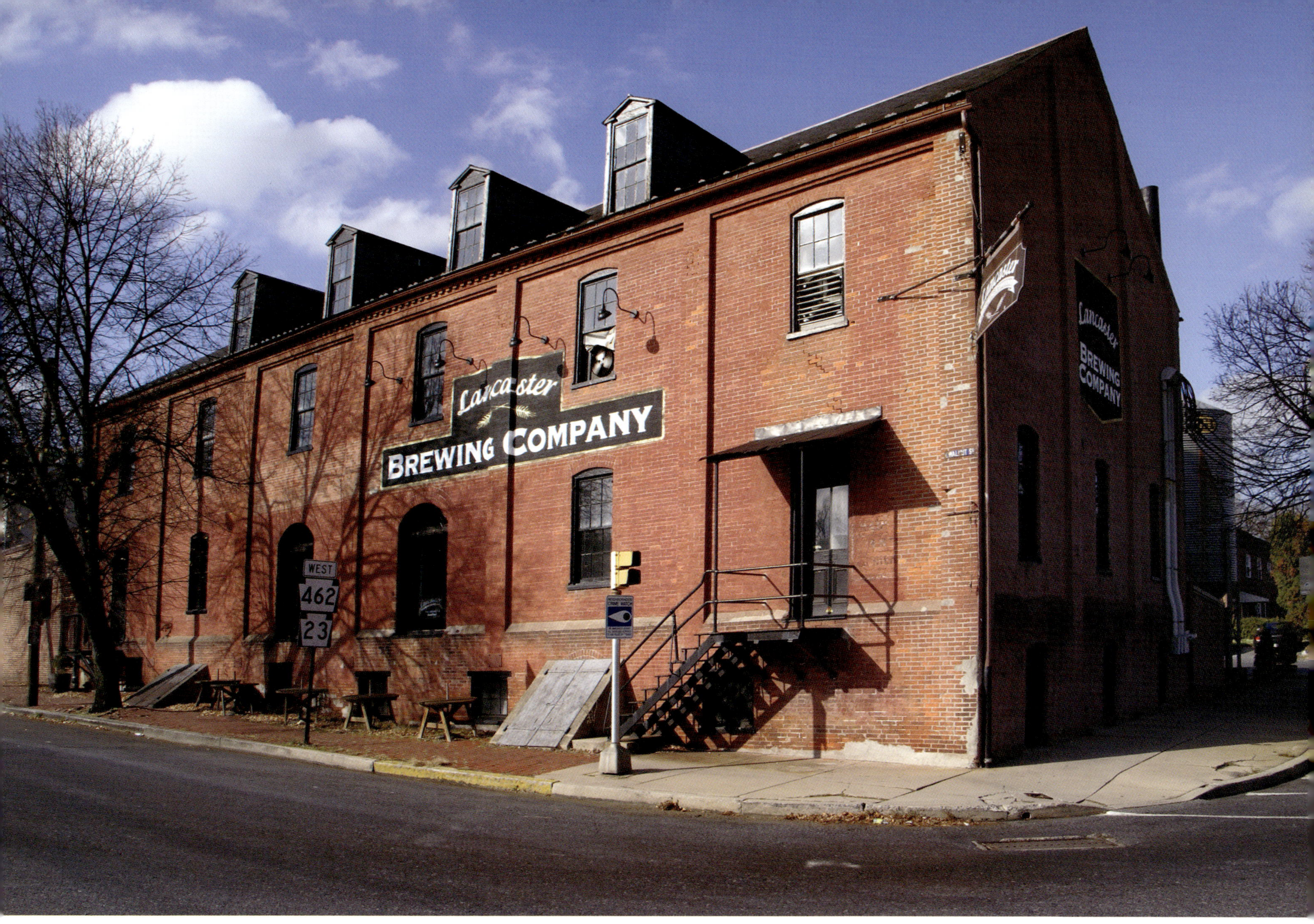

At one time there were more than 100 buildings in Lancaster City connected to the tobacco industry. Today home to the Lancaster Brewing Company, this building at Plum and Walnut Streets was constructed in the 1880s as a tobacco warehouse and later housed prisoners of war during World War II. In 1995, the building found new life as the Lancaster Malt Brewing Company, which was later purchased by the Lancaster Brewing Company.

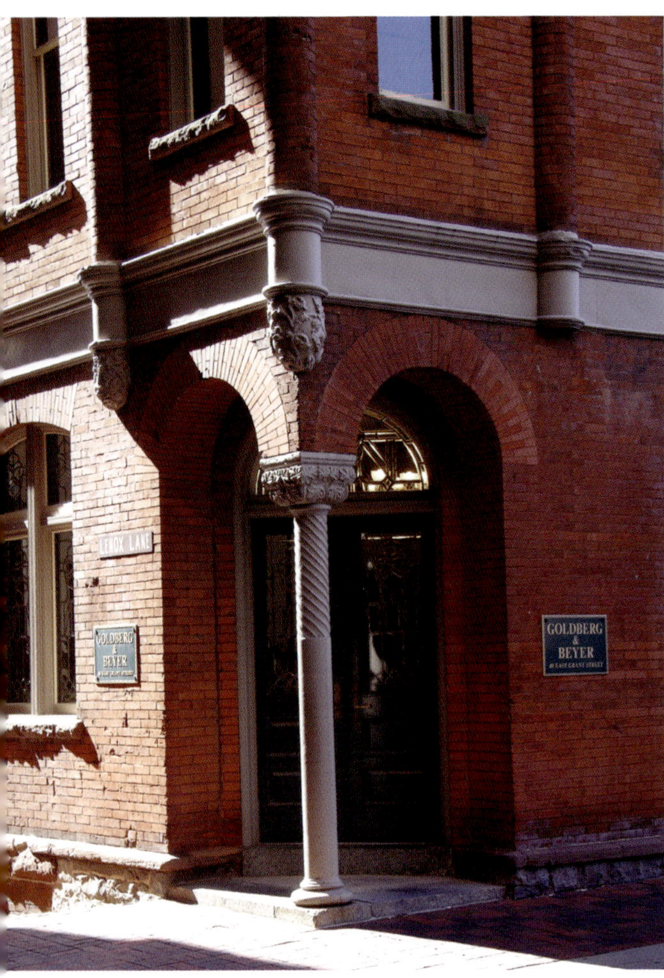

The late-Victorian building at the intersection of Grant Street and Lenox Lane is one of Lancaster's hidden gems. The building was designed by C. Emlen Urban for Charlie Wagner, who operated a tavern and hotel here.

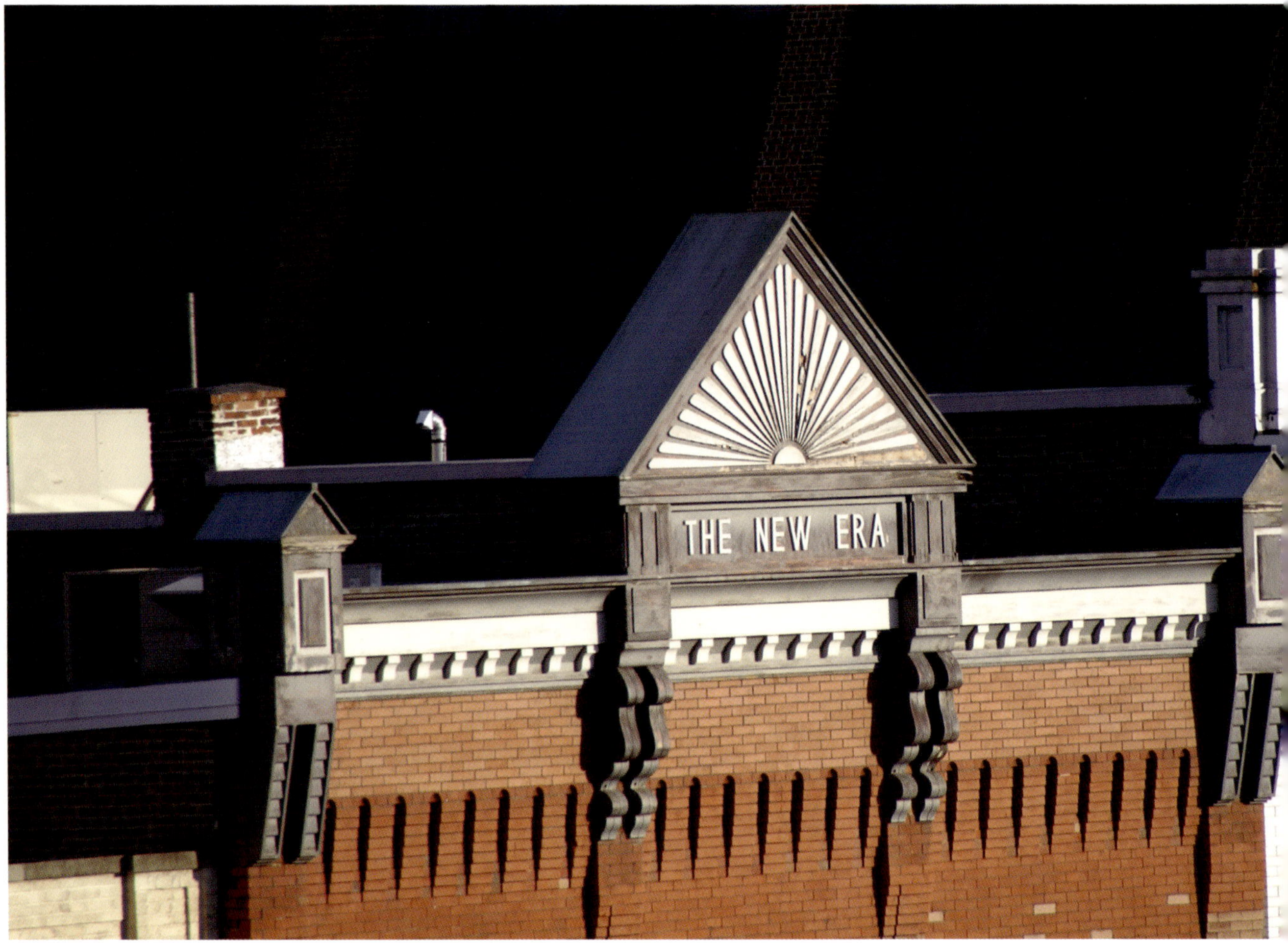

The New Era building on North Queen Street was constructed in 1891. For forty years the *Lancaster New Era* newspaper was printed in the building, as were many national periodicals. The building's most notable feature is a roofline parapet with a sunburst pattern above the words "The New Era." The *Lancaster New Era* was founded in 1877 and purchased by the Steinman family in 1928. The newspaper was published until 2009, when it was merged with the *Intelligencer Journal.*

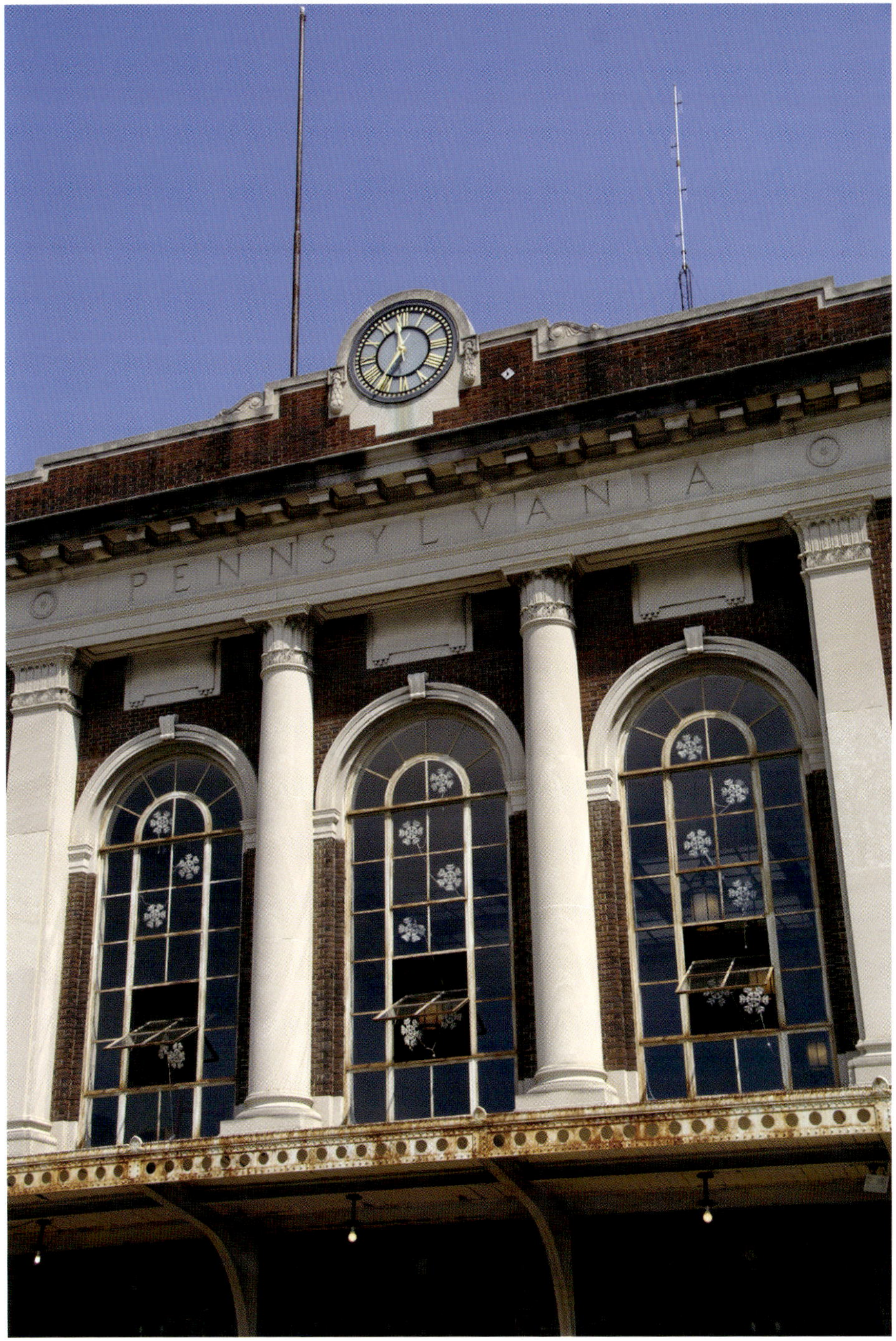

The Lancaster Train Station was built by the Pennsylvania Railroad in 1929 for $1.5 million. The exterior projects a Neoclassical appearance while the interior was inspired by the Art Deco style. Eighty years after it opened, the station underwent a major $12 million renovation and restoration project to preserve its historic charm and modernize it for the next eighty years.

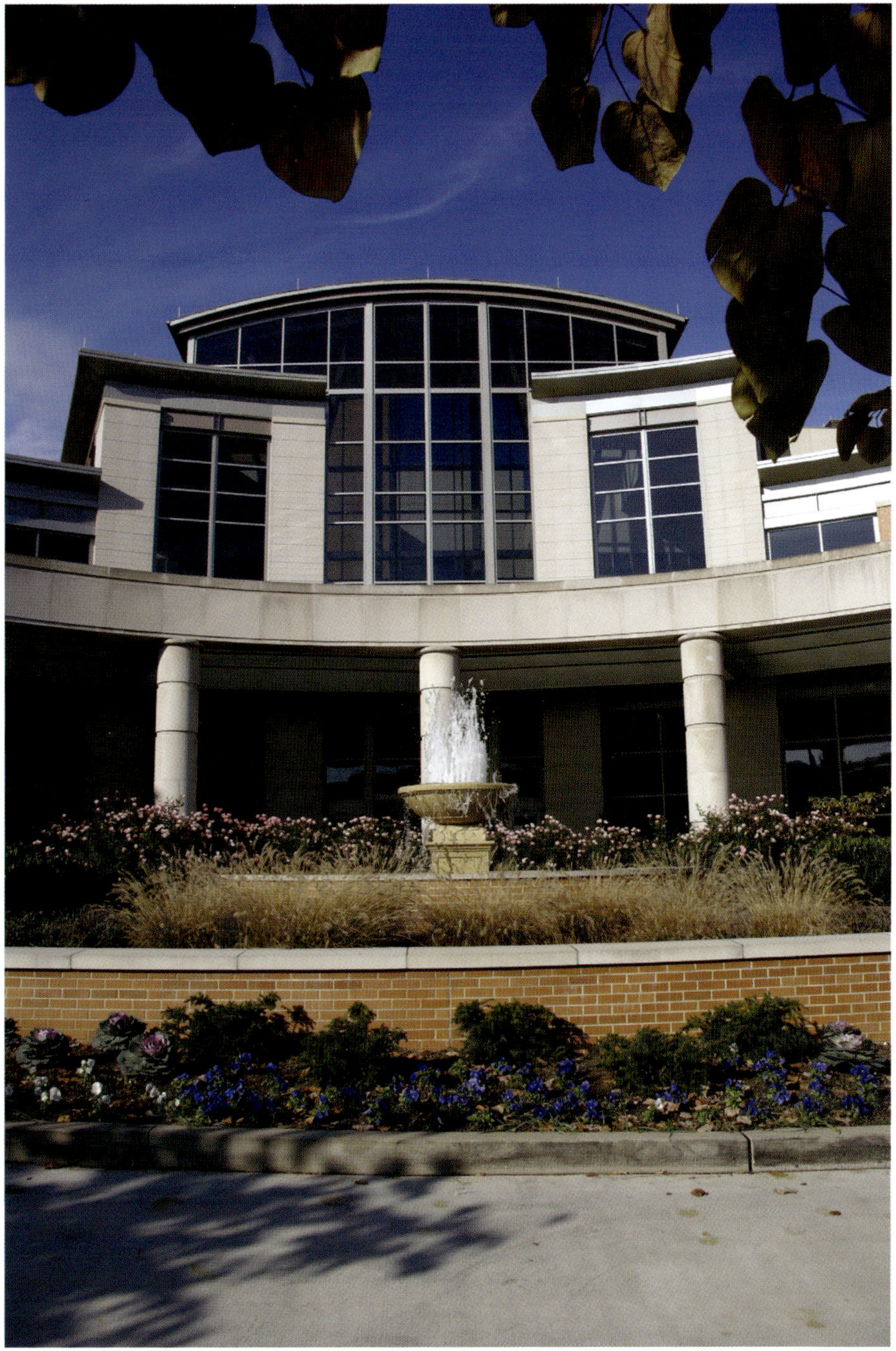

Lancaster General Hospital was founded in 1893 and began operations in a residence on North Queen Street. From those humble beginnings, the institution has grown into Lancaster General Health, a nationally recognized regional healthcare system with multiple locations.

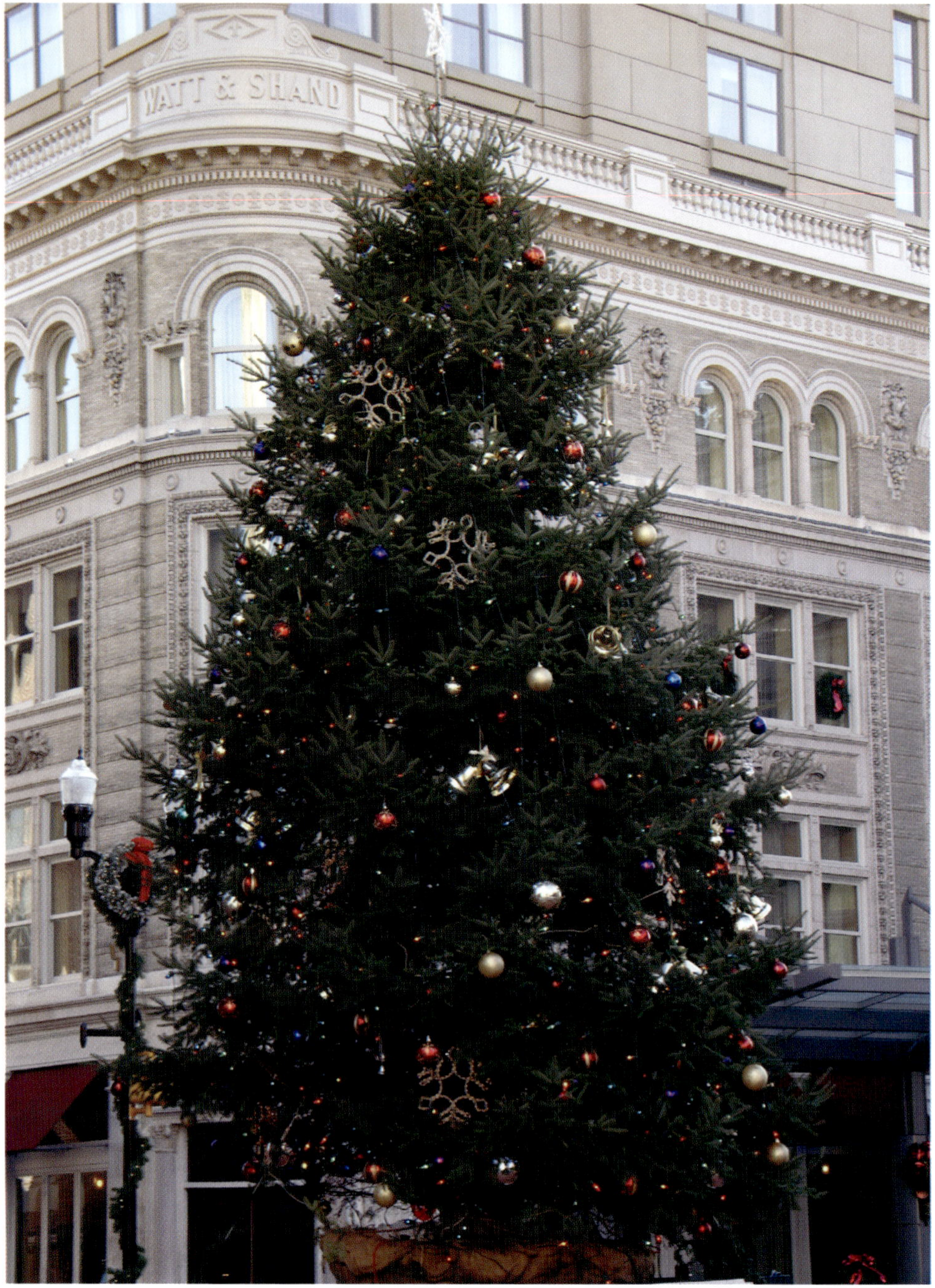

Penn Square sparkles during the holiday season.

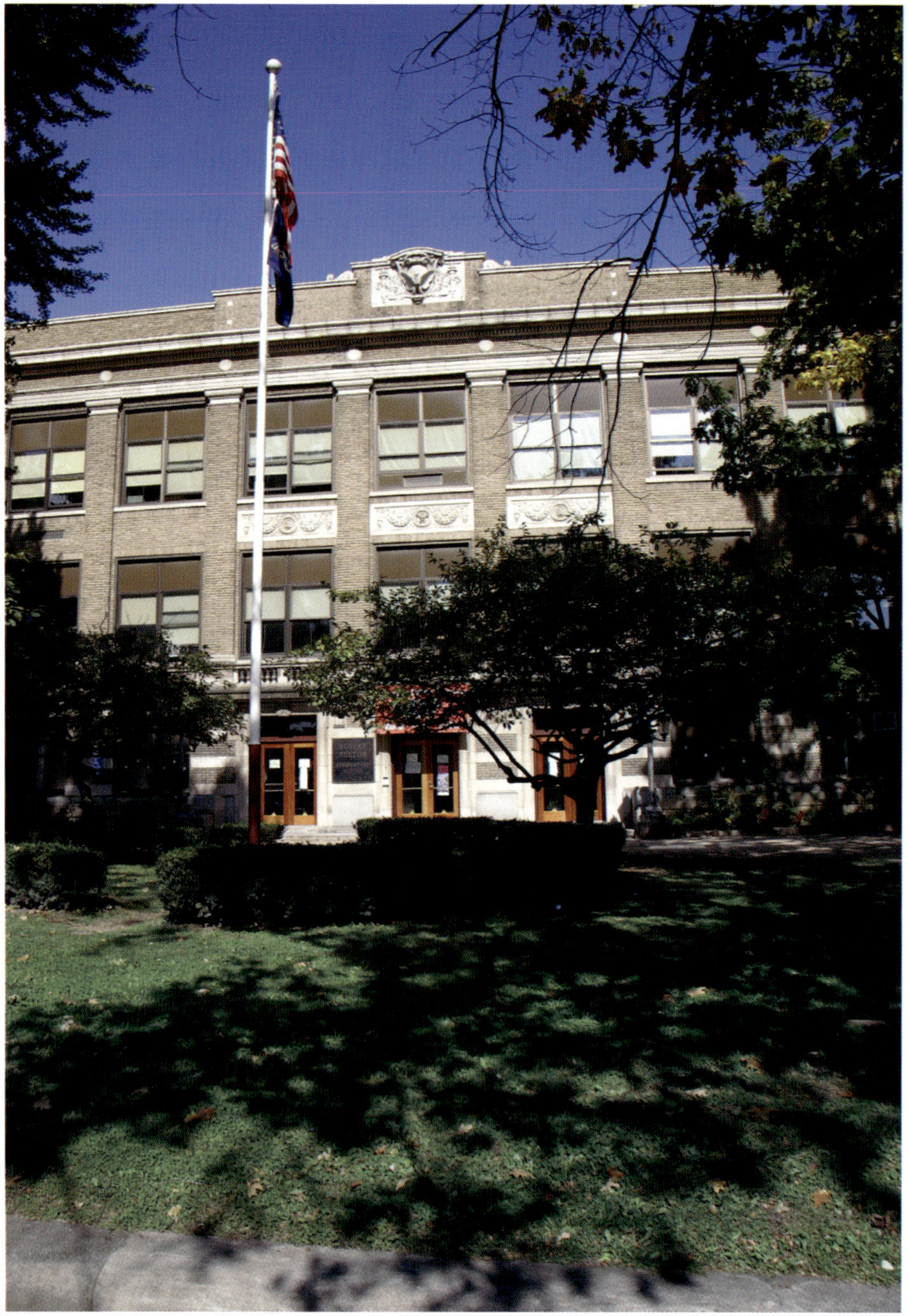

Constructed from 1916 to 1918, the Robert Fulton School is another example of work by Lancaster's most prominent architect, C. Emlen Urban. It was originally built as a high school for boys and later used as an elementary school.

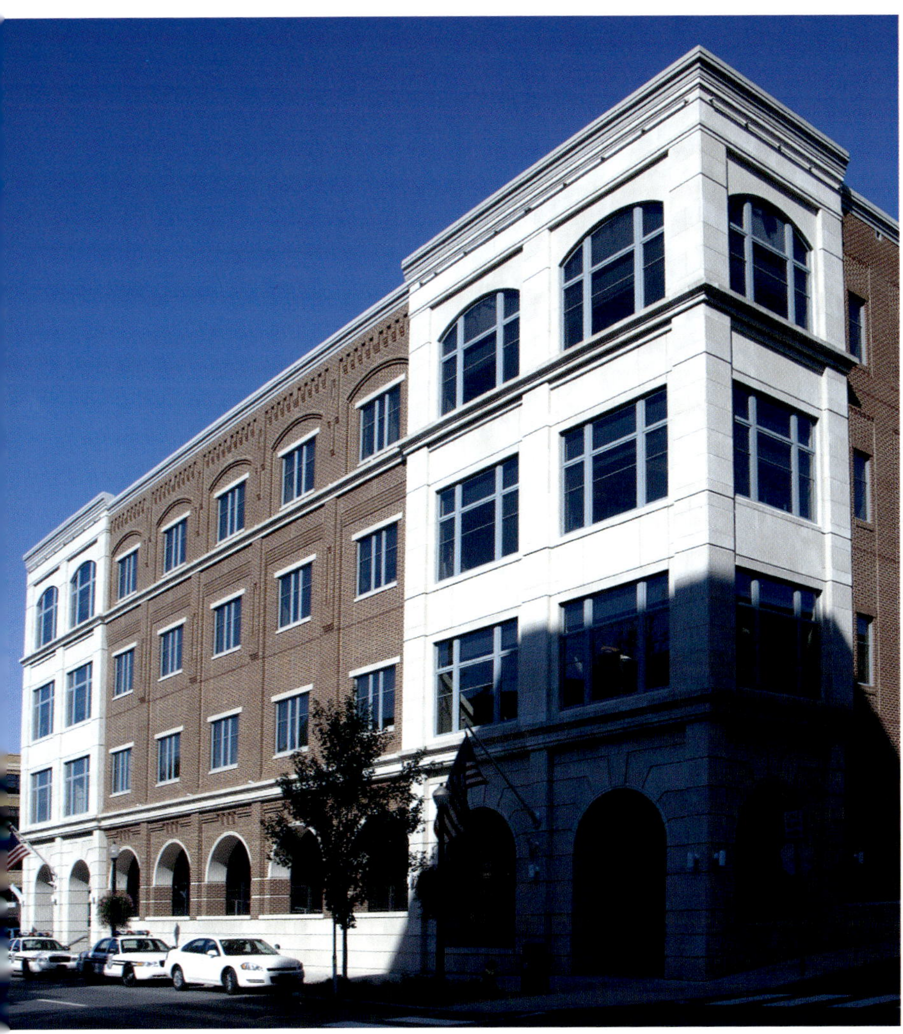

One of the newer buildings in downtown Lancaster is the Lancaster City Police Station on West Chestnut Street. The aesthetic of the building, completed in 2004, complements the historic architecture of the city.

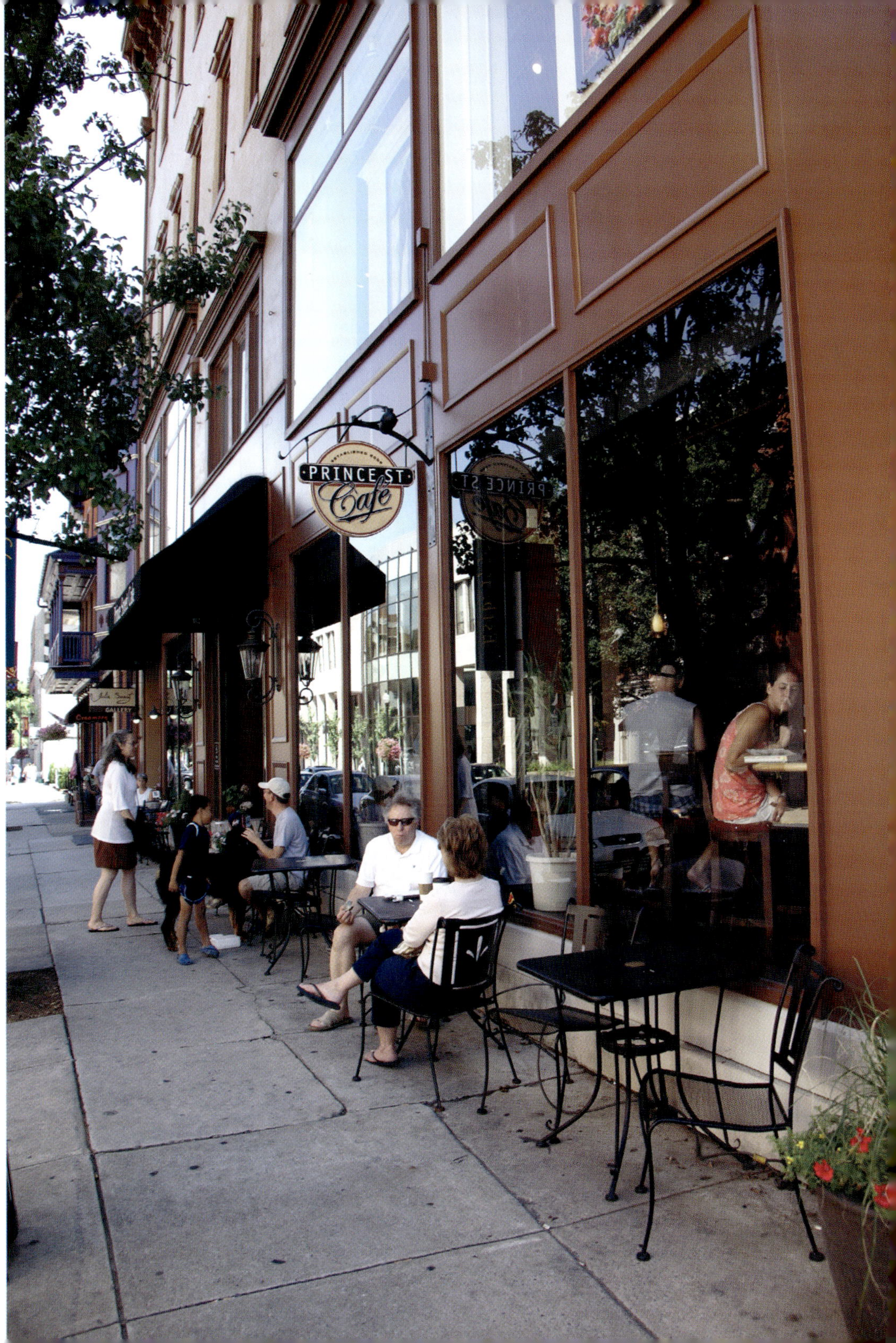

Located across the street from the Fulton Opera House, the Prince Street Café is one of many downtown eateries that offer alfresco dining during the warmer months.

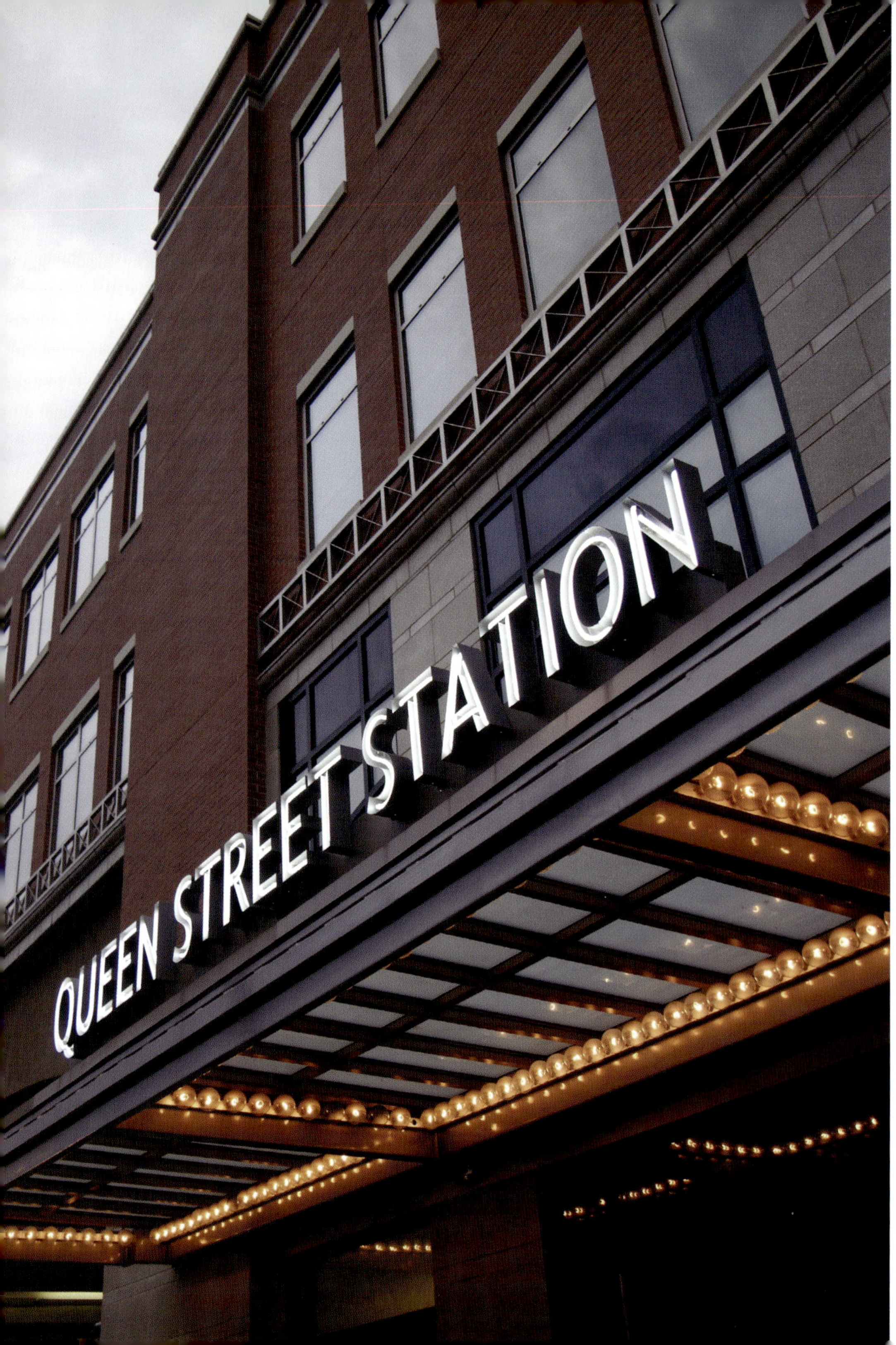

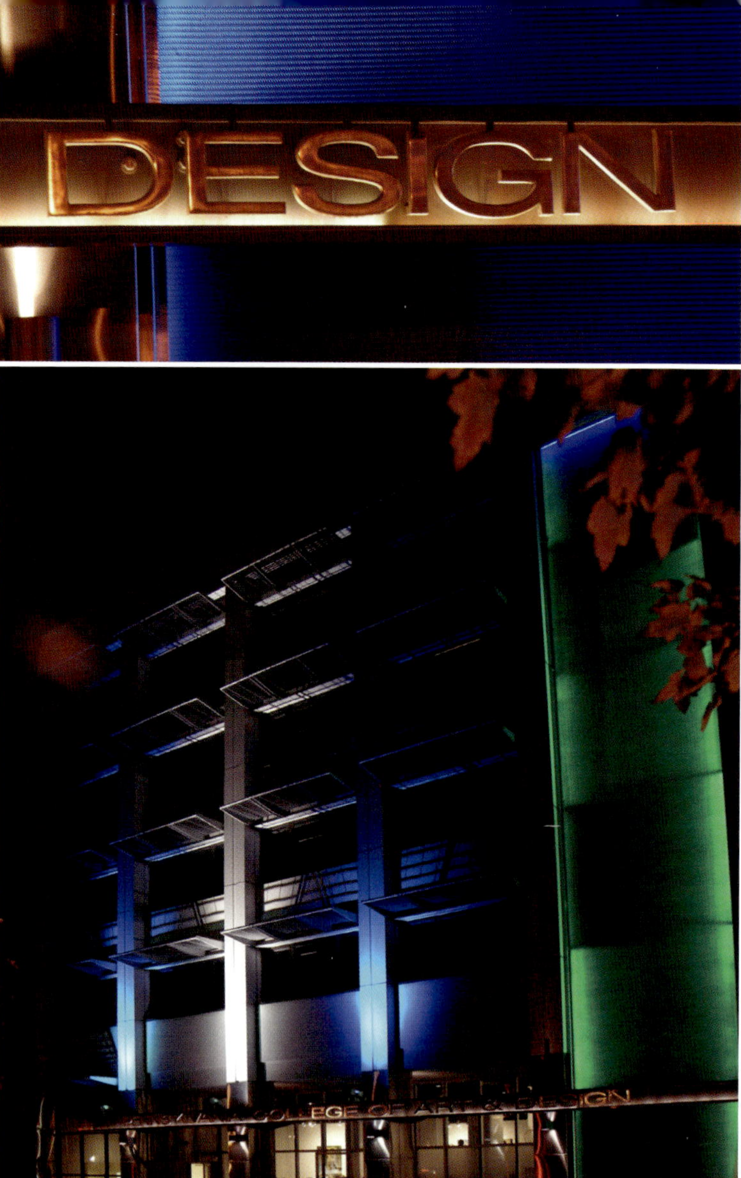

While many cities go dark at night, downtown Lancaster sparkles with illuminated facades, glowing neon, luminous storefronts, pyramids of sodium and mercury vapor streetlight, and a kaleidoscope of color on the Pennsylvania College of Art & Design building.

Built in 2005, the Queen Street Station serves as the Red Rose Transit Authority's downtown transit center. It was constructed on the site of the 1926 Otto Paving and Construction Company building, and some of the materials from that building were reused in the construction. The Authority was formed in 1973 and today offers service throughout Lancaster City and the central portion of Lancaster County. They also operate the Red Rose Trolley, a historic trolley that provides service in downtown Lancaster.

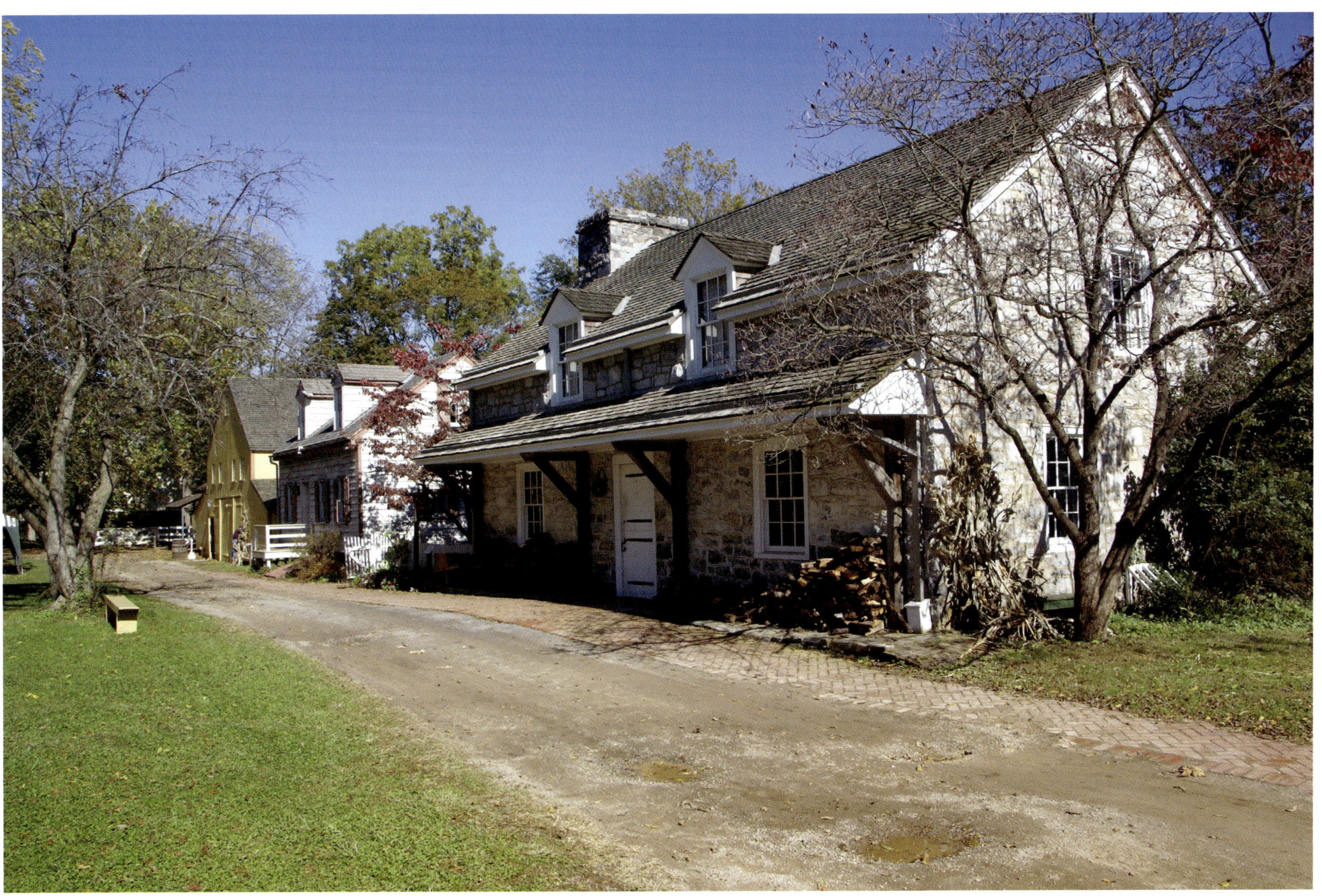

Pennsylvania German heritage comes to life at Landis Valley Village and Farm Museum, a living history attraction located in Manheim Township. Administered by the Pennsylvania Historical and Museum Commission, the property includes several historic houses, an 1856 hotel, a 1890s schoolhouse, firehouse, bank, barn, and more. Some buildings were relocated to the 100-acre property while others were constructed new to expand the interpretation of Pennsylvania German culture from the 1740s through 1940s. *The Tavern, Landis Valley Village and Farm Museum, PHMC, Lancaster County, PA.*

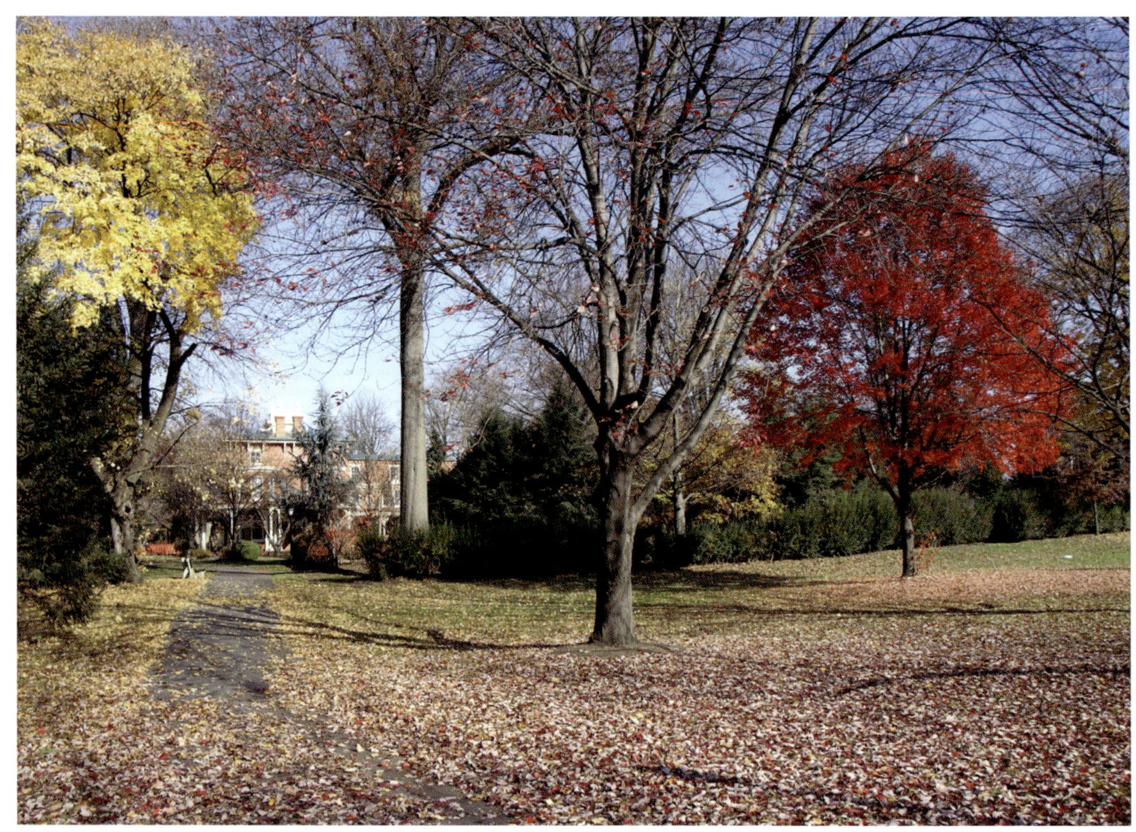

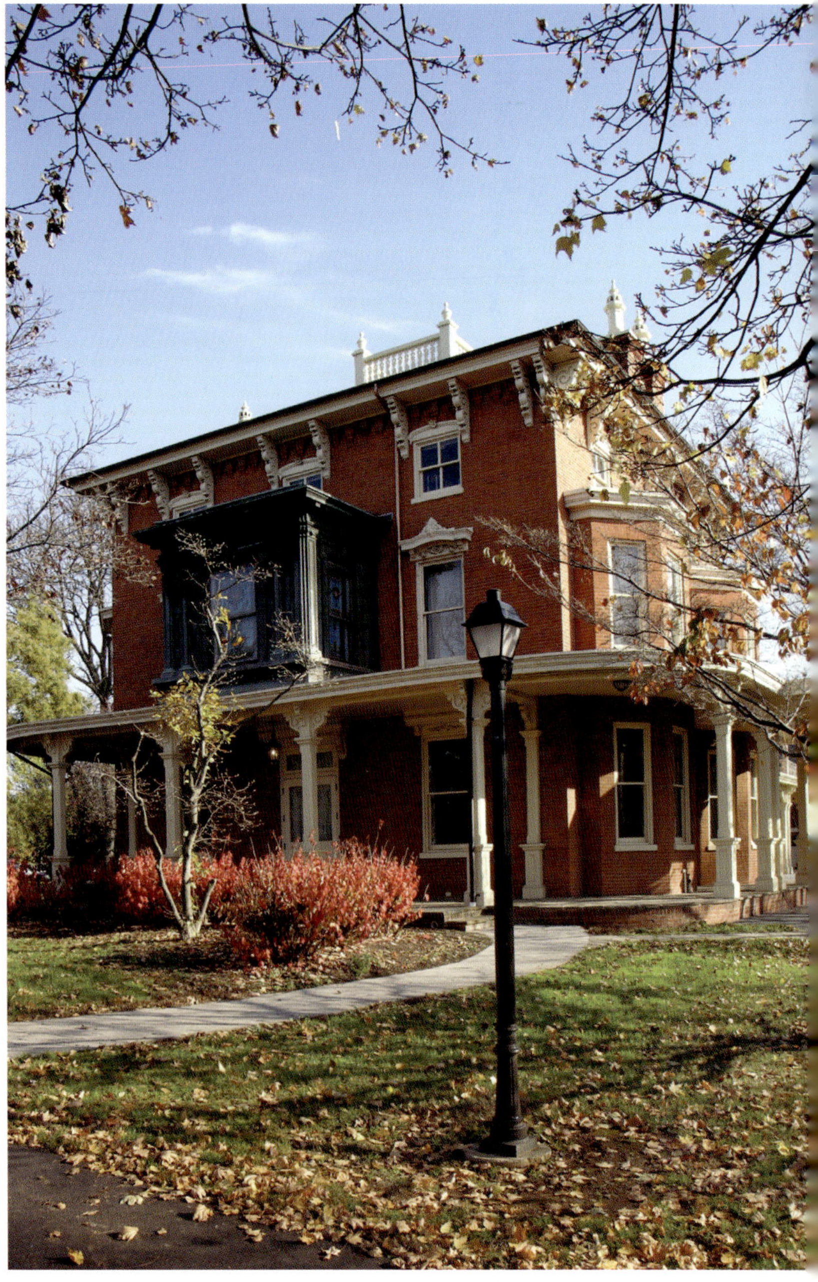

Located within Stauffer Park is a stately Italianate house known as the Stauffer Mansion. The 1870 home was built by John Frederick Sener, a Lancaster businessman. In 1921, he gave the house and property to his daughter and son-in-law, Mr. & Mrs. Grant Stauffer. Their daughter, Elizabeth Ludgate, willed the house and grounds to Manheim Township in 1974. Today the house on Lititz Pike is occupied by Township offices, and the grounds are the eighteen-acre-park known as Stauffer Park.

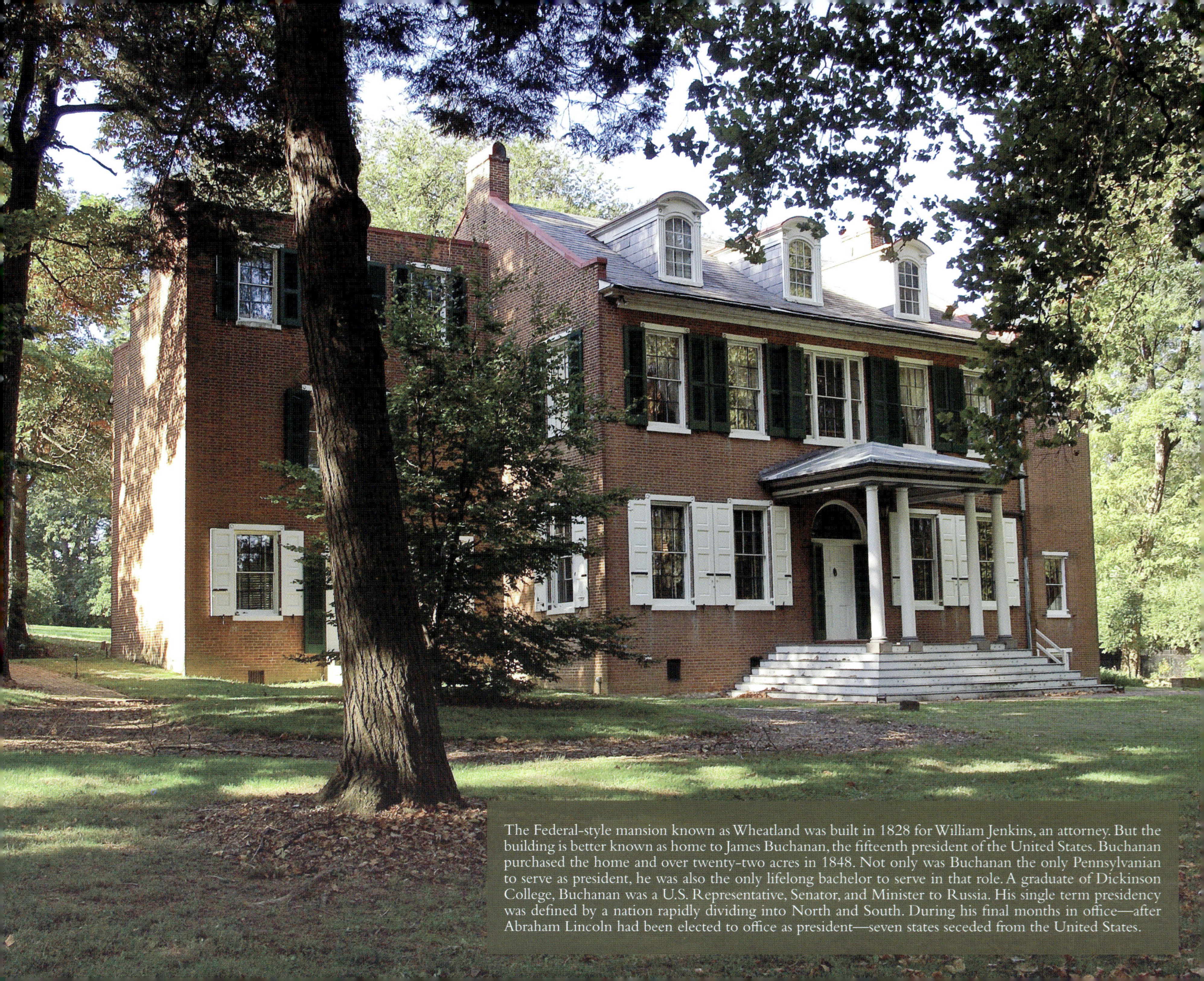

The Federal-style mansion known as Wheatland was built in 1828 for William Jenkins, an attorney. But the building is better known as home to James Buchanan, the fifteenth president of the United States. Buchanan purchased the home and over twenty-two acres in 1848. Not only was Buchanan the only Pennsylvanian to serve as president, he was also the only lifelong bachelor to serve in that role. A graduate of Dickinson College, Buchanan was a U.S. Representative, Senator, and Minister to Russia. His single term presidency was defined by a nation rapidly dividing into North and South. During his final months in office—after Abraham Lincoln had been elected to office as president—seven states seceded from the United States.

LancasterHistory.org was formed through the merger of the Lancaster County Historical Society and James Buchanan's Wheatland. The non-profit's mission is to educate the public about the history of Lancaster County. Their ten-acre-campus includes the Louise Arnold Tanger Arboretum, a research library, archives, and more.

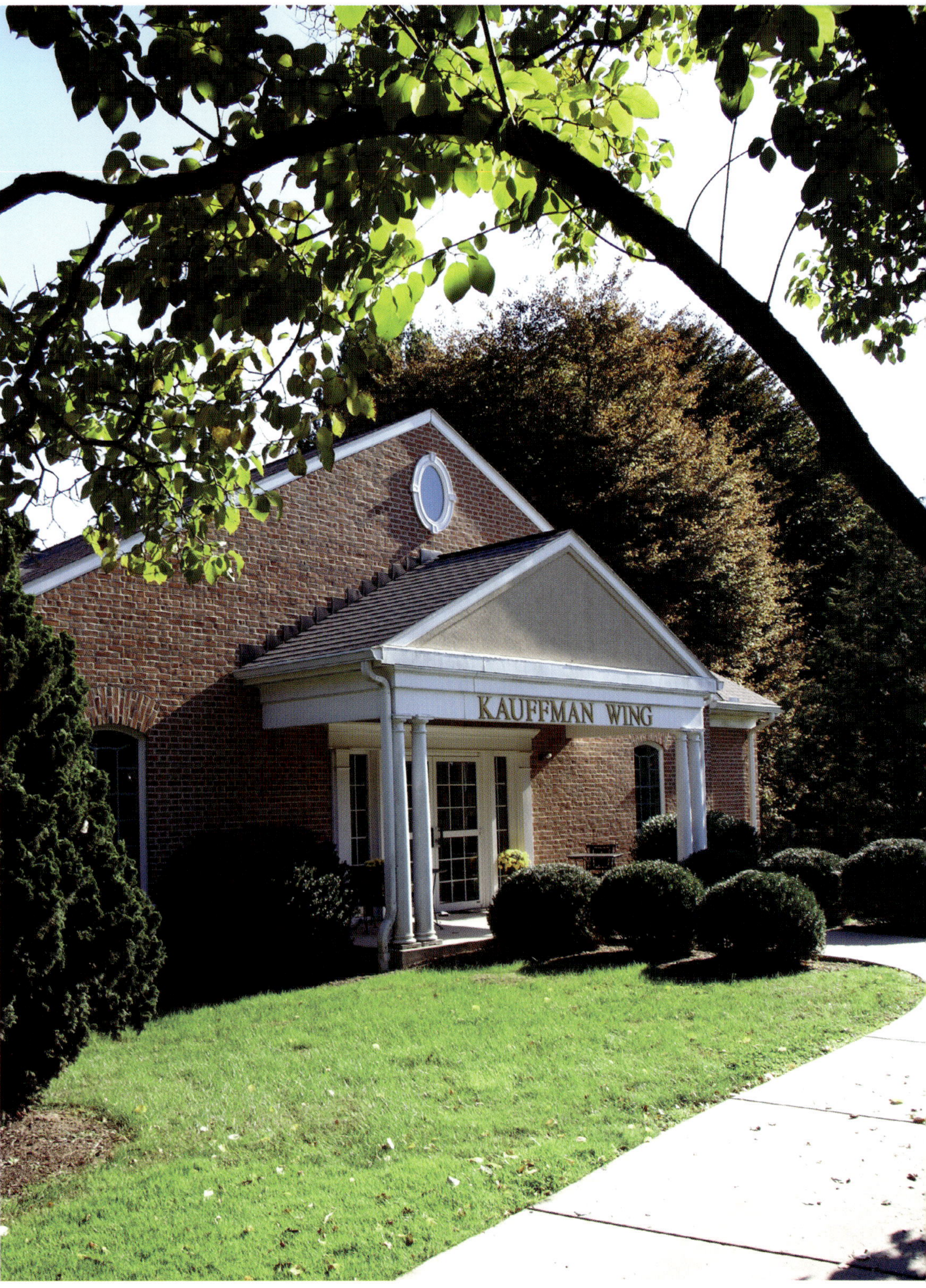

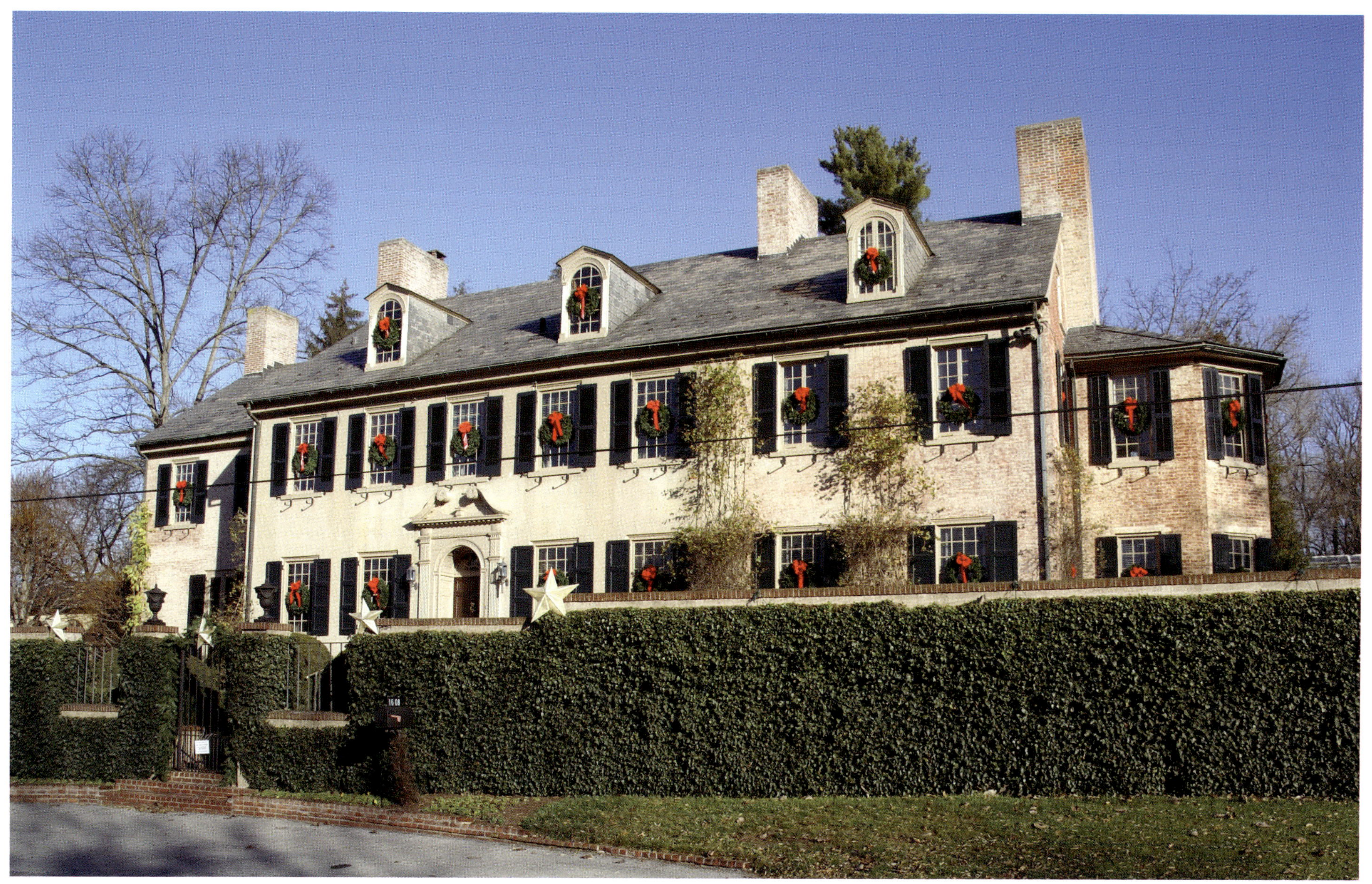

Located on Marietta Avenue west of Lancaster City, the handsome Conestoga House and Gardens was home to the prominent Steinman family for more than fifty years. The Colonial Revival building is the result of a late-1920s project that involved extensive additions and renovations to an existing building. Several years later European-inspired gardens were added, and today the grounds include several unique gardens that are home to more than 3,300 annuals, 400 tropical plants, 160 perennials, and a variety of roses.

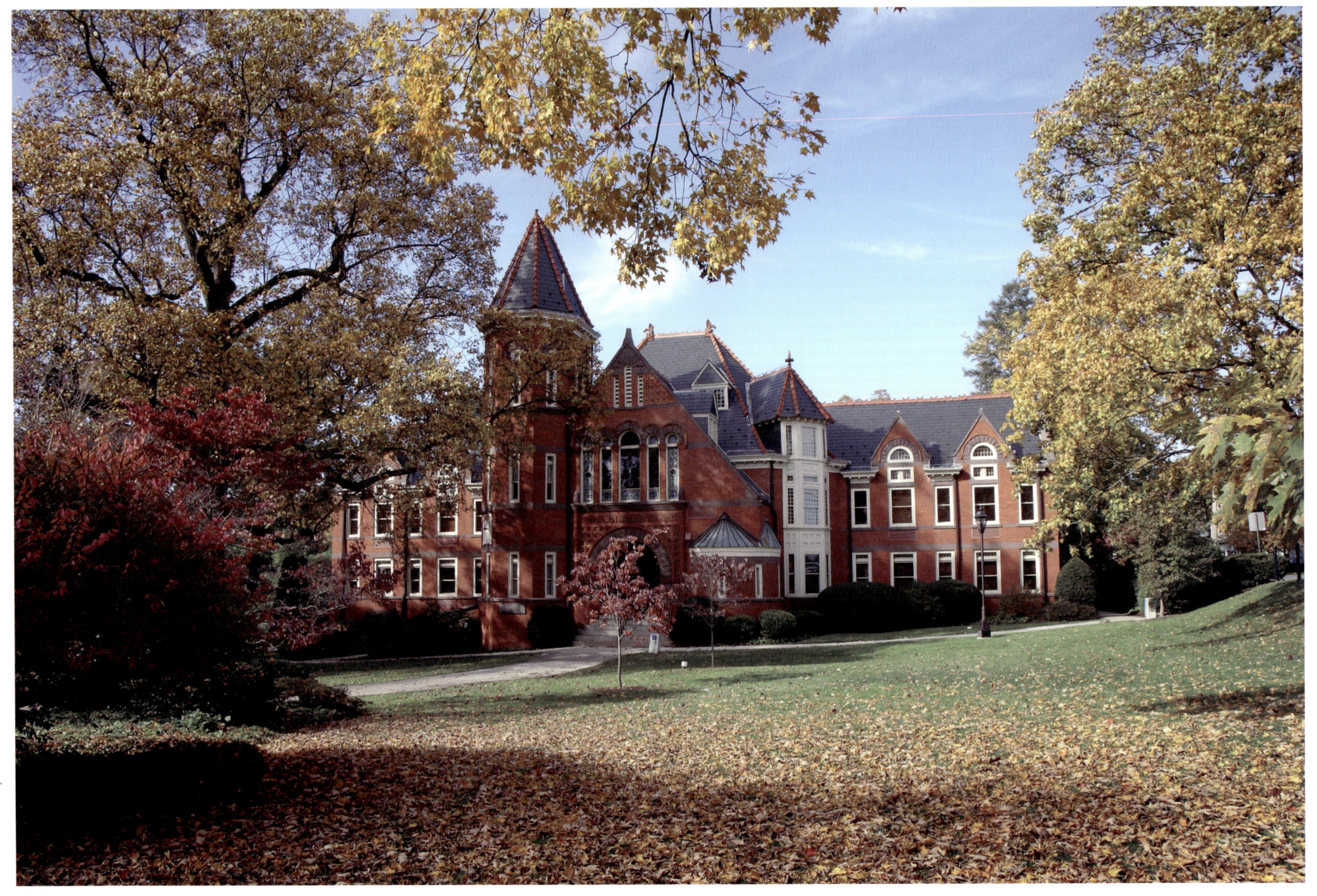

The Biemesderfer Executive Center on the campus of Millersville University was constructed in 1894 and built for $27,500. The Victorian Romanesque building is the centerpiece of the campus, and originally served as the library for the Millersville Normal School.

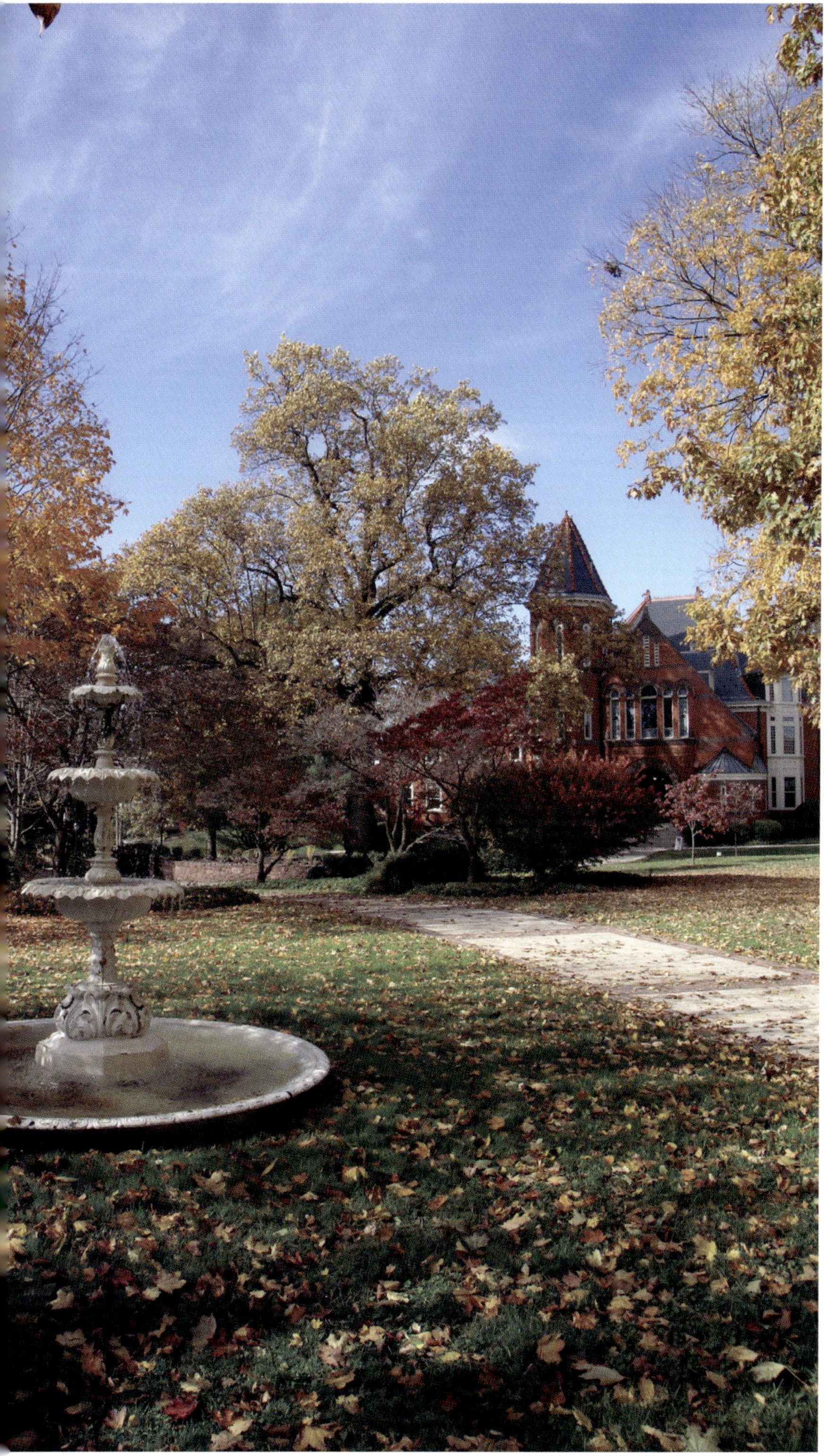

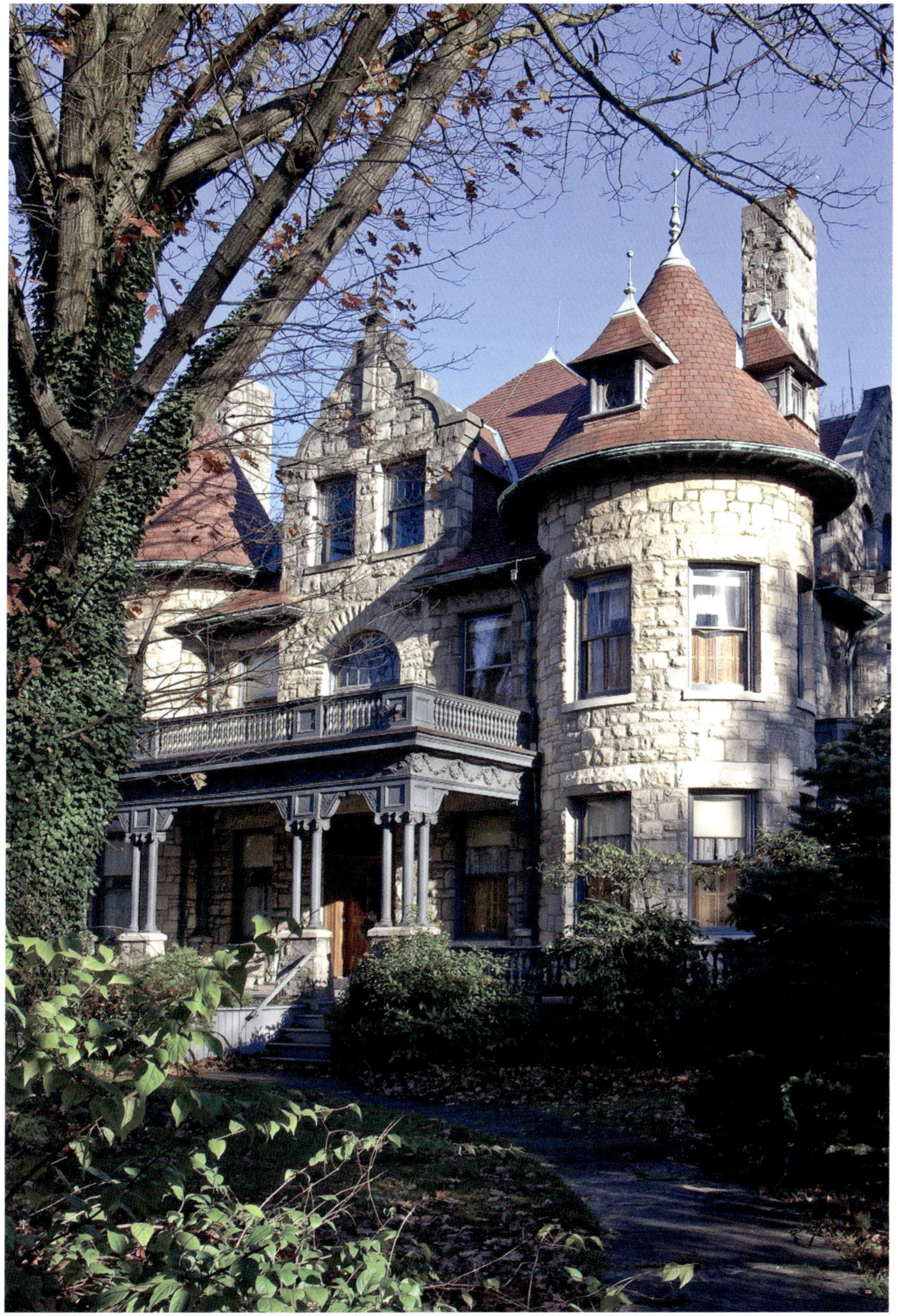

In 1896 the stately mansion known as Roslyn was built for Peter Watt, co-founder of Watt & Shand Department Store. It's a fine example of Chateauesque architecture, a style that drew inspiration from the chateaus of France. C. Emlen Urban was commissioned to design the mansion, which Watt presented to his wife for her birthday. The property remained in the family for the next seventy years.

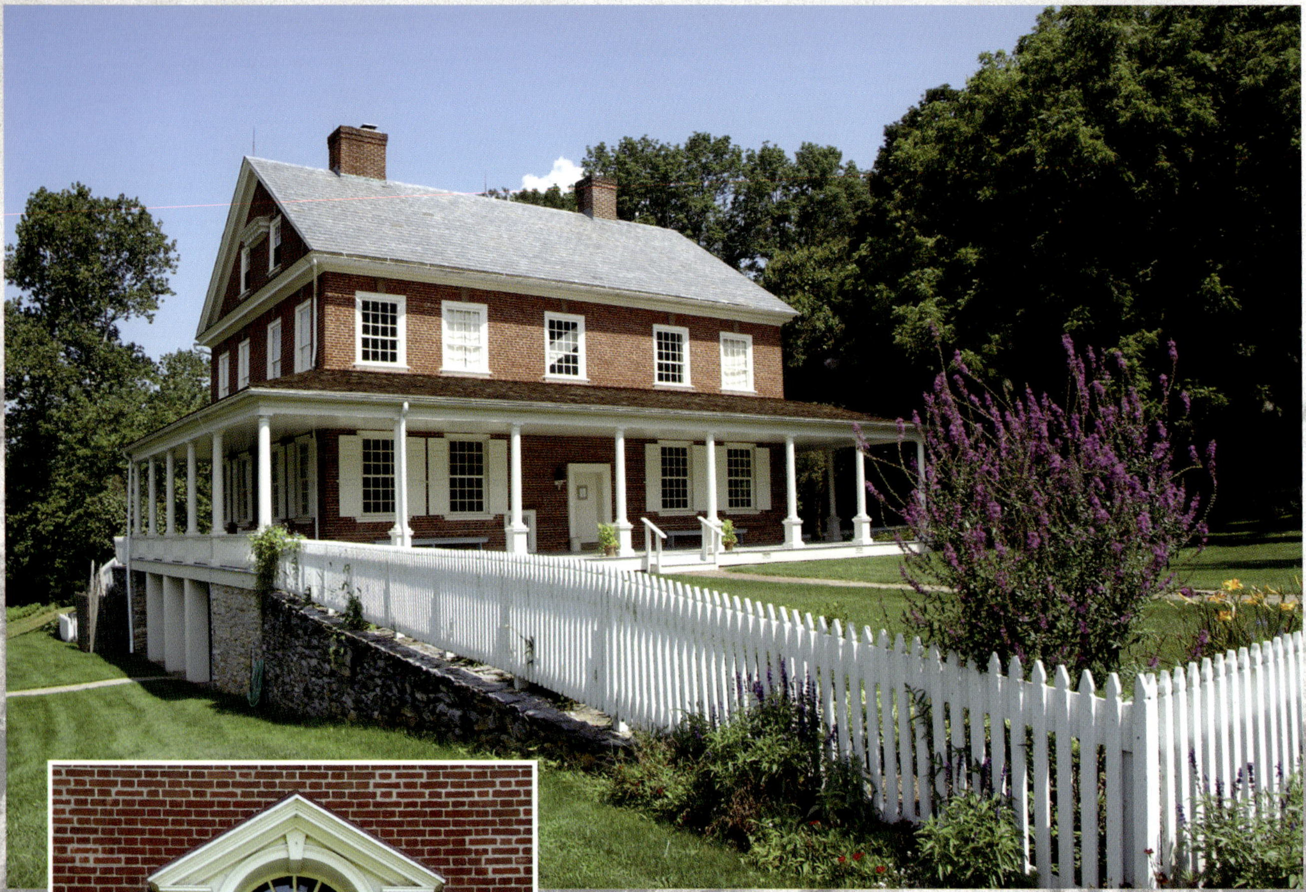

Located in Lancaster County's Central Park, Rock Ford Plantation was the home of Edward Hand, Adjutant General to General Washington during the American Revolution. In 1794, Hand constructed this brick mansion, built in the Georgian style. The building was restored and opened to the public in 1960. The prominent piazzas were restored in 1964.

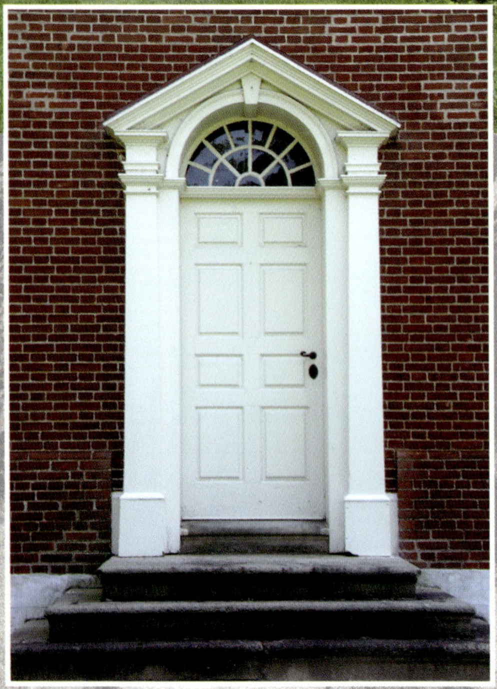

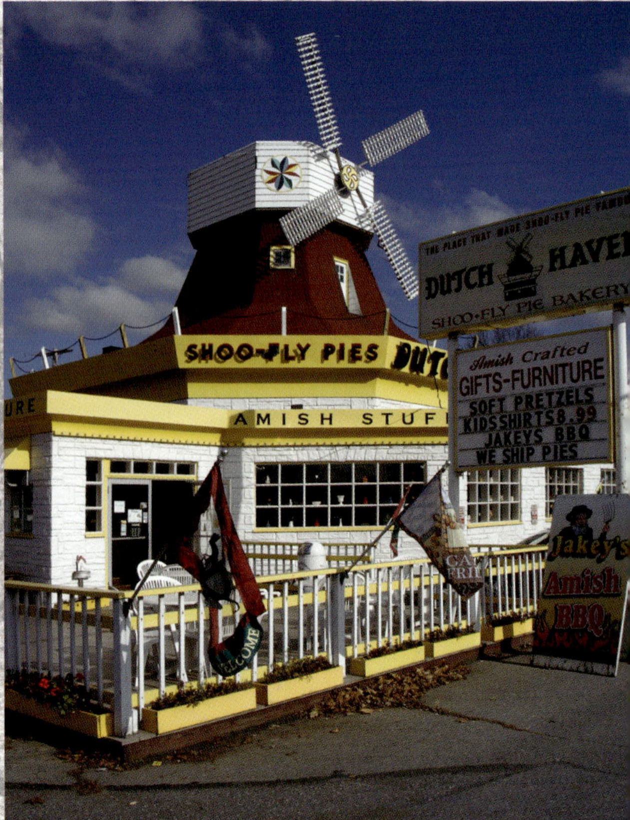

This colorful windmill-topped building on Lincoln Highway in eastern Lancaster County is Dutch Haven, which bills itself as home to America's best shoo-fly pie.

The Hans Herr House was built in 1719 by Christian Herr for he and his wife, Anna. Though named for Christian's father, Hans Herr, it is unknown if Hans actually lived there. Recognized as one of the most important historic homes in Pennsylvania Dutch Country, the building is believed to be the oldest Mennonite meeting house in the Western Hemisphere. The sandstone structure is a notable example of German Colonial architecture, further exemplified by its central chimney and asymmetrical appearance.

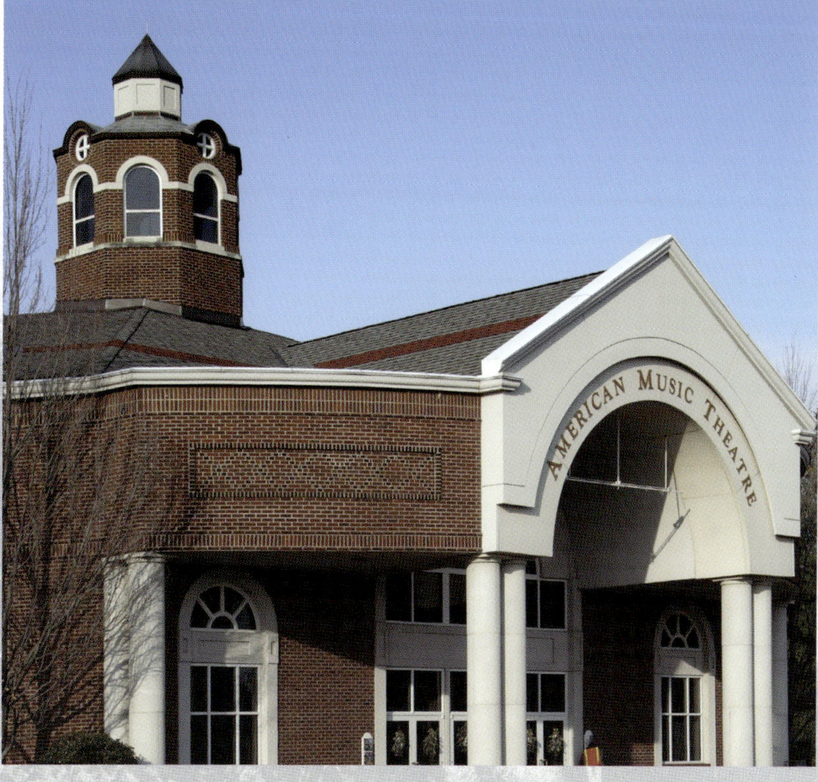

American Music Theater, located east of Lancaster City along Lincoln Highway, is a popular destination for entertainment in Lancaster County. The modern 1600-seat-theater presents original shows, as well as touring Broadway, rock, country, and comedy acts.

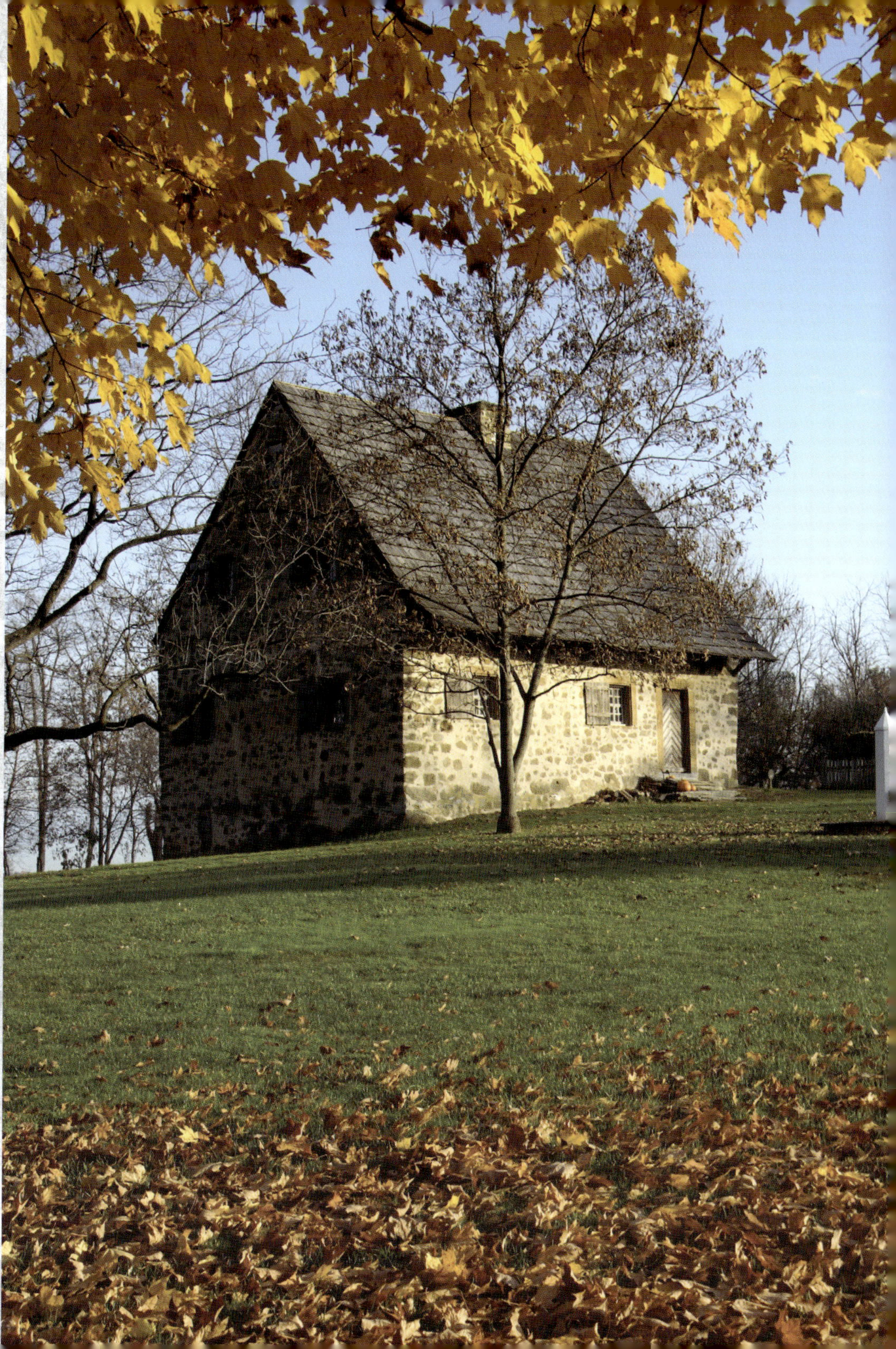

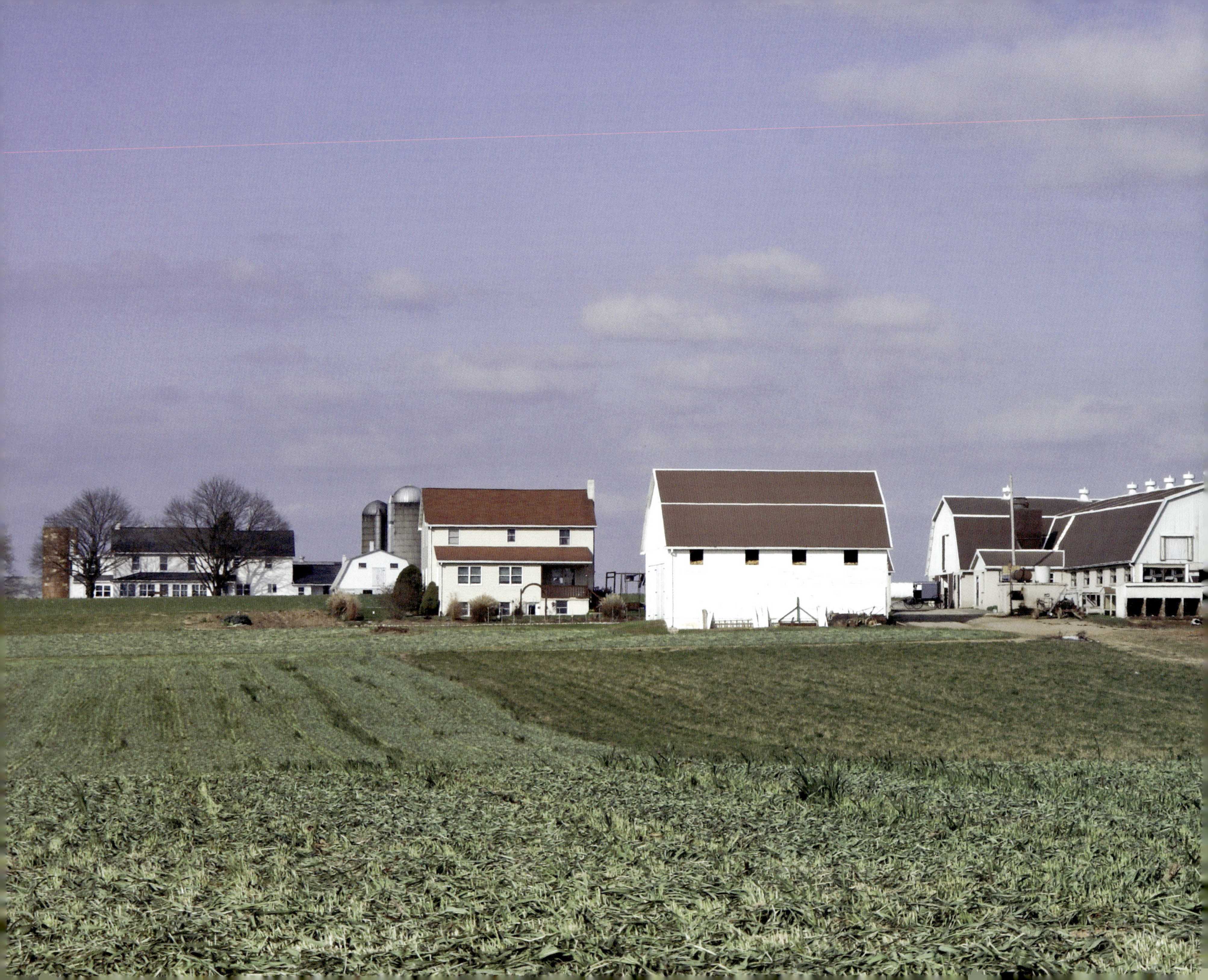

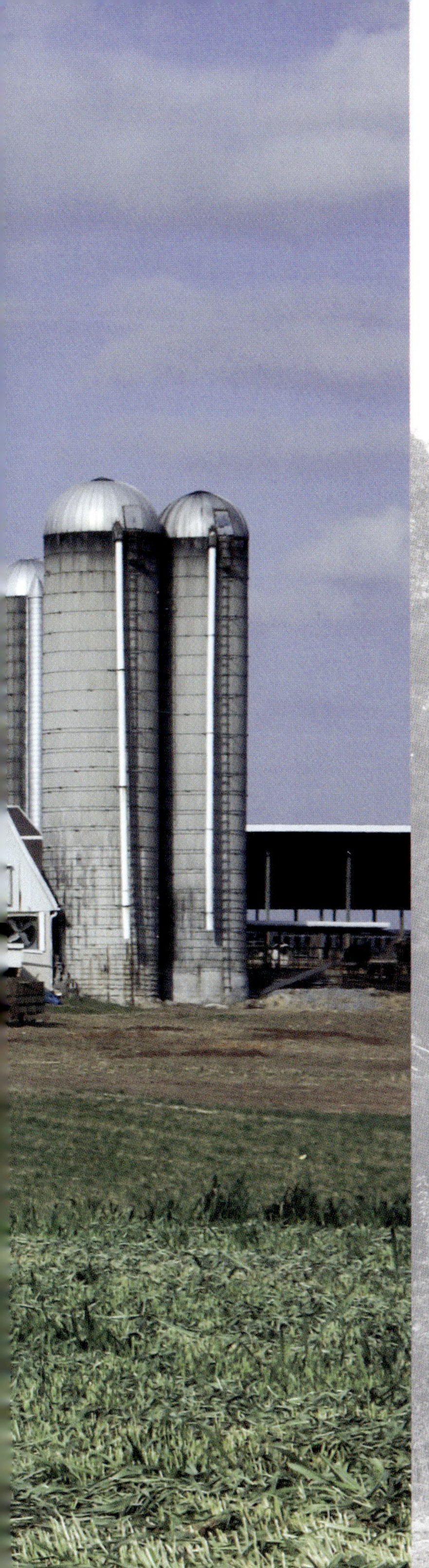

Lancaster County: Towns & Countryside

Pennsylvania's early counties—Philadelphia, Bucks, and Chester—were similar to English shires. When Lancaster County was carved from Chester County in 1729, it was an attempt to try something different in the young colony. The fourth county in Pennsylvania included all or part of modern day Berks, Cumberland, Dauphin, Lebanon, Northumberland, and York Counties. Because Pennsylvania was attractive to diverse European religious groups, Lancaster County became home to several self-contained religious communities like Lititz and the Ephrata Cloister. Other towns, like Columbia and Strasburg, grew because they were on important transportation routes. From its humble beginnings on the western frontier of the American colonies, the 984 square mile Lancaster County has become home to more than half a million residents and is a major tourism destination. Known as "Amish County" for the presence of Old Order Amish and Mennonite families, Lancaster County's towns and villages offer a yesteryear charm that attracts residents and visitors alike.

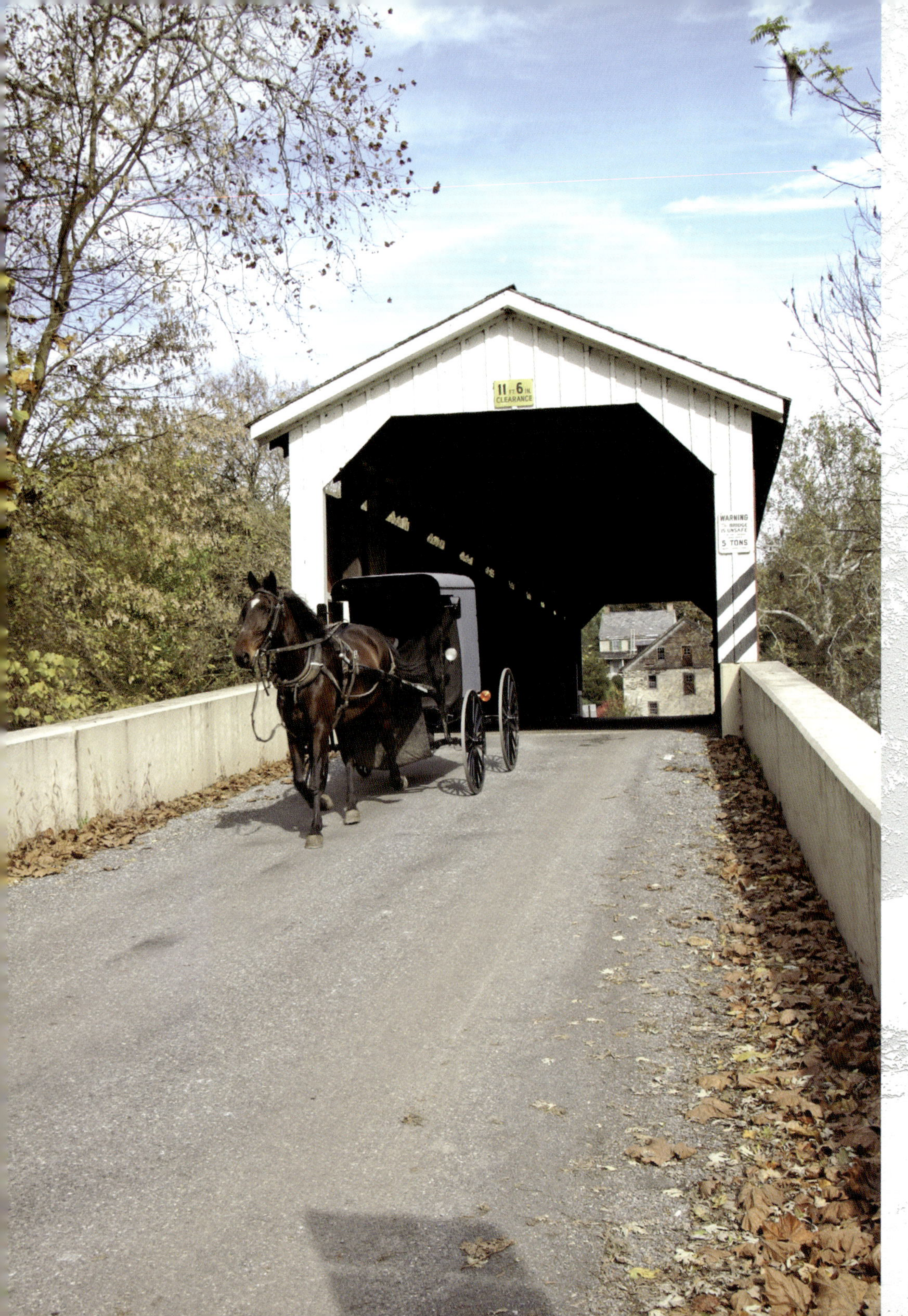

The Plain People

Lancaster County is known throughout the nation as "Amish Country" because of the prevalence of Old Order Amish in many areas of the county. These "plain people" wear simple clothes, do not have electricity or telephones in their homes, and they do not operate automobiles, but instead use horse and buggy for transportation. However, the Old Order groups also include populations of Mennonite and Brethren. All three are Anabaptist groups. In Lancaster County, Old Order Amish drive gray buggies, while Old Order Mennonites drive black buggies.

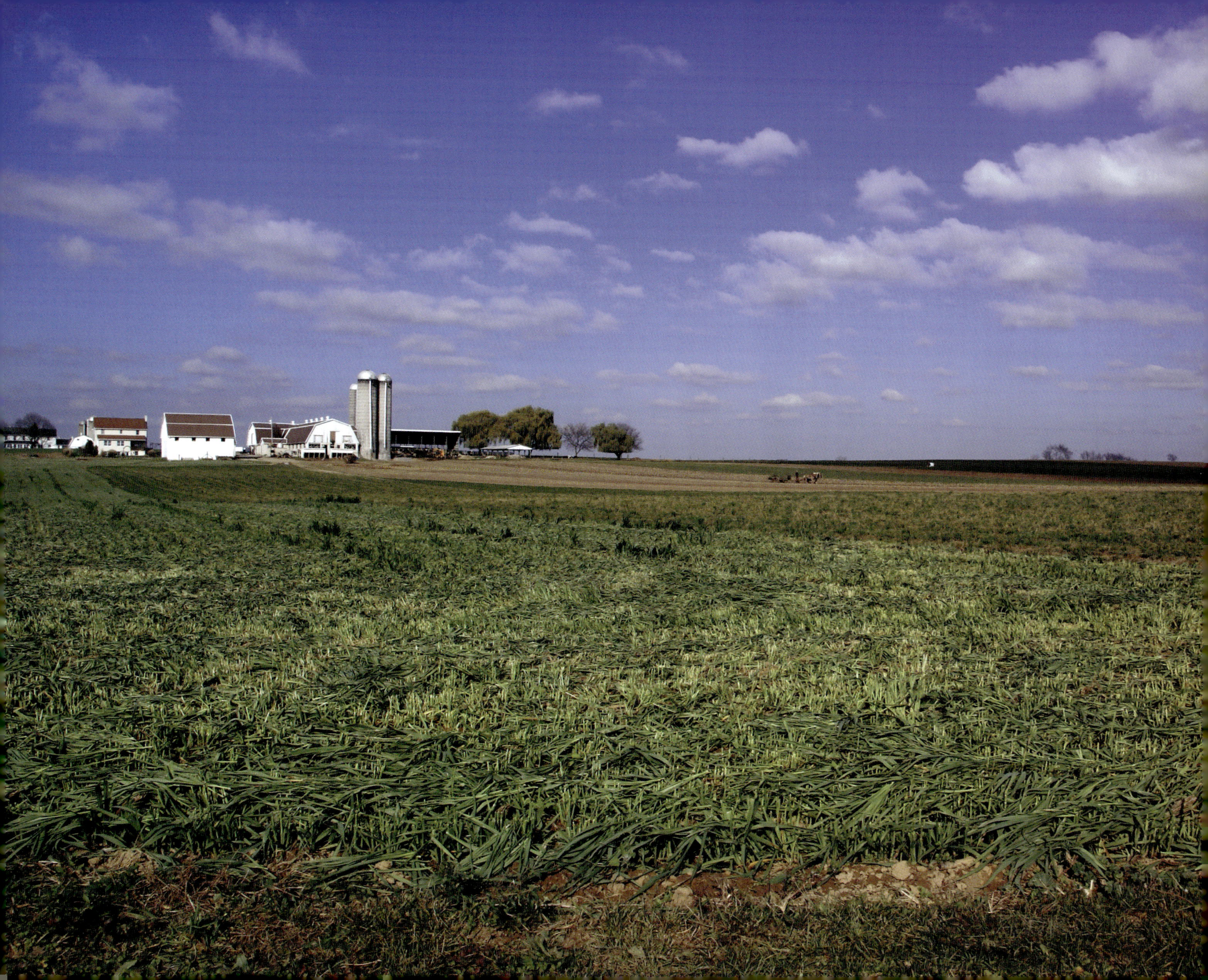

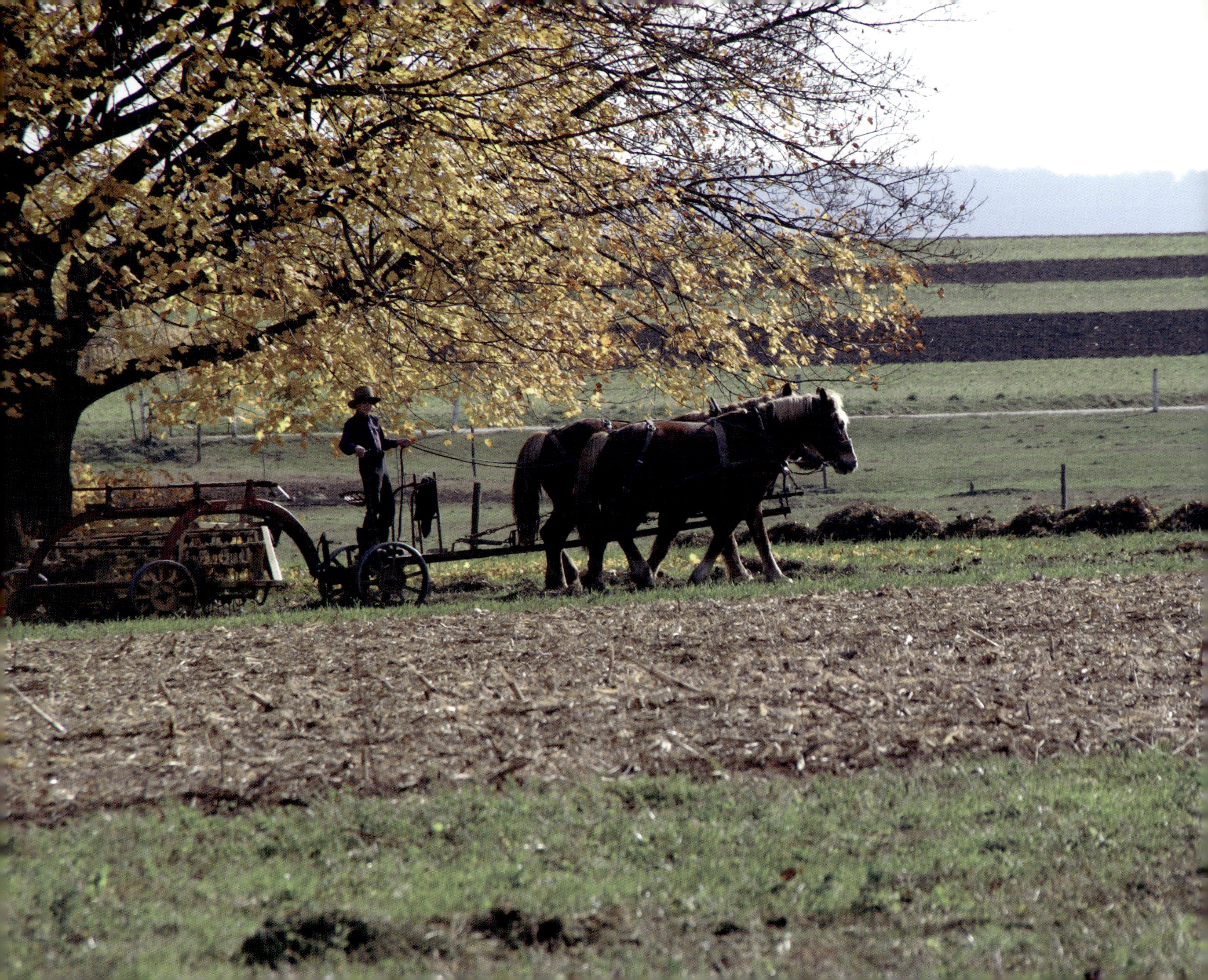

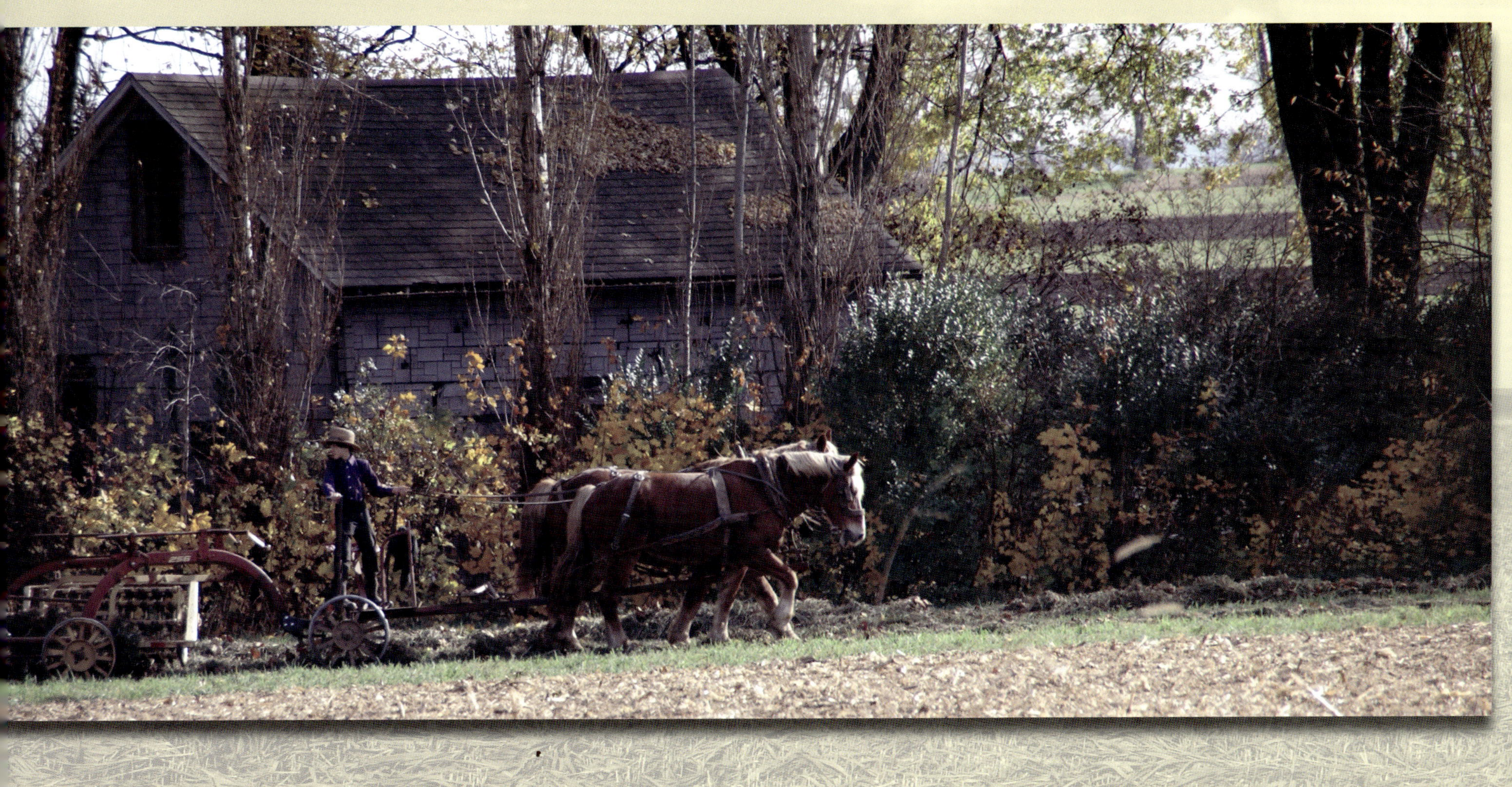

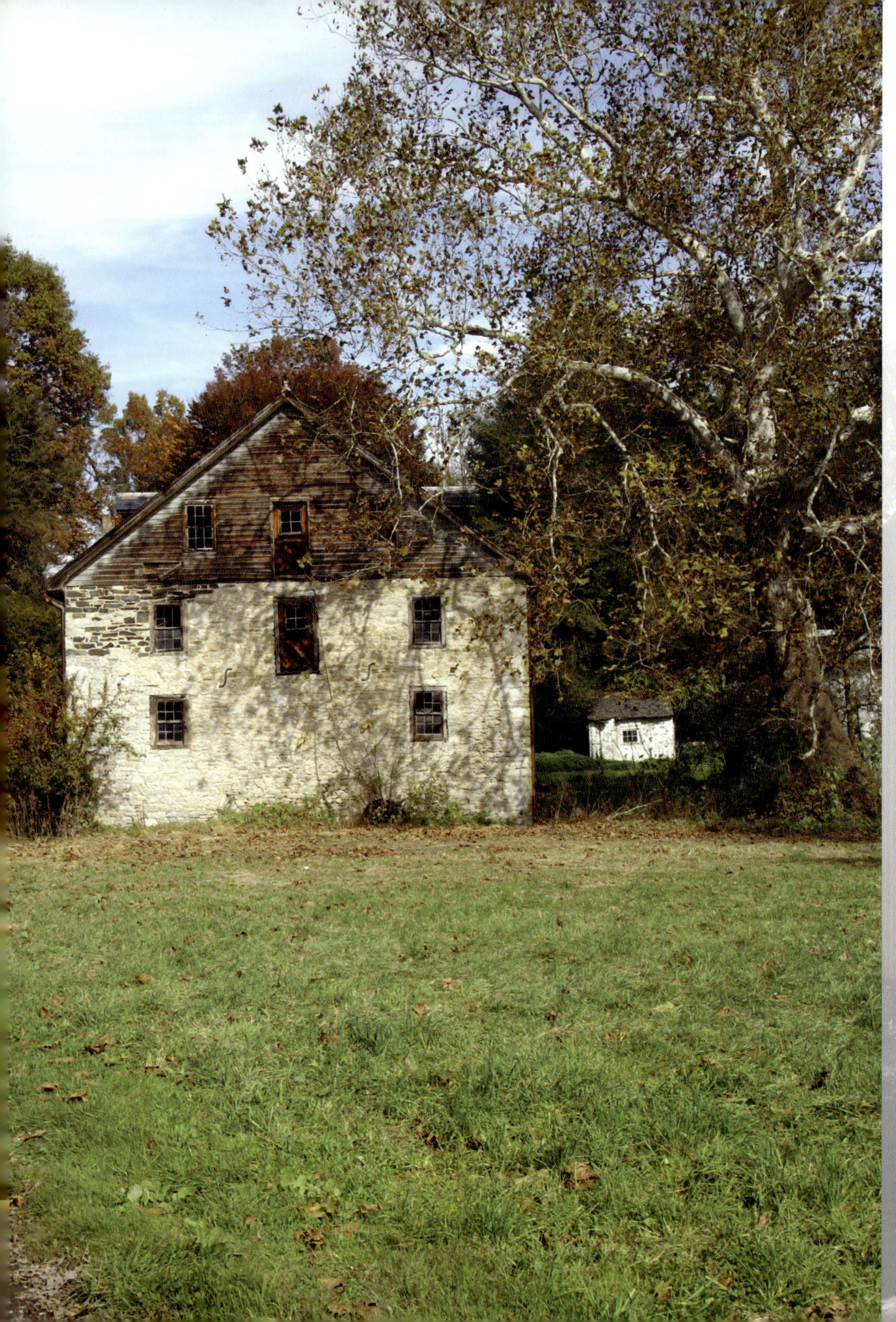

Covered Bridges

With twenty-nine covered bridges, Lancaster County has more covered bridges than any other county in Pennsylvania. The majority of the picturesque structures are listed on the National Register of Historic Places. The traditional paint scheme for county bridges is red sides and white portals, though there are a few exceptions. Most bridges also have vertical sideboards.

This three-story stone mill was built by Jacob Smith and dates from the early 1800s. It was later purchased by Abraham Mylin, who either rebuilt or expanded the mill. It was sold in 1870 to Thomas Baumgardener, for whom the mill—and adjacent covered bridge—is named.

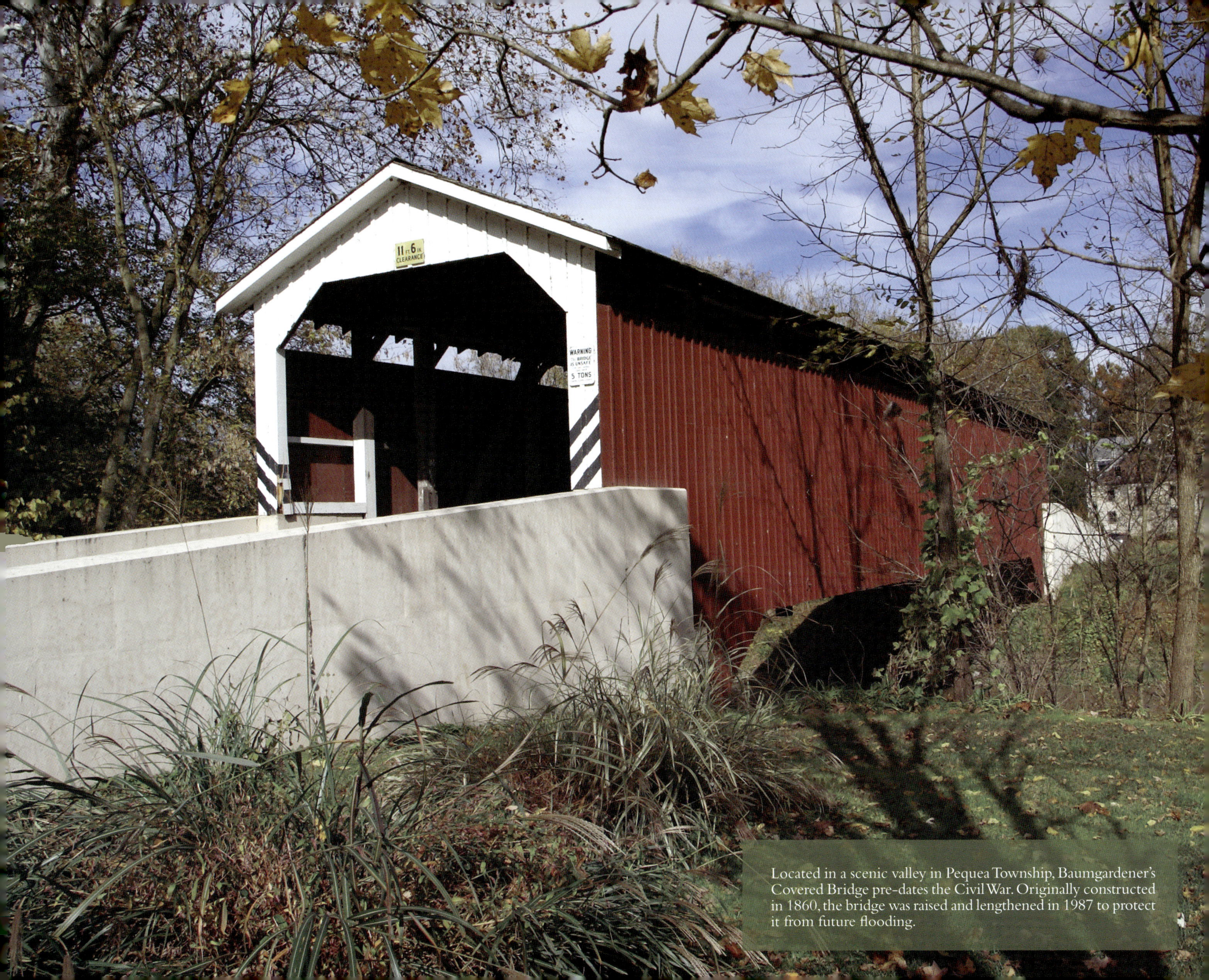

Located in a scenic valley in Pequea Township, Baumgardener's Covered Bridge pre-dates the Civil War. Originally constructed in 1860, the bridge was raised and lengthened in 1987 to protect it from future flooding.

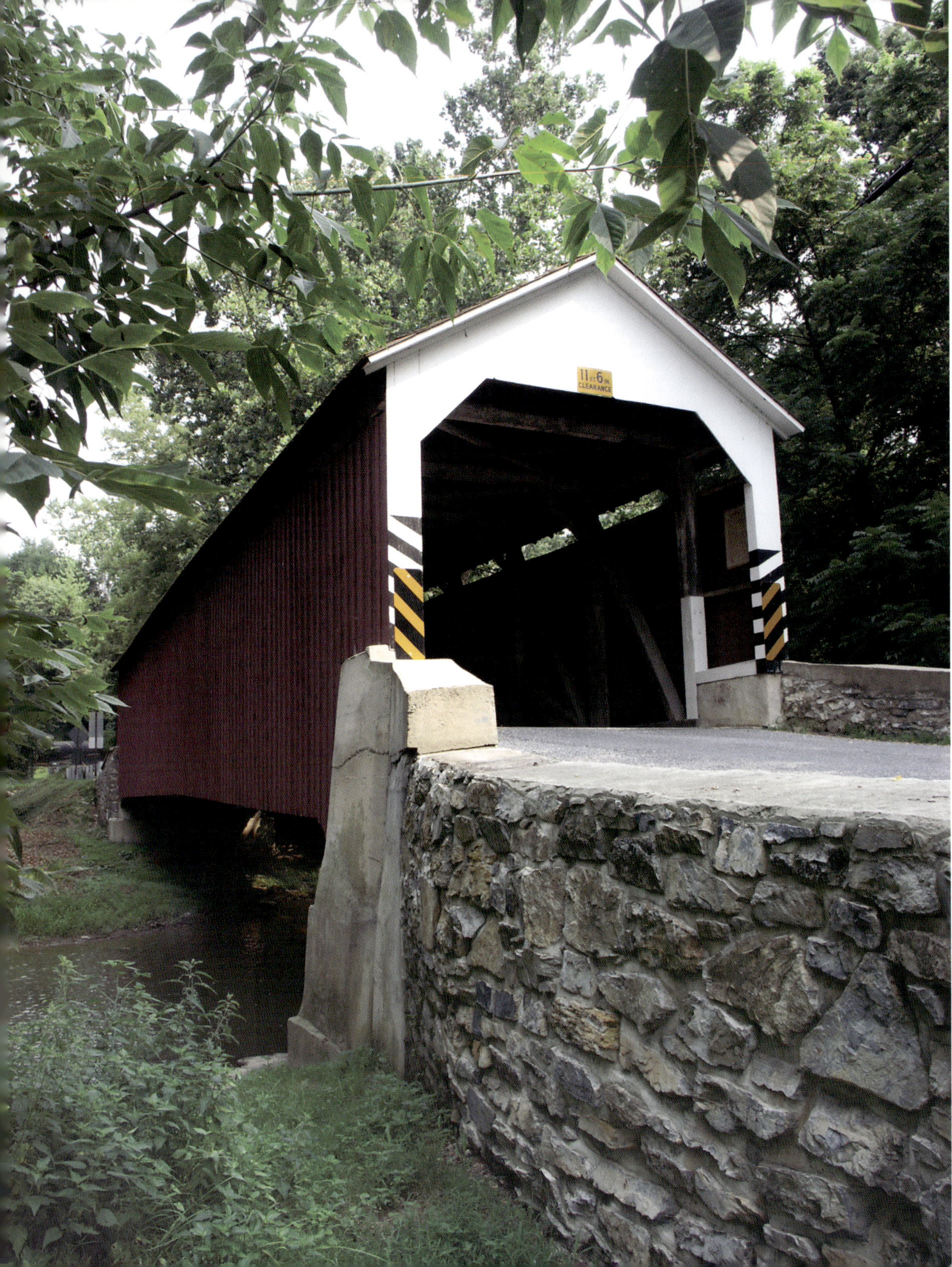

Siegrist's Mill Covered Bridge was originally known as Michael Moore's Mill Bridge when it was built in 1885. The Siegrist family purchased the mill a decade later and changed the name of the bridge.

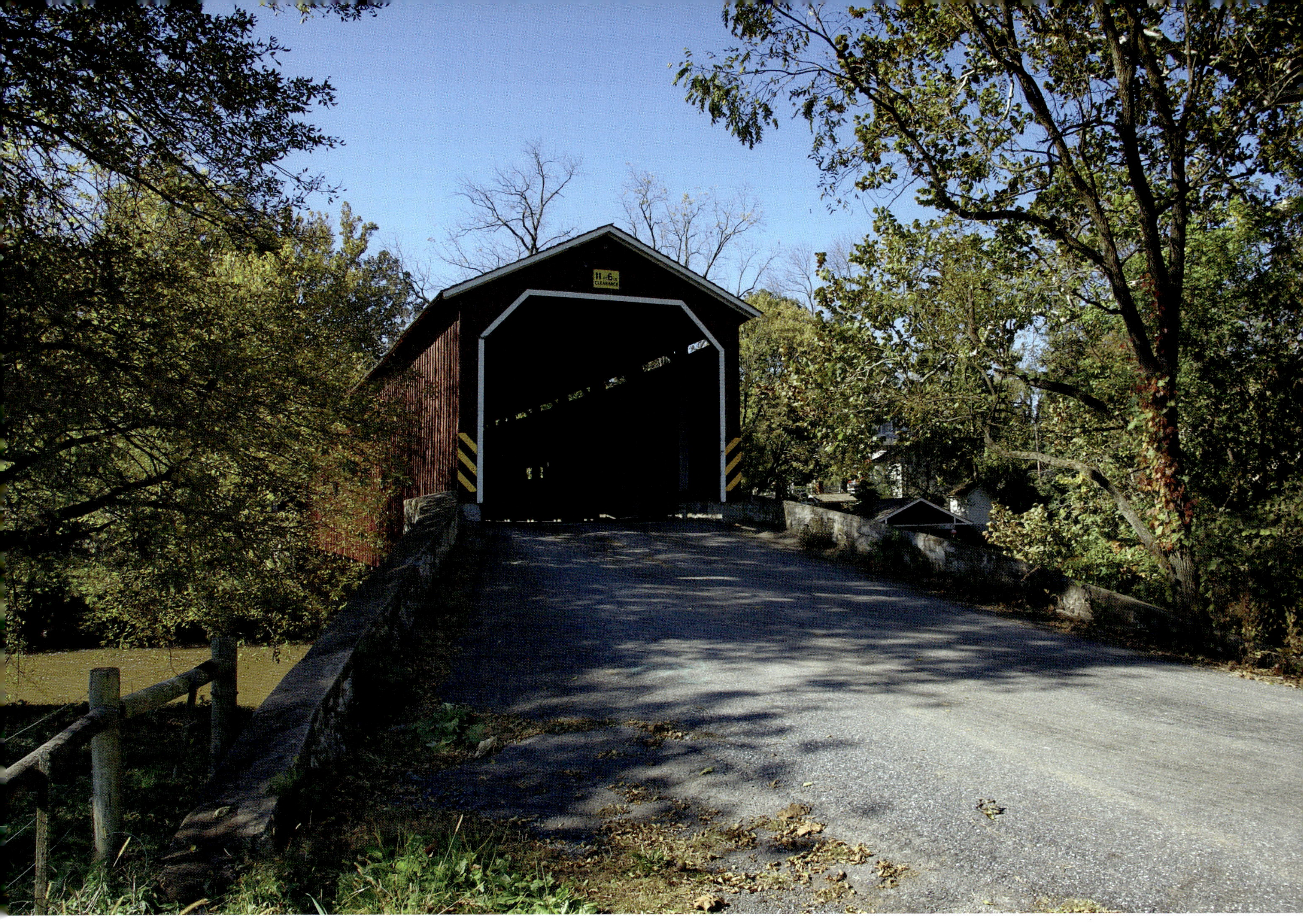

Like other nearby bridges, the Pinetown Covered Bridge was washed off its base in 1972 during the historic flooding caused by Hurricane Agnes. The original bridge was built in 1867 for $4,500.

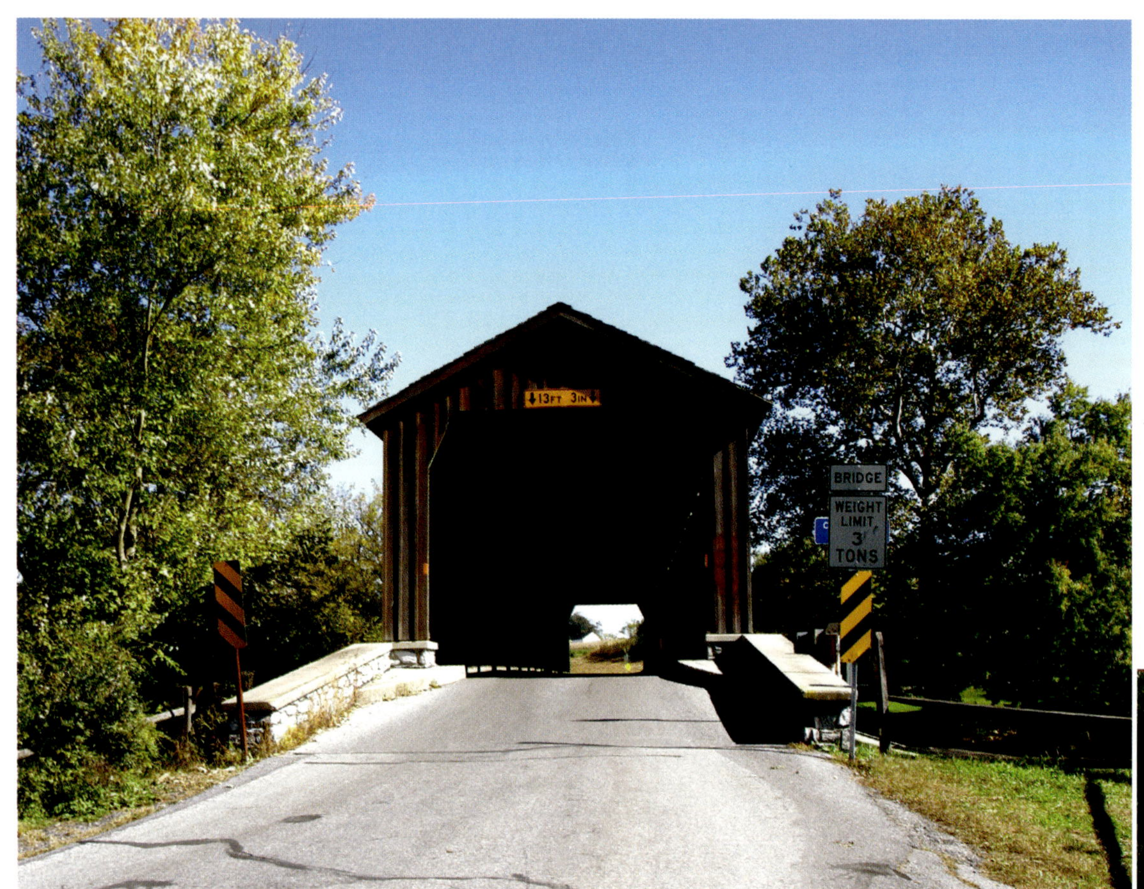

The 180-foot long Hunsecker's Mill Bridge was constructed in 1848 and rebuilt in 1973 after being damaged by Hurricane Agnes. It is the longest single-span covered bridge in Lancaster County.

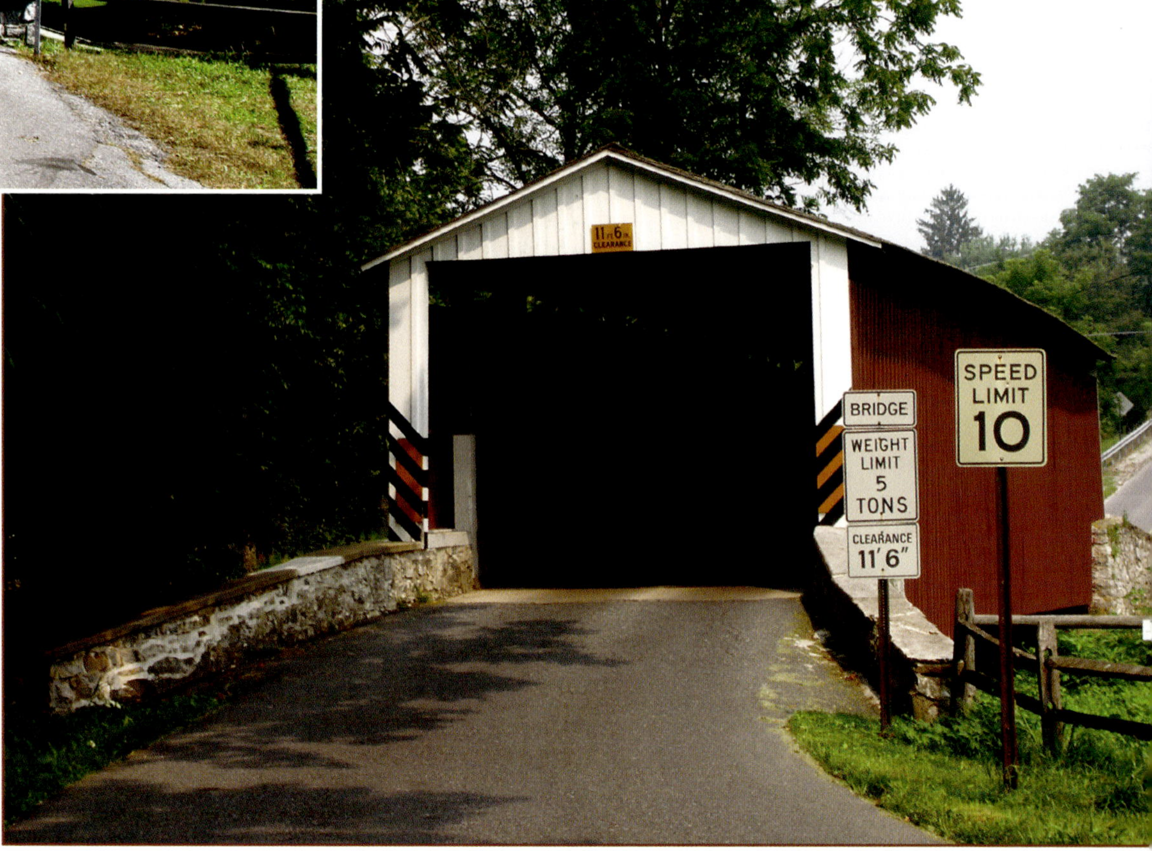

Kauffman's Distillery Covered Bridge was constructed in 1857 and is one of nine area covered bridges built by James Carpenter.

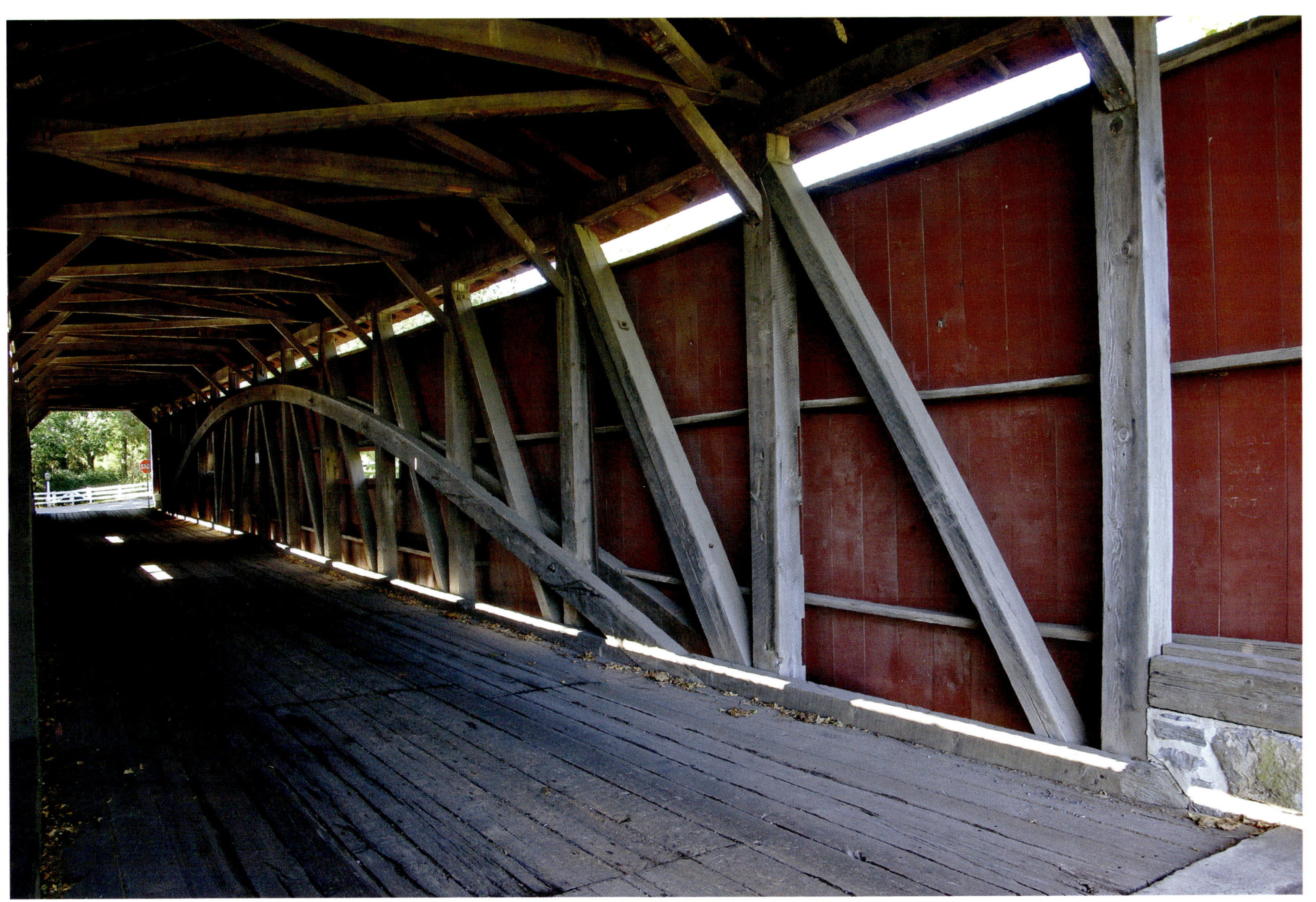

Most covered bridges in Lancaster County were built using the Burr Arched Truss System, which utilizes a single or double arch to hold the load and incorporates trusses to keep the bridge rigid.

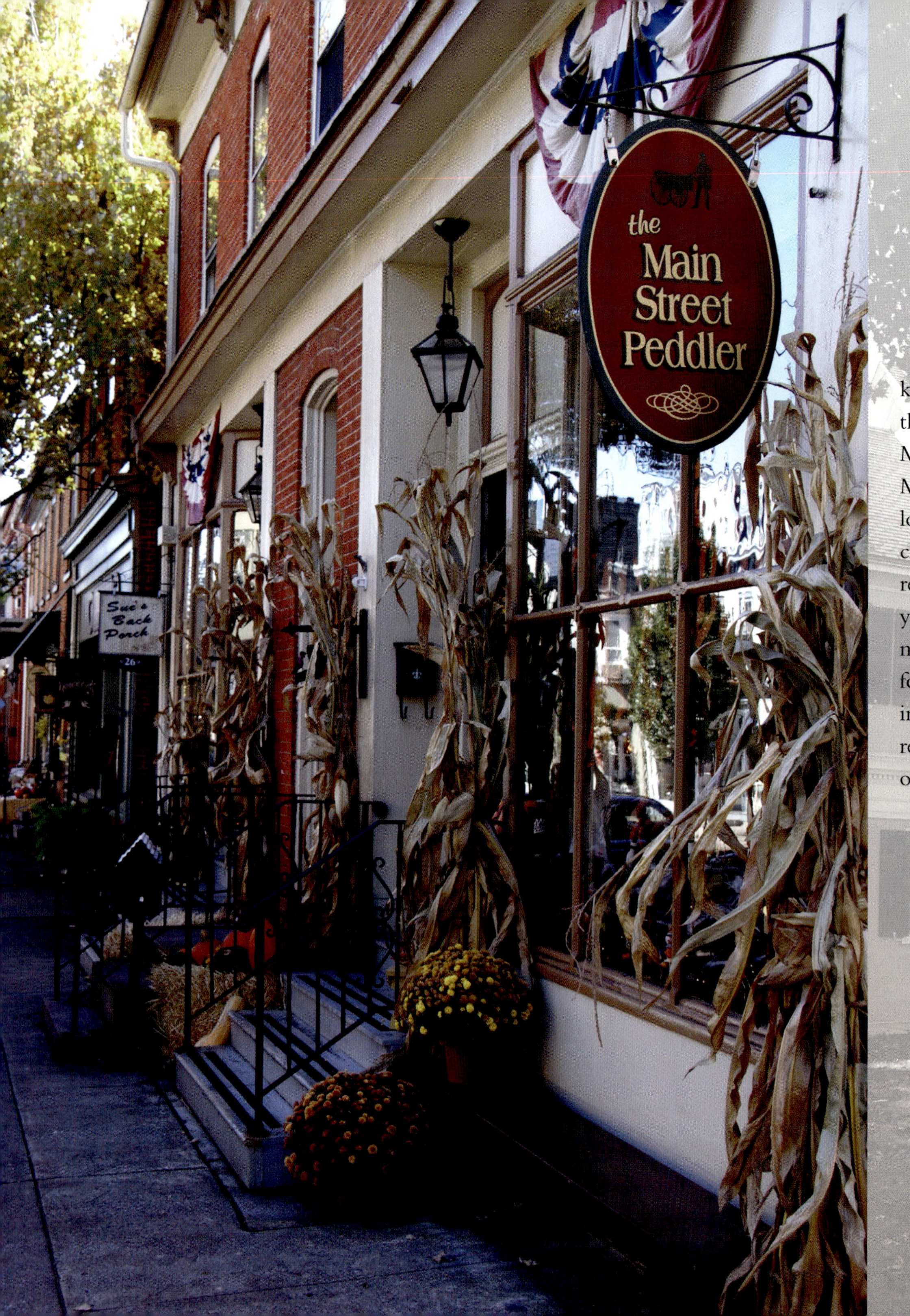

Lititz

In the 1720s, German immigrants began settling in the area that is today known as Lititz. The town of Lititz itself came about in the 1740s, when the visiting Count Nikolaus Von Zinzendorf—organizer of the modern Moravian Church—stopped at a local tavern. He had previously established Moravian communities in Nazareth and Bethlehem, Pennsylvania, and was looking to establish another. This occurred in 1756, and the name Lititz was chosen in homage to a town and castle of the same name in the Bohemian region of what is today known as the Czech Republic. For more than 100 years Lititz was a self-contained religious community. One of the town's most famous residents was John Sutter, the man who found gold in California in 1848, triggering the California Gold Rush. He settled in Lititz in 1871 and is buried in the Moravian cemetery. The charming town was recognized in 2009 by the National Trust for Historic Preservation as one of their Dozen Distinctive Destinations.

Lititz Springs Park is a private seven-acre park that has served the community for more than 200 years. It is owned by the Lititz Moravian Congregation and maintained by the churches of Lititz.

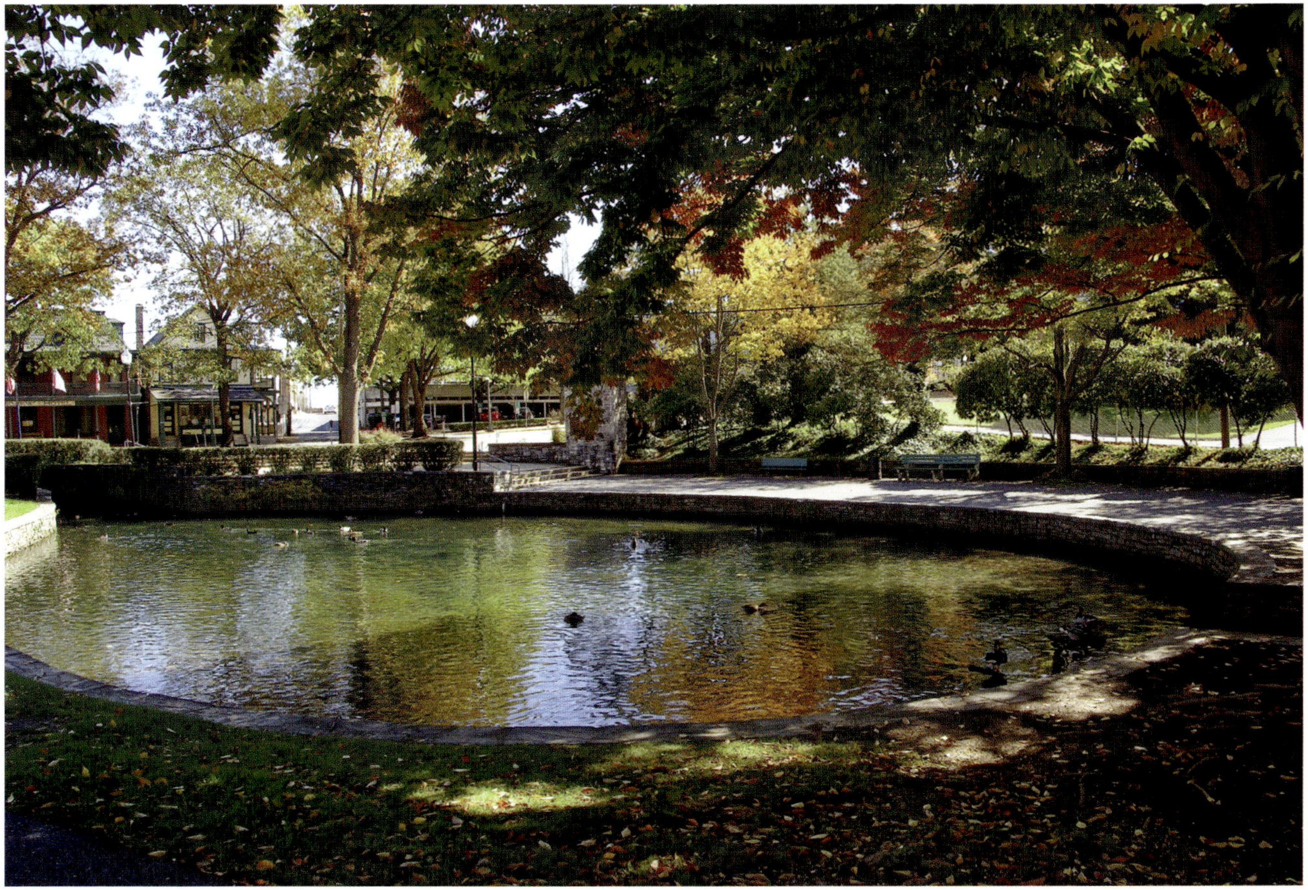

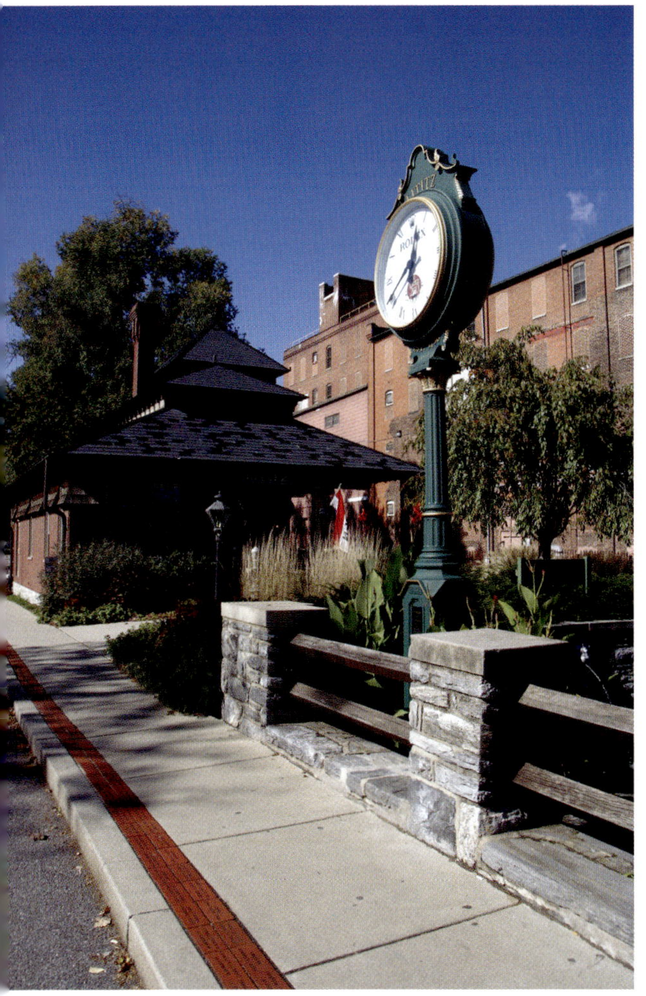

The Lititz Passenger Station is a replica of the original train station that was constructed in 1884 to serve the Reading & Columbia Railroad Company. The last passenger train passed through Lititz in 1952 and the train station was demolished in 1957. This replica station was dedicated in 1999 and is home to the Lititz Welcome Center.

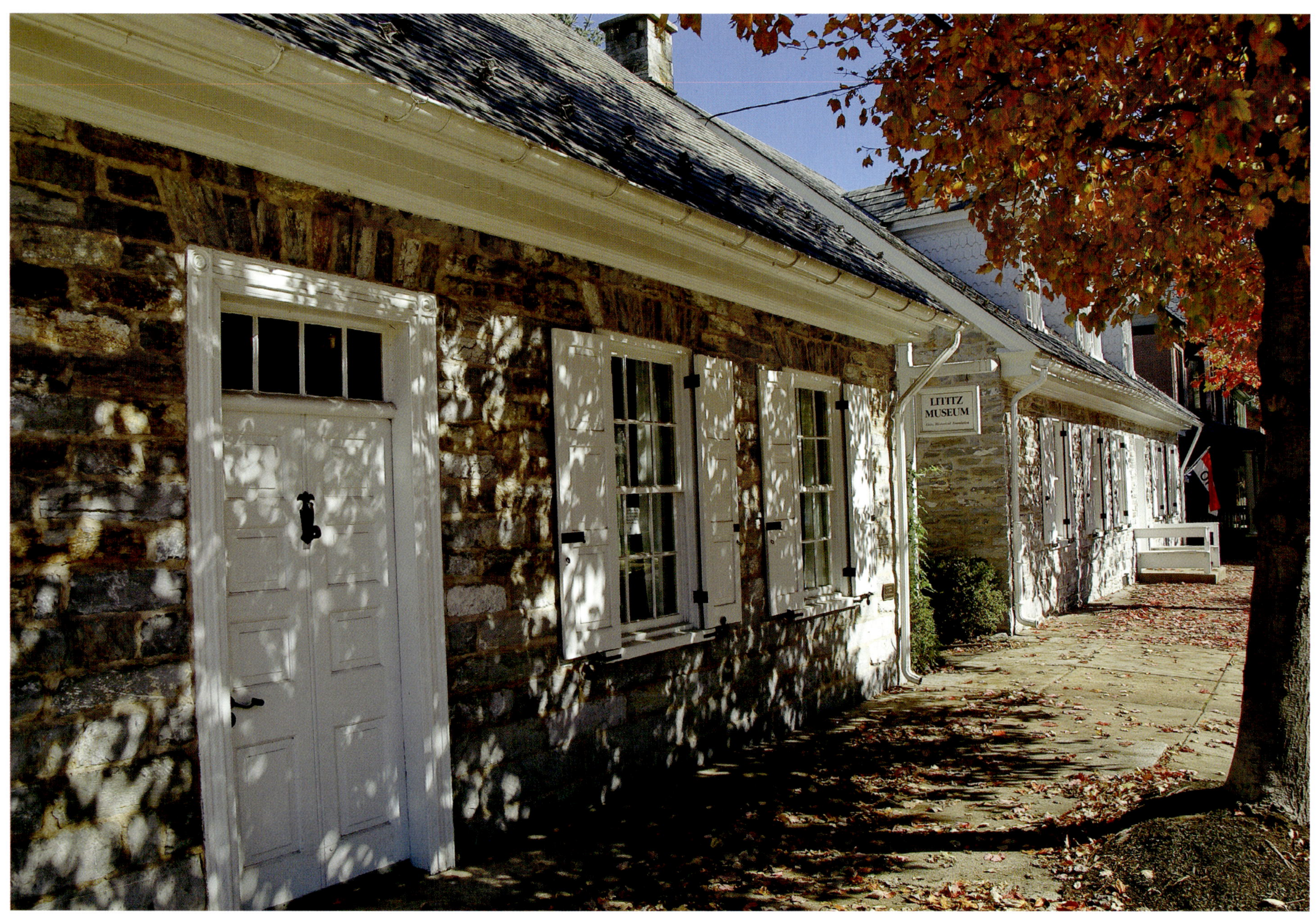

The 1792 Johannes Mueller House retains much of its original architectural character. The house now serves as a museum interpreting the life of an eighteenth-century tradesman and his family in a closed Moravian settlement.

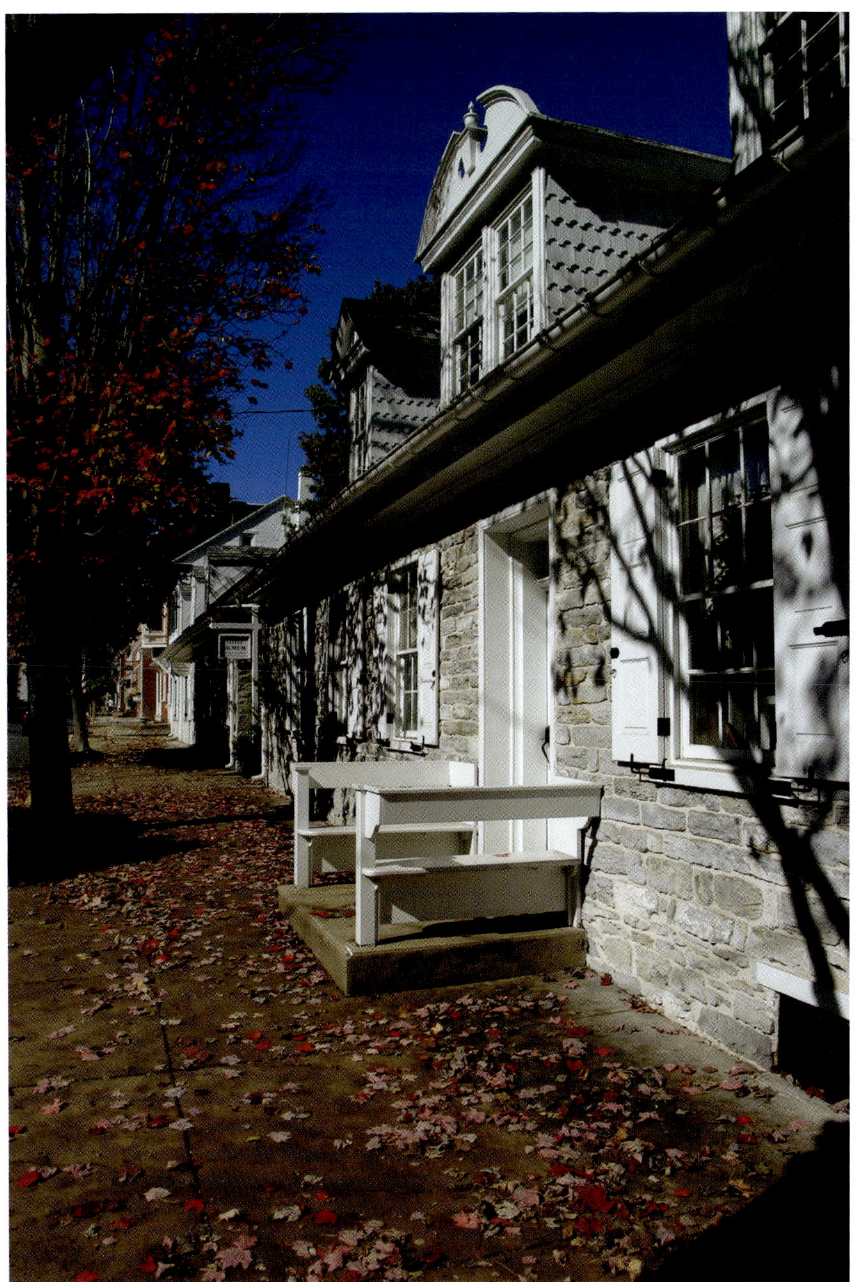

Now the Lititz Museum, the Christian Schropp home was constructed in 1793. A man of many talents, Schropp was a nail smith, schoolteacher, musician, and church organist.

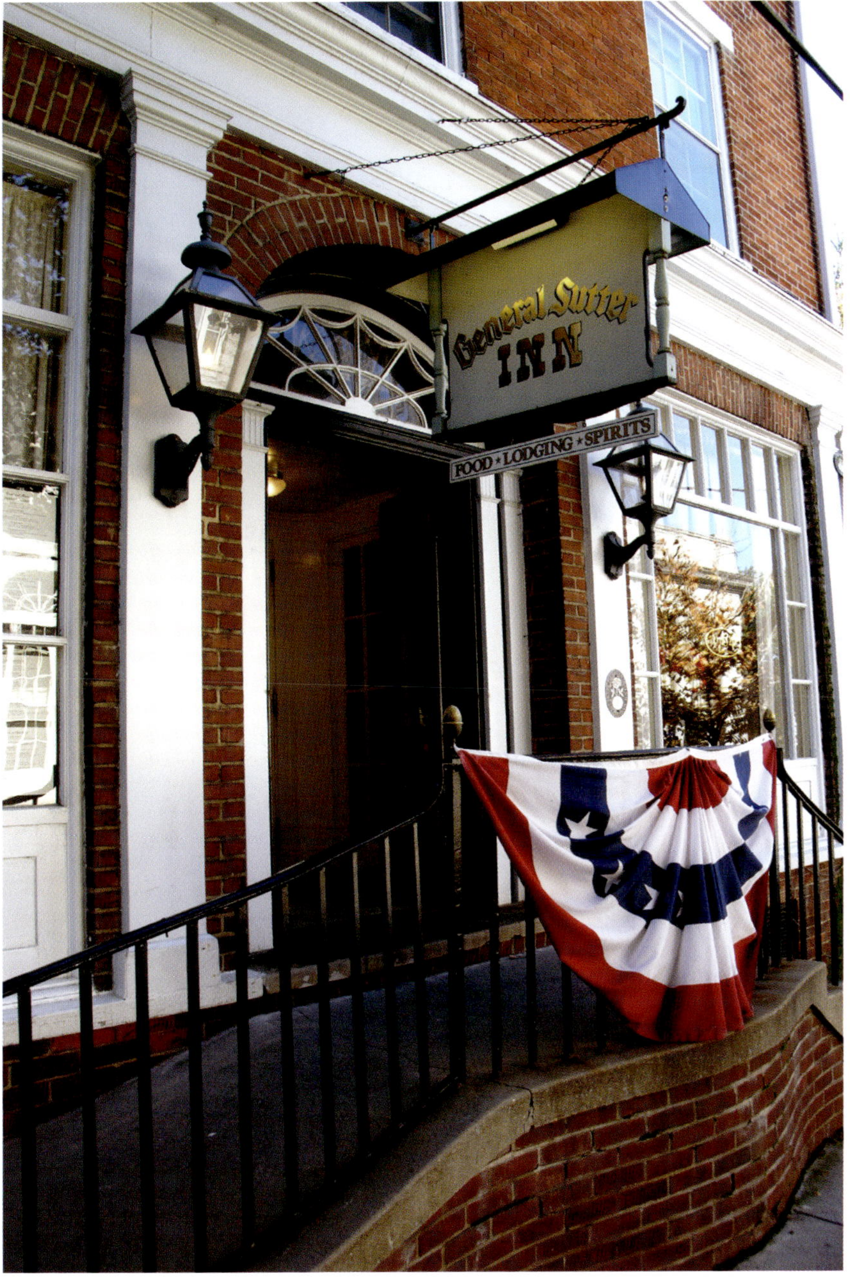

The General Sutter Inn is named for the founder of Sacramento, California, and originator of the California Gold Rush, John Augustus Sutter, who discovered gold at his California mill in 1848. The property was originally home to the Zum Anker Inn, a tavern that was established in 1764. Before becoming the General Sutter Inn, the building was home to the Lititz Springs Hotel.

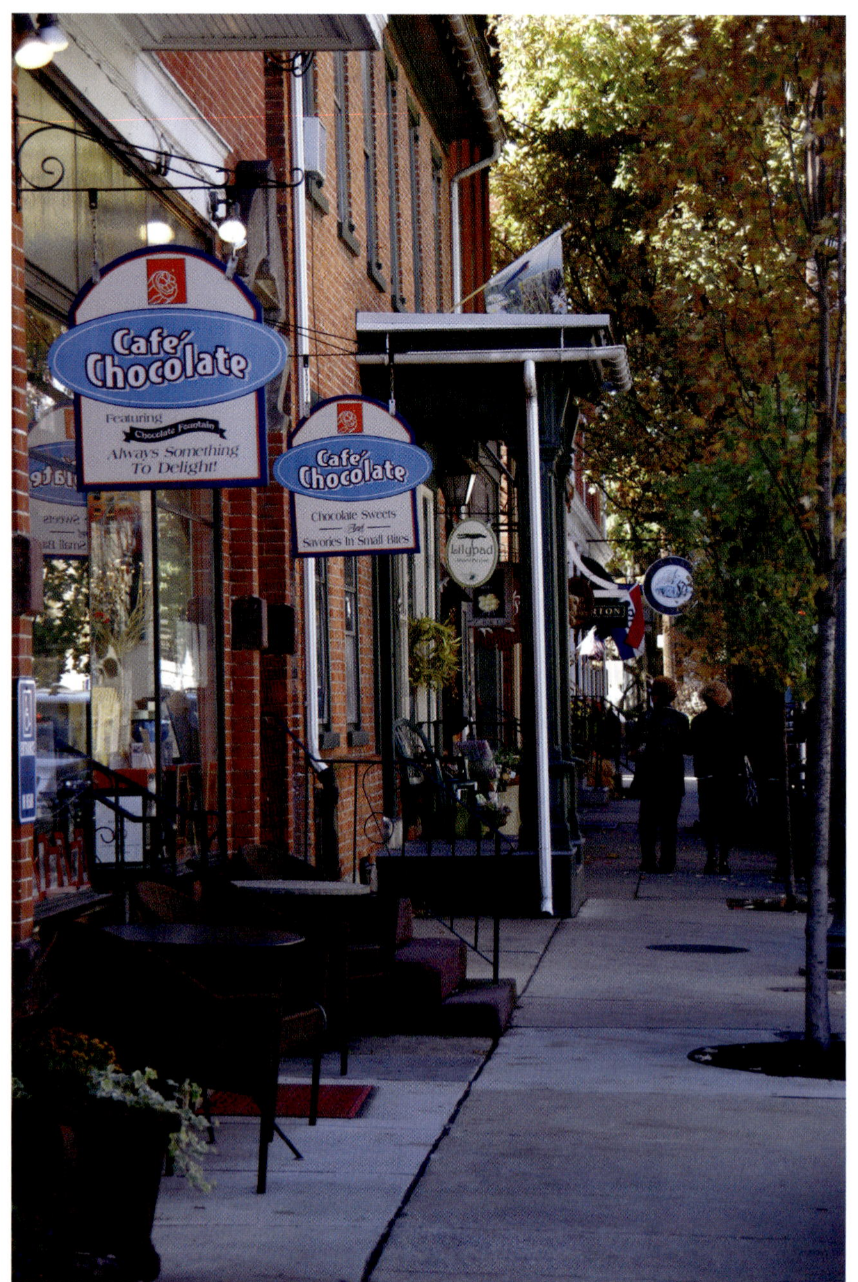

Café Chocolate of Lititz has a simple recipe for success: take a quaint café, season with generous portions of customer service, then coat in chocolate and more chocolate. Offerings like Chili con Chocolate, Chocolate Fondue, and Chocolate Strawberry Lush help the café meet its mission of "Chocolate for life!"

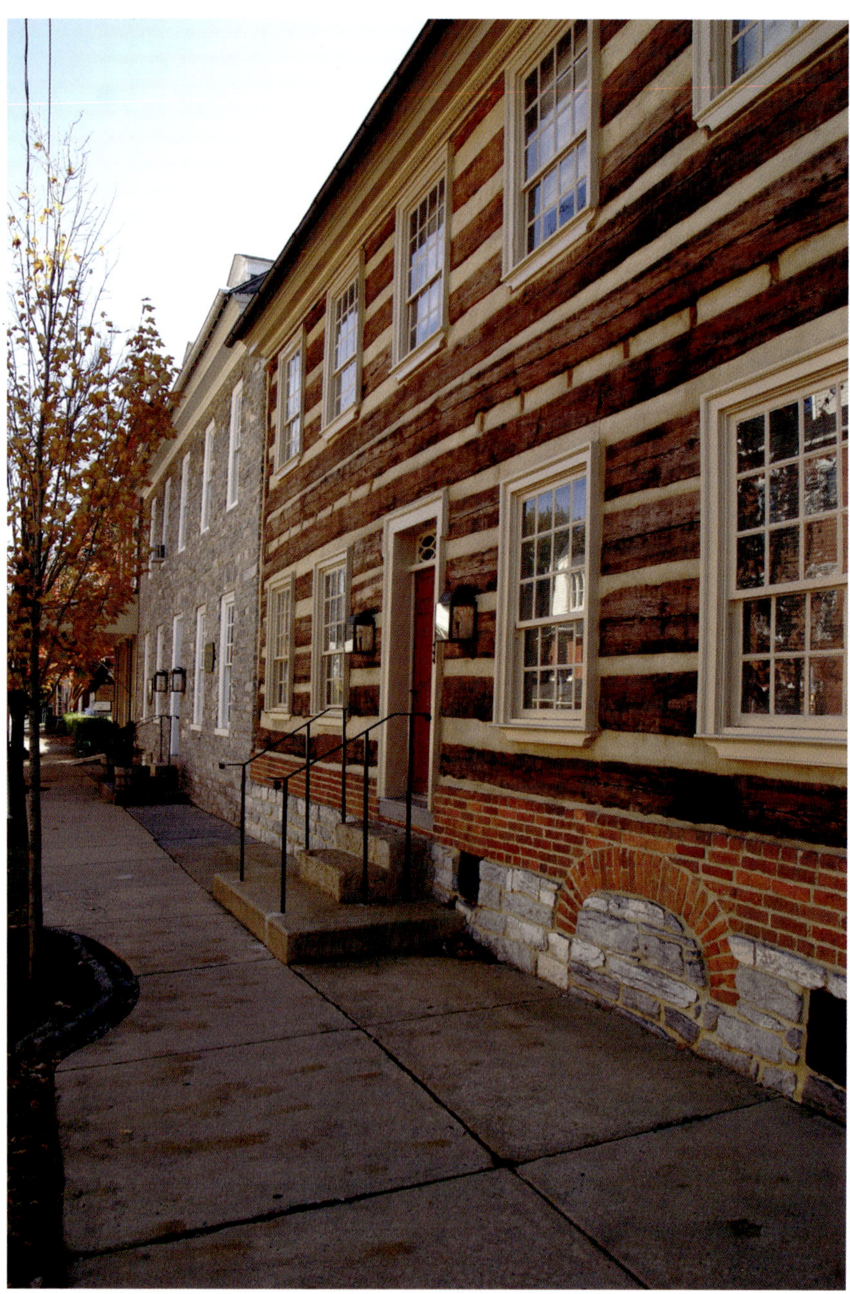

This portion of the Lititz streetscape remains largely unchanged from 1762, when the Moravian Congregational Store was located here.

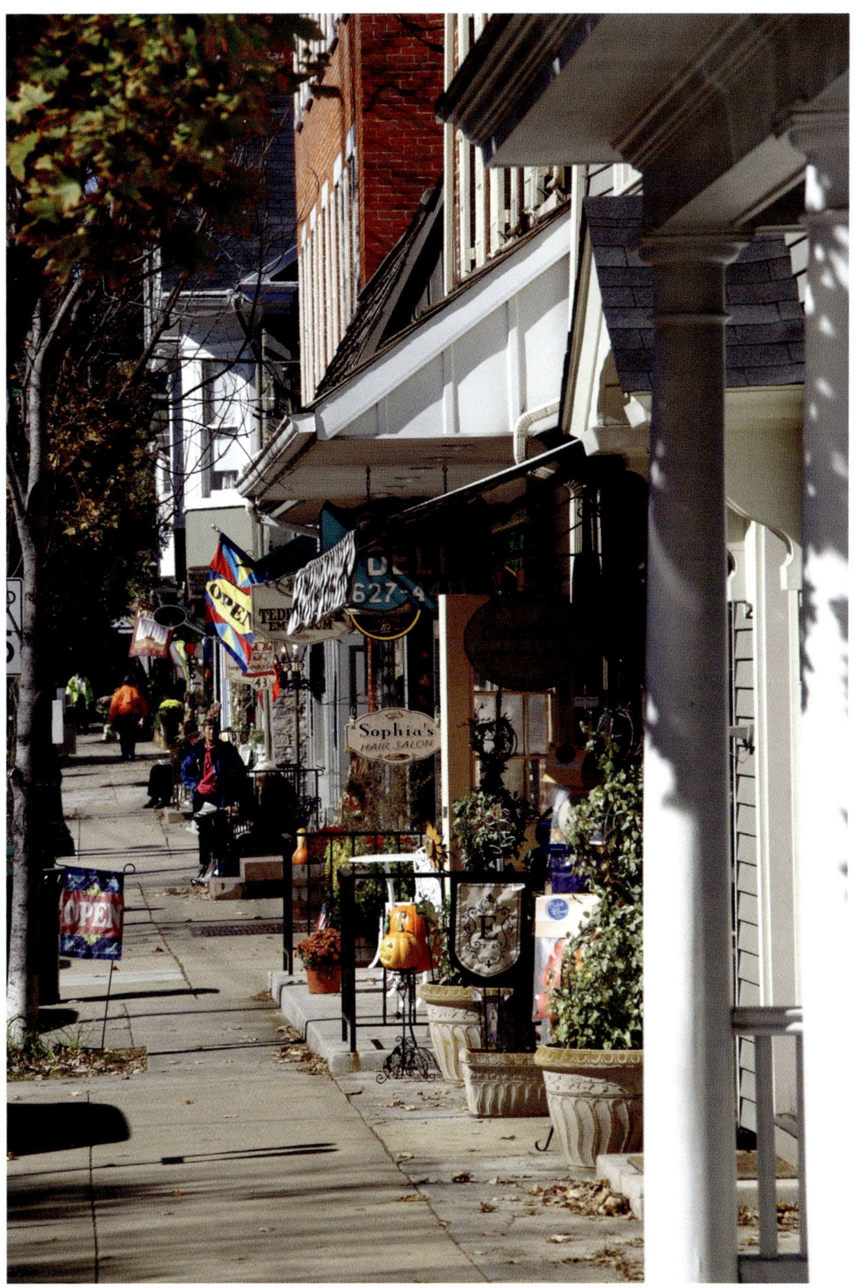

What makes Lititz a Distinctive Destination? According to the National Trust for Historic Preservation, which recognized Lititz in 2009, it is partially due to "the town's mix of independently owned boutiques and galleries, which are emporiums of authentic local country crafts and antiques."

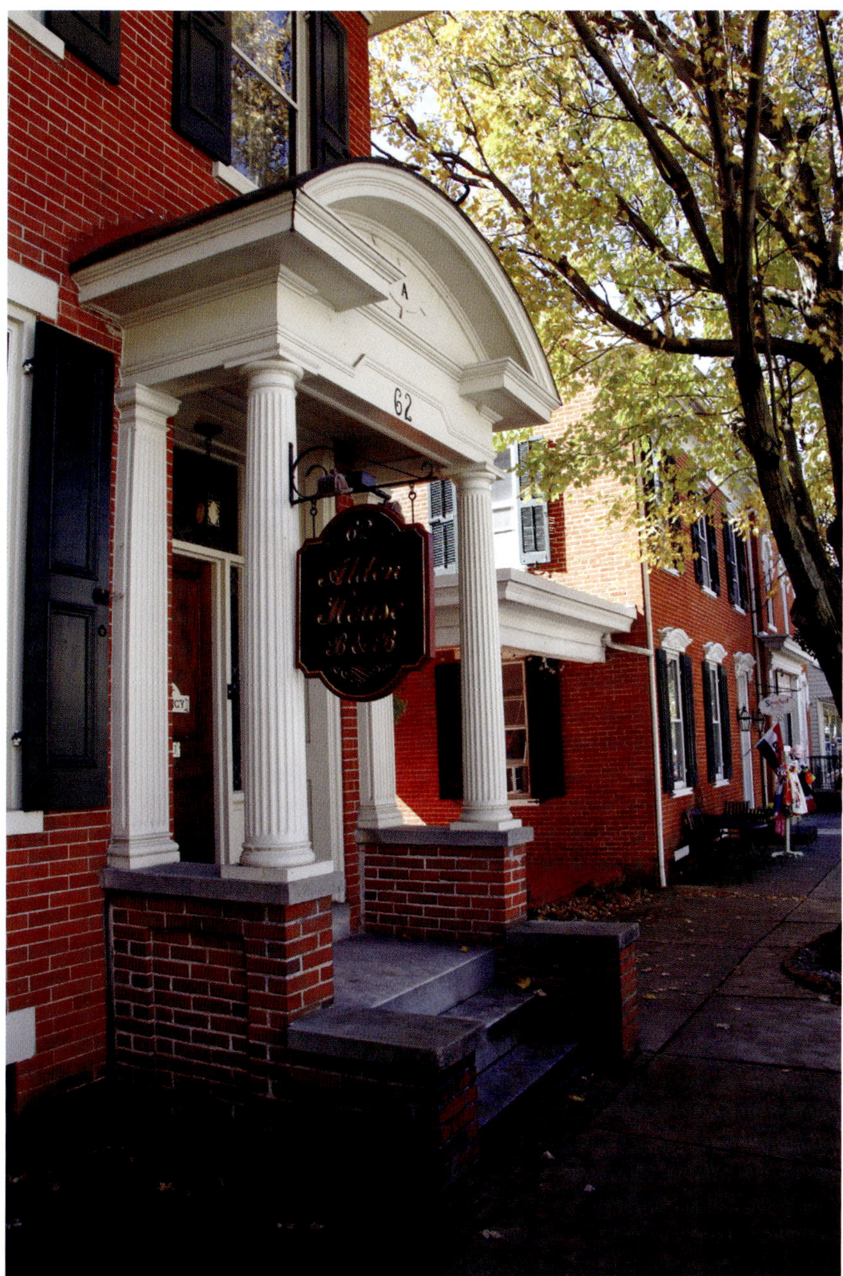

The Alden House is a charming bed and breakfast located in a red brick, mid-nineteenth-century Greek Revival home.

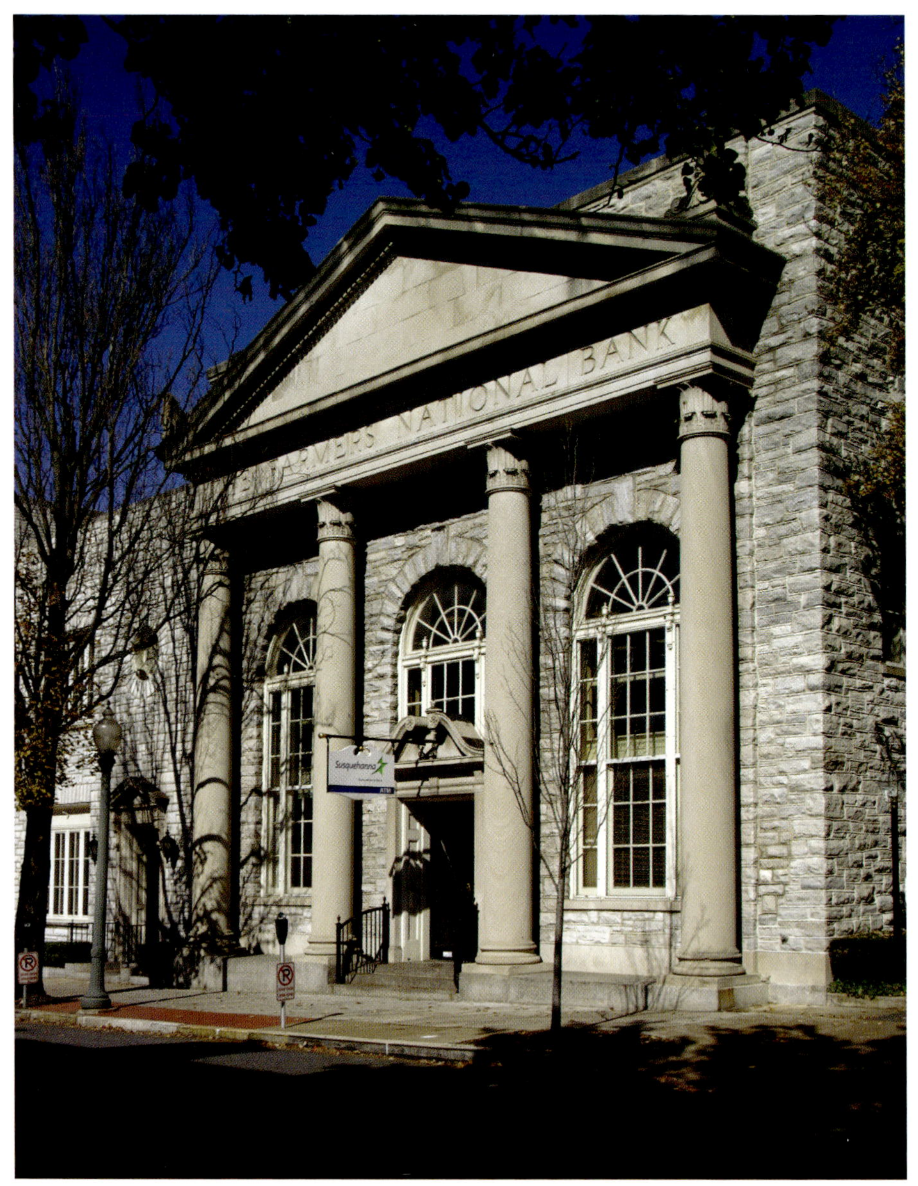

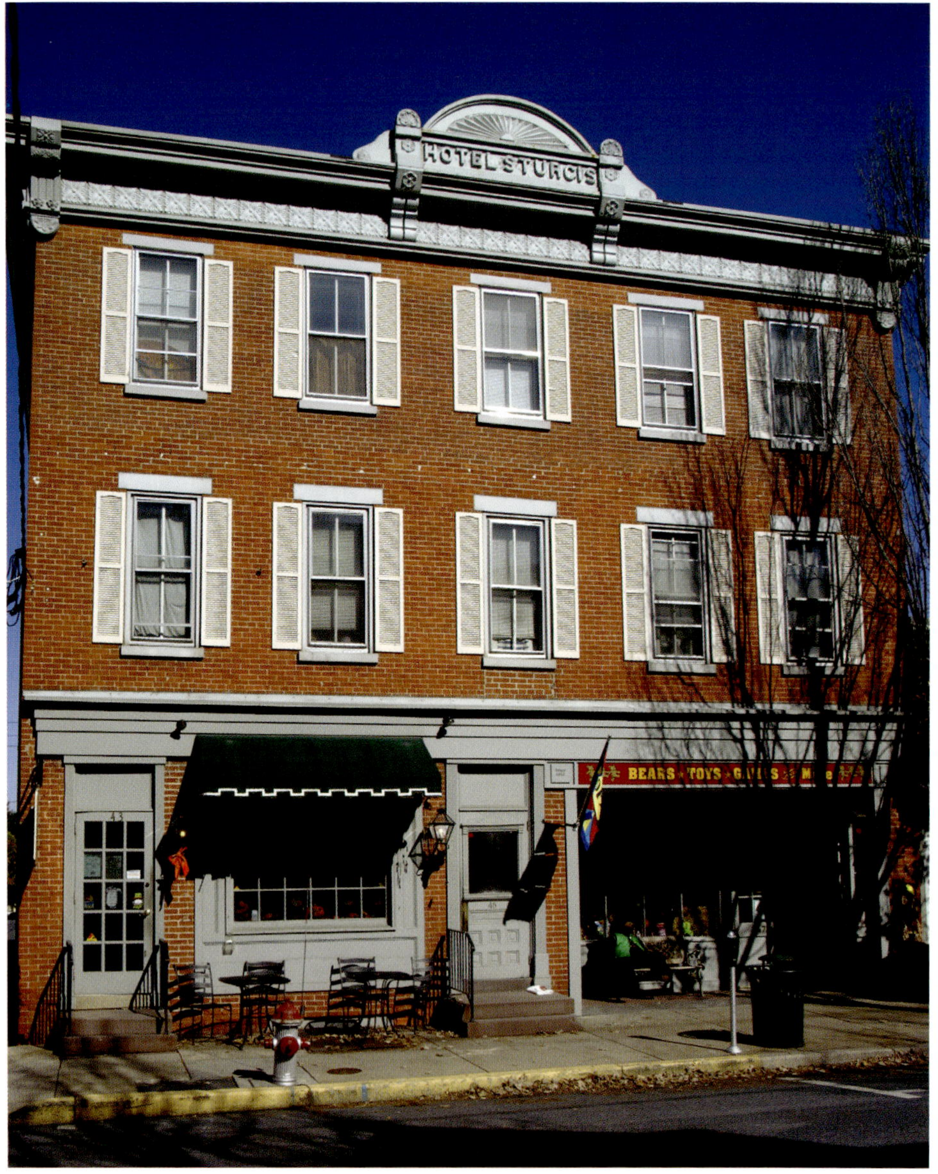

This imposing building was constructed around 1920 as Farmers' National Bank. The stone façade exhibits the Greek temple form common in Neoclassical architecture, but also contains Georgian features like a swan's neck pediment and urn finials, as well as Egyptian inspired capitals atop the columns.

The Sturgis House was built in 1867 by Edward Sturgis to accommodate the expanding need for lodging in Lititz, which by then had gained a reputation as home to the healing waters of the Lititz Springs. Originally two-stories, a third-story was added to the building in 1895 and the name was changed to Hotel Sturgis. In the 1930s, the building became home to a movie theater and restaurant, which operated for several decades.

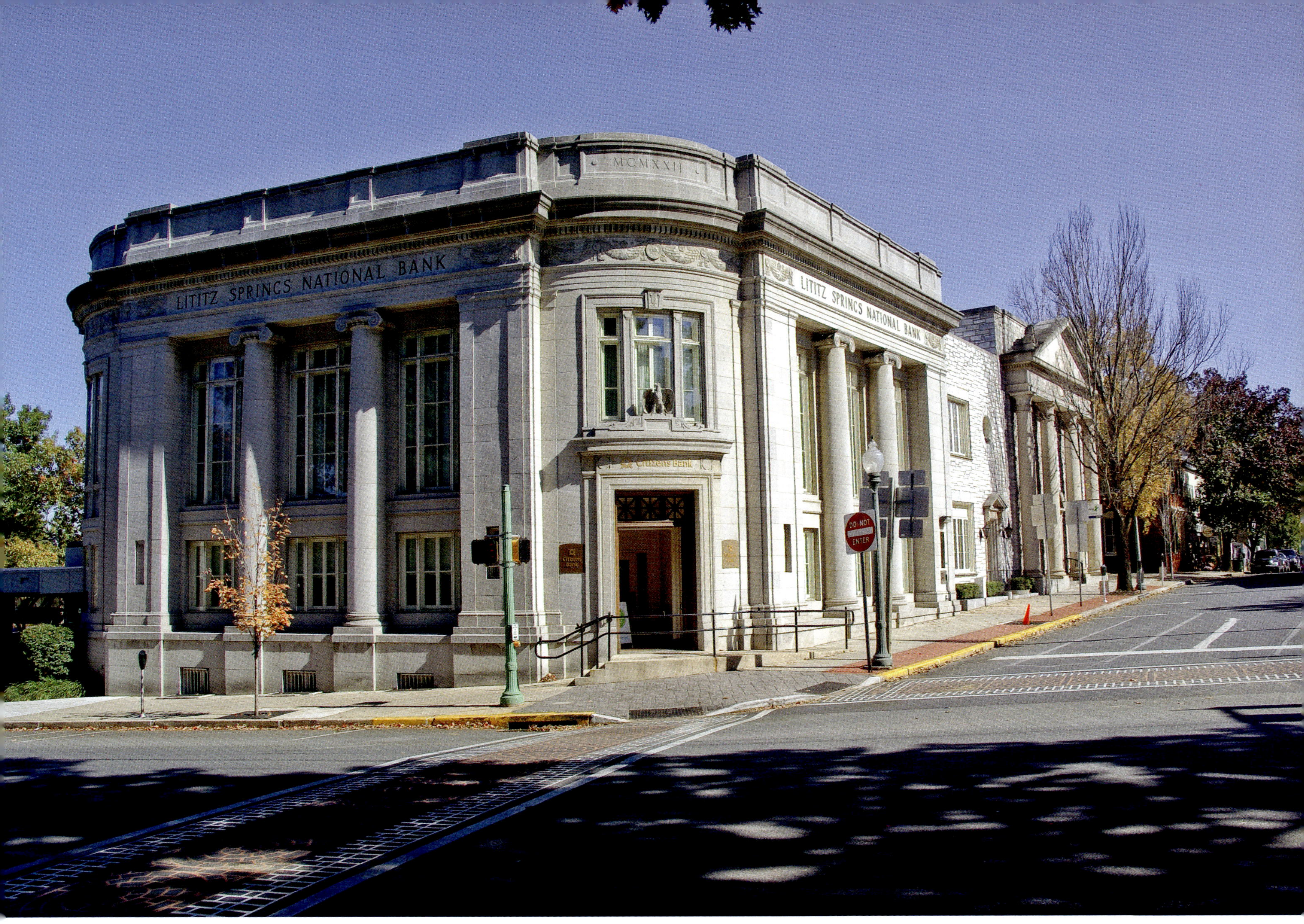

The Neoclassical Revival Lititz Springs National Bank was constructed in 1922. The bank was organized in 1920 with initial capital of $50,000. By the time this building was completed, the bank's capital, profits, and surplus had grown to $183,000.

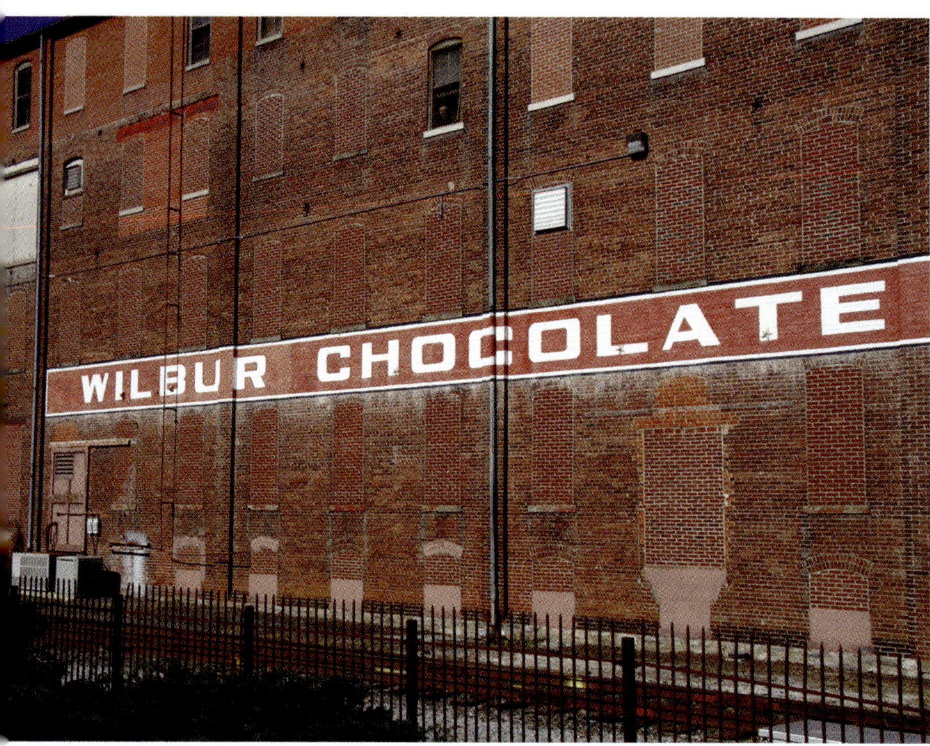

Chocolate manufacturer H.O. Wilbur & Sons was founded in Philadelphia in 1884—a successor to the Croft & Wilbur candy business. While the Wilbur business was growing, a start-up caramel factory, Kendig Chocolate Company, opened in Lititz in 1900. Two years later Kendig became Ideal Cocoa and Chocolate Company. Both Wilbur and Ideal were successful, merging with other companies in the late 1920s. In 1928, Wilber and Ideal came together and then relocated all Philadelphia operations to Lititz in 1930. The flower bud shaped chocolates, known as Wilbur Buds, were introduced in 1894 and are still a popular product.

The Warwick Country Congregation was organized in 1749, and by 1756 the community of Lititz had been laid out. Over the next 100 years, church and community members built their homes on land leased from the church. The present church building was constructed in 1787. A Single Brothers' House and Single Sisters' House were constructed from 1758 to 1759, and both still stand. The Single Brothers' House even served as a military hospital during the American Revolution. Today the congregation is known as Lititz Moravian Church.

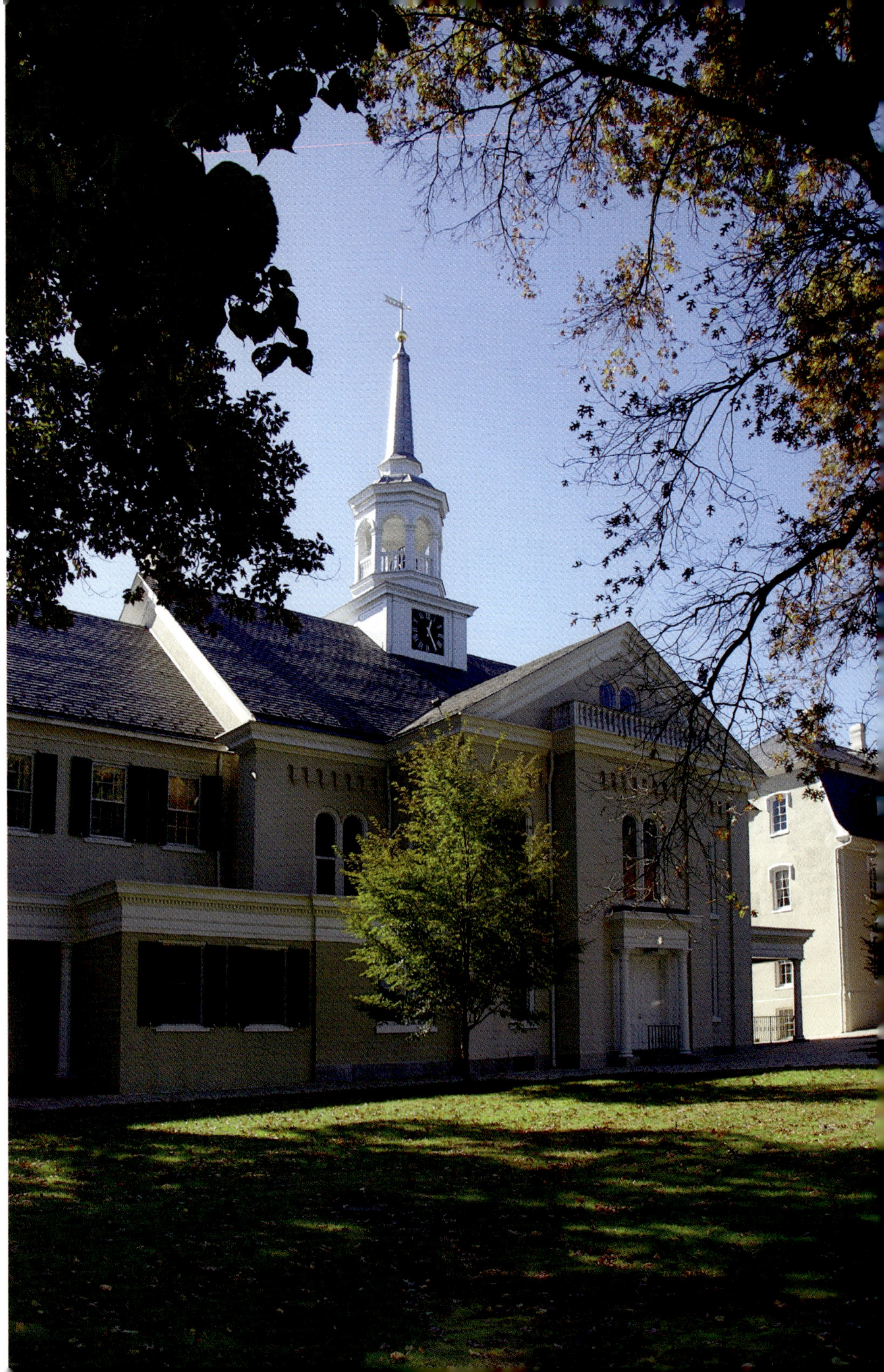

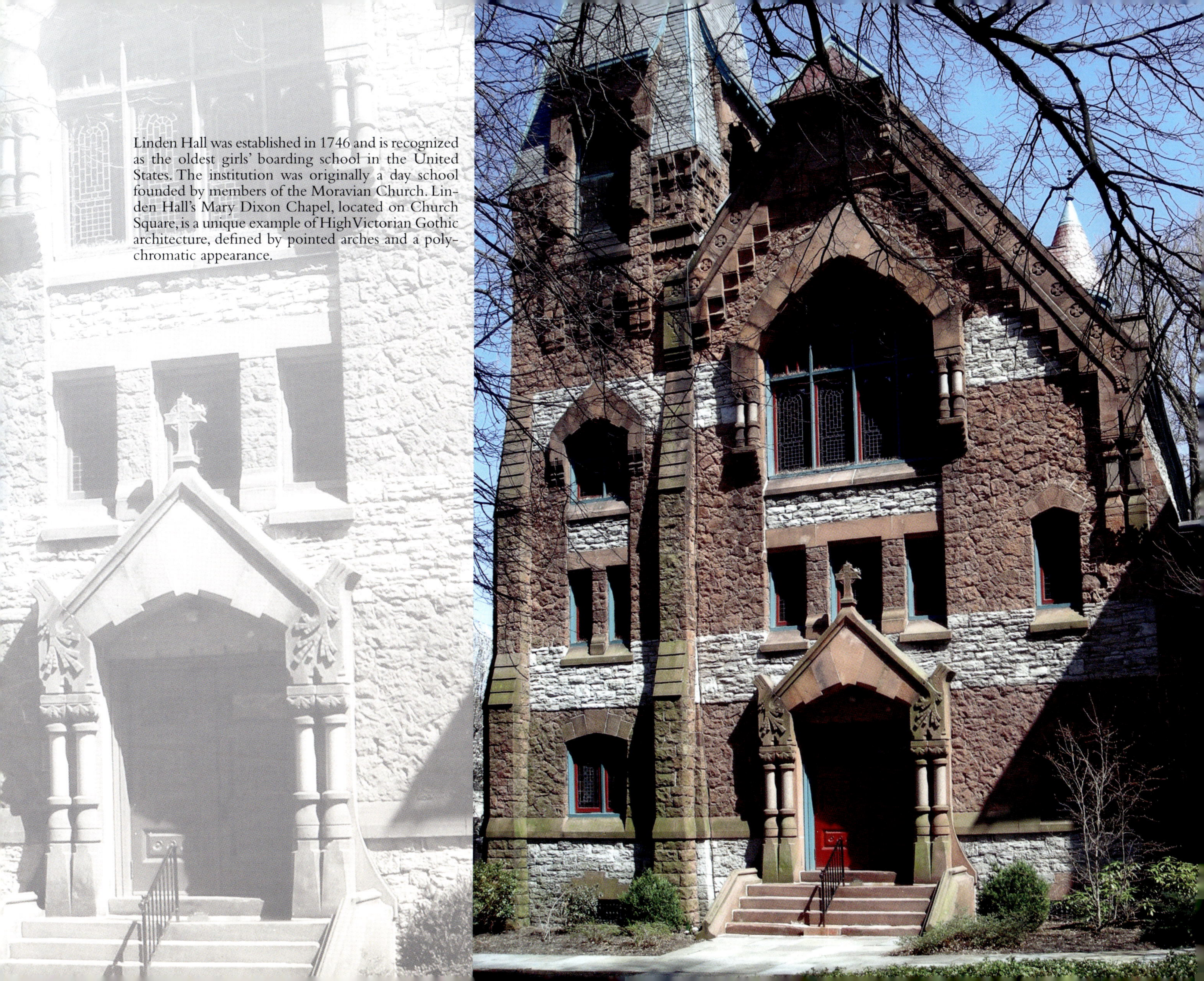

Linden Hall was established in 1746 and is recognized as the oldest girls' boarding school in the United States. The institution was originally a day school founded by members of the Moravian Church. Linden Hall's Mary Dixon Chapel, located on Church Square, is a unique example of High Victorian Gothic architecture, defined by pointed arches and a polychromatic appearance.

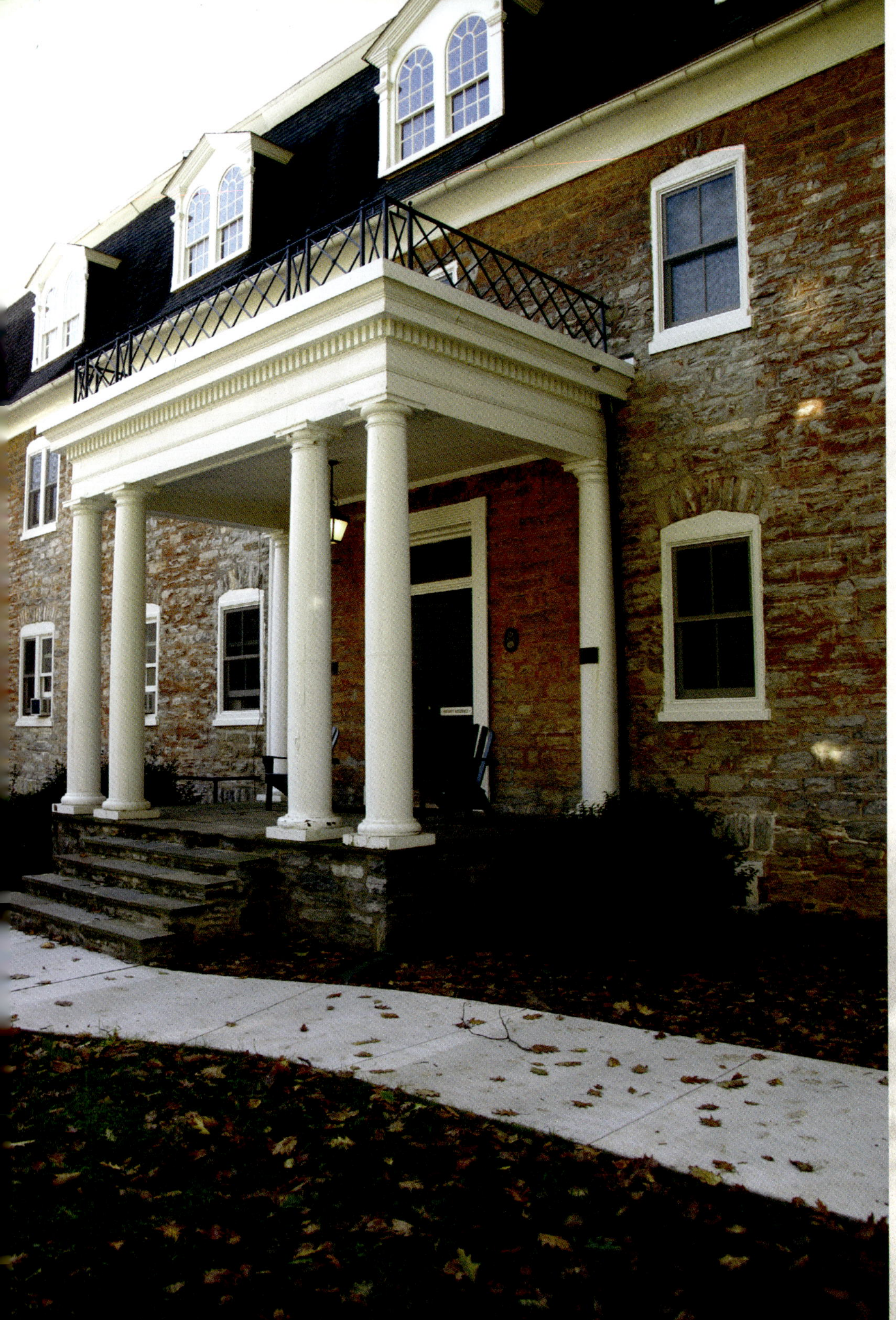

Originally known as the Single Sisters' House, this limestone building dates from 1758 and today is referred to as the Linden Hall Castle.

A depiction of the Moravian Church and Linden Hall school grounds as they would have appeared circa 1804 when the school and church yard occupied a prominent place in the borough of Lititz. *Courtesy of Linden Hall, Lititz, PA.*

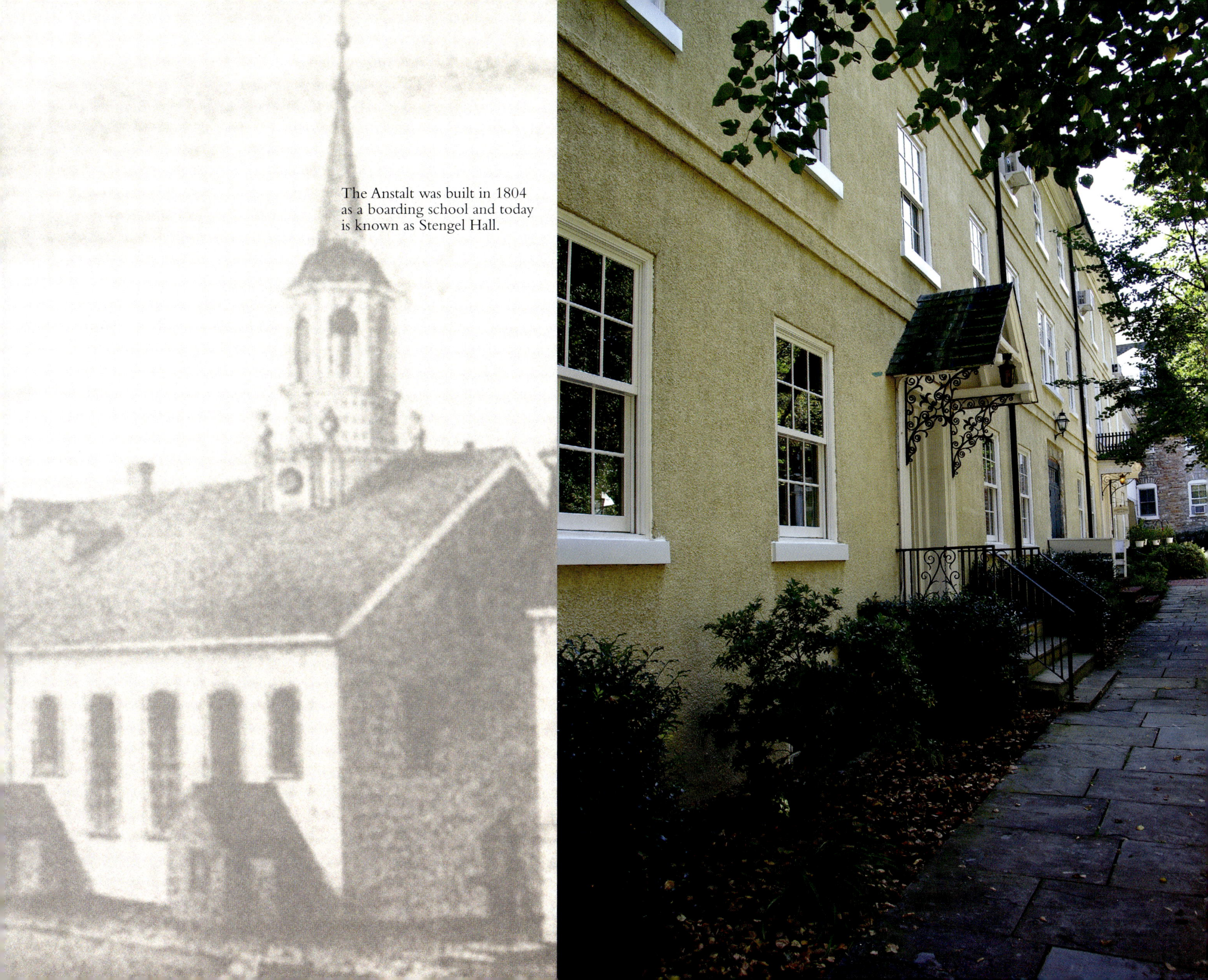

The Anstalt was built in 1804 as a boarding school and today is known as Stengel Hall.

Manheim

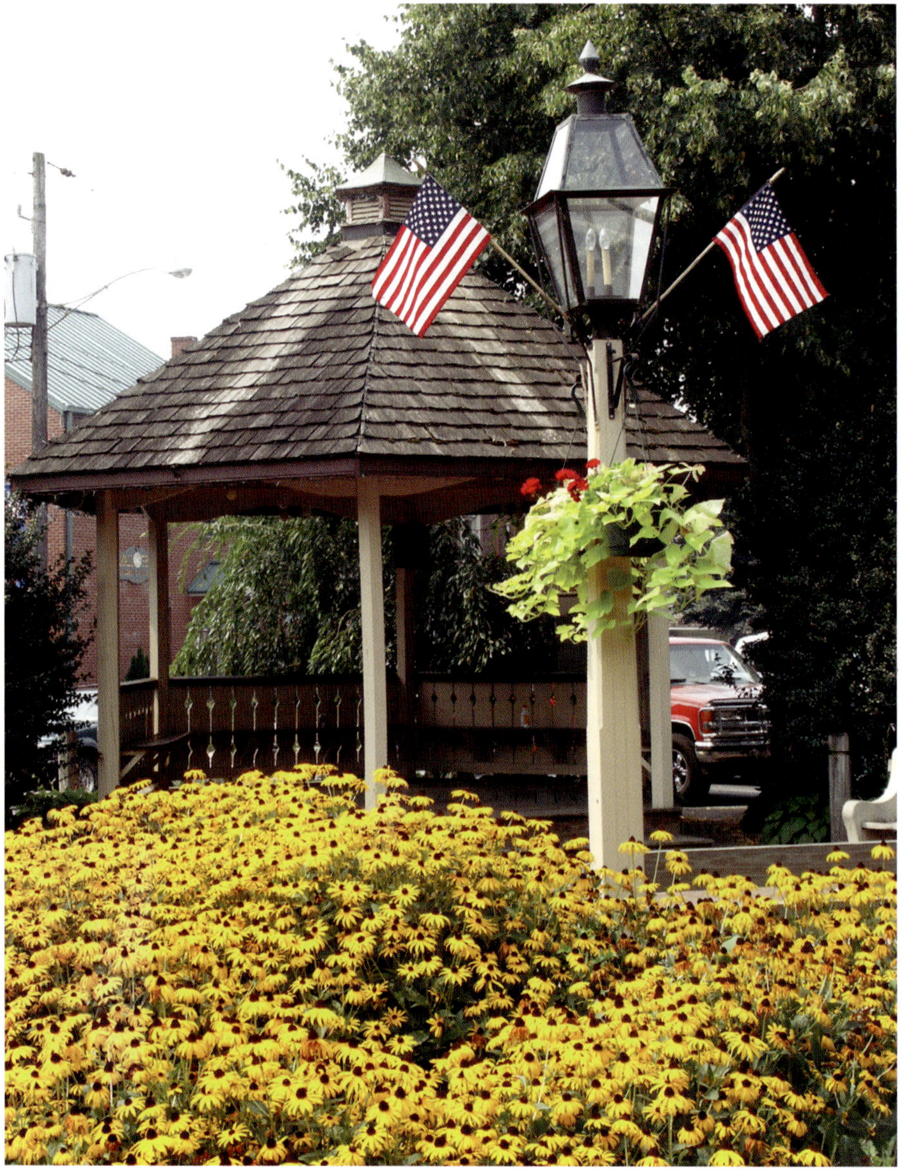

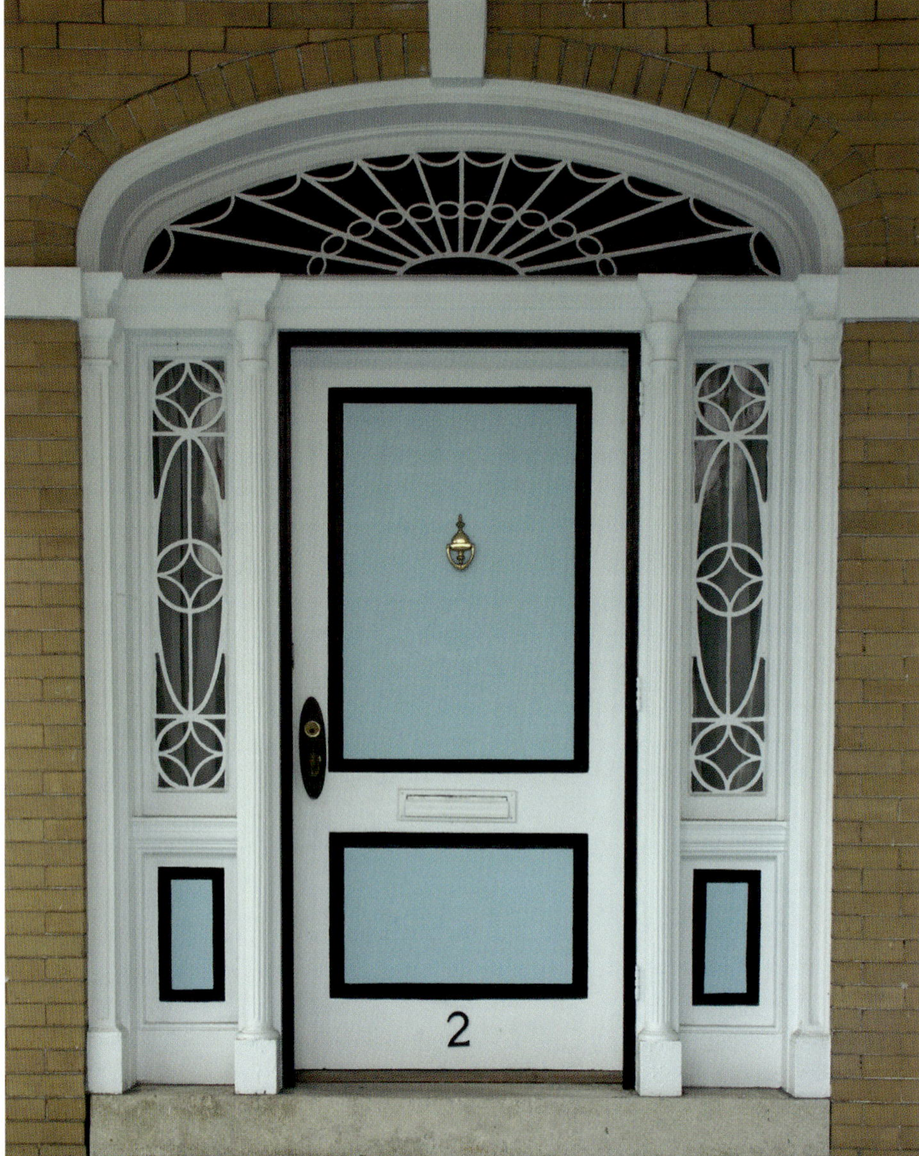

Manheim Borough was founded in 1762 by Henry William Stiegel, a German who arrived in the United States in 1750. Stiegel found success as a glassmaker and was active in the early development of the community. Today, much of the town is located within the Manheim Borough Historic District, listed on the National Register of Historic Places.

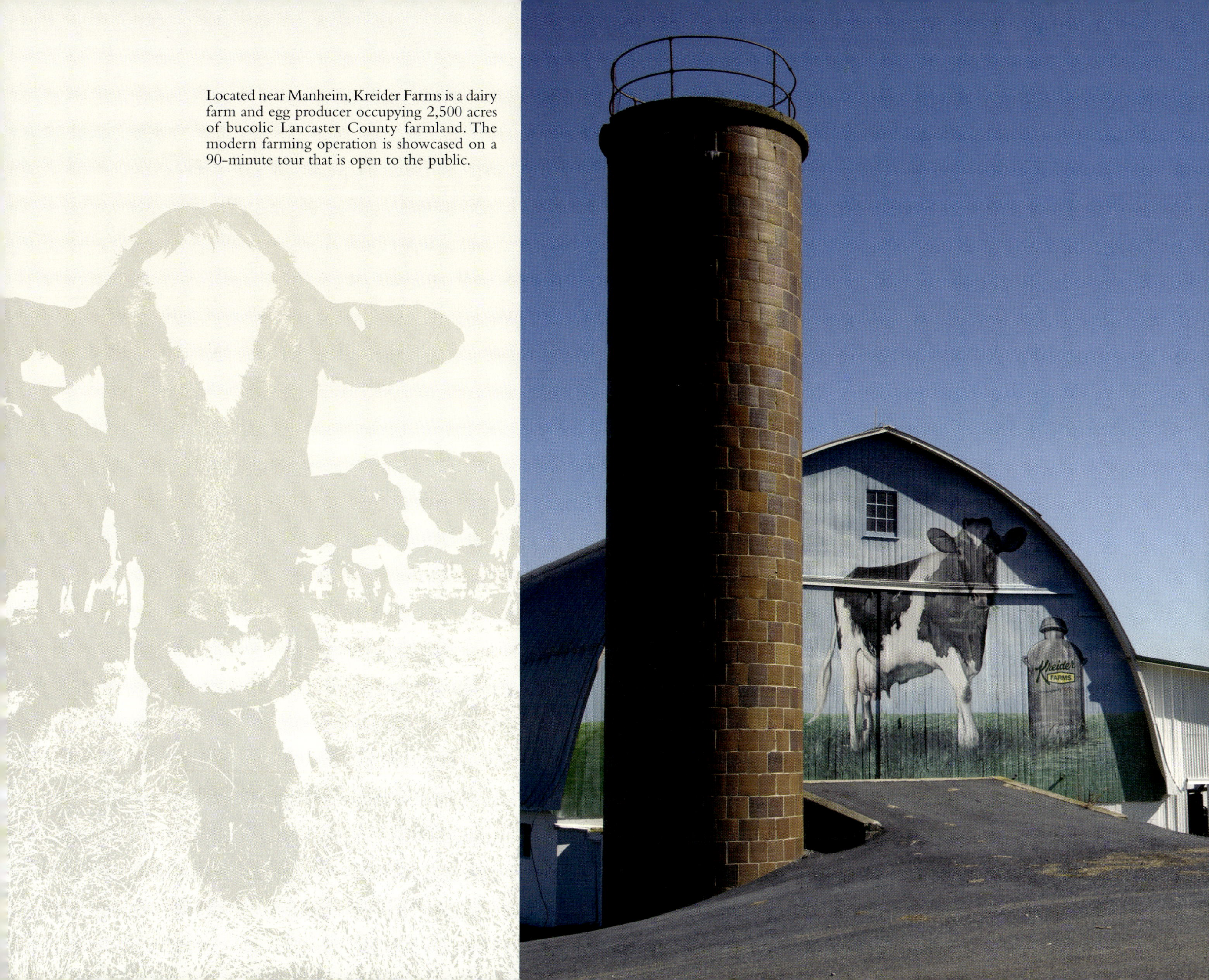

Located near Manheim, Kreider Farms is a dairy farm and egg producer occupying 2,500 acres of bucolic Lancaster County farmland. The modern farming operation is showcased on a 90-minute tour that is open to the public.

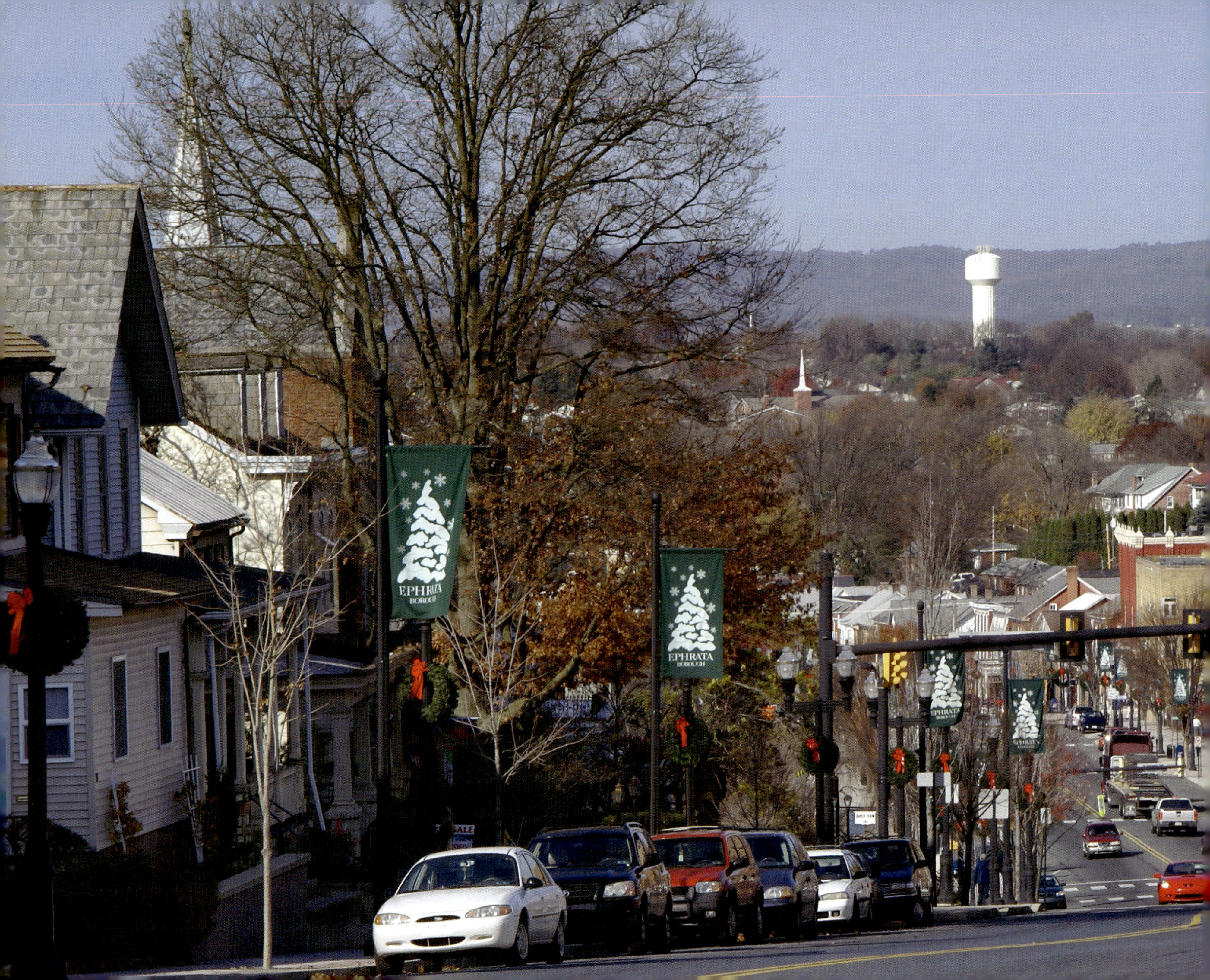
EPHRATA
BOROUGH
EPHRATA
BOROUGH

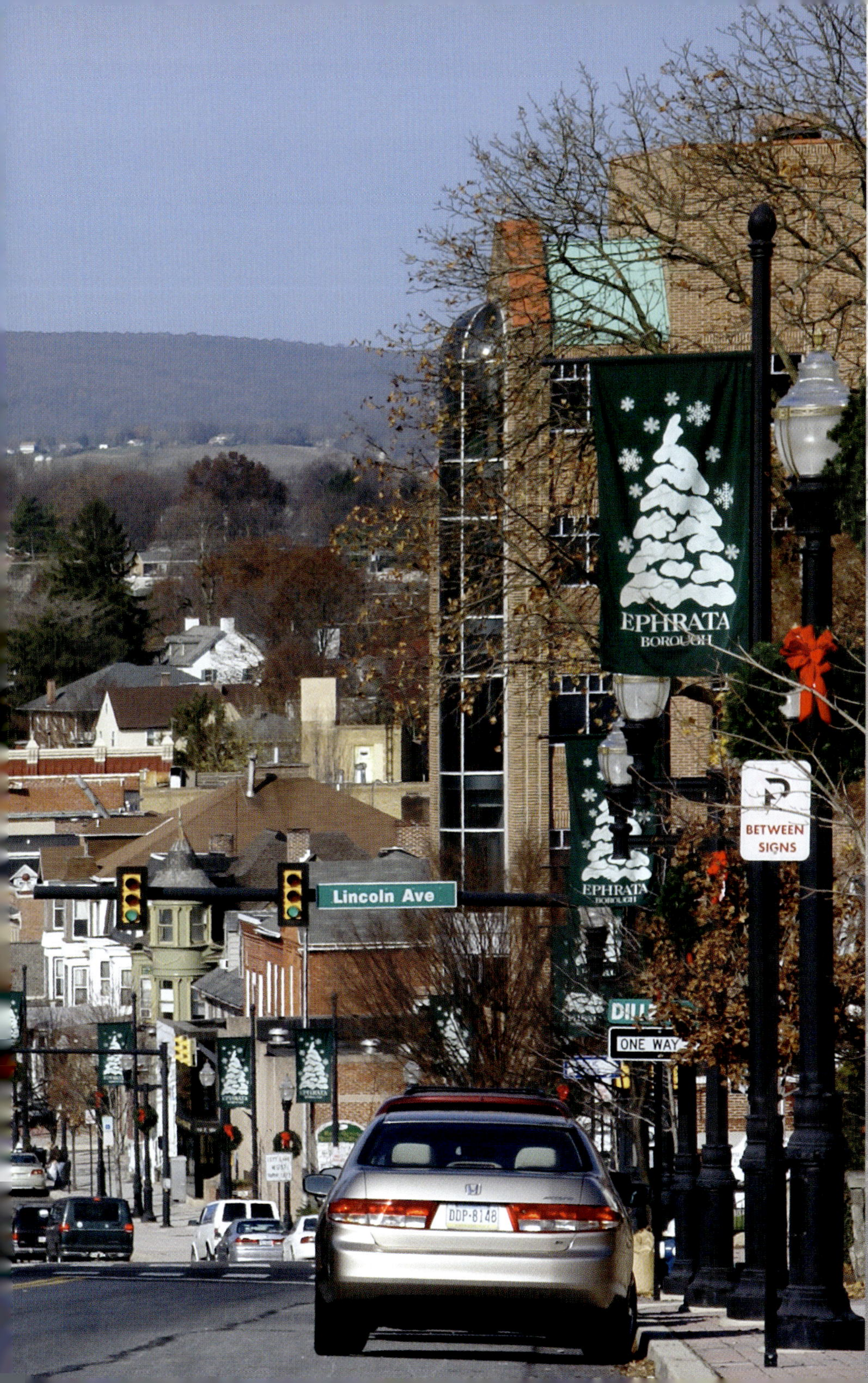

Ephrata

Named after Ephrath, a Biblical town in present-day Israel, Ephrata owes its beginnings to mystic Conrad Beissel, who founded the Ephrata Cloister. A nearby village sprang up and grew throughout the nineteenth century due to the presence of two resorts and a train station on the Reading & Columbia Railroad. Ephrata was incorporated as a borough in 1891. Today the town, which sits comfortably among the famous rolling hills of central Pennsylvania, has an alluring tree-lined streetscape with historic façades.

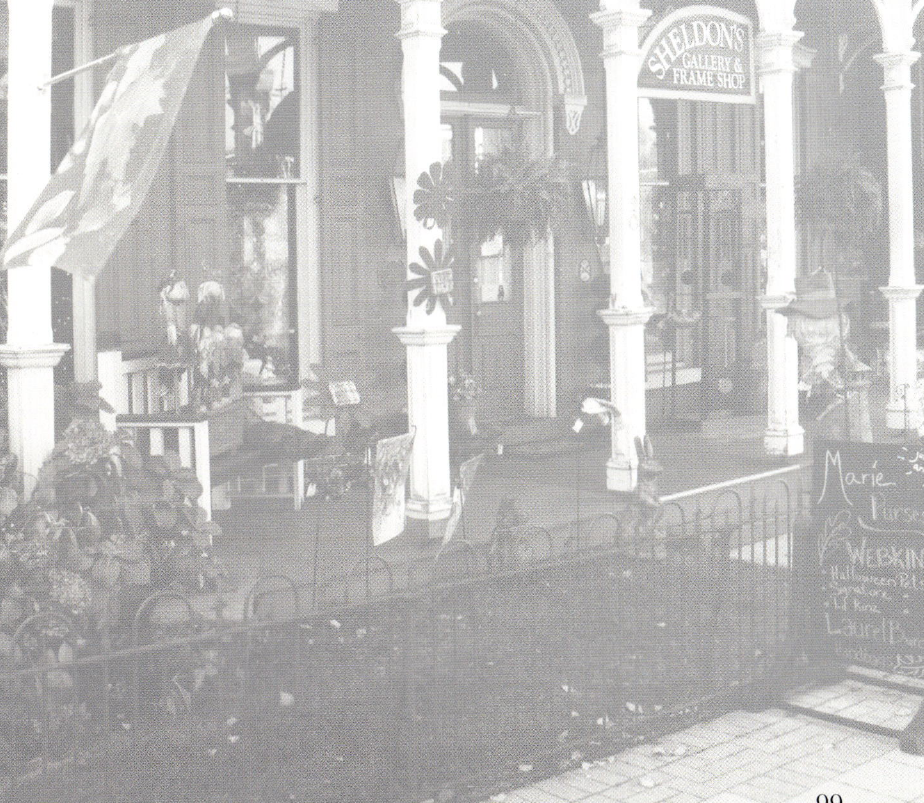

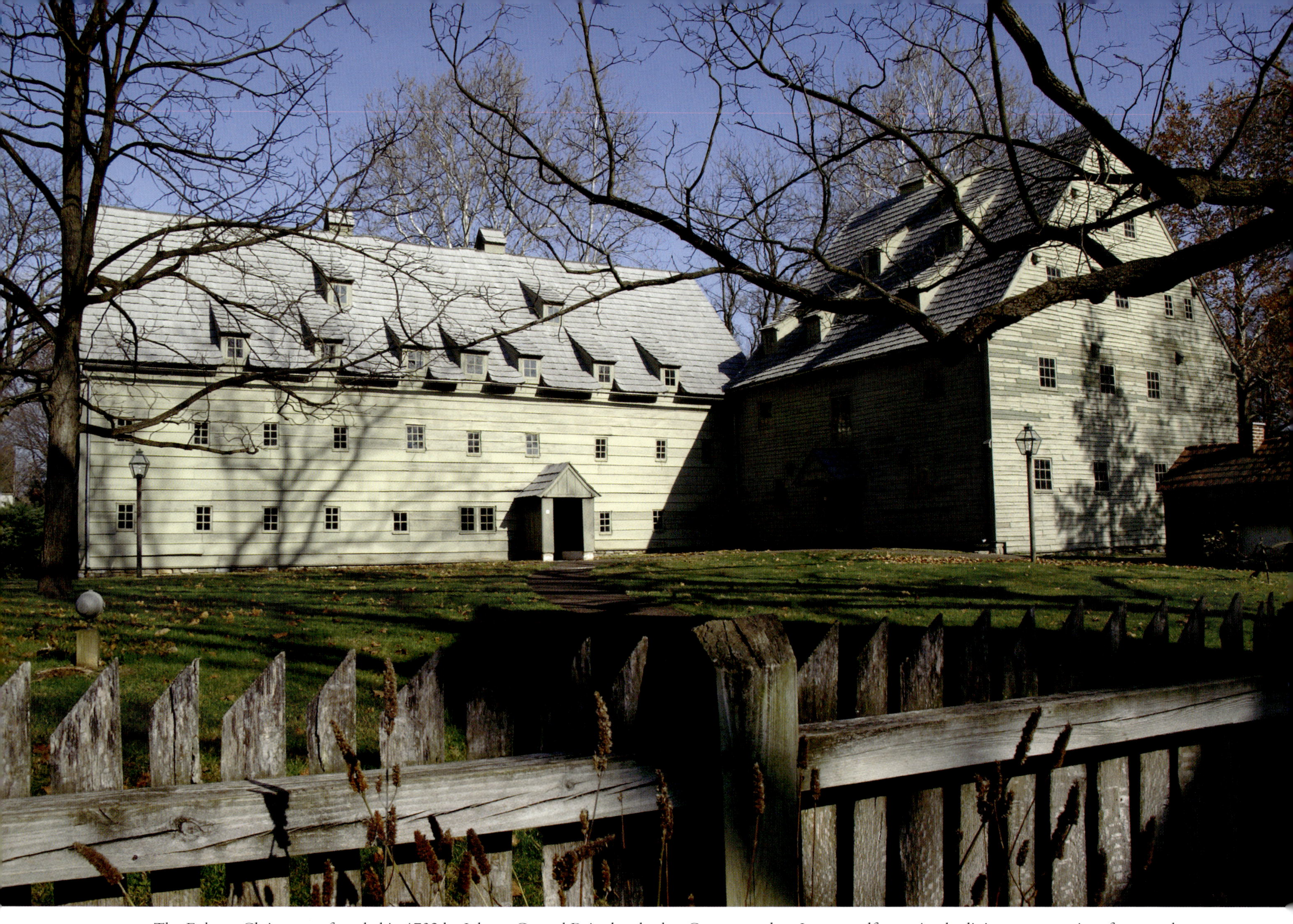

The Ephrata Cloister was founded in 1732 by Johann Conrad Beissel and other German settlers. It was a self-contained religious community of men and women—brothers and sisters who chose a life of celibacy and worshipped on Saturdays. Among the surviving buildings are the Saron, or Sisters' House, and adjacent Saal, or Meetinghouse. The Saron was built in 1743 while the Saal dates from 1741. The Ephrata Cloister was one of the earliest religious communities in America and is today a National Historic Landmark. *Ephrata Cloister, Pennsylvania Historical and Museum Commission, Ephrata, PA.*

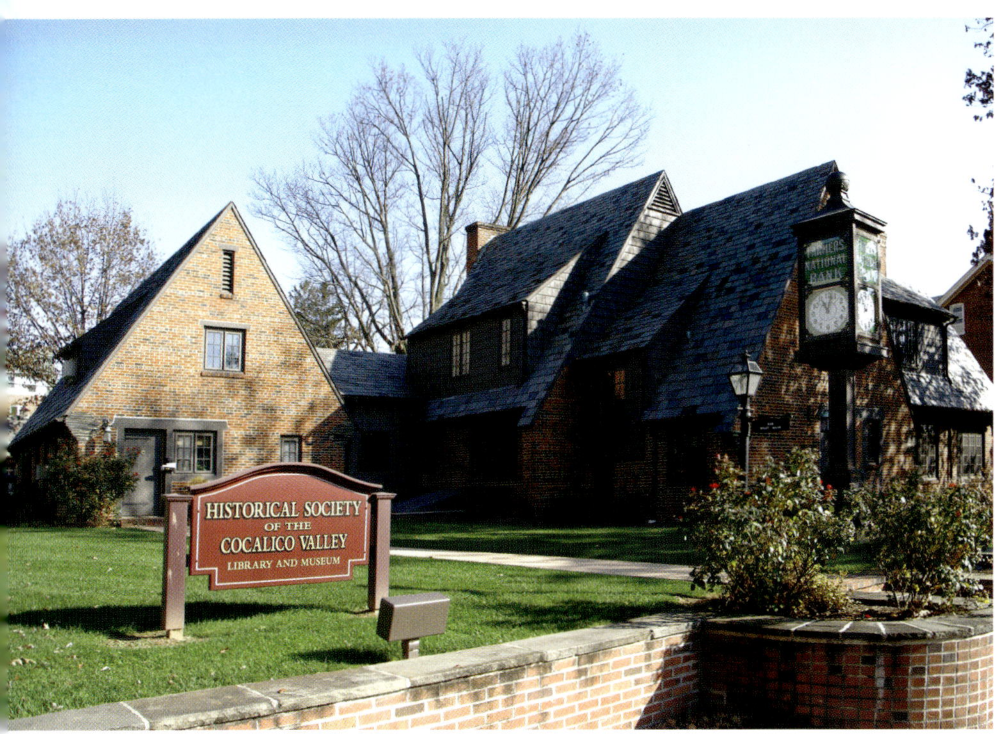

Property administered by the Historical Society of the Cocalico Valley includes the historic Moore Connell Mansion, as well as a library, archives, and museum. The Connell Mansion was built in 1868 and designed in the Italianate style.

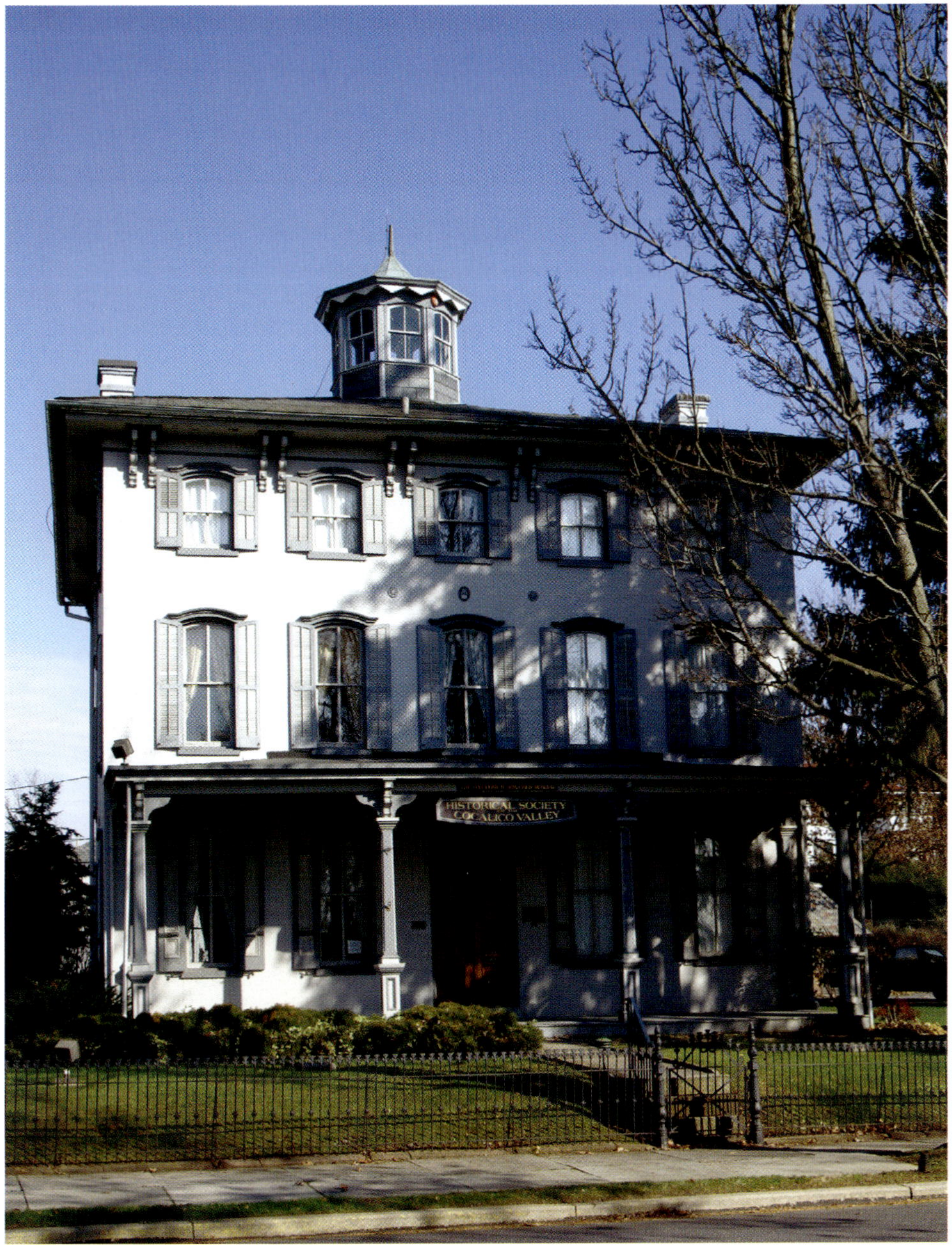

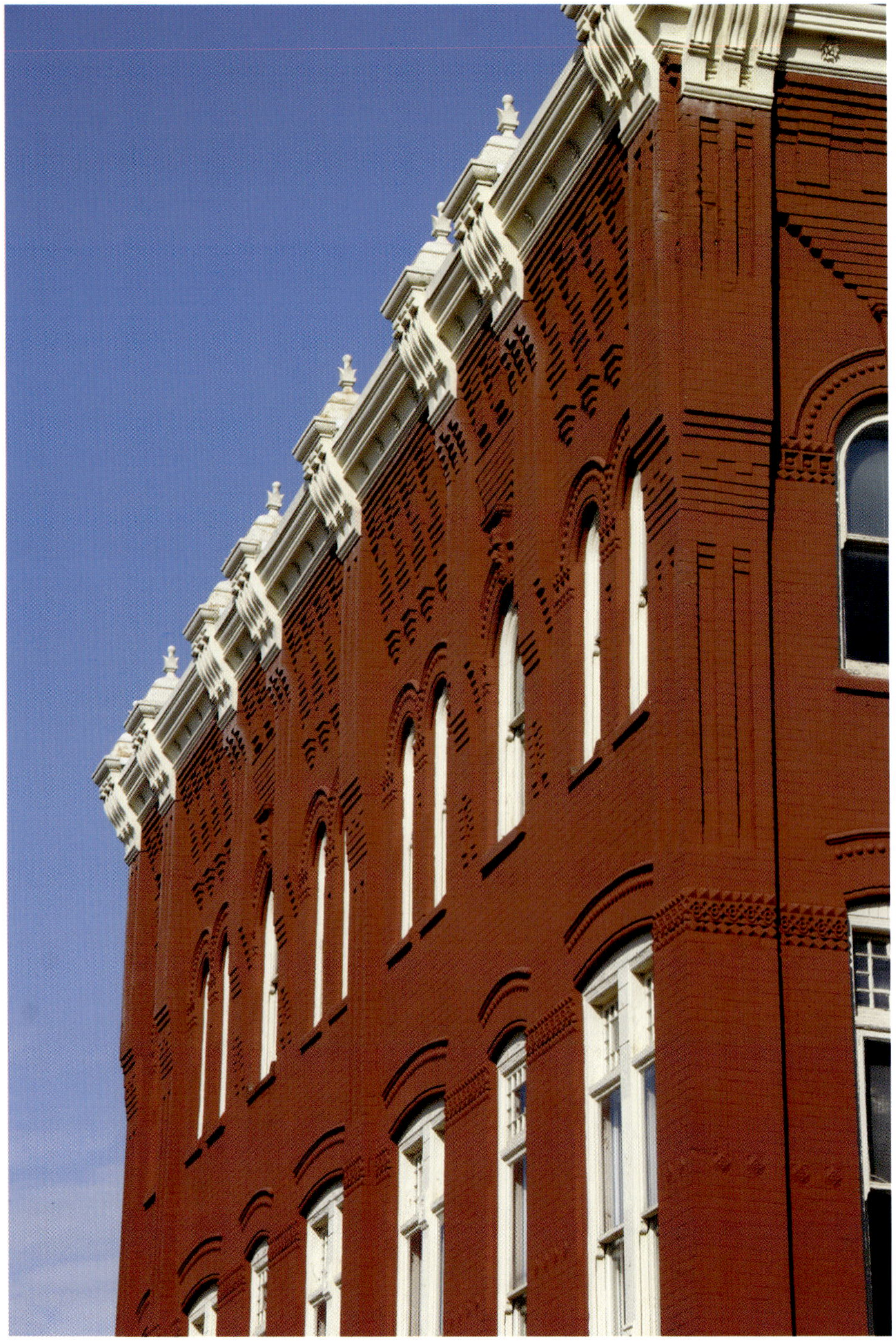

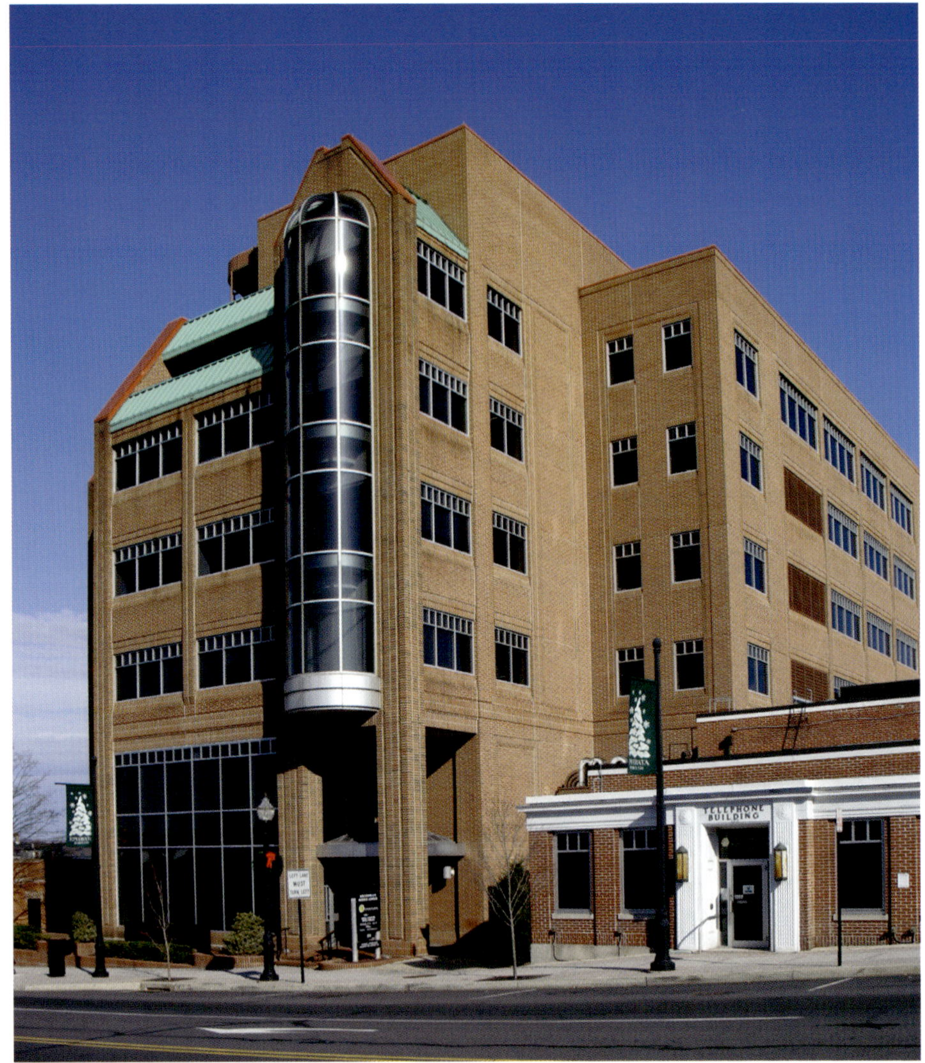

The Brossman Business Complex is named for Mr. and Mrs. William Brossman and Bertha Brossman Blair. William Brossman was founder of the Denver & Ephrata Telephone Company. The modern office complex was constructed on the site of the Art Deco-style Main Theatre.

Designed by Lancaster architect Clifton Evans, the Mentzer Building was constructed in 1889 by Allen Mentzer, a local merchant. The architecture is Italianate in style and features corbelled brickwork and a cornice topped with a series of decorative finials.

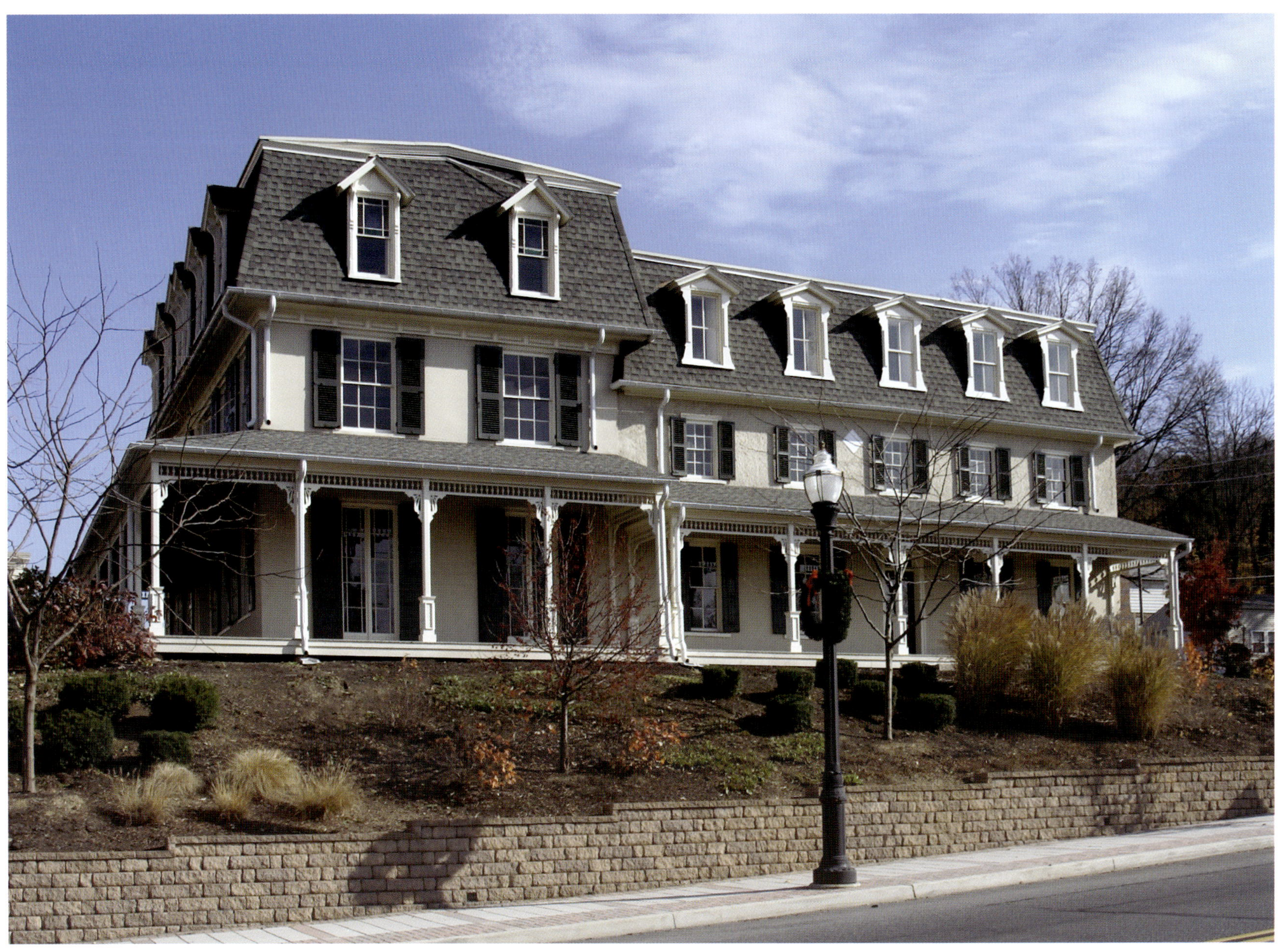

In 1848, Pennsylvania Senator Joseph Konigmacher built the Konigmacher Mansion as a summer resort. Over the next decade, the resort grew into a 400-room hotel that entertained such notable figures as Presidents Abraham Lincoln, Ulysses Grant, and James Buchanan. In the twentieth century, it briefly served as a hospital. After falling into a state of disrepair, much of the property was demolished in 2004. A portion of the main building, however, was restored in 2005.

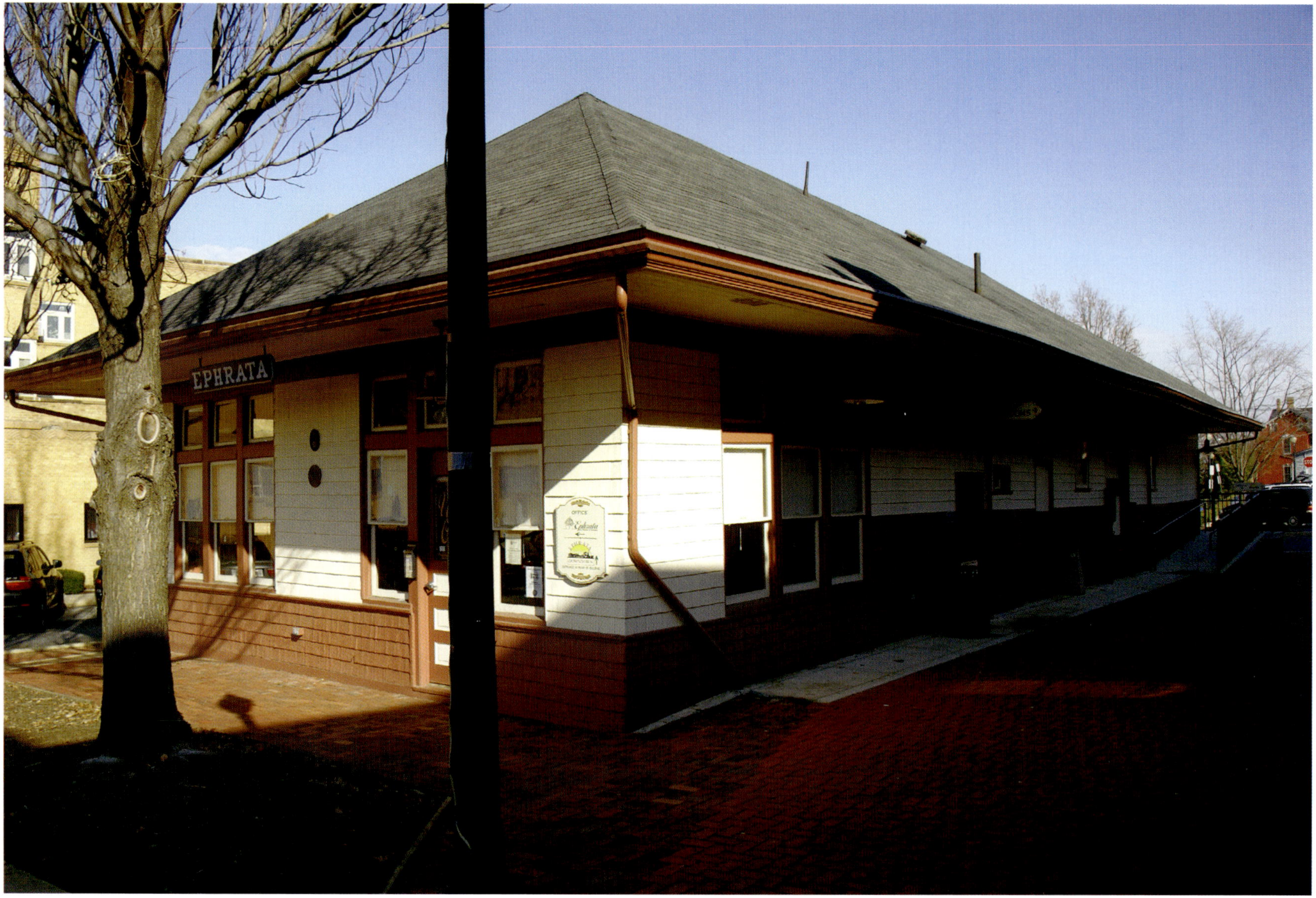

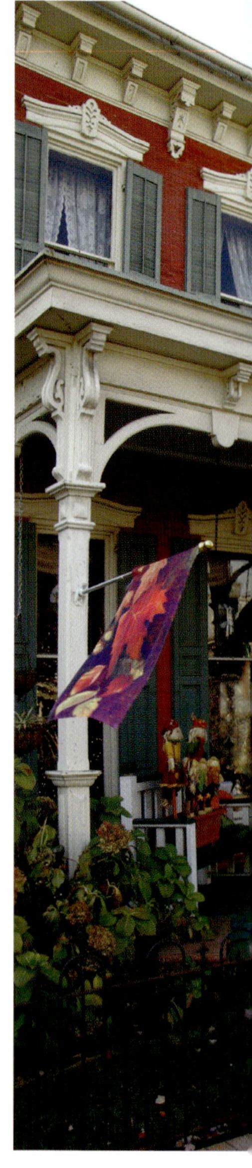

This train station was constructed in 1889 for use by the Reading and Columbia Railroad. Today the building is occupied by the Ephrata Chamber of Commerce and Downtown Ephrata, Inc. and serves as the Ephrata visitor's center.

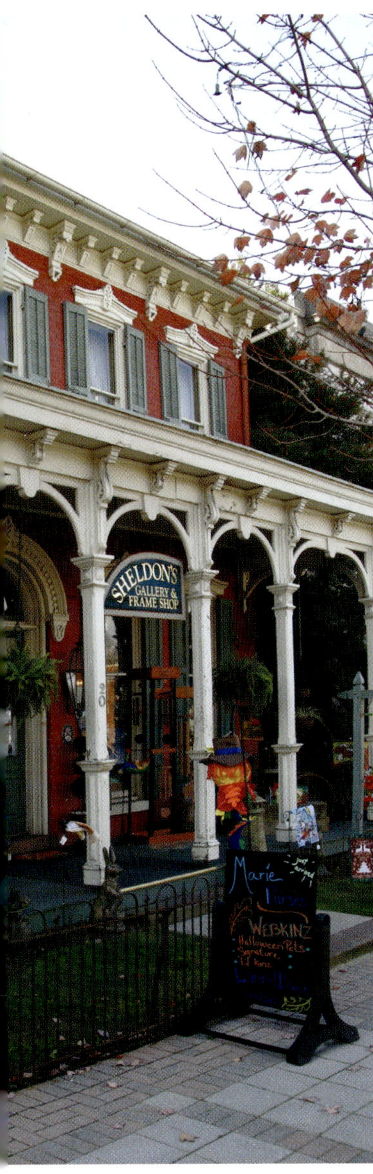

is attractive Italianate home on West ain Street was constructed for Andrew ker and now houses Sheldon's Gallery d Frame Shop.

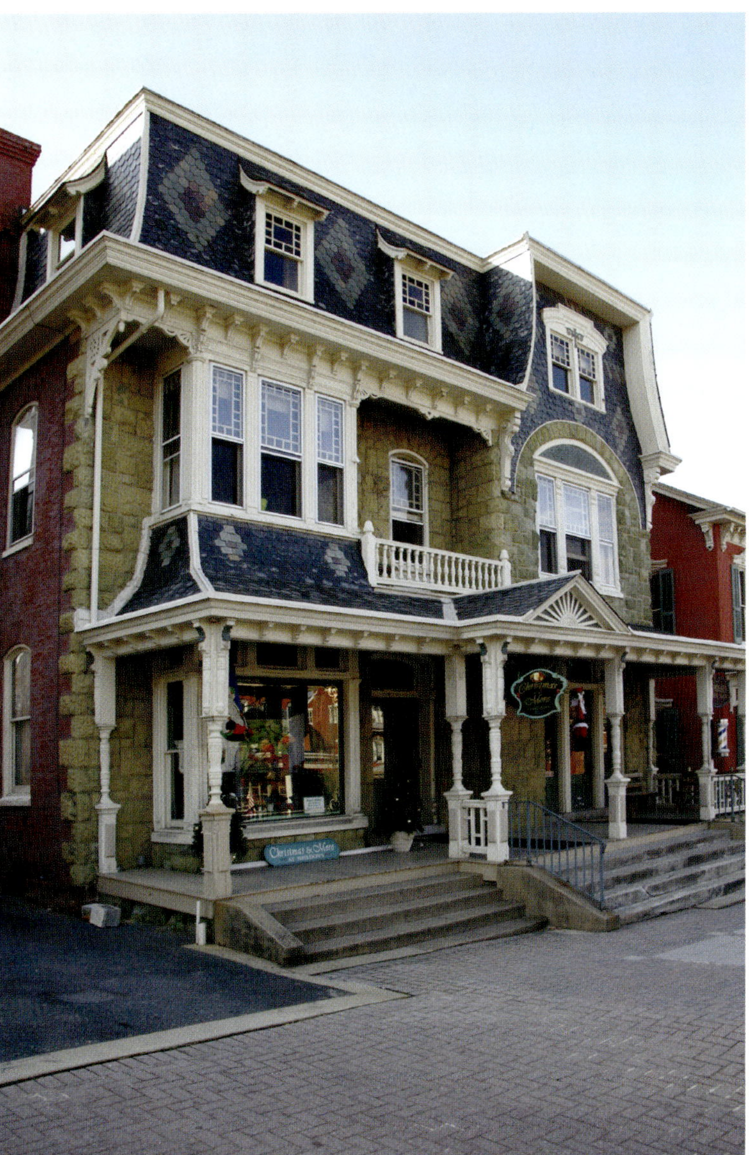

Known historically as the Baker-Groff Building, this Second Empire-style building was built in 1891 by Andrew Baker.

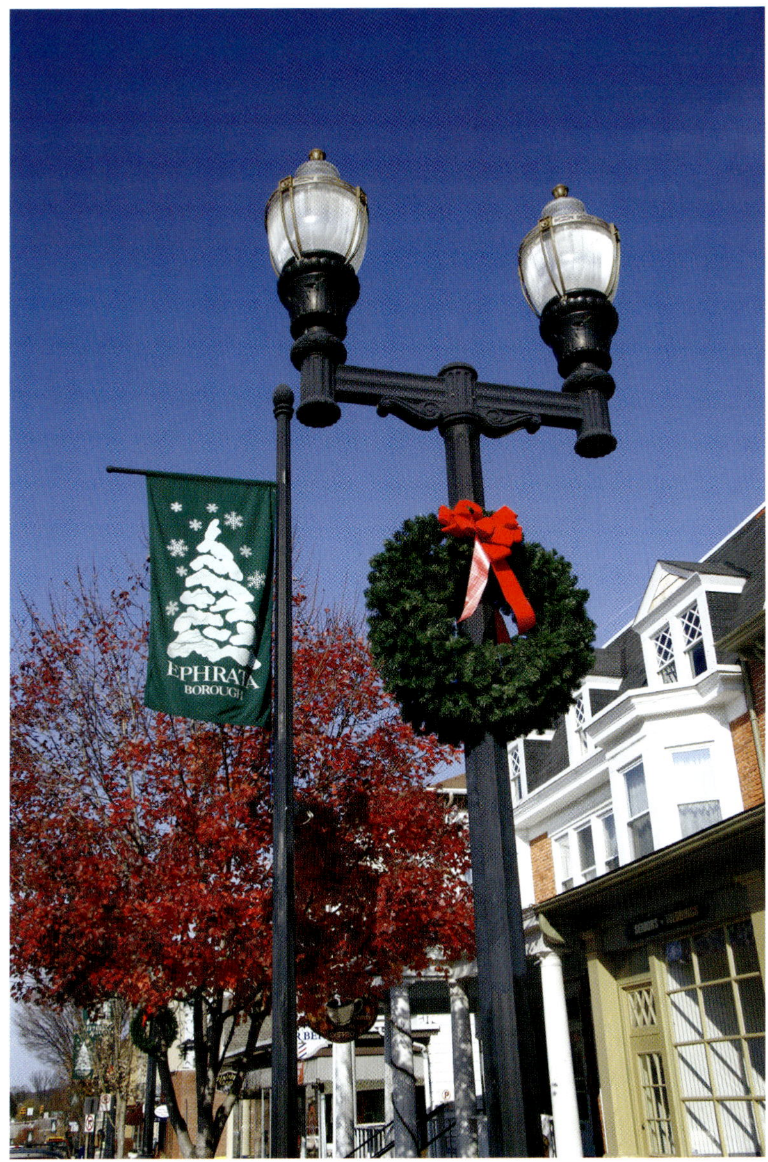

As the seasons change, orange and red foliage give way to green and red holiday decorations along Ephrata's Main Street.

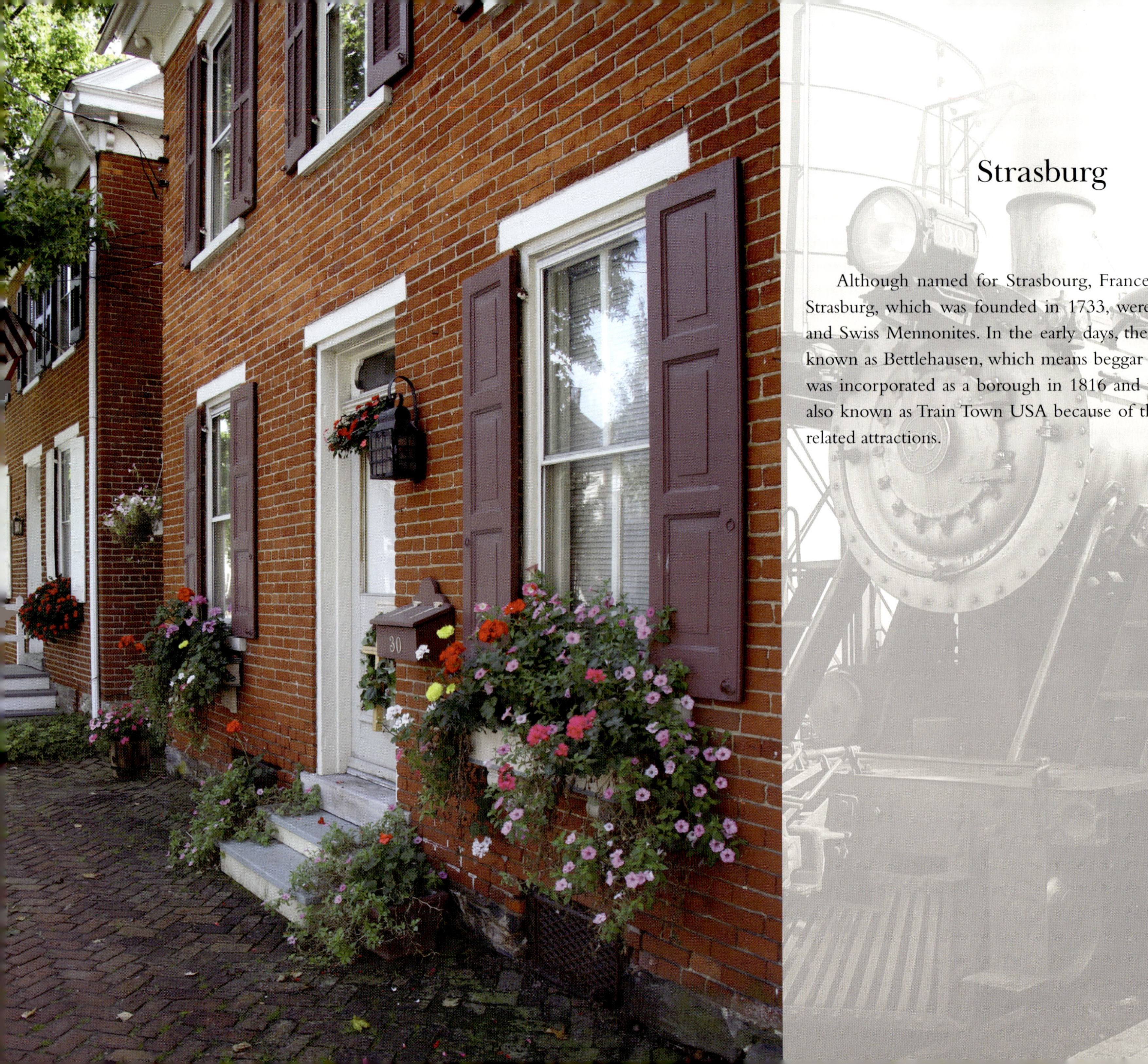

Strasburg

Although named for Strasbourg, France, early settlers of Strasburg, which was founded in 1733, were mainly German and Swiss Mennonites. In the early days, the small village was known as Bettlehausen, which means beggar houses. The town was incorporated as a borough in 1816 and today Strasburg is also known as Train Town USA because of the many railroad-related attractions.

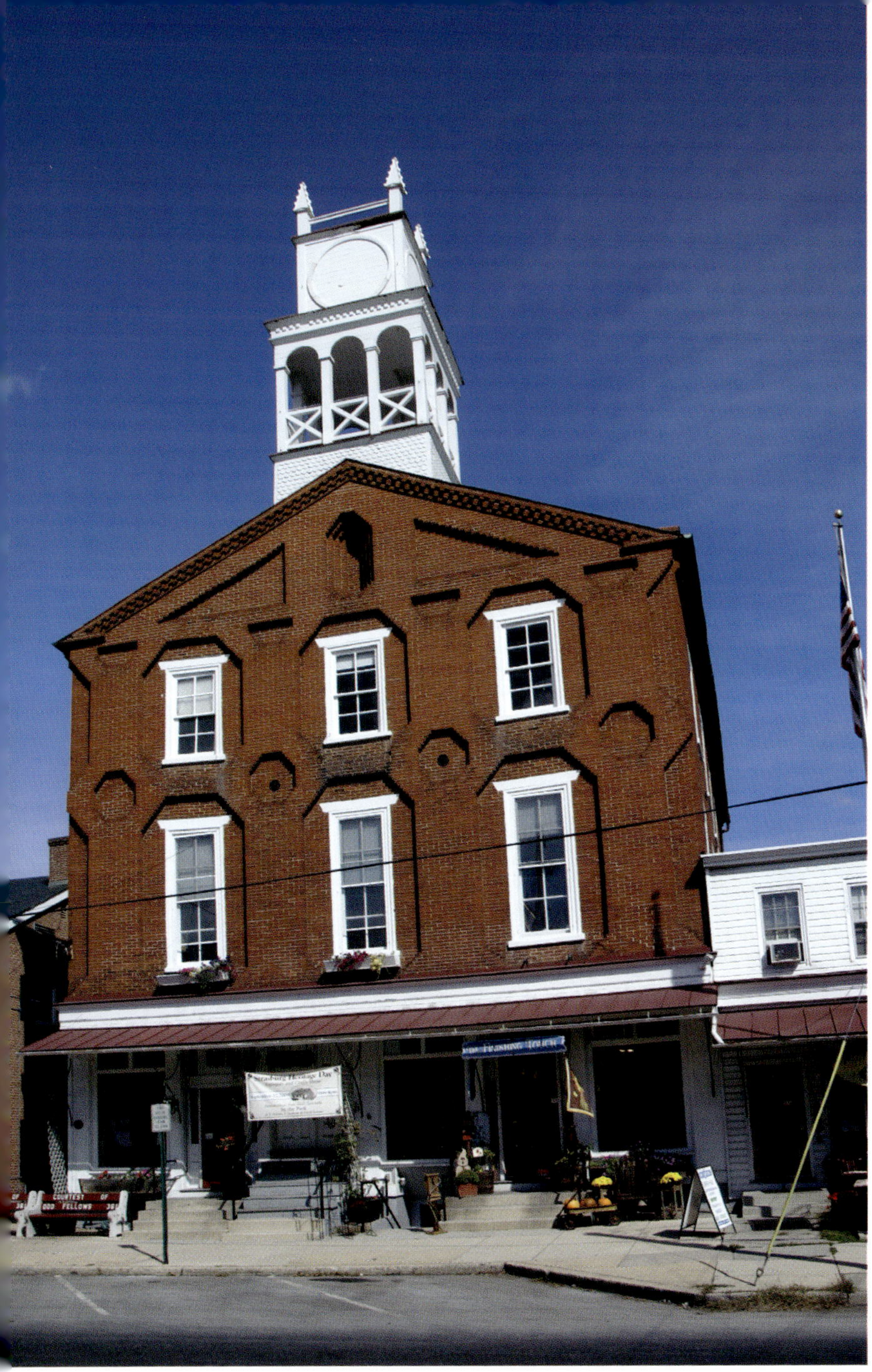

This large building in Strasburg's Center Square spent much of its life as a community center for the borough. Constructed in 1856, the brick building, known as Massasoit Hall, also housed an auditorium and stage on the second floor. Massasoit was a Wampanoag Indian Chief who maintained peaceful relations with the English settlers of Plymouth, Massachusetts.

The oldest documented building in Strasburg Borough is the Jacob Pfoutz (or Fouts) house, which was built around 1754. The building is constructed of red sandstone and rubble stone and exhibits a number of German colonial features, including a central chimney.

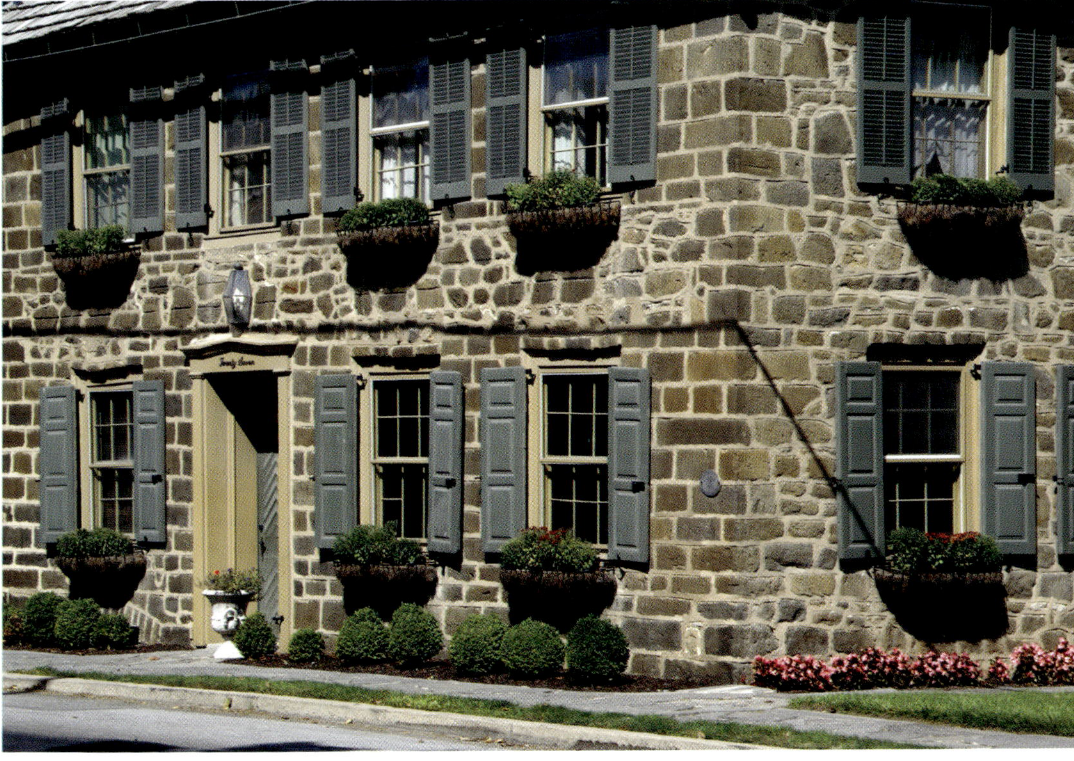

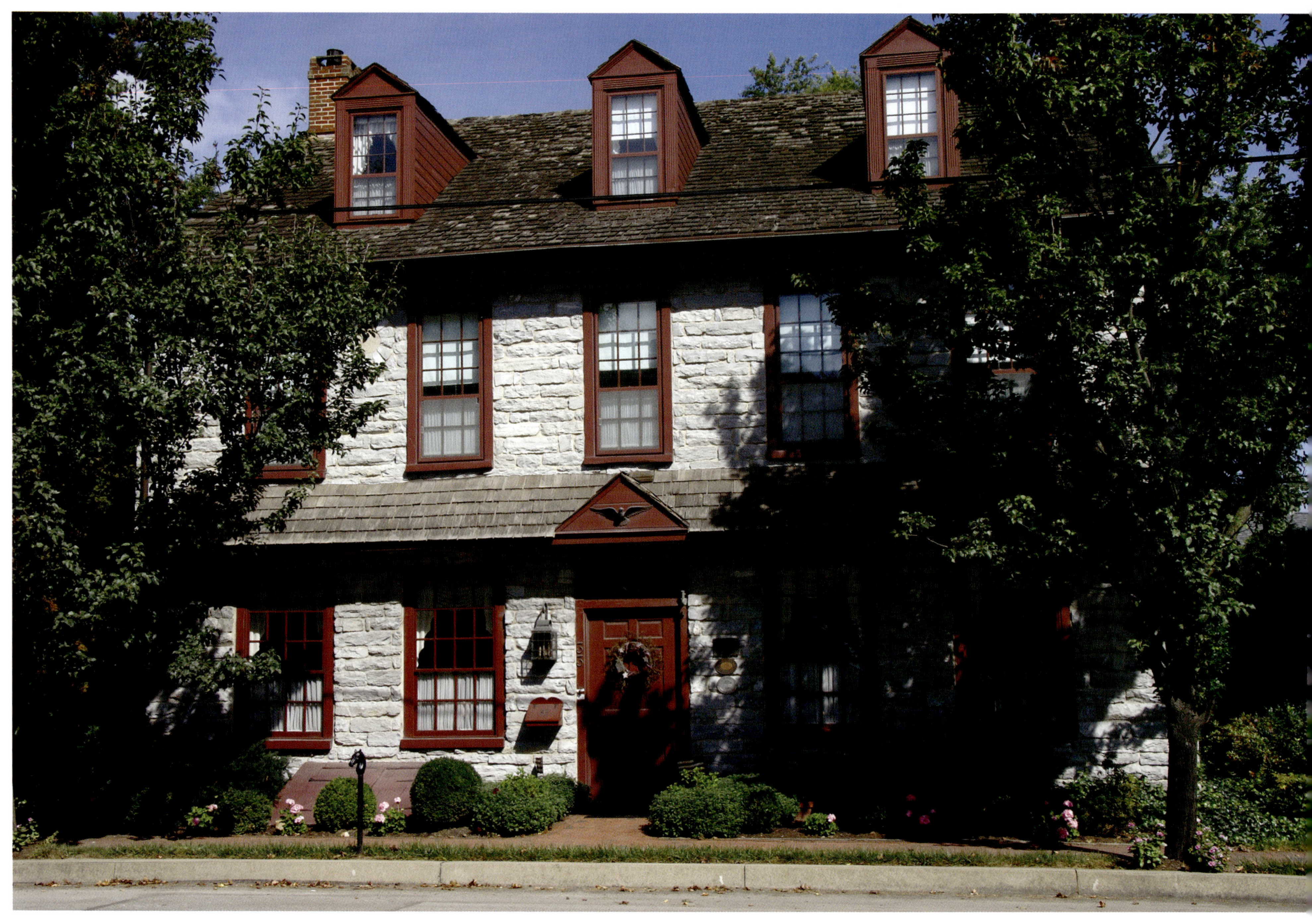

In 1786, Jacob Pfoutz constructed this building for his son, Martin, who operated a store here. James Whitehall, the first chief burgess of Strasburg, also lived here. In 1839, the Georgian house became part of the Strasburg Academy. Today the building is home to the Limestone Inn Bed & Breakfast.

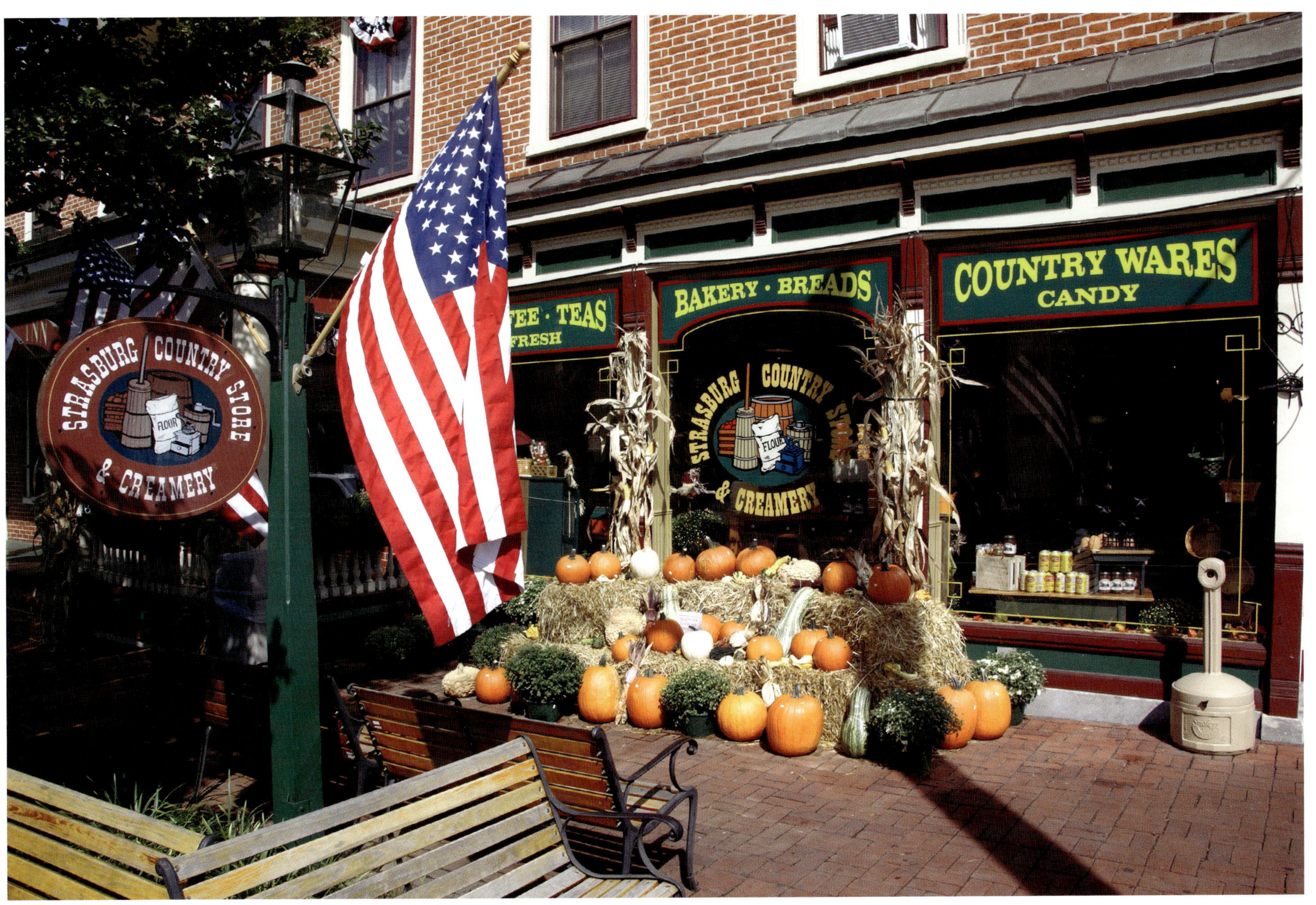

Originally known as the Thomas Crawford Tavern, this building on the northwest corner of Center Square was constructed in the early nineteenth century and throughout its life housed the Strasburg Borough Council, a post office, and a general store. Now it's home to the Strasburg Country Store & Creamery.

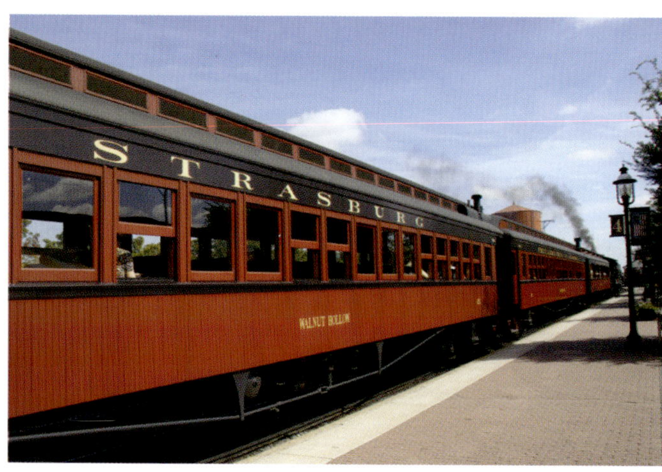

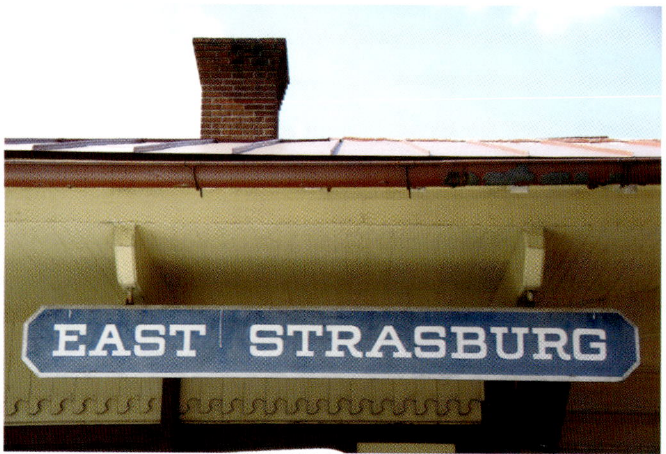

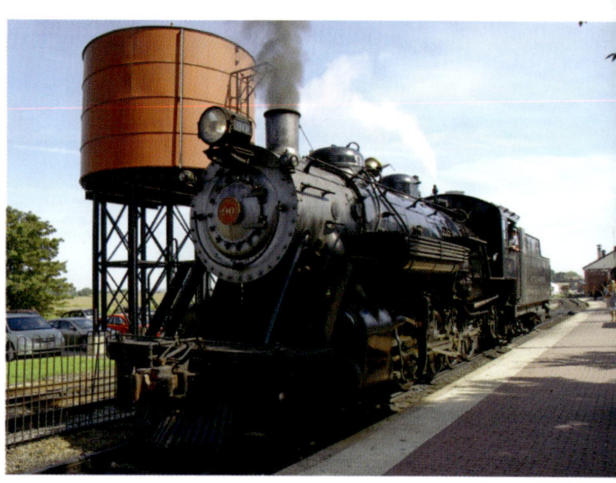

Recognized as America's oldest short-line railroad, the Strasburg Railroad dates from 1832 and today offers visitors the opportunity to ride in authentically restored cars pulled by a coal-burning locomotive.

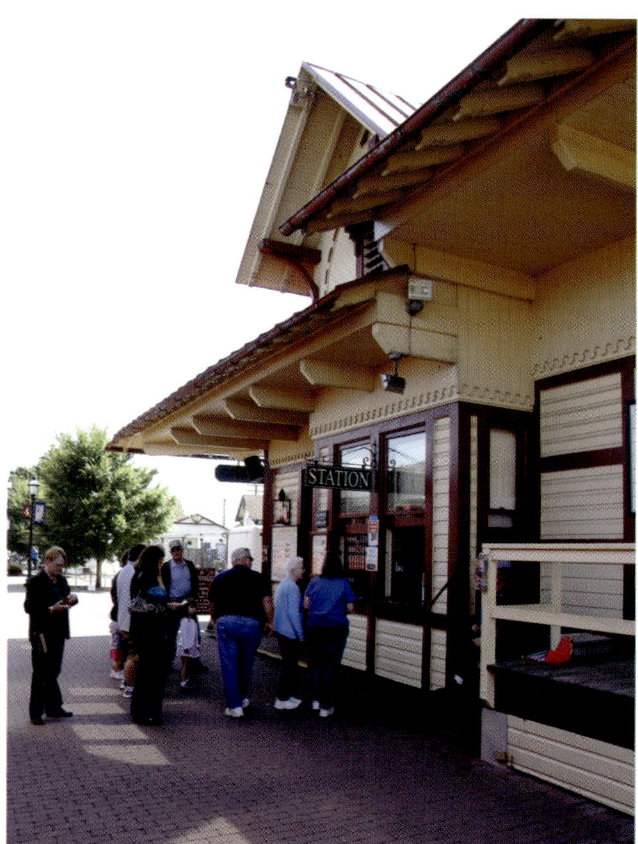

Visitors to the Strasburg Railroad can experience the 1915 East Strasburg Station, browse a number of specialty shops, visit the switch tower, and take a behind-the-scenes tour of the mechanical shop.

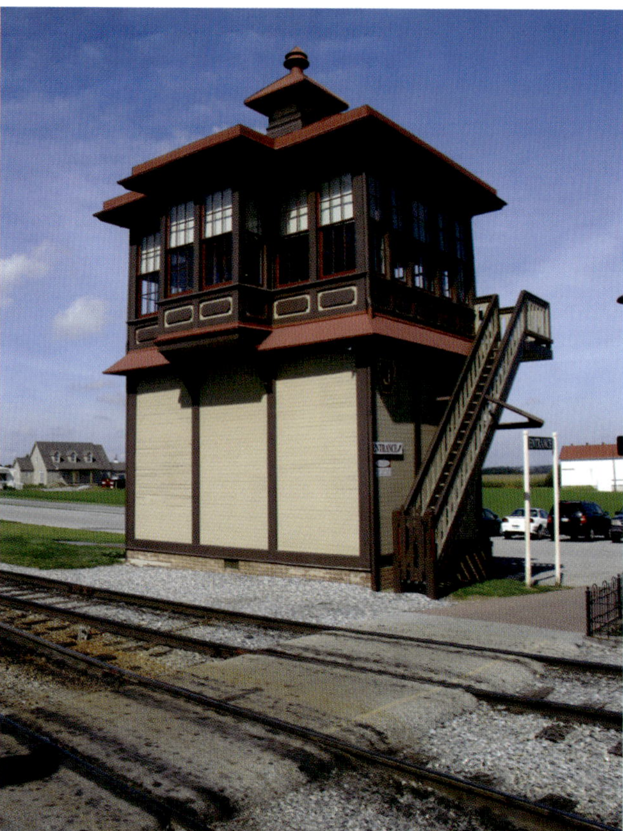

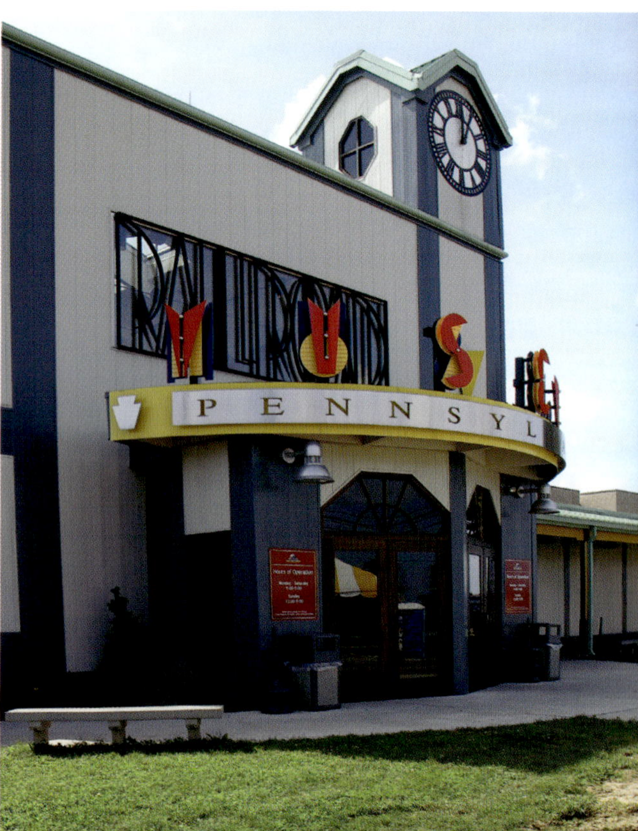

Located outside of Strasburg Borough, the Railroad Museum Pennsylvania is a popular destination for railroad enthusiasts. T museum features more than 100 locomotives and cars from th mid-nineteenth through twentieth centuries.

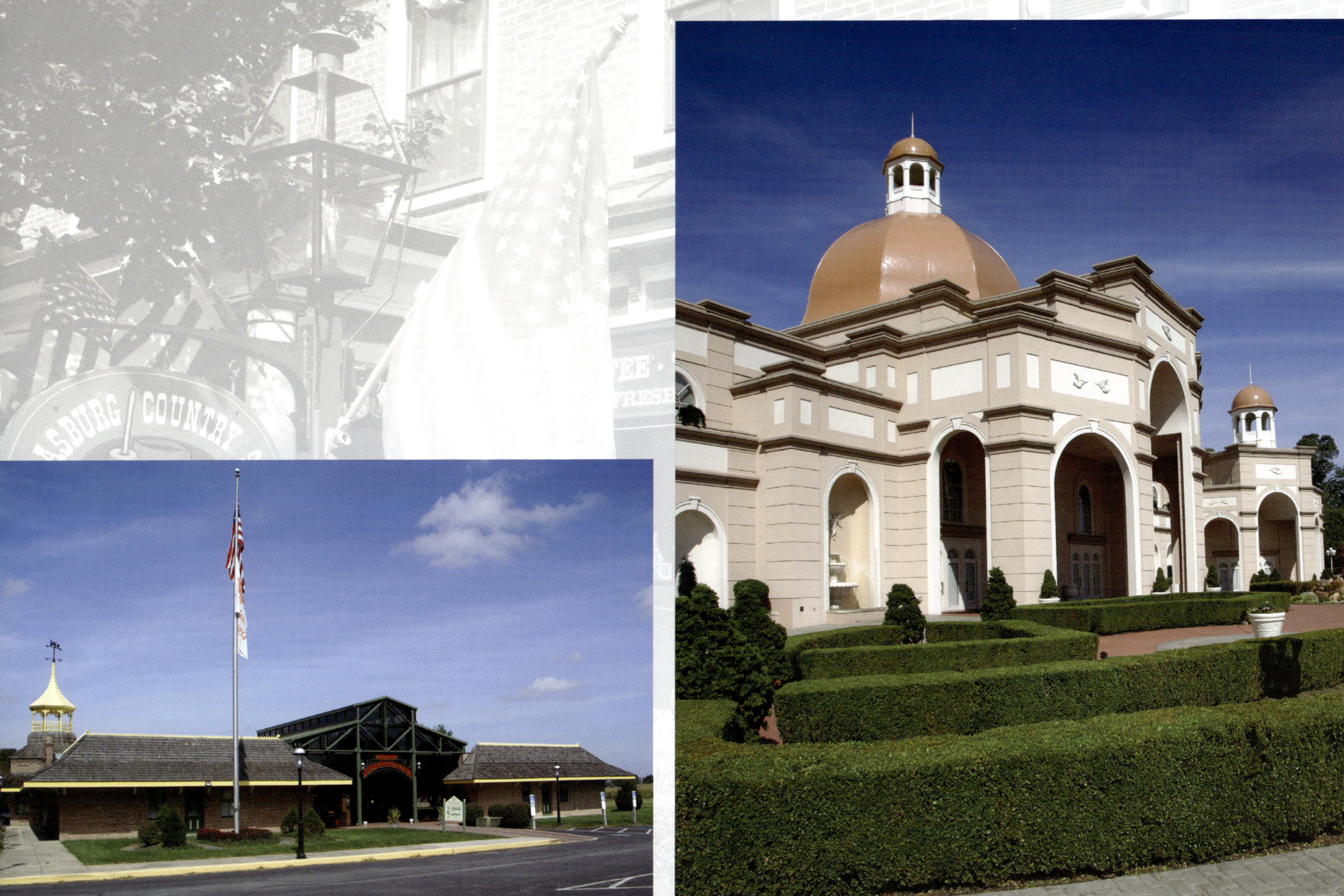

The National Toy Train Museum features one of the most extensive toy train collections in the world. Five large train track layouts showcase different gauges from the large "G" to tiny "Z".

With over 2,000 seats and a 300-foot stage, the Sight & Sound Theatre provides Christian and Biblical-themed entertainment at its Millennium Theatre. The venue opened in 1998 after a devastating fire destroyed an earlier theater.

Columbia

Located at the intersection of the Lincoln Highway and Susquehanna River, the Borough of Columbia has played an important role in transportation for several centuries. In 1730, an English Quaker named John Wright established a ferry that provided access to the western frontier on the opposite side of the Susquehanna River. Wright's grandson, Samuel Wright, laid out a town in 1788 and named it Columbia in honor of Christopher Columbus. In 1814, a covered bridge over a mile in length was constructed over the Susquehanna River, connecting Columbia and Wrightsville. By 1833 the Pennsylvania Canal was operating, creating a canal system that started in Columbia and connected with the Juniata River forty miles to the north. The Susquehanna and Tidewater Canal opened in 1840 on the west side of the river, and a towpath was established on the bridge. Horses and mules walking on the bridge would pull the canal boats, which were then able to travel south to Baltimore and the Chesapeake and Delaware Canal system. During the Civil War, a Confederate advance eastward was thwarted with the burning of the Columbia-Wrightsville Bridge. General John B. Gordon's Georgians didn't reach Lancaster County, and instead concentrated two days later with the Confederate Army near a little town known as Gettysburg. In 1913, Columbia's transportation legacy was enhanced when the borough became a stop on the Lincoln Highway, the nation's first coast-to-coast highway.

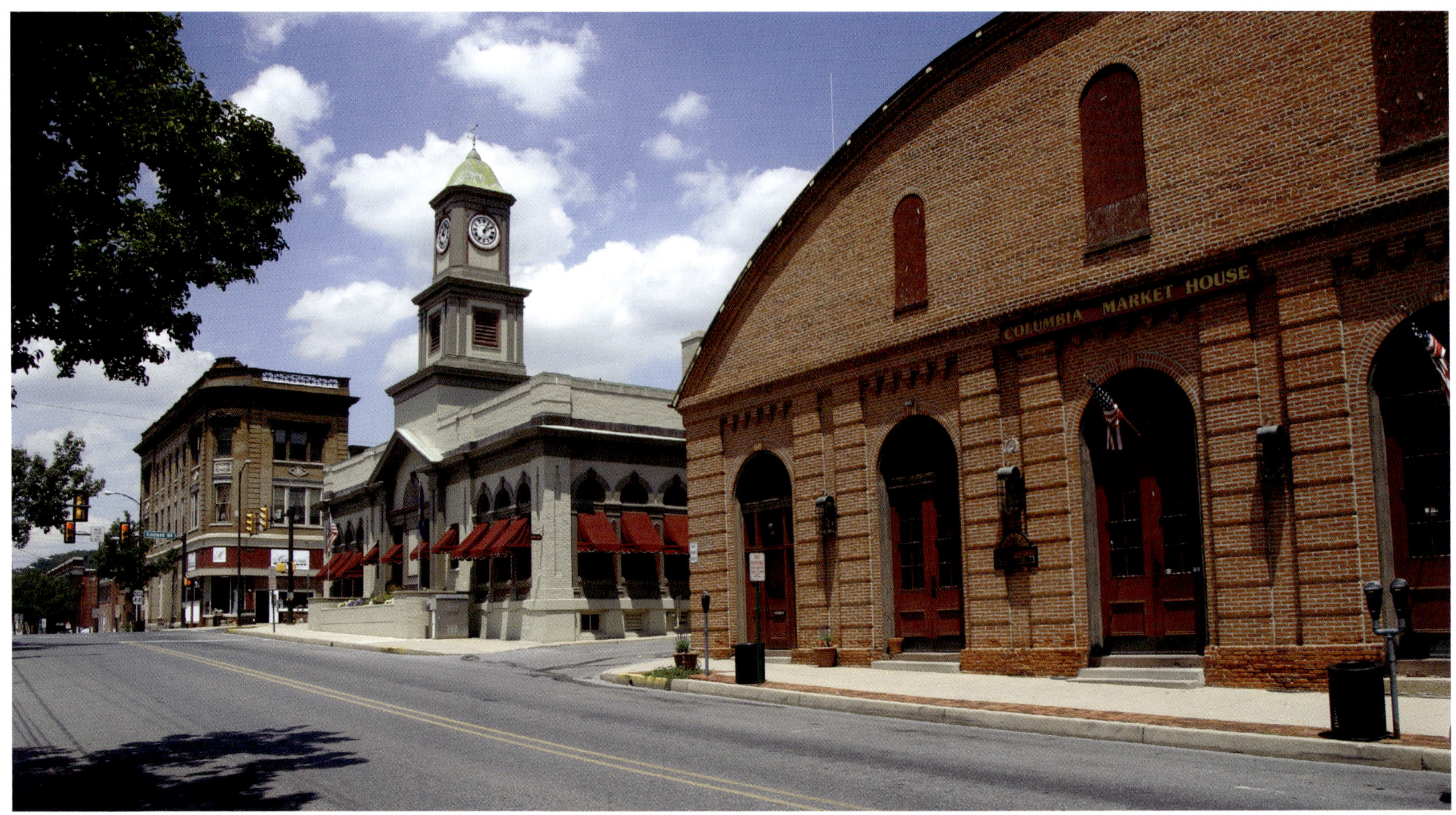

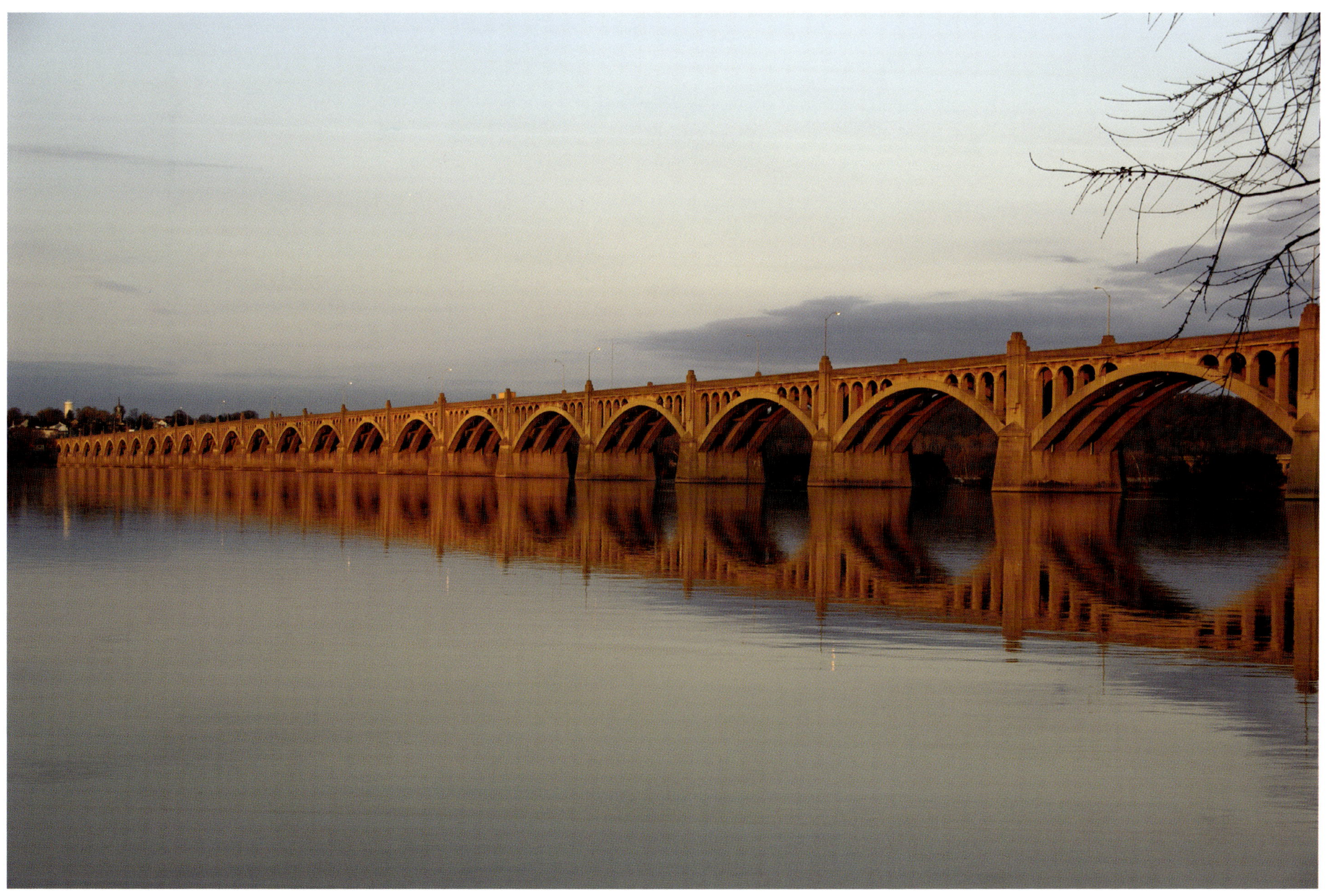

The Columbia-Wrightsville Bridge, or Veterans Memorial Bridge, is a Historic Civil Engineering Landmark and listed on the National Register of Historic Places. Designed by James B. Long, the bridge was built from 1929 to 1930 for $2.5 million. The mile-long arched bridge is actually the fifth bridge to span the Susquehanna River at this location. The first and second bridges were covered and completed in 1814 and 1834, respectively. The second bridge was destroyed during the Civil War to prevent a Confederate advance into Lancaster County, which could have resulted in an attack on Philadelphia or Harrisburg. The third bridge was completed in 1868 and destroyed by a hurricane twenty-eight years later. The fourth bridge, constructed of iron and steel, opened in 1897. When the Lincoln Highway was completed, traffic on the bridge greatly increased, necessitating the larger Columbia-Wrightsville Bridge that exists today. The piers that supported the earlier bridges are still visible.

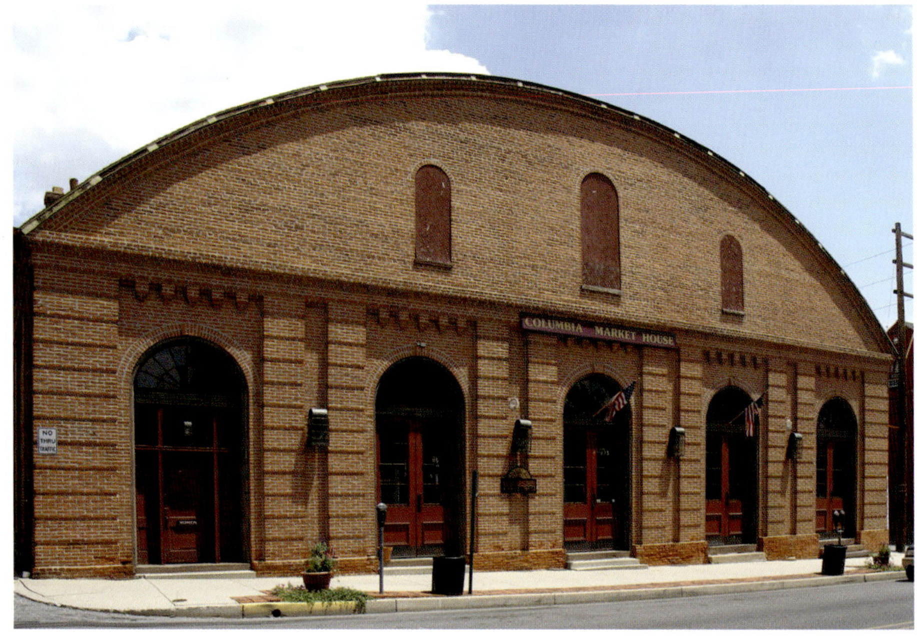

This historic market house on 3rd Street was constructed in 1869 for $20,000. Today it hosts a farmers' market on Thursdays and Fridays.

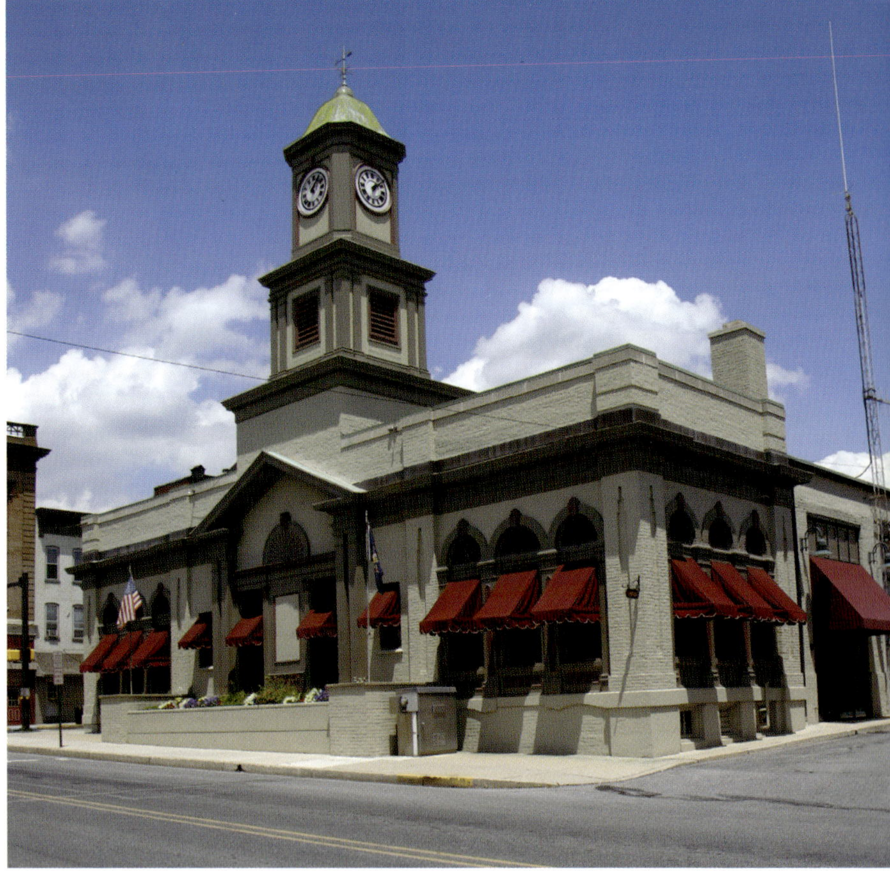

In 1875 a new building opened in the Borough. Topped with a 140-foot tower, it served as town hall, opera house, and office building. The building was destroyed by fire in the mid-twentieth century and replaced with this building, which still houses the Borough offices.

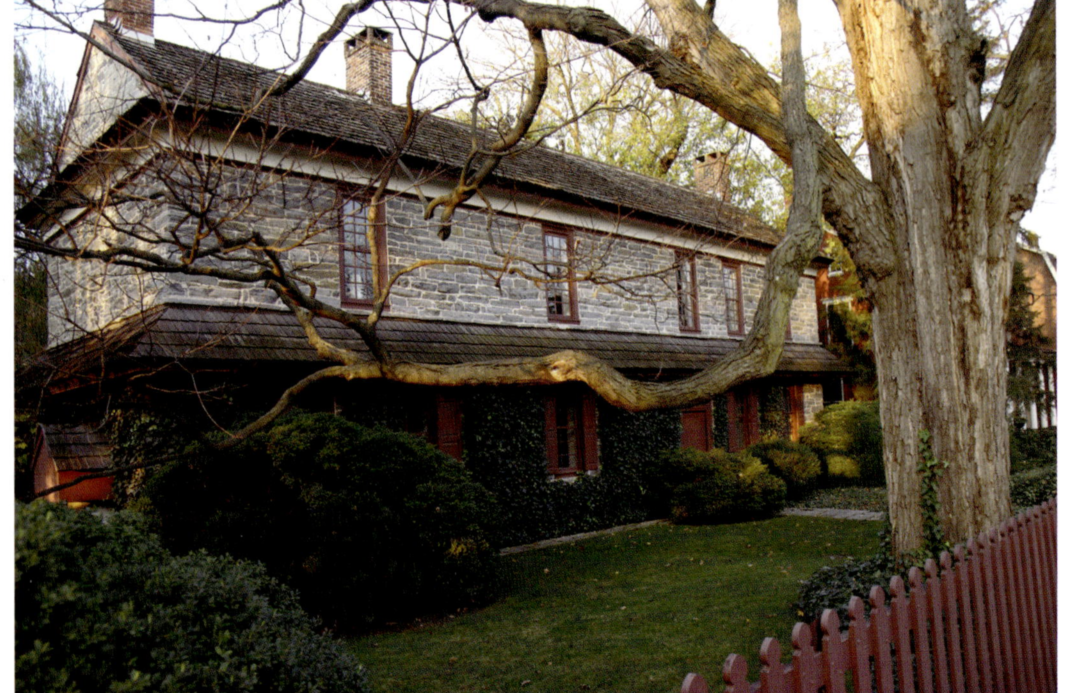

The stone Wright's Ferry Mansion was built in 1738 and was home to Susanna Wright. Its size and details are notable for any building constructed during that period, but its presence is even more remarkable because it was on the frontier where there were more Native Americans than European settlers. Today the restored home is a museum operated by the Louise Steinman von Hess Foundation.

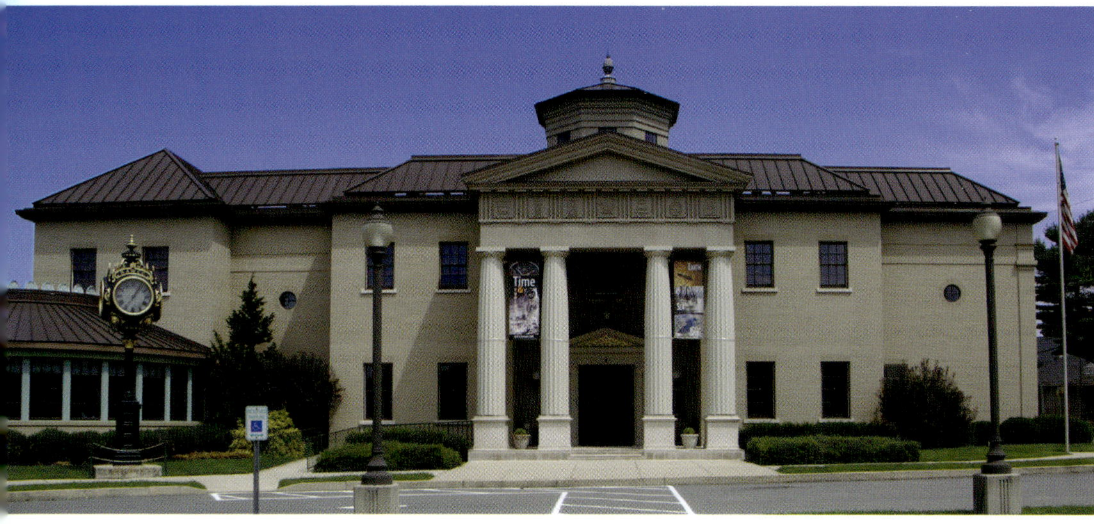

The National Watch and Clock Museum was constructed in 1977 and expanded in 1999. Home to a collection of more than 12,000 items, the museum exhibits clocks, watches, and other time-keeping pieces built throughout the world.

Originally built in 1850, the former First English Lutheran Church is now home to the Columbia Museum of History, which houses a collection of historic photos, railroad and canal memorabilia, and more.

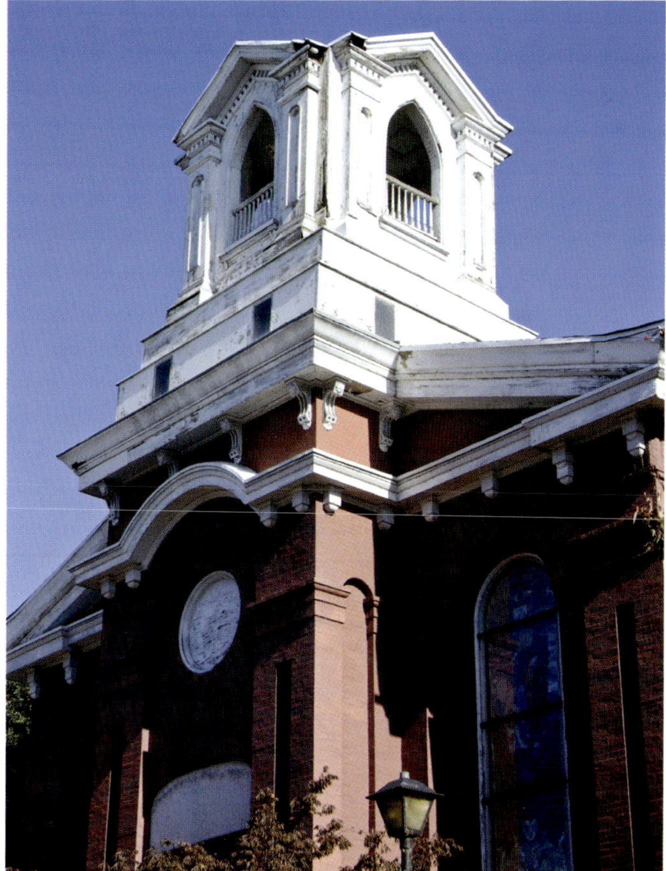

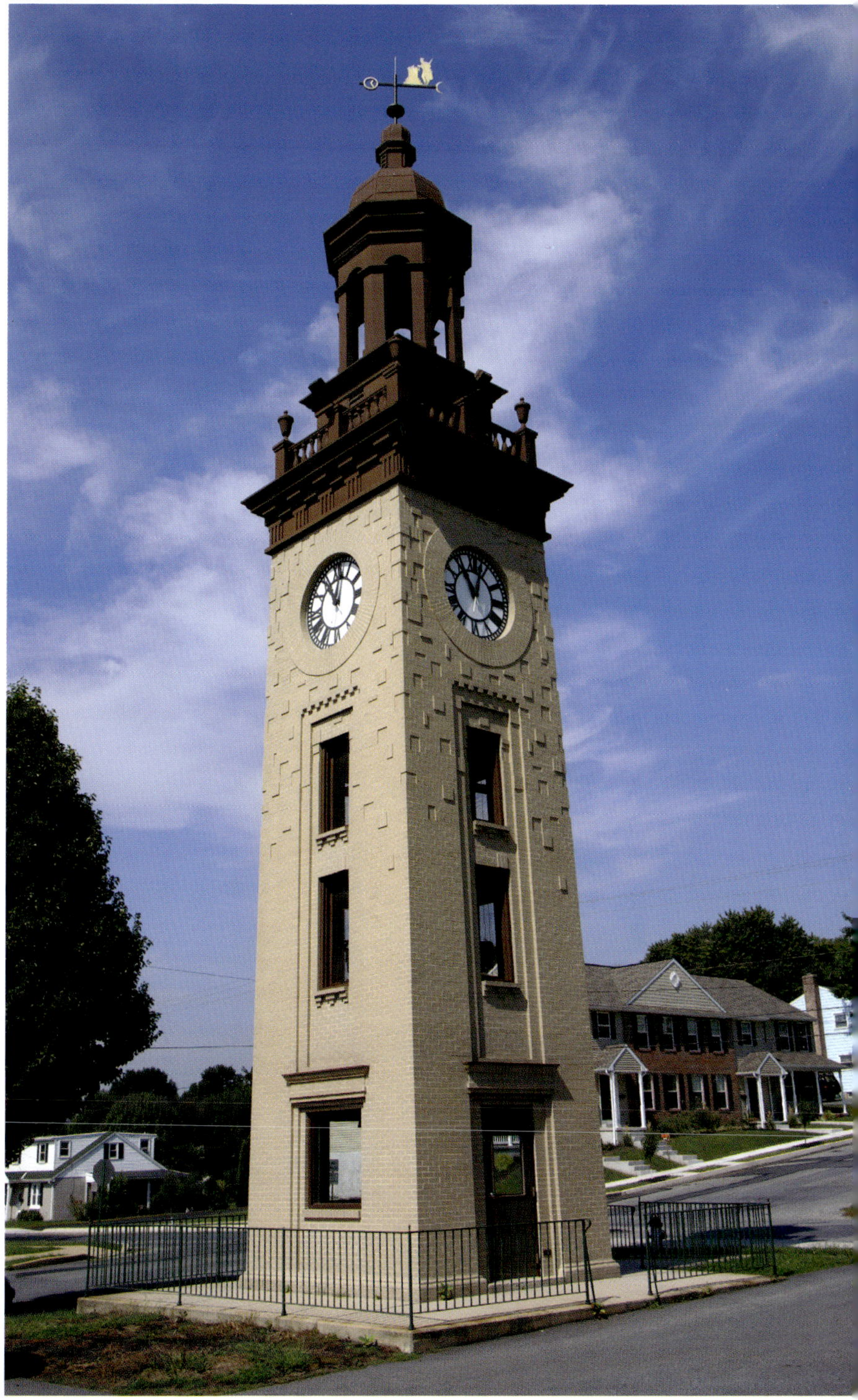

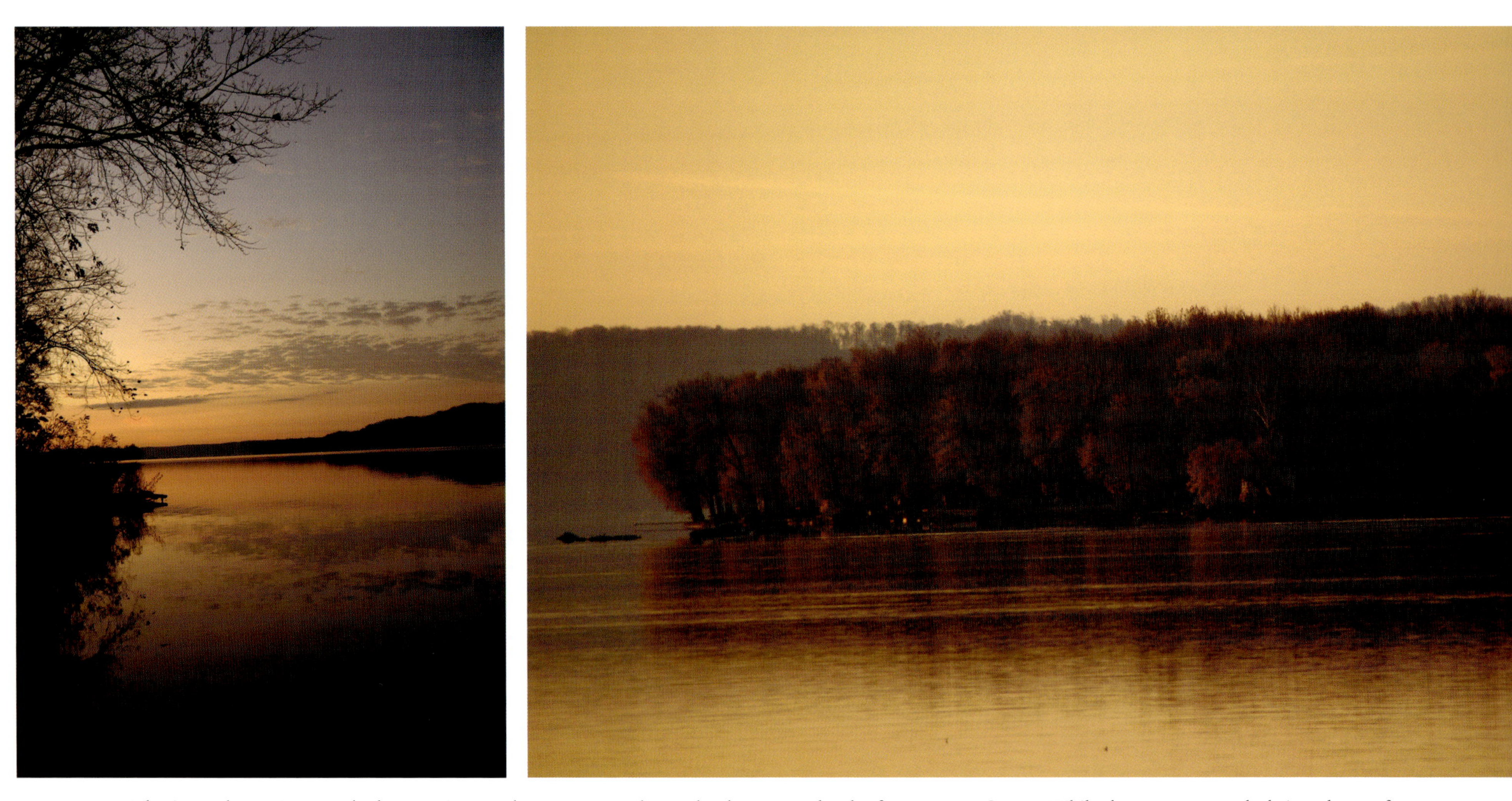

The Susquehanna River is the longest river on the east coast and provides the western border for Lancaster County. While the warmer months bring plenty of boaters, fishers, and picnickers to the river and its shores, there's always an opportunity to enjoy the solitude of a vibrant sunrise, when nature's artistry is on display.

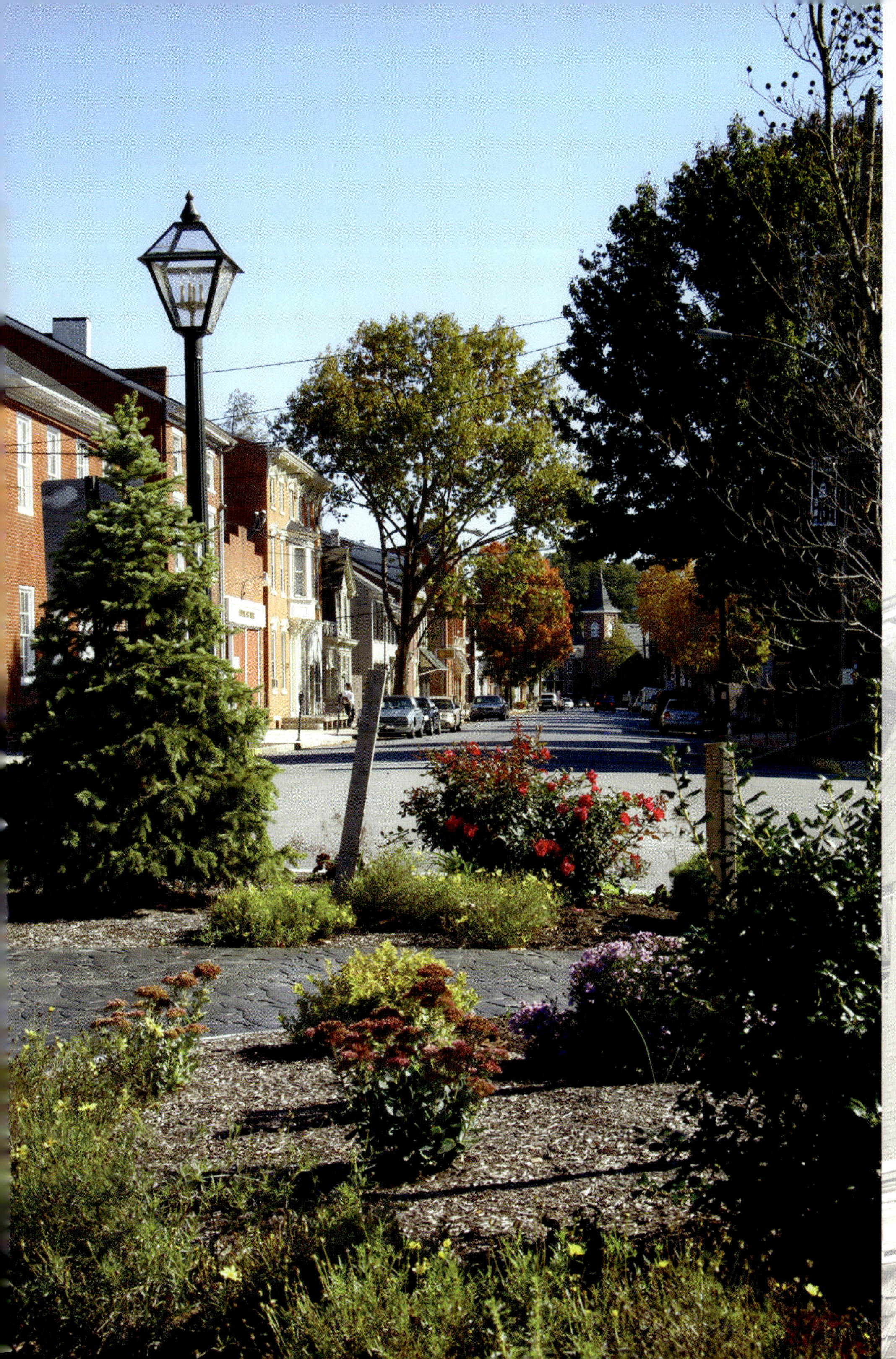

Marietta

With an area less than one square mile, the Borough of Marietta qualifies as small. Yet this small borough has an abundance of beautiful architecture—almost half of the town is listed on the National Register of Historic Places. Its history dates from 1736, when the village of Anderson's Ferry was established by James Anderson, who ran a ferry across the Susquehanna River to the present-day Accomac Inn in York County. The area was later known as Waterford, named by Scotch-Irish immigrants. The borough of Marietta was established and named in 1812, when the towns of Waterford and New Haven merged. Two other small towns, Moravian Town and Irishtown, later became part of Marietta. The town is unique in that it is two and a half miles long and only half a mile wide. The lumber and iron industries drove the local economy and created wealth that can still be seen today in many of the beautiful old homes.

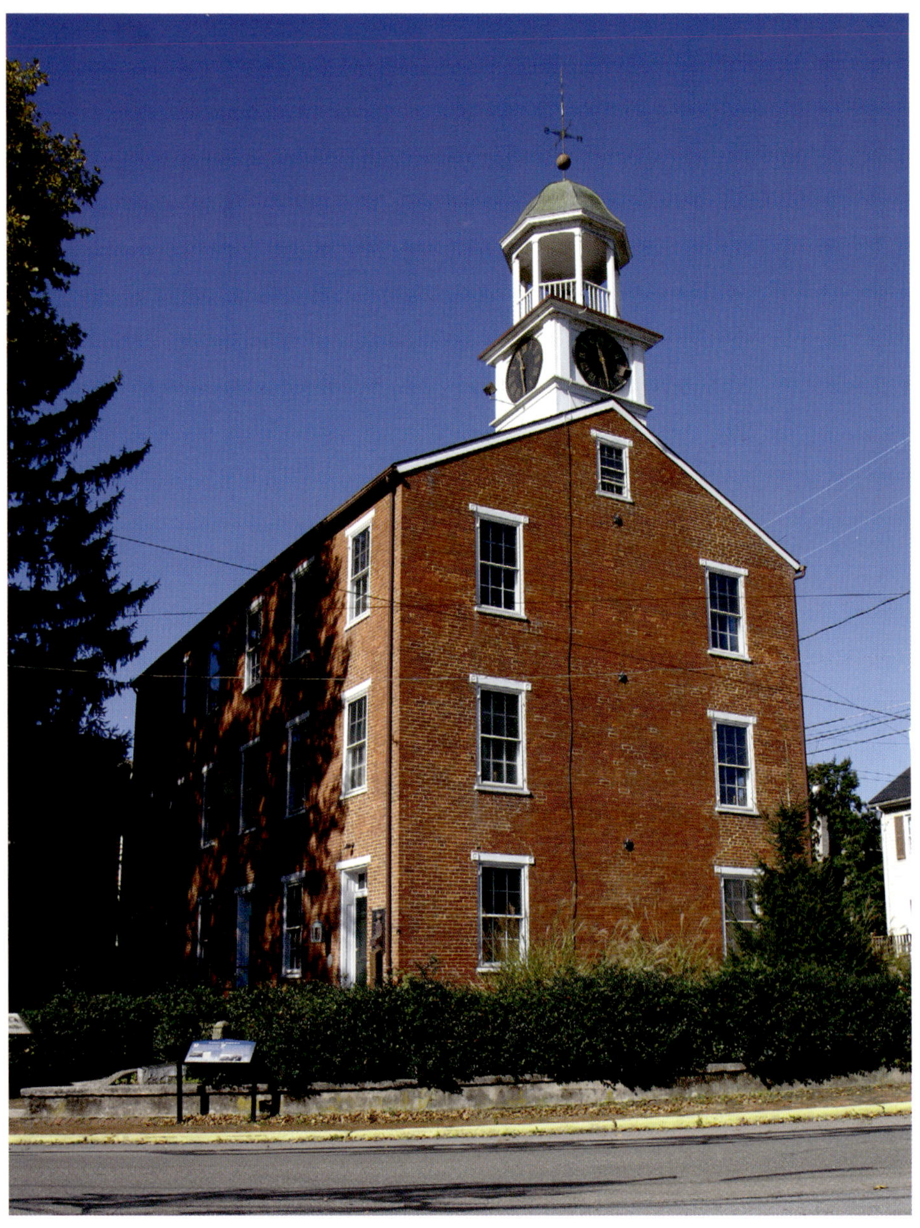

The Old Town Hall was built in 1845, and the town clock was added eight years later. Today the building is home to the Marietta Museum, the result of a 1987 agreement between the Borough and Marietta Restoration Associates, which restored the building and opened a museum.

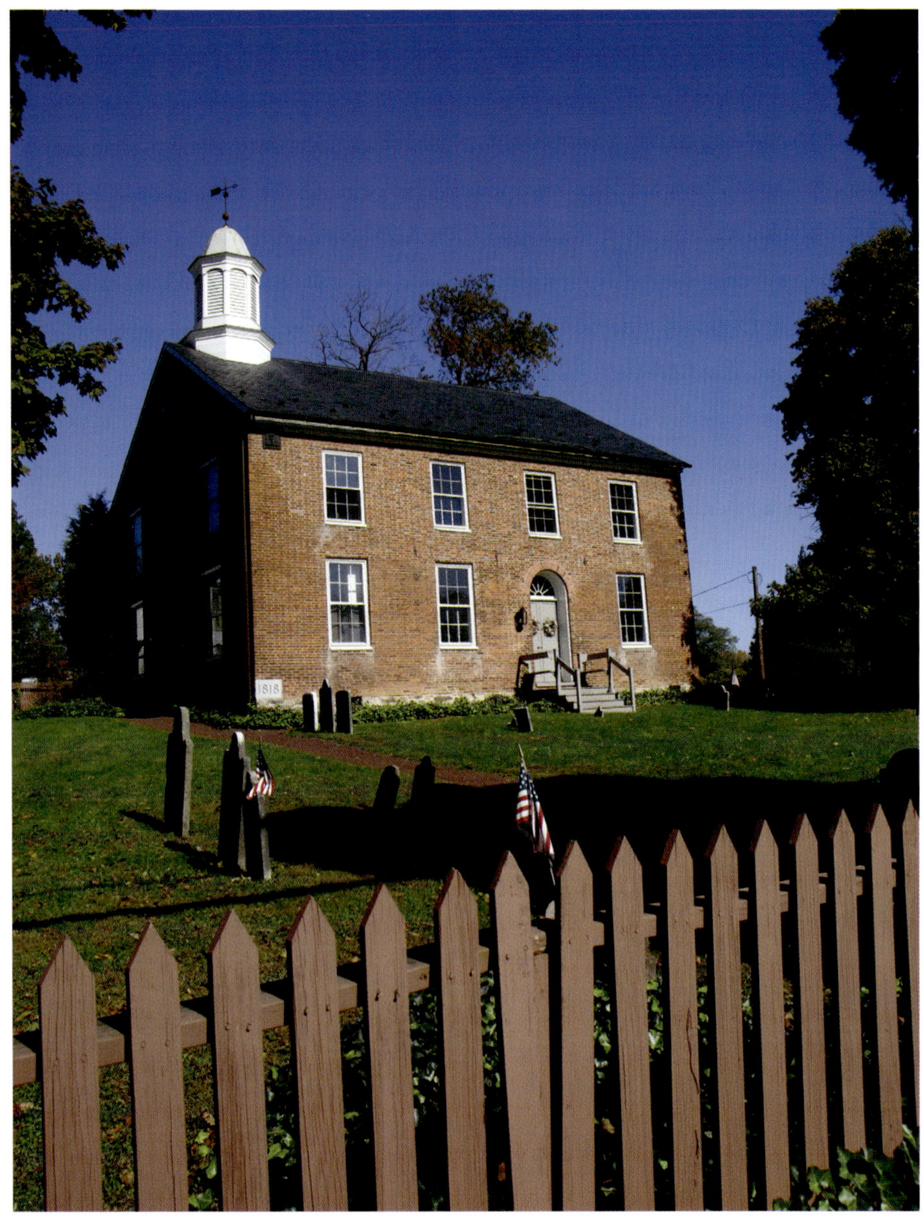

Opened in 1818, the Union Meeting House was originally home to several local Protestant congregations. The Federal-style building was restored in 1982 by Marietta Restoration Associates.

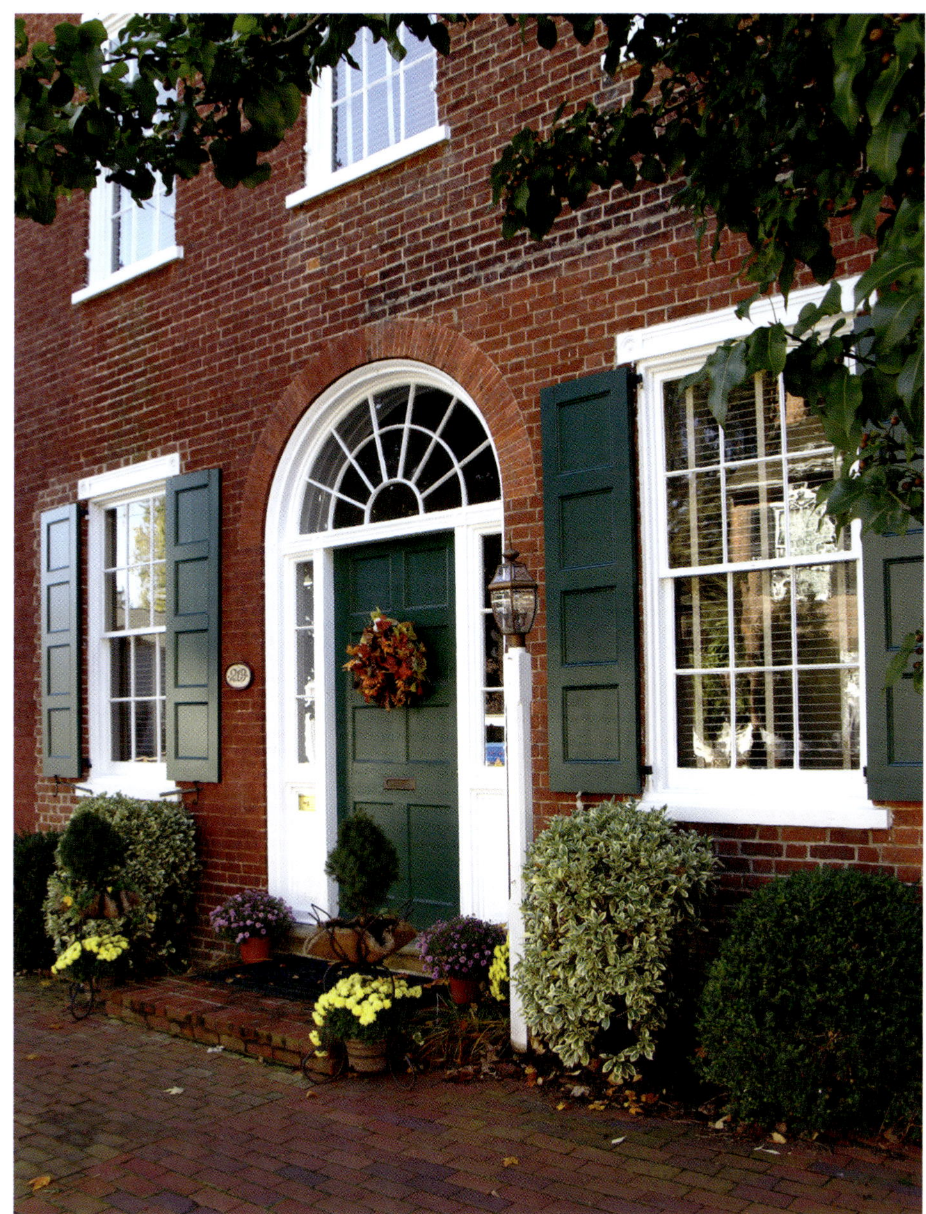

The Ascot House is a charming Bed & Breakfast located in a historic home. It is a noteworthy example of Federal architecture dating from 1800. The fanlight above the door is common to the Federal style, which was popular in the United States from the end of the American Revolution until the early nineteenth century.

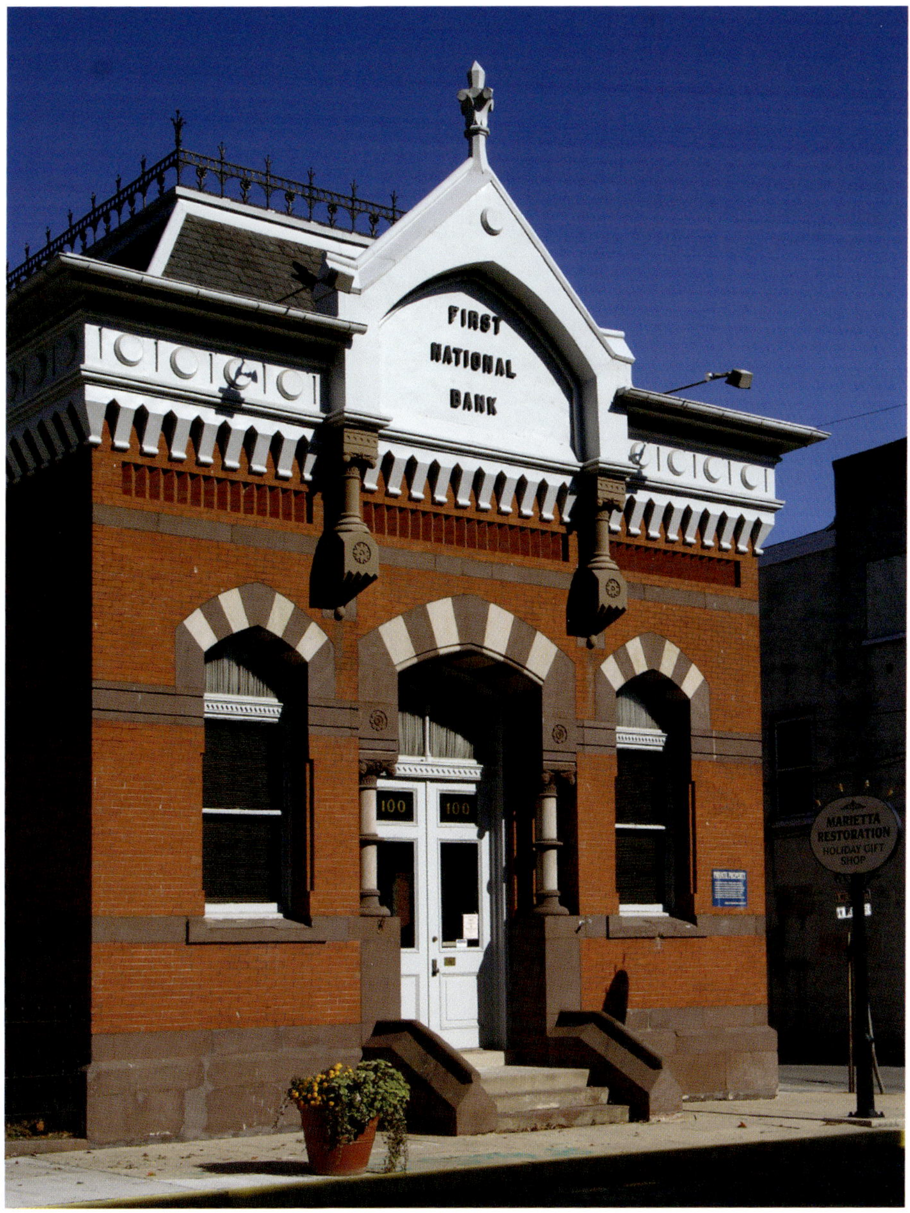

In 1863, First National Bank of Marietta became the first federally-chartered bank in Lancaster County and the twenty-fifth chartered bank in the United States. In 1875, the bank constructed a new building on West Market Street. After the bank was closed in 2001, the building was donated to Marietta Restoration Associates and today it houses their offices and gift shop.

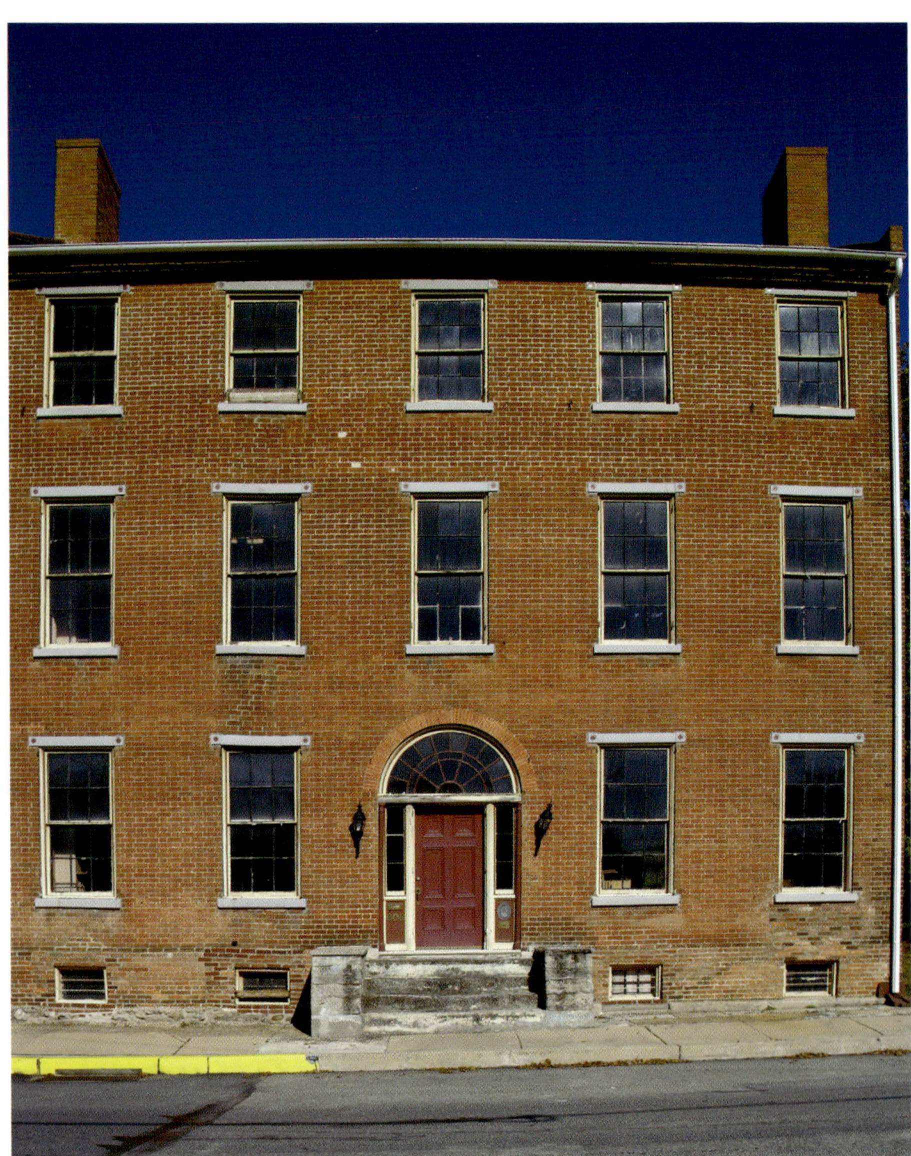

Known as the Linden House, this building was constructed for Henry Cassel around 1814. Cassel was a coal and lumber merchant, and his home is considered an important surviving example of Lancaster County's Federal-style architecture.

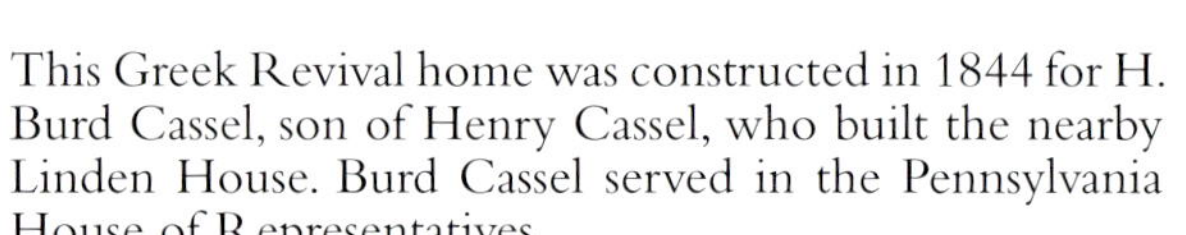

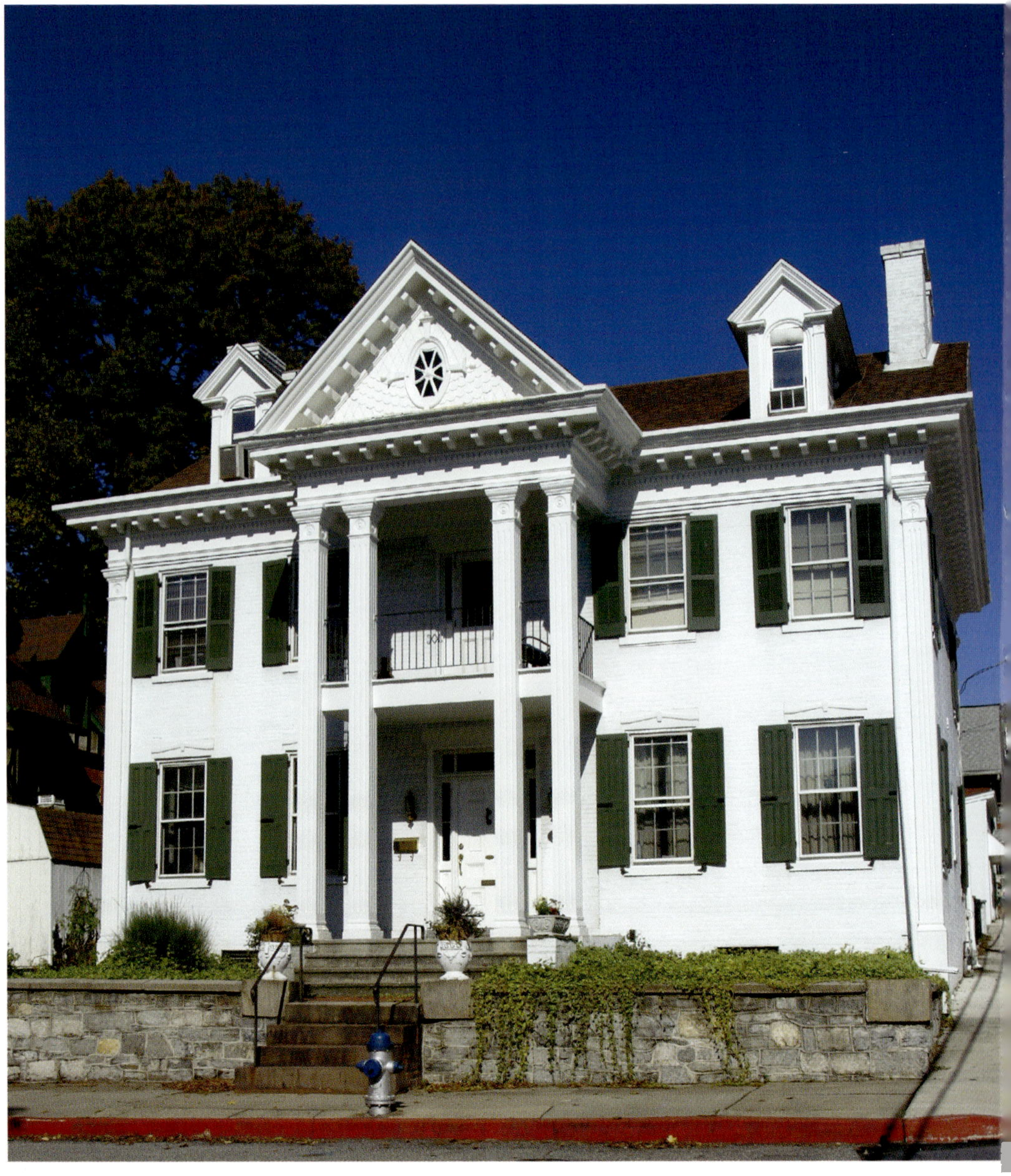

This Greek Revival home was constructed in 1844 for H. Burd Cassel, son of Henry Cassel, who built the nearby Linden House. Burd Cassel served in the Pennsylvania House of Representatives.

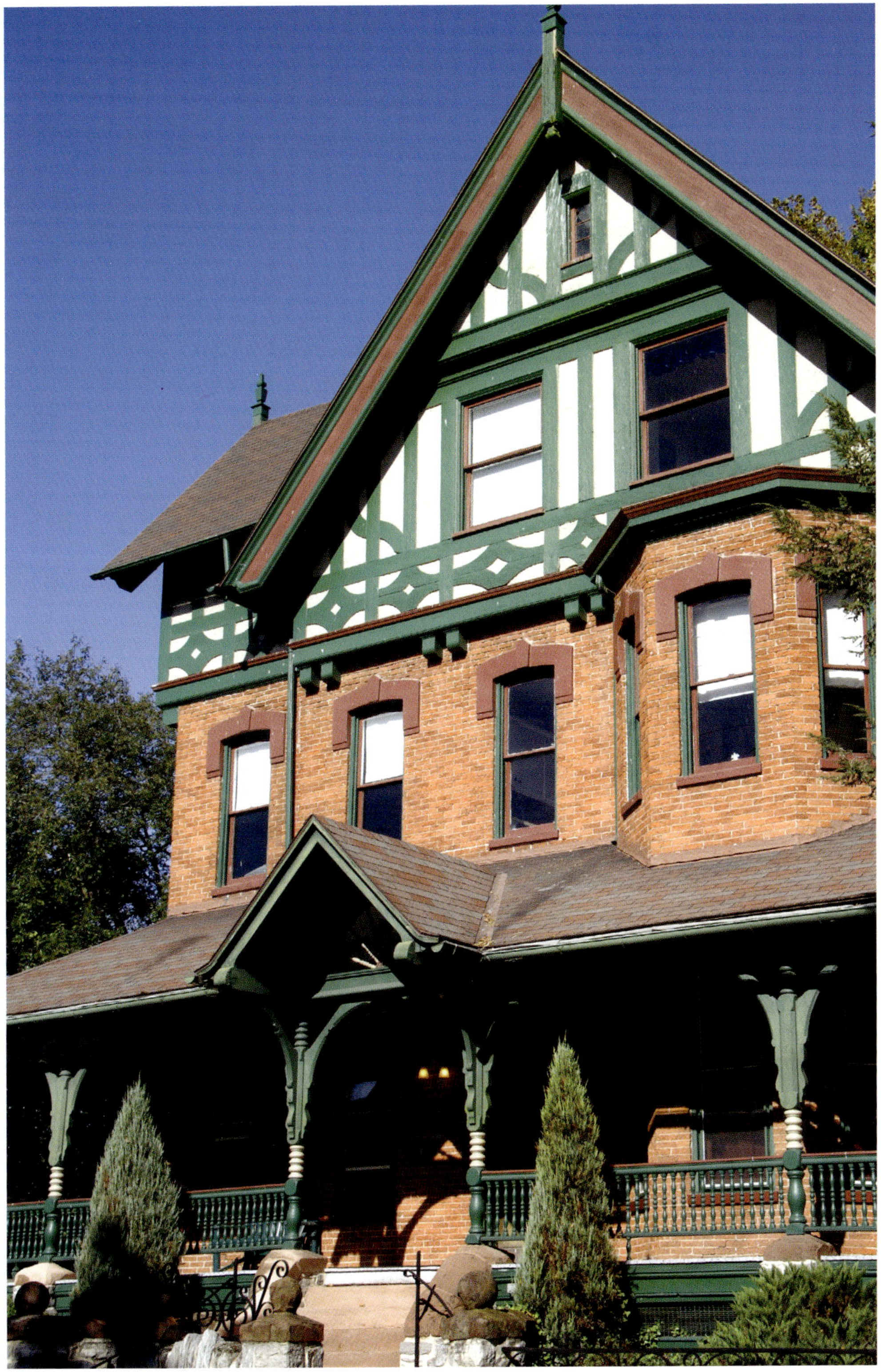

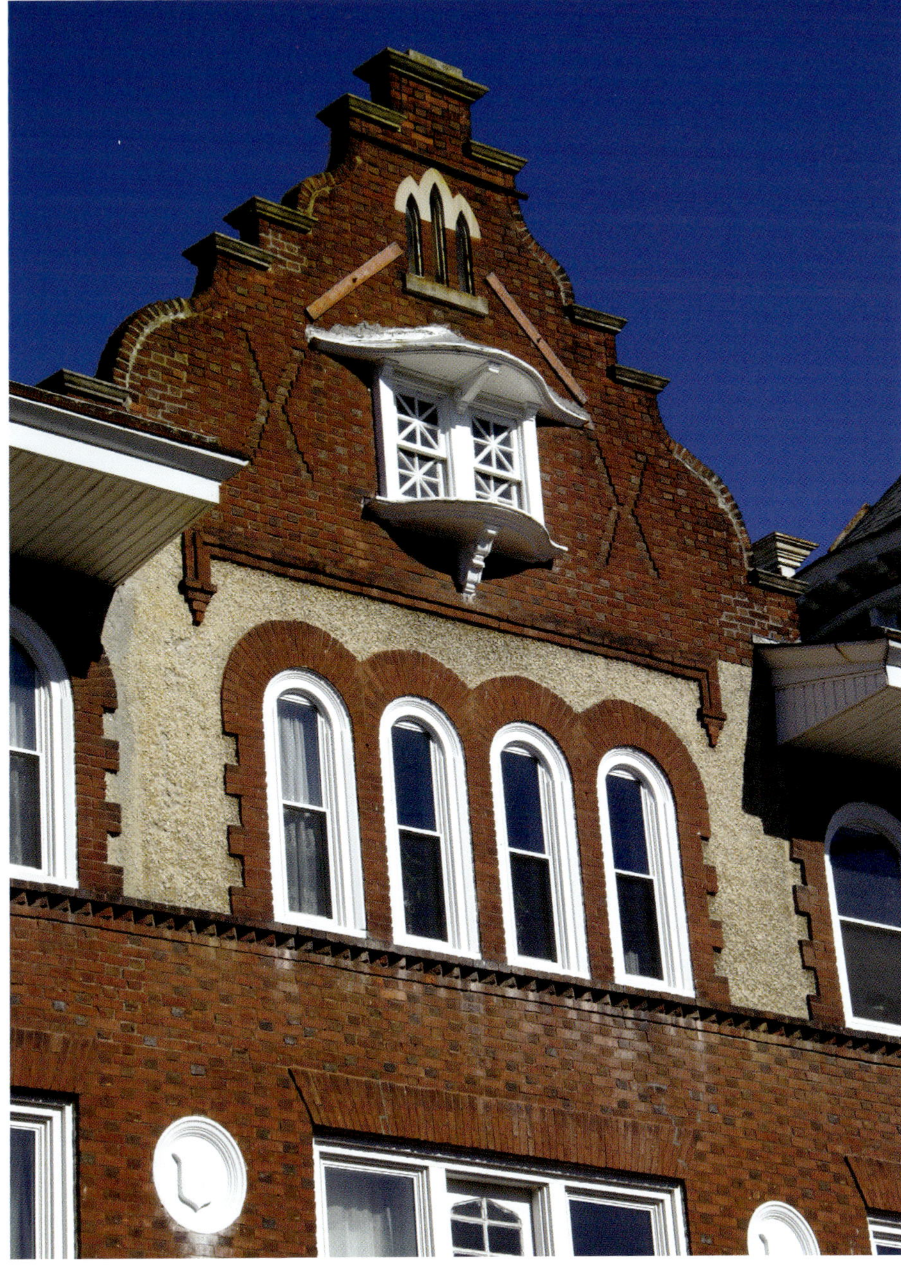

This Victorian building was constructed in the late nineteenth century and operated as the Exchange Hotel.

This picturesque Victorian home was constructed by Henry Cassel's grandson in the late 1890s.

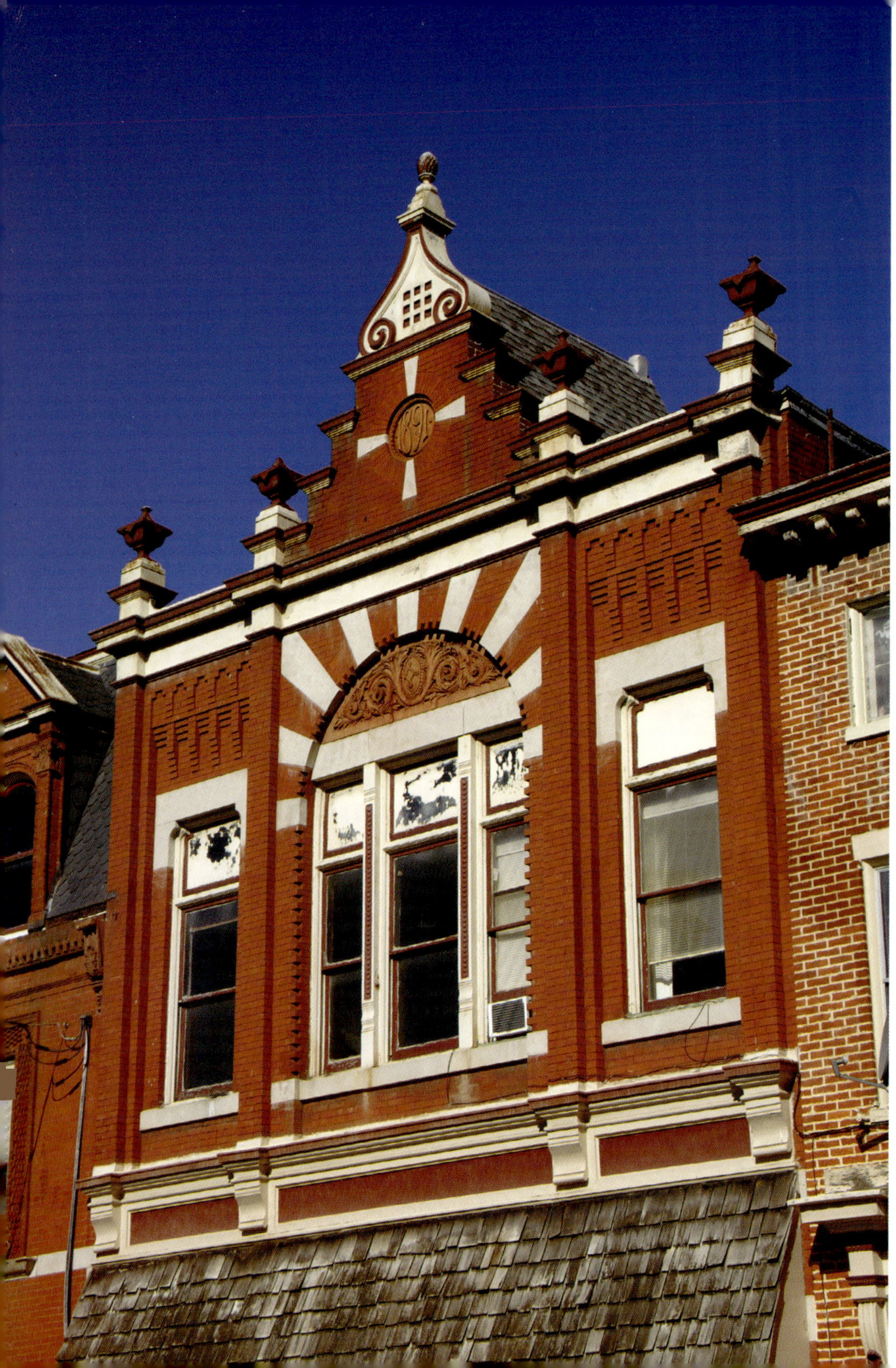

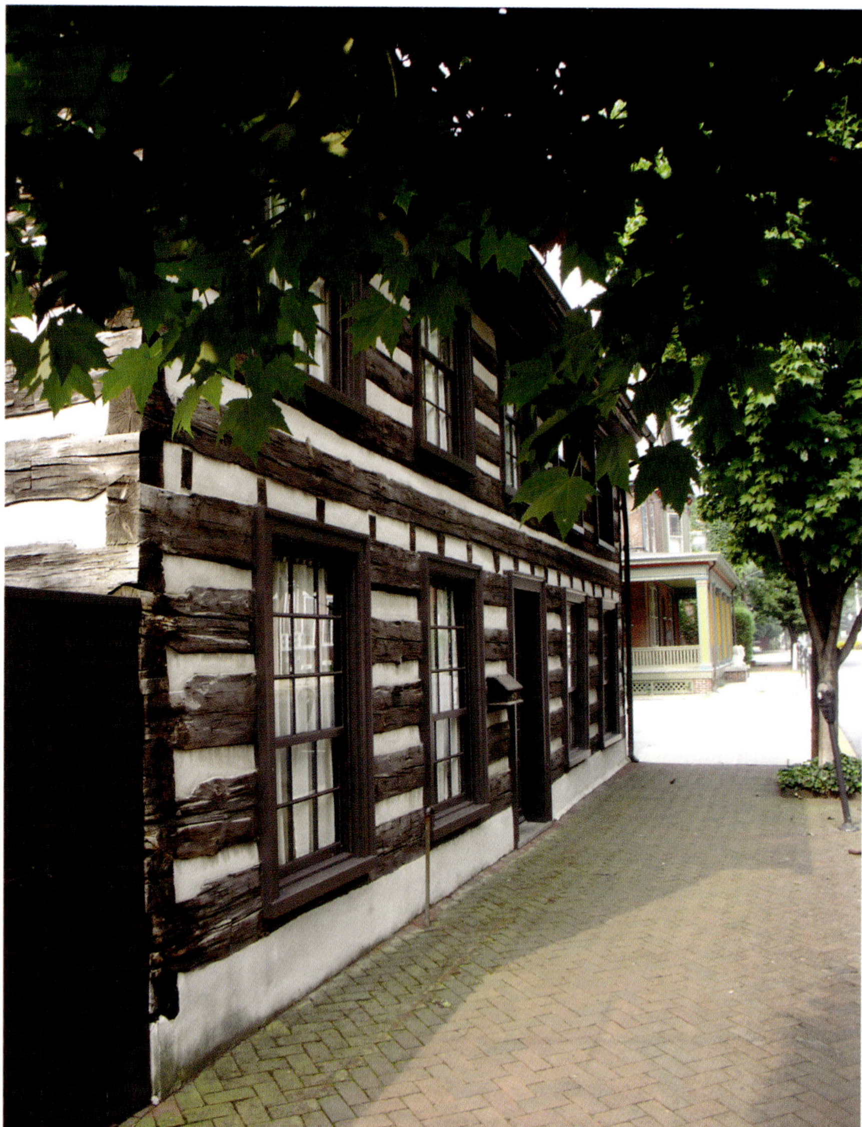

Log houses like this one in Marietta were common throughout early Lancaster County. Lumber was plentiful and the houses could be quickly constructed. The typical log home was made from hewn timbers and an infill known as chinking and daubing, which was made from a variety of materials including stones, wood, moss, and clay.

One of Marietta's many interesting buildings is this eclectic Victorian structure that dates from 1891.

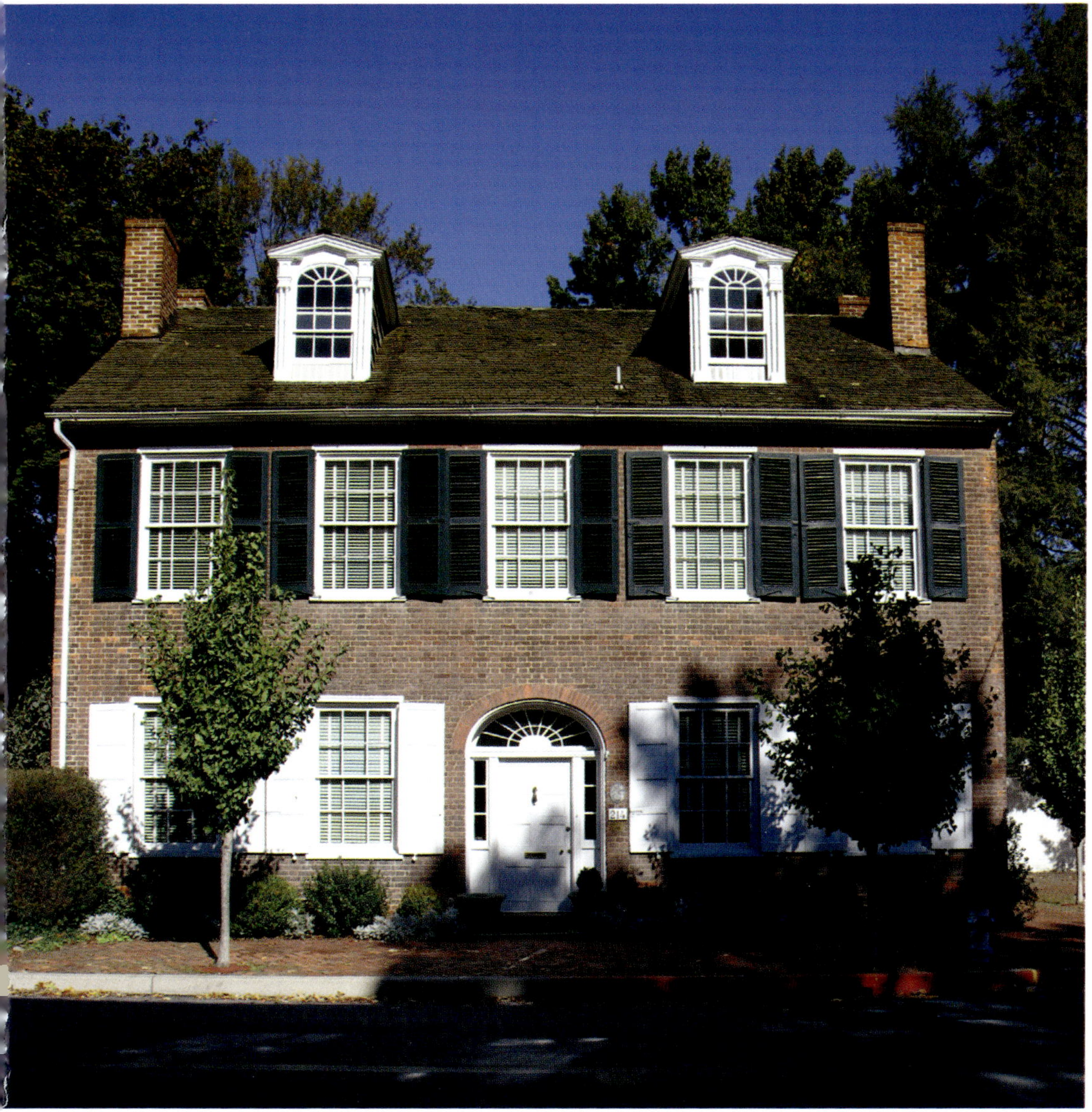

Marietta's town square is actually a circle, surrounded by several notable buildings, including the 1811 Federal-style Samuel Houston House. Houston was a successful businessman who used the nearby Susquehanna River for his shipping business.

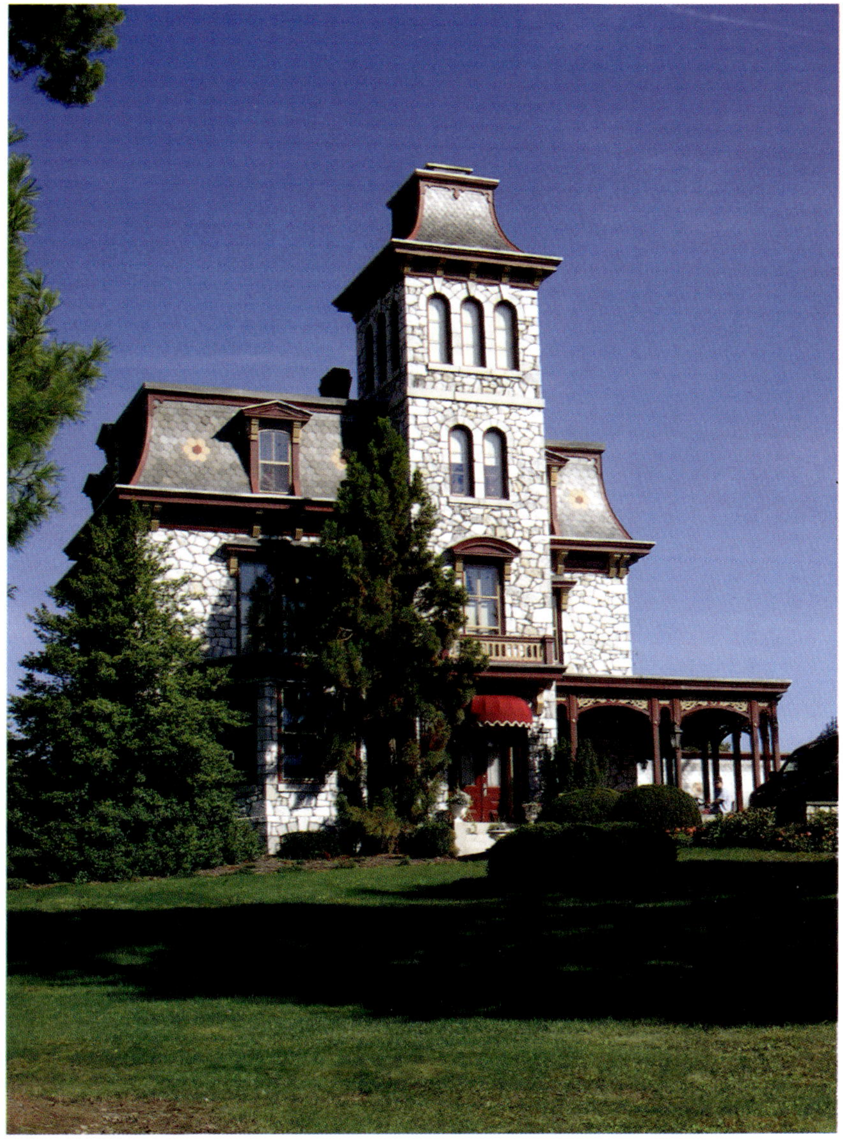

The beautiful mansion known as Riverview has been watching over the Susquehanna River near Marietta since 1860. It was built for Henry Miller Watts, a local ironmaster who had also served as Minister to Austria under President Andrew Johnson. Inspired by the architecture of Austria, Watts had stone imported from that country for construction of his Second Empire-style home.

Maytown and Mt. Joy

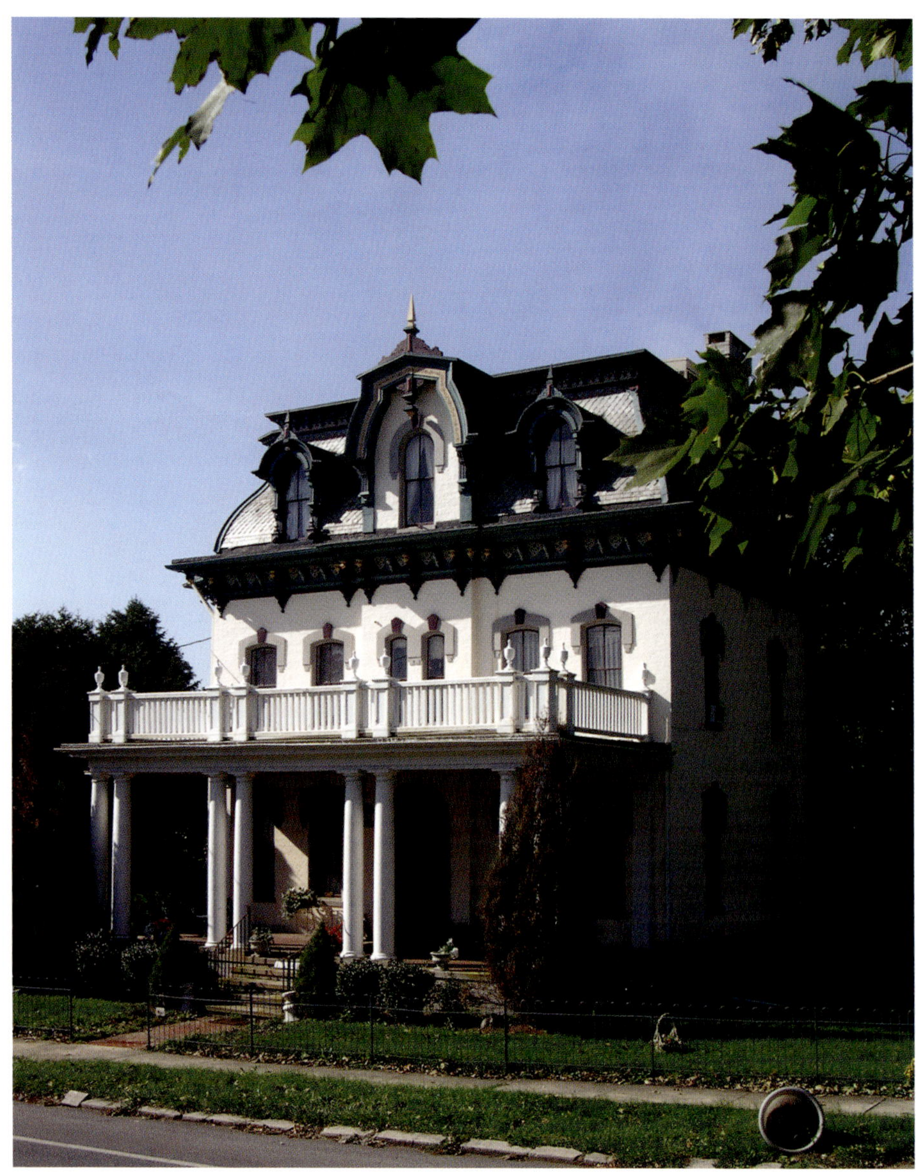

The Grove Mansion in Maytown is listed on the National Register of Historic Places. The home was constructed for David Grove in the early 1880s and designed in the picturesque Second Empire style. He didn't get to enjoy it for long, however. By 1887 Grove had fallen into financial hardship and the mansion was sold at a sheriff's sale.

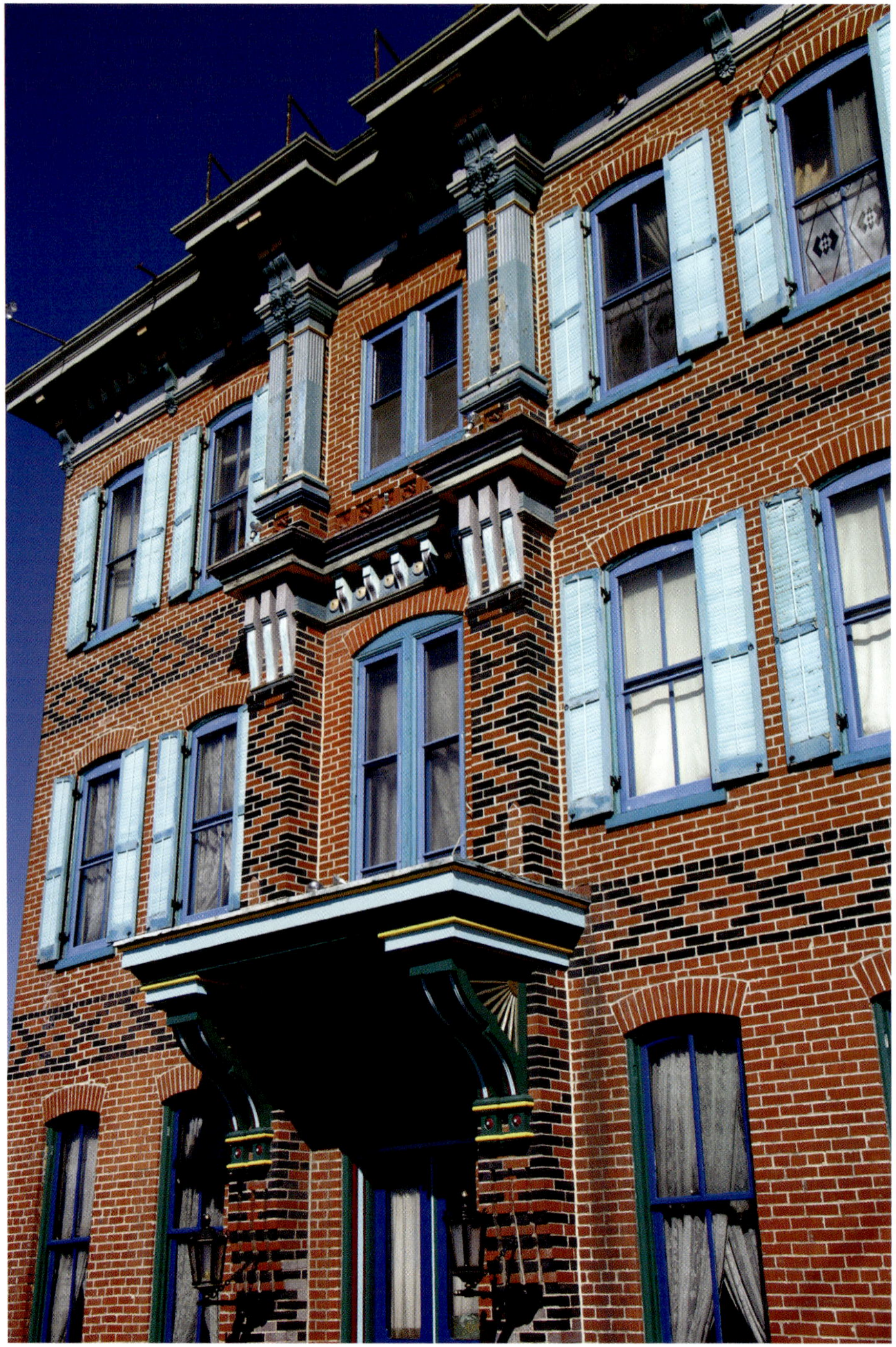

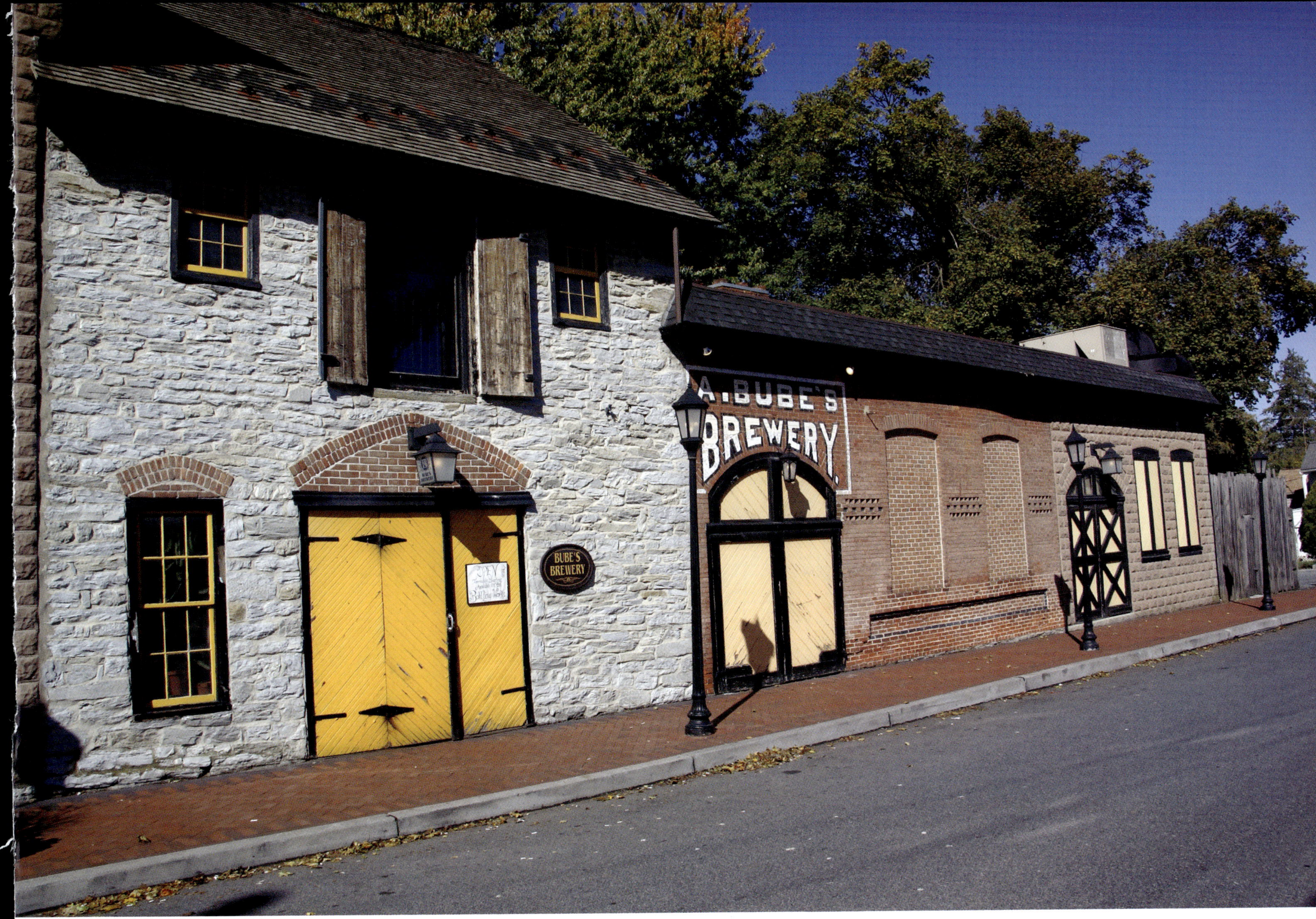

Above and oppposite page: In 1876, Alois Bube, a German immigrant, purchased a small brewery in Mt. Joy. He expanded it several times and also built the Central Hotel next to the brewery in 1880. Though he died in 1908, and Prohibition spelled an end to the brewery, family members continued to live here until the 1960s, making few alterations to the property. Restoration of the complex began in 1968, and today, Bube's Brewery is home to several restaurants, a museum, microbrewery, martini bar, and more.

Bibliography

Books

Christopher, Lisa M. *Historic Towns & Villages of Lancaster County Pennsylvania* (Lancaster, PA: Lancaster County Heritage Partnership, Pennsylvania Heritage Tourism Initiative, 2003).

City of Lancaster, Pennsylvania. *To Build Strong and Substantial: The Career of Architect C. Emlen Urban* (Lancaster, PA: The City of Lancaster, 2009).

Kauffman, Henry J. *Architecture of the Pennsylvania Dutch Country 1700-1900* (Elverson, PA: Olde Springfield Shoppe, 1992).

Snyder, John J., Jr. *Lancaster Architecture 1719-1927; A Guide to Publicly Accessible Buildings in Lancaster County* (Lancaster, PA: Historic Preservation Trust of Lancaster County, 1979).

Websites

"1786 The Limestone Inn B&B: Strasburg, Lancaster County—In The Heart Of Amish Country," (The Limestone Inn B&B: www.thelimestoneinn.com, accessed November 19, 2009).

"Alden House Bed & Breakfast," (www.aldenhouse.com, accessed February 20, 2010).

"The Amish and the Plain People of Lancaster County, PA," (Pennsylvania Dutch Country Welcome Center: www.800padutch.com, accessed November 26, 2009).

"Amish History & Beliefs in Lancaster, PA," (Pennsylvania Dutch Welcome Center: www.padutchcountry.com, accessed November 26, 2009).

"Borough of Marietta Town Life," (Borough of Marietta, PA: www.boroughofmarietta.com, accessed November 4, 2009).

"Borough of Strasburg," (Borough of Strasburg, PA: www.co.lancaster.pa.us, accessed November 26, 2009).

"Bube's Brewery, Alois, The Catacombs, Bottling Works, and Restaurants," (Bube's Brewery: www.bubesbrewery.com, accessed November 19, 2009).

"The Buildings," (Franklin and Marshall College: www.fandm.edu, accessed November 20, 2009).

"Café Chocolate of Lititz," (www.chocolatelititz.com, accessed February 20, 2010).

"Colombia Borough," (Borough of Columbia, Pennsylvania: http://psabcontent.com, accessed November 4, 2009).

"Columbia Museum of History," (Lancaster County Heritage: www.lancastercountyheritage.com, accessed November 4, 2009).

"Columbia, PA, Market House, Farmers Market, and Historic Columbia, PA," (www.columbiamarkethouse.com, accessed November 4, 2009).

"Congregation Shaarai Shomayim," (Congregation Shaarai Shomayim: http://shaarai.org, accessed November 21, 2009).

"Covered Bridges by Lancaster County Pennsylvania Visitors Center," (Pennsylvania Dutch Convention & Visitors Bureau: www.padutchcountry.com, accessed November 18, 2009).

Deel, Jane. "Steinman Park an Oasis in Lancaster," (Landscape Communications, Inc., www.landscapeonline.com, accessed November 21, 2009).

"The Demuth Museum," (The Demuth Museum: www.demuth.org, accessed November 17, 2009).

"Downtown Ephrata, PA, Ephrata Business District, and Lancaster County," (Downtown Ephrata, Inc.: www.downtownephrata.org, accessed November 22, 2009).

"Dozen Distinctive Destinations, Lititz 2009," (National Trust for Historic Preservation: www.preservationnation.org, accessed February 20, 2010).

"Ephrata Borough: At A Glance," (Borough of Ephrata: www.ephrataboro.org, accessed November 28, 2009).

"Franklin & Marshal: The Buildings," (Franklin & Marshall College: www.fandm.edu, accessed November 19, 2009).

"Franklin & Marshall, Musser Park," (Franklin & Marshall College: www.fandm.edu, accessed November 19, 2009).

"The Fulton," (Fulton Opera House Foundation: www.thefulton.org, accessed November 19, 2009).

"The General Sutter Inn History," (The General Sutter Inn: www.generalsutterinn.com, accessed November 16, 2009).

"Heritage Center Museum, Lancaster, PA," (Heritage Center of Lancaster County, Inc.: www.heritagecentermuseum.com, accessed November 19, 2009).

"Historical and Pictorial Lititz," (American Libraries Internet Archives: www.archive.org, accessed February 20, 2010).
"The Historic Preservation Trust of Lancaster County," (Historic Preservation Trust of Lancaster County: www.hptrust.org, accessed November 20, 2009).
"Historic Rock Ford Plantation, Home of Revolution War General Edward Hand, Lancaster, PA," (Rock Ford Foundation: www.rockfordplantation.org, accessed November 20, 2009).
"Holy Trinity Evangelical Lutheran Church, Lancaster, PA," (The Evangelical Lutheran Church of the Holy Trinity: www.trinitylancaster.org, accessed November 20, 2009).
"Kreider Farms, Lancaster County, PA," (Kreider Farms: www.kreiderfarms.com, accessed November 21, 2009).
"Lancaster Brewing Company: The Only Beer Brewed and Bottled in Lancaster, Pennsylvania," (Lancaster Brewing Company: www.lancasterbrewing.com, accessed November 20, 2009).
"Lancaster City: An Overview of Lancaster's Architectural Heritage," (City of Lancaster, Pennsylvania: www.co.lancaster.pa.us, accessed June 3, 2009).
"Lancaster City: Downtown Lancaster Tour: Three Centuries in Four Blocks," (City of Lancaster, Pennsylvania: www.co.lancaster.pa.us, accessed November 17, 2009).
"Lancaster County Convention Center: Lancaster, Pennsylvania," (Lancaster County Convention Center: www.lancasterconventioncenter.com, accessed November 16, 2009).
"Lancaster County, PA, Bed and Breakfast: Marietta Bed and Breakfast," (Ascot House Bed and Breakfast: www.ascothousebandb.com, accessed November 4, 2009).
"Lancaster General Hospital," (Lancaster General: www.lancastergeneral.org, accessed November 19, 2009).
"Lancaster Living: Historic Lancaster City," (Lancaster Living: www.lancastercityliving.org, accessed November 28, 2009).
"Lancaster Timeline: Concurrent U.S., State, and Local Events," (City of Lancaster, PA: www.co.lancaster.pa.us, accessed November 29, 2009).
"Landis Valley Museum, Pennsylvania German Heritage, Lancaster County Tourism, PA," (Landis Valley Museum: www.landisvalleymuseum.org, accessed November 20, 2009).
"Linden Hall: Lititz, PA," (Linden Hall: www.lindenhall.com, accessed November 4, 2009).
"Lititz," (Pioneers and Patriarchs: Pennsylvania Dutch History, Genealogy and Culture: www.horseshoe.cc, accessed November 22, 2009).
"Lititz Historical Foundation, The Lititz Museum, Johannes Mueller House, Lititz, PA, Lancaster," (Lititz Historical Foundation: www.lititzhistoricalfoundation.com, accessed November 4, 2009).
"The Lititz Moravian Congregation," (Lititz Moravian Congregation, Lititz, PA: www.lititzmoravian.org, accessed February 20, 2010).
"Lititz Springs Park History," (Lititz Springs Park: www.lititzspringspark.org, accessed November 22, 2009).
"A Look Through Baumgardners Mill Bridge," (Red Rubble: www-0.redbubble.com, accessed November 22, 2009).
"Manheim Township," (Manheim Township, PA: www.manheimtownship.org, accessed November19, 2009).
"Marietta Restoration Associates: History," (Marietta Restoration Associates: www.mariettarestoration.org, accessed November 4, 2009).
"Musser Park: An Enduring Gift to the City of Lancaster," (Franklin and Marshall College: www.fandm.edu, accessed November 18, 2009).
"National Toy Train Museum: Toy Trains for All Ages," (The National Toy Train Museum: http://nttmuseum.org, accessed November 16, 2009).
"National Watch & Clock Museum," (National Association of Watch & Clock Collectors, Inc.: www.nawcc.org, accessed November 4, 2009).
"A New Beginning for Lancaster: New Era," (LancasterOnline.com, http://articles.lancasteronline.com, accessed November 19, 2009).
"Our Building History," (Spill the Beans Café: www.spillthebeanscafe.com, accessed November 22, 2009).
Parrish, Marilyn M. "The Library at Millersville," (Friends Folio: www.library.millersville.edu, accessed November 21, 2009).
"Pennsylvania Academy of Music," (Pennsylvania Academy of Music: www.pamusacad.org, accessed November 20, 2009).
"Pequea Township," (Pioneers and Patriarchs: Pennsylvania Dutch History, Genealogy and Culture: www.horseshoe.cc, accessed November 22, 2009).
"Prison Portal: History," (Lancaster County Government: www.co.lancaster.pa.us, accessed November 19, 2009).
"Railroad Museum of PA: Welcome," (Railroad Museum of Pennsylvania: www.rrmuseumpa.org, accessed November 16, 2009).
Savery, Kat. "A Brief History of the Mountain Springs Hotel," (The Muse's Wings: www.3catsstudios.com, accessed November 22, 2009.)
"A Short History of the College Library," (Franklin and Marshall College: http://library.fandm.edu, accessed November 16, 2009).
"Sight & Sound Theatres," (Sight & Sound Theatres www.sight-sound.com, accessed November 16, 2009).
"Strasburg Rail Road: Lancaster County, Pennsylvania," (The Strasburg Railroad: www.strasburgrailroad.com, accessed November 16, 2009).
"A Strolling Tour of Strasburg's Historic District," (Strasburg Heritage Society: www.strasburgheritagepa.org, accessed November 19, 2009).
"Thaddeus Stevens Biography," (Thaddeus Stevens College of Technology, www.stevenscollege.edu, accessed November 18, 2009).
"Theater, Dance & Film Facilities," (Franklin and Marshall College: http://tdf.fandm.edu, accessed November 16, 2009).
"Towns of Lancaster County, PA: Lancaster City," (EZSolution Corp., www.yourlancaster.

com, accessed November 21, 2009).
"Welcome to First Reformed Church United Church of Christ," (The First Reformed Church United Church of Christ: www.firstreformedlancaster.org, accessed November 19, 2009).
"Welcome to Lancaster Museum of Art," (Lancaster Museum of Art: www.lmapa.org, accessed November 19, 2009).
Wikipedia Contributors. "List of Covered Bridges in Lancaster County, Pennsylvania," (Wikipedia: http://en.wikipedia.org, accessed November 18, 2009).
Wikipedia Contributors. "Mountain Springs Hotel," (Wikipedia: http://en.wikipedia.org, accessed November 22, 2009).
Wikipedia Contributors. "Thaddeus Stevens," (Wikipedia: http://en.wikipedia.org, accessed November 18, 2009).

Pamphlets & Unpublished Works

Aleci, Eugene L. "National Register of Historic Places: Inventory Nomination Form, Farmers' Southern Market," (Lancaster, PA, 1986)
Behling, Robert M. "National Register of Historic Places: Inventory Nomination Form, Lancaster County Courthouse," (Lancaster, PA: Lancaster County Planning Commission, 1978).
Dawson, Christopher, AIA. "National Register of Historic Places: Registration Form, W.W. Griest Building," (Lancaster, PA: Hammel Associates, Architects, 1997).
Greenwood, Richard. "National Register of Historic Places: Inventory Nomination Form, Fulton Opera House," (Washington, DC: Landmark Review Task Force, 1974).
Hamel, Ken & Richard Levengood. "National Register of Historic Places: Inventory Nomination Form, Sprenger Brewery," (Lancaster, PA: Levengood Associates, Architects, 1979).
Jarvis, Sarah M. "National Register of Historic Places: Inventory Nomination Form, Original Buildings of Franklin & Marshall College," (Lancaster, PA: The North Museum, Franklin & Marshall College, 1975).
Klein, Frederic S. "National Register of Historic Places: Inventory Nomination Form, Soldiers and Sailors Monument.," (Lancaster, PA: Historical Preservation Trust of Lancaster County, 1970).
Kurtz, Sarah M. "National Register of Historic Places: Registration Form, Lancaster City Historic District.," (Lancaster, PA: City of Lancaster, 2001).
Lancaster County Heritage Partnership. *Freedom of Religion Walking Tour* (Lancaster, PA: Lancaster County Heritage Partnership/Downtown Lancaster City Ministerium, 2001).
Lancaster County Planning Commission/Lancaster County Cultural Heritage Plan Task Force. *The Cultural Heritage Element: A Strategy for Preserving Our Sense of Place, The Comprehensive Plan for Lancaster County, Pennsylvania* (Lancaster, PA: Lancaster County Planning Commission, 2006).
Lititz Historical Foundation. *The Lititz Historical Foundation Invites You to Stroll Down Main Street and Relive a Way of Life Before 1800.*
Stallings, Suzanne. *A Self-Guided Walking Tour along Historic East King Street from Penn Square to Broad Street* (Lancaster, PA: City of Lancaster, Pennsylvania, 2007).
Pennsylvania Register of Historic Sites and Landmarks. "National Register of Historic Places: Inventory Nomination Form, Central Market," (Harrisburg, PA: Pennsylvania Historical and Museum Commission, 1972).
Pennsylvania Register of Historic Sites and Landmarks. "National Register of Historic Places: Inventory Nomination Form, Old City Hall," (Harrisburg, PA: Pennsylvania Historical and Museum Commission, 1972).
Schneider, David B. "National Register of Historic Places: Registration Form, Watt and Shand Department Store," (Beaufort, SC, 1998).
Smith, Janet C. "National Register of Historic Places: Inventory Nomination Form, Old Dorm, Lutheran Theological Seminary," (Harrisburg, PA: Pennsylvania Historical and Museum Commission, 1973).
Snyder, John J., Jr. "National Register of Historic Places: Inventory Nomination Form, Lancaster Historic District (annex)," (Lancaster, PA: Historic Preservation Trust of Lancaster County, 1983).
Snyder, John J., Jr. "National Register of Historic Places: Inventory Nomination Form, United States Post Office, Lancaster," (Lancaster, PA: Historic Preservation Trust/Lancaster County, 1980).
Snyder, John J., Jr. "National Register of Historic Places: Inventory Nomination Form, New Era Building," (Lancaster, PA: Historic Preservation Trust of Lancaster County, 1983).
Snyder, John J., Jr. "National Register of Historic Places: Inventory Nomination Form, Stevens High School (also, Girls High School)," (Lancaster, PA: Historic Preservation Trust of Lancaster County, 1983).
Snyder, John J., Jr. "National Register of Historic Places: Inventory Nomination Form, West Lawn," (Lancaster, PA: Historic Preservation Trust of Lancaster County, 1983).
Stacks, David C. "National Register of Historic Places: Inventory Nomination Form, Lancaster Historic District," (Mechanicsburg, PA, 1978).
Wiley, Mary T. "National Register of Historic Places: Inventory Nomination Form, Follmer, Clogg & Company Umbrella Factory," (Lancaster, PA: Historic Preservation Trust of Lancaster County, 1986).

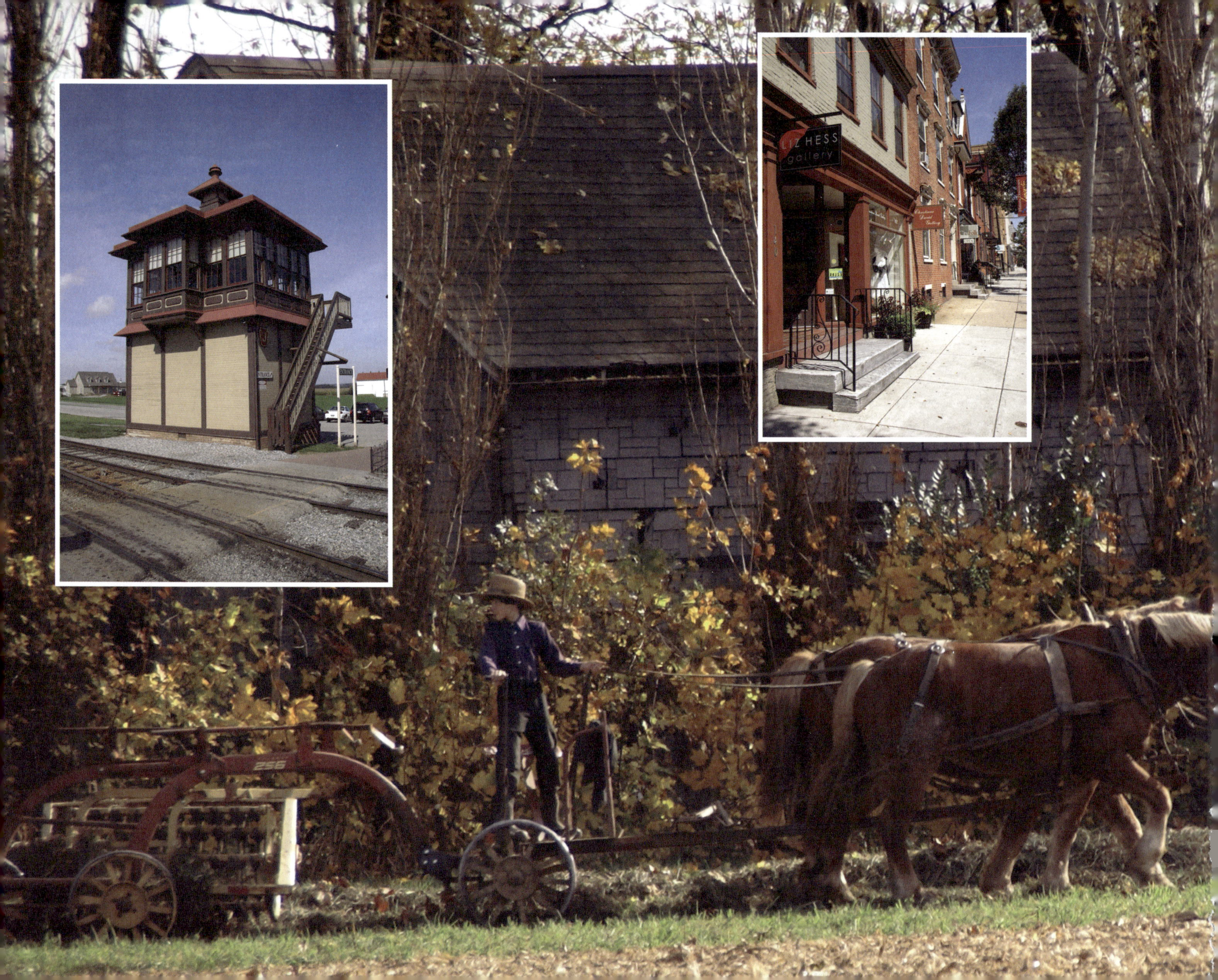
LIZ HESS
gallery